MAKING, SELLING AND WEARING BOYS' CLOTHES IN LATE-VICTORIAN ENGLAND

T0300368

In memory of Charles I Rose, 1901–2004

Making, Selling and Wearing Boys' Clothes in Late-Victorian England

CLARE ROSE

Routledge
Taylor & Francis Group

LONDON AND NEW YORK

First published 2010 by Ashgate Publishing

2 Park Square, Milton Park, Abingdon, Oxon OX14 4RN
711 Third Avenue, New York, NY 10017, USA

Routledge is an imprint of the Taylor & Francis Group, an informa business

First issued in paperback 2016

British Library Cataloguing in Publication Data
Rose, Clare.
  Making, selling and wearing boys' clothes in late-Victorian England. –
  (The history of retailing and consumption) 1. Boys' clothing–England–
  History–19th century.
  2. Children's clothing industry–England–History–19th century.
  I. Title II. Series
  687'.08341'0942–dc22

Library of Congress Cataloging-in-Publication Data
Rose, Clare.
  Making, selling, and wearing boys' clothes in late-Victorian England / Clare Rose.
    p. cm. — (The history of retailing and consumption)
  Includes bibliographical references and index.
  ISBN 978-0-7546-6444-4 (hardcover : alk. paper) 1. Boys' clothing—
  England—History. 2. Clothing trade—England—History. I. Title.

TT630.R67 2010
646.4'020942—dc22

2009050046

ISBN 13: 978-0-7546-6444-4 (hbk)
ISBN 13: 978-1-138-26186-0 (pbk)

Contents

The History of Retailing and Consumption
General Editor's Preface

It is increasingly recognized that retail systems and changes in the patterns of consumption play crucial roles in the development and societal structure of economies. Such recognition has led to renewed interest in the changing nature of retail distribution and the rise of consumer society from a wide range of academic disciplines. The aim of this multidisciplinary series is to provide a forum of publications that explore the history of retailing and consumption.

Gareth Shaw, University of Exeter, UK

List of Tables

Acknowledgements

This book, and the PhD from which it came, have been long projects that could not have been sustained or completed without the help and encouragement of many institutions and individuals. I am very grateful to the Arts and Humanities Research Council for the award of a research studentship; to the Pasold Research Fund for their award to support the collections research; to the School of Historical and Critical studies at Brighton for additional funding; and to the Scouloudi Fund for supporting the illustrations in this book. At Ashgate, I would like to thank Tom Gray for guiding the project through to completion and Mary Murphy for her meticulous editing.

I would like to thank my doctoral supervisors, Lou Taylor and Anna Davin, for their support, encouragement, and constructive criticism throughout the project. Their clear views of what was needed have helped to guide me through the research jungle, and their high standards spurred me on. Andrew Godley and Hugh Cunningham have been sources of inspiration through their work on childhood and on the clothing industry, and have offered support for my efforts. I have also benefited from the expertise and generosity of others working on the history of the clothing industry, notably Christopher Breward, Katrina Honeyman, Sarah Johnson and the late Anne Buck OBE. I have benefited greatly from discussions in the seminars hosted by John Benson and Laura Ugolini at the Centre for the History of Retailing and Distribution, University of Wolverhampton, and by Kelly Boyd at the Institute of Historical Research, London. I am grateful to Amy Miller and Dr Robert Blyth of the National Maritime Museum for reading an earlier version of the section on maritime history, and to Dan Cook for discussions on consumption and childhood.

The three major archives used for this research were the commercial documents registered by the Board of Trade and by the Worshipful Company of Stationers, held at The National Archives; photographs of children entering Dr Barnardo's Homes, held at the charity's headquarters in Barkingside; and the John Johnson Collection of Ephemera at the Bodleian Library. Viewing and recording the very numerous images in these documents raised many logistical problems, and I am very grateful for the assistance I received. At The National Archives I would like to thank Curator Carole McCormack, and Chris Cooper, Head of Reader Services, for permission to photograph documents. I would also like to thank Hugh Alexander, in the Image Library, for introducing me to the Stationers' Hall documents. At Barnardo's, I am very much indebted to Paul Carr and Marisa Dowling in the photographic department for their loan of space and equipment to peruse their unparalleled archive, and to Stephen Pover for negotiating permissions to publish images. Discussions with Caroline Bressey of University College London, with

Lydia Murdoch of Vassar College and with Mrs Esther Kwizera of Muhabura Diocese, Uganda, were invaluable in clarifying the interpretation of this material. At the Bodleian, Julie Anne Lambert, Librarian of the John Johnson Collection, shared her expertise and facilitated access to this major resource.

This project also made use of historic garments held in museum collections throughout England. Finding and studying these would have been impossible without the help and encouragement of many curators, especially: Penelope Byrde and Rosemary Harden at the Museum of Costume Bath; Noreen Marshall at the V&A Museum of Childhood; Joanna Hashagen of the Bowes Museum; Rosemary Allan, Beamish North of England Open Air Museum; Alison Carter, Hampshire County Museums Service; Jane May, Leicester Museums; Edwina Ehrman, then at the Museum of London; Anthea Jarvis and Miles Lambert, Gallery of Costume, Manchester; Sheila Shreeve OBE, Walsall; Ann Wise, then at Worthing Museums; Josie Sheppard, York Castle Museum. I am grateful to all of them for their interest and support.

I would also like to acknowledge the advice and assistance of Audrey Linkman at the Documentary Photography Archive in accessing this important collection. The patience and professionalism of the desk staff at the British Library, Children's Society archives, Guildhall Library, London Metropolitan Archives, National Art Library, Oldham Local Studies Library, and The Women's Library was also much appreciated.

Access to texts was facilitated by Monica Brewis at the University of Brighton; Tania Olsson at Chelsea College of Art; Donna Keniger at the University of Winchester; Catherine Polley at Winchester School of Art Library; and the inter-library loans service of Hampshire County Libraries.

This lengthy and arduous project would never have been finished without the unfailing support of my parents, and of William Brook-Hart, Nicholas and Rosemary. They have dealt cheerfully with my absence and preoccupation, and provided me with the best possible basis for understanding what family life should be, now or in the past.

Currency

Prices given in historic documents have been cited in pounds, shillings and pence (£ s d) without conversion to decimal currency as this can be misleading. The purchasing power of £1 varied over the period, but might represent a family's weekly income as late as 1913, as demonstrated by Maud Pember Reeves' classic study *Round About a Pound a Week* (London, 1913).

The divisions of £1 were as follows:

> 20 shillings (20s) = £1 pound (£1)
> 12 pence (12d) = 1 shilling (1s or 1/-)
> 21 shillings (21s) = 1 guinea (1 gn)

Items costing over £1 were sometimes priced in shillings – thus 21/6d for £1 1s 6d.

List of Abbreviations

BATH	Museum of Costume, Bath
BC	Books Commercial
BEA	North of England Open Air Museum, Beamish
BT	Board of Trade
Copy 1	Stationers' Hall Archive, The National Archives
DPA	Documentary Photography Archive, Manchester
Evan	Evanion Collection, the British Library
GCM	Gallery of Costume, Manchester
HCMS	Hampshire County Museums Service
HF	House of Fraser Collection, Scottish Business Archive, University of Glasgow Archives
JJ	John Johnson Collection, Bodleian Library
LEIC	Leicester City Museums
LMA	London Metropolitan Archives
MC	Men's Clothing
MOL	Museum of London Archive
NMM	National Maritime Museum, Greenwich
NPG	National Portrait Gallery, London
OT	Oxford Trades
TNA	The National Archives, Kew
VAMC	V&A Museum of Childhood
WIN	Winchester City Museum
Win Bills	Window Bills
WOR	Worthing Museums

Introduction

In September 1882, the editor of a woman's magazine advised her readers about the latest fashions for boys who were still young enough to wear dresses:

> The following dress has been made for such a child, a beautiful boy of three, and consists of crimson satin and cream lace; the skirt is lightly gathered over an embroidered satin band worked in black silk, the casaque being crenelated over it, each tab embroidered with a flower in black silk, and a black satin scarf is tied loosely round the hips in a large knot behind; beneath the tabs is sewn a full flounce of cream lace, and a very large handsome collar and cuffs of lace complete a costume which though showy is the very thing for the handsome little man, thus coloured both by art and nature as richly as a tropical butterfly.[1]

For poorer families, clothing choice was dictated less by fashion than by physical and economic constraints:

> I watched a sobbing little girl whose legs were being sponged down by one of the teachers.. It was a little boy, she said, not a little girl; and he had had an accident … these were the boys who went to school at the age of two and a half and, even so, could not yet be regarded as 'house-trained'.[2]

These contrasting passages remind us that gender and social status are both historically constructed, and constructed through clothing. An understanding of historic clothing practices can illuminate the ways in which social changes were experienced and conceptualised by individuals. This is particularly true of changes in family and personal life, which may be hard to access by other means.

The late nineteenth century was a period when childhood was at the forefront of public debate in Britain, from the Education Act of 1870 to the 'degeneration' controversy of the Boer War. There were great efforts to save distressed children, with the foundation of Dr Barnardo's Homes (1874), The Church of England Central Society for Providing Homes for Waifs and Strays (1881; later the Church of England Waifs and Strays Society and now The Children's Society), and the National Society for the Prevention of Cruelty to Children (1889). Changes in employment patterns, with women challenging men for the new clerical jobs, led to anxieties about the undermining of conventional masculinity. At the same time changes in production, distribution and retailing practices instigated an era of truly

---

[1] *Myra's Mid-Monthly Journal* September 1882, p. 256.

[2] C.H. Rolph, *London Particulars* (Oxford, 1980), p. 26.

mass consumption of standardised goods from bars of soap to suits of clothes. Each of these areas is currently being actively investigated by historians working in different fields. Outlines of some of the key methodological issues and debates for each area are provided below.

This book will use boys' clothing as a lens through which all of the above factors can be examined, assessed and re-evaluated. It will investigate the clothing worn by boys of all classes – not just the wealthy elite – in England between 1870 and 1900.[3] This period has been chosen as one in which new educational legislation and concerns about health made childhood the focus of national debate and political scrutiny. The age range of the 'boys' studied is bounded by toilet training and puberty – roughly three to thirteen years of age. This spans the ages at which a typical boy would enter and finish schooling and commence work, allowing us to examine the ways in which these life stages were conceptualised in clothing. For this age group clothing consumption was largely determined by the family rather than the individual, which raises interesting issues in consumption that have not been examined elsewhere.

Moreover, consumption was central to children's social identity, allowing them to integrate with their peer group in school or in the street. Indeed, consumption was one of the factors that defined these groups, with older and younger children separated by distinctive choices of clothing. Consumption also expressed family relationships, with family solidarity and prosperity expressed by dressing siblings to match. When times were hard, families made carefully calibrated judgements about clothing consumption to maximise potential earnings or charitable handouts. As nineteenth-century writers recognised all too well, clothing is essential to the staging of the self. This book will examine the means by which clothing was produced, marketed and consumed by families across the social spectrum. In doing so it will pose questions and offer answers that are applicable to other goods and times – perhaps even our own.

Historiographies

Histories of Childhood

The history of childhood has recently been opened up by some interesting cross-disciplinary initiatives. In the USA there is a Society for the History of Children and Youth (2001) with more than 200 international members and a Center for Childhood Studies at Rutgers University, which brings together historians with experts in childhood development and educationalists. In the UK there is a Centre

---

[3]   The enquiry was restricted to England because of the different educational and employment legislation affecting Scotland. The sources for consumption practice are largely concerned with major urban centres such as London, Manchester and Leeds. The PhD on which this book is based covered the period 1840–1900, but documentation before 1870 was found to be sparse and inconsistent.

for the History of Childhood at Oxford University (2003) and a Society for the Study of Childhood in the Past (2007).[4] During 2006, BBC Radio 4 broadcast a series on 'The Invention of Childhood' researched by Hugh Cunningham, and accompanied by a website, CD and book.[5] These initiatives are particularly valuable for the ways in which they set out to draw parallels across time and space, and to address the gap between readers' lived experience of childhood and the historiography.

Hugh Cunningham has identified two main approaches for writing about the history of childhood since the publication of Phillipe Ariès' *Centuries of Childhood* in 1960.[6] The first approach, typified by Carolyn Steedman,[7] is principally concerned with 'the cultural construction of ideas to do with childhood',[8] and uses cultural artefacts including literary texts, images and even toys as sources. These sources relate mostly to middle-class families. The second approach, typified by Viviana Zelizer,[9] uses quantitative sources, primarily economic in nature, to examine the family strategies that shaped children's roles. Family strategy studies have been used by Anna Davin and Ellen Ross to answer questions about social as well as economic relations.[10] In this book qualitative and quantitative methodologies will be combined in order to examine the interaction between economic and cultural forces in shaping children's experience.

The cultural history of childhood was developed by Linda Pollock, who identified a progressivist narrative in many histories of childhood.[11] Cunningham has followed Pollock's identification of a shaping 'romance' in the historiography of

---

[4]   Websites at: http://www.h-net.org/~child/SHCY/index.htm; http://children.camden.rutgers.edu/index.htm; http://www.history.ox.ac.uk/research/clusters/history_childhood/description.htm; http://www.sscip.bham.ac.uk

[5]   Hugh Cunningham and Michael Morpurgo, *The Invention of Childhood* (London, 2006); http://www.bbc.co.uk/radio4/history/childhood/.

[6]   Hugh Cunningham, 'Histories of Childhood', *American Historical Review*, 103/4 (1998): 1195–208.

[7]   Carolyn Steedman, *Strange Dislocations: Childhood and the Idea of Human Interiority, 1780–1930* (Cambridge, MA, 1995).

[8]   Cunningham, 'Histories of Childhood', p. 1195.

[9]   Viviana Zelizer, *Pricing the Priceless Child, The Changing Social Value of Children* (New York, 1985).

[10]   Anna Davin, *Growing Up Poor, Home, School and Street in London 1870–1914* (London, 1996); Ellen Ross, *Love and Toil, Motherhood in Outcast London 1870–1918* (Oxford, 1993); *eadem*, '"Fierce Questions and Taunts": Married Life in Working-class London, 1870–1914', *Feminist Studies*, 8/3 (1982): 575–602; *eadem*, 'Survival Networks: Women's Neighbourhood Sharing in London Before World War I', *History Workshop Journal*, 15 (1983): 4–28.

[11]   Linda Pollock, *Forgotten Children, Parent–Child Relations from 1500 to 1900* (Cambridge, 1983), p. 12.

childhood.[12] This 'romance' first appeared around 1847, and by 1857 writers were identifying their present as the 'Happy Ever After', foreclosing any possibility of further improvements.[13] This romance had one hero, Lord Shaftesbury, and working-class parents were either cast as villains, or written out altogether.[14] Cunningham's identification of an accepted historical narrative as 'romance' highlights the ambiguities in historic discussions of children. This affected even the definition of childhood: in the debates on the 1833 Factory Act childhood ended at age 14, around the age of puberty, but young workers were described as 'infants' by reformers.[15] The terminology used for discussing working-class childhood was further clouded by contemporary definitions of 'race' that elided class status and ethnicity. Cunningham has pointed out the extent to which even sympathetic observers such as Lord Ashley and Mayhew conflated class and race, calling poor children 'savages'.[16] The characterisation of the poor as a separate race was strengthened in the 1860s with Haekel's formulation 'ontogeny recapitulates phylogeny', in which 'savages' represented the childhood of humanity, and 'the child therefore represents the adult of an earlier period – the savage'.[17]

There was another concept of the poor child, identified by Cunningham from the 1860s onwards, which focused on the child as a victim. The discourse of the child-victim was fostered by Evangelical reformers such as Lord Shaftesbury and 'Dr' Barnardo, building on literary prototypes such as Dickens' Jo the crossing-sweeper in *Bleak House*. Narratives and images of the 'waif' child were immensely popular and profitable for fundraising.[18] In this model, the deviation from expected norms of childhood was identified with the parents, who were cast as 'savages'.[19] The foundation of the East End Juvenile Mission (Dr Barnardo's Homes) in 1871, the National Society for the Prevention of Cruelty to Children in 1879 and the Church of England Waifs and Strays Society (CEWSS) in 1881 helped to consolidate the new view of childhood.[20]

---

[12]   Hugh Cunningham, *The Children of the Poor: Representations of Childhood since the Seventeenth Century* (Oxford, 1991); Eric Hopkins, *Childhood Transformed: Working Class Children in Nineteenth-Century England* (Manchester, 1994).

[13]   Ibid., p. 12.

[14]   Ibid., p. 16.

[15]   Ibid., p. 94.

[16]   Ibid., pp. 94–109, citing H. Mayhew, *The Unknown Mayhew*, ed. E. Yeo and E.P. Thompson (London, 1971).

[17]   Ibid., p. 127, citing Stephen Jay Gould, *Ontology and Phylogeny* (Cambridge, MA, 1977).

[18]   Alfred Alsop, a Manchester evangelist, claimed to have sold 25,000 copies of one such narrative in less than a year; ibid., p. 141.

[19]   Ibid., p. 133.

[20]   Ibid., p. 136. See also June Rose, *For the Sake of the Children, Inside Dr Barnardo's: 120 Years of Caring for Children* (London, 1987); John Stroud, *Thirteen Penny Stamps:*

Carolyn Steedman finds evidence of the 'romance' of childhood in Mayhew's account of the 'little watercress girl', concluding that she is best understood not as an individual human being, but as an embodiment of the damaged child who was presented elsewhere in Victorian popular culture.[21] Diana Gittins has taken Steedman's work a stage further, distinguishing between the child as a physical or 'embodied' being; as a representation; and as a memory in the consciousness of the adult reader.[22] Gittins highlights the gap between representations and reality, with photographs a particularly problematic source because of their claims of 'scientific objectivity'.[23] This raises the issue of how historians can address the embodied experience of a child, rather than cultural constructs of it.

Sources for childhood practices have been examined by a series of American historians starting with Jay Mechling and continuing with Sally Helvenston, Jo Paoletti and Christina Bates. Mechling maintained that childcare texts are primarily self-referential, and should only be used as evidence of 'manual-writing values'.[24] This is true for aspects of childcare such as feeding schedules where externally verified evidence is hard to obtain. It is less of a problem for clothing, where evidence of behaviour can be found in portraits or manufacturers' catalogues.[25] Christina Bates has unpicked the assumed link between the clothing discussed by theorists such as dress reformers, and the clothing actually worn.[26] She found that where these coincided, as with the loose smock dresses adopted by young girls in the 1890s, the motivation was not theoretical but pragmatic: loose dresses were easier and cheaper to make and to wear than fitted ones. Bates' work has provided a model for the evaluation of the meanings of the sailor suit and the kilt in Chapter 8.

Gendered Childhoods

One of the key issues in the history of childhood is historical constructions of gender, in which clothing practices play a major part. Gender practices also tended to be class-specific, and have been examined separately in the context of middle-class and working-class families. In their seminal study of early-Victorian middle-class families, Leonore Davidoff and Catherine Hall examined the ways in which

---

The Story of the Church of England Children's Society (Waifs and Strays) from 1881 to the 1970s (London, 1971); Gillian Wagner, *Barnardo* (London, 1979).

[21] Steedman, *Strange Dislocations*, p. 174.

[22] Diana Gittins, *The Child in Question* (Basingstoke, 1998), p. 12.

[23] Ibid., pp. 119, 27–30.

[24] Jay Mechling, 'Advice to Historians on Advice to Mothers', *Journal of Social History*, 9 (1975), p. 55.

[25] Sally Helvenston, 'Advice to American Mothers on the Subject of Children's Dress, 1800–1920', *Dress*, 7 (1981): 30–46.

[26] Christina Bates, 'How to dress the Children? A Comparison of Prescription and Practice in Late-Nineteenth-Century North America', *Dress*, 24 (1997), p. 43.

the needs of parents, children and siblings worked with and against each other.[27] John Tosh has followed this with several detailed studies of Victorian fatherhood, and of the gendered division of emotional labour within middle-class families after 1860.[28] In *A Man's Place*, Tosh examined in more detail the transition between boyhood and manhood, and identified a shift in the late nineteenth century to a gendered view of early childhood.[29] He saw this change reflected in changes in the practice of 'breeching', young boys' passage from toddlers' dresses to male trousers:

> In many ways petticoats for little boys were a conservative residue of the past, rather than an accurate indicator of Victorian attitudes to gender. Prevailing conceptions of a deep divide between the sexes were founded on a theory of natural or biological difference. Logically this extended to children and should have encouraged markers of sexual difference from birth.[30]

The shift from gradualism to essentialism in gender identity by the 1890s is seen by historians using different types of sources. Karin Calvert has used portraits, furniture and toys to show how material culture embodies and amplifies abstract concepts of childhood.[31] In the 1890s she sees a restating of masculine identity in boys' clothes, accompanied by an anxiety about avoiding 'effeminacy'.[32] Claudia Nelson has examined children's literature, which presented models of both childhood and of adult male and female behaviour.[33] For Nelson, the 1890s ideal of boyhood was typified by the adventure novels of G.F. Henty and by the stories of *The Boys' Own Paper*, with an Imperial dimension added by the work of Rudyard Kipling and Robert Baden-Powell.[34] However this interpretation is complicated by the co-existence of multiple models of masculinity in popular literature: Frances

---

[27]   Leonore Davidoff and Catherine Hall, *Family Fortunes: Men and Women of the English Middle Class 1780–1850* (London, 1987).

[28]   John Tosh, 'Domesticity and Manliness in the Victorian Middle Class, the Family of Edward White Benson', in Michael Roper and John Tosh (eds), *Manful Assertions: Masculinities in Britain since 1800* (London, 1991), pp. 44–74; *idem*, 'Authority and Nurture in Middle-Class Fatherhood: the Case of Early and Mid-Victorian England', *Gender and History*, 8/1 (1996): 48–64; *idem, A Man's Place, Masculinity and the Middle-Class Home in Victorian England* (New Haven, 1999).

[29]   Tosh, *A Man's Place*, p. 90.

[30]   Ibid., p. 103.

[31]   Karen Calvert, *Children in the House: The Material Culture of Early Childhood, 1600–1900* (Boston, 1992).

[32]   Calvert suggests that this was based on a waning of religious values and the waxing of 'a more strictly human, and hence gender-specific, image of their young'; ibid., p. 110.

[33]   Claudia Nelson, *Boys will be Girls: The Feminine Ethic and British Children's Fiction, 1857–1917* (New Brunswick, 1990).

[34]   Ibid., p. 110; pp. 79–81.

Hodgson Burnett's *Little Lord Fauntleroy*, with its redemptive boy-hero, went to 18 editions between 1883 and 1890.[35] Jo Paoletti, who has examined gendered clothing practices for children, agrees with Tosh and Nelson in seeing a growing essentialism expressed in boys' clothing in the 1890s.[36] This was particularly apparent in a lowering of the age for gender-distinct clothing. Age-related rites of passage in boys' clothing will be considered in Chapter 6 of this book.

The ways the ideology of Empire affected masculine behaviour has been a fruitful source of study since the work of John Mackenzie.[37] He mapped out the ways in which militarism permeated children's literature, education and leisure activities. Other historians such as Andrew Thompson and Bernard Porter have challenged this view, suggesting that there was significant working-class resistance to official propaganda on Empire.[38] Graham Dawson has contributed an examination of the role of heroes and of the imagination in supporting Imperial ideologies: 'Masculinities are lived out in the flesh, but fashioned in the imagination.'[39] Dawson's analysis of the performative aspect of masculinity has an obvious relevance to the history of dress.[40] Michael Paris has focused on the presentation of actual conflicts through the imaginary media of popular fiction, art and advertising.[41] Heather Streets has examined the particular place of Highland soldiers in British military ideology and popular culture, particularly in the aftermath of the Indian Mutiny.[42] Each of these studies has informed the book as a whole, but particularly the interpretation of the cultural meanings of boys' sailor suits and kilts in Chapter 7.

---

[35] Information from the British Library catalogue.

[36] Jo B. Paoletti, 'Clothes Make the Boy, 1869–1910', *Dress*, 9 (1983): 16–20; Jo B. Paoletti and Carol L. Kregloh, 'The Children's Department', in Claudia Kidwell and Valerie Steele (eds), *Men and Women, Dressing the Part* (Washington DC, 1989), pp. 22–41.

[37] John Mackenzie, *Propaganda and Empire: The Manipulation of British Public Opinion 1880–1960* (Manchester, 1984); *idem* (ed.), *Imperialism and Popular Culture* (Manchester, 1986).

[38] Andrew Thompson, *The Empire Strikes Back? The Impact of Imperialism on Britain from the Mid-nineteenth Century* (Harlow, 2005), esp. Chapter 4; Bernard Porter, *The Absent-Minded Imperialists: Empire, Society and Culture in Britain* (Oxford, 2004), esp. Chapter 9.

[39] Graham Dawson, *Soldier Heroes: British Adventure, Empire, and the Imagining of Masculinity* (London, 1994) p. 1.

[40] Ibid., p. 23. Dawson's insistence on the 'distinctions between fantasies and real relationships and actions with consequences in the social world' (p. 17) is particularly helpful for understanding the fantasy element of boys' clothes.

[41] Michael Paris, *Warrior Nation, Images of War in British Popular Culture 1850–2000* (London, 2000).

[42] Heather Streets, *Martial Races: The Military, Race and Masculinity in British Imperial Culture, 1857–1914* (Manchester, 2004).

Masculinity in the Working-class Family

Childhood experience in the nineteenth century was defined not only by gender but also by class, as was demonstrated by the pioneering work of Standish Meacham.[43] In working-class households gender relations were often underpinned by economic relations, as Anna Clark has showed.[44] Ellen Ross has demonstrated that many working-class families functioned as two economic units, one with the husband and the other with the wife and children.[45] Ross saw the difficulties this situation posed for adolescent boys, pulled between the need to contribute to the family budget and the desire for marks of individual status such as new clothes.[46] The role of clothing in demarcating the passage from dependant to wage-earner will be evaluated through an analysis of Barnardo's entry photographs in Chapter 4.

Anna Davin takes as her subject the encounter between middle-class and working-class experiences of childhood on the shared territory of the Board School.[47] The gulf between class-specific childhoods was exaggerated by the rhetoric of philanthropic organisations and state agencies, who stigmatised models of childhood and parenting that did not conform to their own.[48] This creates a real problem in the discussion of past childrearing practice, since many of the available sources are heavily biased. Davin deals with this problem by comparing the evidence on working-class behaviour produced by outsiders (teachers' reports) and insiders (oral histories and autobiographies).

Steve Humphries used personal histories to question the view of working-class behaviour presented by middle-class observers.[49] Humphries has a clear view of the elements of class control at work in institutions such as schools, and of the dangers of a 'Whig' historiography of childhood.[50] He identifies the late nineteenth-century 'discovery' of adolescence as a class-based ideology with 'little explanatory power when applied to a working-class culture typified by group solidarity and a rapid transition from childhood to adulthood.'[51] The reaction of working-class boys to middle-class initiatives on their behalf has been examined in detail by John Springhall, who analysed the ways in which late nineteenth-century militarism and imperialism and masculinity were enacted in a network of overlapping and

---

[43]   Standish Meacham, *A Life Apart, The English Working Class 1890–1914* (London, 1977).

[44]   Anna Clark, *The Struggle for the Breeches: Gender and the Making of the British Working Class* (Berkeley, 1995).

[45]   Ross, 'Fierce Questions', p. 576.

[46]   Ross, *Love and Toil*, pp. 148–60.

[47]   Davin, *Growing up Poor*, p. 1.

[48]   Ibid., pp. 7–8 and 134.

[49]   Stephen Humphries, *Hooligans or Rebels? An Oral History of Working-Class Childhood and Youth 1889–1939* (Oxford, 1981).

[50]   Ibid., p. 2.

[51]   Ibid., p. 17.

competing organisations including the YMCA, the Boys' Brigade, the Church Lads' Brigade and the Catholic Boys' Brigade.[52] Springhall was particularly aware of the performative aspects of these organisations with their emphasis on parades and uniforms.[53] He was clear about the degree to which ideals of masculinity remained class-bound:

> The majority of working class youth shared a different concept of manliness from that embodied in the Boys' Brigade or the *Boys' Own Paper*. Manliness, as understood in this environment, was often identified by the middle class as synonymous with hooliganism.[54]

The work of Springhall, Ross, Davin and Humphries on the interaction between families and institutions has informed the discussions of the 'street arab' in Chapter 1 and of institutional photographs in Chapter 6.

Masculinity and Clothing

Historians of male clothing have paid close attention to the interaction between clothing practices and changes in social hierarchies. John Harvey has shown how the dark clothing of Victorian professional men was used by contemporary writers as a metaphor for the bureaucratisation and Puritanism of their society.[55] David Kuchta has demonstrated that sobriety in clothing also had political meanings after the French Revolution, helping to create a new type of elite masculine virtue which excluded both proletarian men and aristocratic women.[56] When working men tried to assimilate the elite model of dress, as British agricultural workers did in the 1880s by adopting wool lounge suits instead of corduroy trousers, this was seen as a political act and the elite responded with an elaboration of dress and behavioural codes.[57]

Christopher Breward's work is important for its use of theories of masculinity based on the twentieth century to open up the study of the nineteenth.[58] Using

---

[52]   John Springhall, 'Building Character in the British Boy: the Attempt to Extend Christian Manliness to Working-class Adolescents, 1880–1914', in Roper and Tosh, *Manful Assertions*, pp. 52–74; idem, *Youth, Empire and Society: British Youth Movements, 1883–1940* (London, 1977). See also Michael J Childs, *Labour's Apprentices: Working-Class Lads in Late Victorian and Edwardian England* (Montreal, 1992).

[53]   Springhall, 'Building Character', p. 60.

[54]   Ibid., pp. 69–70.

[55]   John Harvey, *Men in Black* (Chicago, 1995); David Kuchta, *The Three-Piece Suit and Modern Masculinity, England 1550–1850* (Berkeley, 2002).

[56]   Kuchta, *The Three-Piece Suit*, pp. 147–9 and 167–9.

[57]   Diana De Marly, *Fashion for Men, An Illustrated History* (London, 1985), p. 100.

[58]   Christopher Breward, *The Hidden Consume:, Masculinities, Fashion and City Life 1860–1914* (Manchester, 1999); see also Frank Mort, *Cultures of Consumption: Masculinities*

sources from texts to shop flyers to music hall songs, he has uncovered a plurality of masculine identities based on class, age and location.[59] His work has been crucial in highlighting the importance of clothing consumption in the formation of masculine identities, and examining the business of fashion retailing for men in the early twentieth century.[60] Laura Ugolini has amplified several of Breward's themes, notably the importance of clothing consumption in defining male social roles, and the problems when consumption was limited by age, poverty or war.[61] She also acknowledges the role of social groups (including families) in defining and enforcing norms of individual consumption.[62] These studies illuminating the meanings in male clothes have proved useful in articulating the discussion of social and gender distinctions in clothing in Chapters 6 and 7.

Producing Male Clothing

Ugolini's work forms a bridge between studies of clothing consumption following cultural history methods and studies of clothing production using economic history methods, particularly in her discussion of the challenges faced by bespoke tailors increasingly challenged by ready-to-wear manufacturers.[63] Important studies by Beverley Lemire and Stanley Chapman have established the existence of an organised trade in ready-made clothing in Britain by 1800, with centres in London, Leicester, Leeds and Manchester.[64] Phillipe Perrot and Farid Chenoune recognise Britain as the source for the ready-made men's clothing that dominated the French market from the 1860s onwards.[65] Chenoune sees ready-made manufacturers as fashion innovators, originating new garments like the loose 'paletot' that suited industrial production methods.[66] The relationship between industrial and bespoke clothing

---

and Social Space in Late Twentieth Century Britain (London, 1996).

[59]   Breward, *Hidden Consumer*, pp. 170–73 and 201–10.

[60]   Ibid., pp. 100–151.

[61]   Laura Ugolini, *Men and Menswear: Sartorial Consumption in Britain 1880–1939* (Aldershot, 2007) especially pp. 19–45; 'Men, Masculinities and Menswear Advertising, c.1890–1914', in John Benson and Laura Ugolini (eds), *A Nation of Shopkeepers, Five Centuries of British Retailing* (London, 2003).

[62]   Ugolini, *Men and Menswear*, pp. 47–70.

[63]   Ibid., pp. 99–124.

[64]   Beverley Lemire, *Dress, Culture and Commerce: The English Clothing Trade Before the Factory, 1660–1800* (Basingstoke, 1997); Stanley Chapman, *Merchant Enterprise in Britain from the Industrial Revolution to World War I* (Cambridge, 1992); *idem*, 'The Innovating Entrepreneurs in the British Ready-made Clothing Industry', *Textile History*, 24/1 (1993): 5–25.

[65]   Philippe Perrot, *Fashioning the Bourgeoisie: A History of Clothing in the Nineteenth Century* (Princeton, 1994 [1981]), pp. 68–9; Farid Chenoune, *A History of Men's Fashion* (Paris, 1993), p. 67.

[66]   Chenoune, *History of Men's Fashion*, p. 66–8.

producers, and their respective roles in design innovation for boys, will be examined in Chapters 2 and 3.

Detailed studies of British ready-to-wear clothing manufacturers by Andrew Godley and Katrina Honeyman have singled out Leeds as a centre that specialised in menswear from the 1850s.[67] Honeyman's research has identified Leeds manufacturers as innovators not only in production methods, but in new types of retailing such as chain stores and 'wholesale bespoke'.[68] Honeyman also notes that boys' suits were a specialism of major Leeds firms such as John Barran and Blackburn.[69] Sarah Levitt, who has worked extensively on the Board of Trade Archive of Registered Designs, suggests that this concentration on boys may have provided the ready-to-wear trade with an entrée to middle-class adult custom.[70]

These historians have noted the innovations in promotion and retailing that accompanied developments in production, from Moses' versified advertisements in the 1840s onwards.[71] The scale of clothing retailers' spending on advertising (up to £10,000 in 1850)[72] indicates that they may not have been selling on price alone. This raises the issue of the role of design in the growth of ready-to-wear. Ben Fine and Ellen Leopold have seen early menswear as characterised by 'unchanging high-volume output of standardised, machine-made garments' while women's clothing was subject to fashionable variation.[73] This raises the issue as to whether boys' clothing fit the male or the female model.

Levitt's work on the Board of Trade Archive of Registered Designs has demonstrated the full engagement of clothing manufacturers with design copyrighting from the 1840s onwards.[74] However, the implications of this source

---

[67]   Andrew Godley, 'The Development of the UK Clothing Industry, 1850–1950: Output and Productivity Growth', *Business History*, 37 (1995): 46–63; 'The Emergence of Mass Production in the UK Clothing Industry', in Ian Taplin and Jonathan Winterton (eds), *Restructuring within a Labour Intensive Industry: The UK Clothing Industry in Transition* (Aldershot, 1996): 8–23; *The History of the Ready-Made Clothing Industry* (Leeds, 1997); 'The Development of the Clothing Industry: Technology and Fashion', *Textile History*, 28/1 (1997): 3–9; 'Foreign Multinationals and Innovation in British Retailing: 1850–1962', *Business History*, 45 (2003): 80–100; with R. Church, *The Emergence of Modern Marketing* (London, 2003).

[68]   Katrina Honeyman, *Well Suited: A History of the Leeds Clothing Industry, 1850–1990* (Oxford, 2000); 'Following Suit: Men, Masculinity and Gendered Practices in the Clothing Trade in Leeds, England, 1890–1940', *Gender and History*, 14/3 (2002): 426–46.

[69]   Honeyman, *Well Suited*, pp. 21, 33, 248–305.

[70]   Sarah Levitt, *The Victorians Unbuttoned* (London, 1986), p. 101; see also *eadem*, 'Clothing', in Mary Rose (ed.), *The Lancashire Cotton Industry, A History Since 1700* (Lancaster, 1996), pp. 168, 175.

[71]   Chapman, 'Innovating Entrepreneurs', p. 23.

[72]   Godley, 'Development of the Clothing Industry', p. 6.

[73]   Ben Fine and Ellen Leopold, *The World of Consumption* (London, 1993), pp. 231–6.

[74]   Levitt, *Victorians Unbuttoned*, p. 1.

have not been fully taken into account by other historians. Honeyman, while acknowledging the ways that menswear retailers adjusted their displays to attract different market segments, concluded that the industry benefited from a degree of 'style monotony' as a stabilising force.[75] The quantitative analysis of Registered Designs in Chapter 2 will allow us to reconsider the role of design in boys' clothing, and the role of boys' clothing in the garment industry as a whole.

Alongside the burgeoning mass-produced sector, nineteenth-century consumers had access to made-to-order clothing from both male tailors and female dressmakers. Young boys' clothing, which occupied a half-way point between dresses and suits, was a frequent subject of contention between these two sets of professionals.[76] In the late nineteenth century, the position of bespoke tailors was progressively undermined both by the growth of ready-to-wear and by developments such as paper patterns for dressmakers. Dressmaking patterns were available to amateur dressmakers as well as professionals, but the extent to which they were used for boys' clothing is unclear. Indeed the scope of both professional and amateur dressmaking practice remains undefined, in spite of groundbreaking studies by Wendy Gamber, Barbara Burman, Beth Harris and others.[77] The evidence for dressmaking practices will be discussed as part of the evaluation of the production of boys' clothing in Chapter 2.

Consuming Boys' Clothing

Clothing, with its social and symbolic meanings and its built-in obsolescence, provides fertile ground for theorists of consumption. One of the main figures in the field is Daniel Miller, an anthropologist of contemporary Britain who sees consumption as 'key to an understanding of contemporary society and of culture itself'.[78] Miller builds on Pierre Bourdieu's concept of the habitus which 'tends to generate all the "reasonable", "common-sense" behaviours … which are likely

---

[75]   Katrina Honeyman, 'Style Monotony and the Business of Fashion: The Marketing of Menswear in Inter-war England', *Textile History*, 34/2 (2003): 171–91.

[76]   This was already an issue in the 1840s: see Joseph Couts, *A Practical Guide for the Tailor's Cutting-Room, being a treatise on Measuring and Cutting Clothing in all styles, and for Every Period of Life from Childhood to Old Age* (Glasgow, 1850), p. 29; A Lady, *The Workwoman's Guide, by a Lady* (London, 1838) [Doncaster, 1975].

[77]   Wendy Gamber, *The Female Economy: the Millinery and Dressmaking Trades, 1860–1930* (Urbana, 1997); Barbara Burman (ed.), *The Culture of Sewing: Gender, Consumption and Home Dressmaking* (Oxford, 1999); Beth Harris (ed.), *Famine and Fashion: Needlewomen in the Nineteenth Century* (Aldershot, 2005). See also Kevin Seligman, 'Dressmakers' Patterns: The English Commercial Paper Pattern Industry, 1878–1950', *Costume,* 37 (2003): 95–113.

[78]   Daniel Miller, *Material Culture and Mass Consumption* (Oxford, 1987), p. 76. See also Miller, *Acknowledging Consumption* (London, 1995); Miller (ed.), *Material Cultures, Why Some Things Matter* (London, 1996).

to be positively sanctioned'.[79] Bourdieu's concepts of the habitus and of distinction between social groups have been recognised as important models for theorising the consumption of clothing.[80] A refinement to this theory has been provided by Colin Campbell, who has explored the gap between the meaning of the goods consumed and the meaning of the act of consumption: 'All too often observers presume that, since they have no difficulty in ascribing meaning to an item of clothing, they can, by a simple process of extrapolation, also understand the meaning of an individual's action in selecting and displaying it.'[81] Campbell highlights the importance of acknowledging 'instrumental meaning' based on pragmatic factors such as cost and ease of wear, which may limit the consumer's ability to express 'symbolic meaning' through their choice of goods.[82] Campbell's understanding of the multiple intentions expressed in a single act of consumption has been used to shape the analysis of consumption practices and their meanings in Chapters 5 and 6.

Clothing has also been identified as an important marker for shifts in historic consumption practices by John Styles, Neil Mc Kendrick, John Brewer and Maxine Berg.[83] Fine and Leopold have insisted on the primacy of mass consumption (rather than technical advances) as a driver of mass production.[84] This is borne out by work on the eighteenth-century clothing industry by Beverly Lemire.[85] However, it is generally agreed that changes in production and distribution, as well as a gradual erosion of income differentials, created a marked change in consumption patterns in the late nineteenth century.[86] Diana Crane has made an important contribution to the study of clothing consumption in this period, using surveys of French and American households which give detail of clothing consumption by individuals.[87]

[79] Pierre Bourdieu, *The Logic of Practice* (Cambridge, 1990), pp. 55–6.

[80] Pierre Bourdieu, *Distinction: A Social Critique of the Judgement of Taste* (London, 1984). See Joanne Entwistle, *The Fashioned Body: Fashion, Dress and Modern Social Theory* (London, 2000), p. 36.

[81] Colin Campbell, 'The Meaning of Objects and the Meaning of Actions, a Critical Note on the Sociology of Consumption and Theories of Clothing', *Journal of Material Culture*, 1/1 (1996): 93–105. See also *idem*, 'When the Meaning is not a Message: A Critique of the Consumption as Communication Thesis', in Mica Nava et al., *Buy This Book, Studies in Advertising and Consumption* (London, 1997): 340–52.

[82] Campbell, ' Meaning of Objects', pp. 97–100.

[83] Neil McKendrick, John Brewer and J.H. Plumb, *The Birth of a Consumer Society: The Commercialization of Eighteenth-century England* (London, 1982); John Brewer and Roy Porter, *Consumption and the World of Goods* (London, 1993); John Styles, 'Dress in History: Reflections on a Contested Terrain', *Fashion Theory*, 2/4 (1998): 383–9; Maxine Berg and Elizabeth Eger, *Luxury in the Eighteenth Century: Debates, Desires and Delectable Goods* (Basingstoke, 2003).

[84] Fine and Leopold, *World of Consumption*, p. 66.

[85] Lemire, *Dress, Culture and Commerce*.

[86] John Benson, *The Rise of Consumer Society in Britain, 1880–1980* (London, 1994); Harold Perkin, *The Rise of Professional Society; England since 1880* (London, 1989).

[87] Diana Crane, *Fashion and Its Social Agendas* (Chicago, 2000), pp. 30–98.

Crane's use of this quantitative data has provided a model for the analysis of clothing consumption in Chapters 4–6.

The history of marketing and of sales practices is an area that has developed in tandem with the history of consumption, but with an emphasis on methods from business history rather than sociology.[88] Advertising documents used to sell clothing and other goods have been studied in their own right for many years,[89] and three major collections have been partially published.[90] Advertisements were used as a major source in studies of clothing consumption of clothing in Britain by Breward and Ugolini.[91] However, the most detailed analysis of the way that late nineteenth-century clothing advertising worked is found in Rob Schorman's study of America.[92] He argues that these advertisements communicated much more than the prices of goods on offer:

> Advertising added yet another layer of meaning and interpretive necessity to the dress code at the same time that it made the forms of fashion available to an unprecedented range of people. At the end of the nineteenth century, fashion, advertising, and image-making forged a strategic alliance so strong that it eventually made them seem virtually interchangeable.[93]

Schorman's analysis of advertisers' visual strategies has provided a model for the interpretation of British advertising documents in Chapter 7.

---

[88]   Useful overviews of the field are given by John Benson and Laura Ugolini, *A Nation of Shopkeepers: Five Centuries of British Retailing* (London, 2003), esp. pp. 1–25; Bill Lancaster, *The Department Store, A Social History* (Leicester, 1995); Richard Coopey, Sean O'Connell, and Dilwyn Porter, *Mail Order Retailing in Britain: A Business and Social History* (Oxford, 2005).

[89]   T.R. Nevett, *Advertising in Britain, a History* (London: Heinemann, 1982); Paul Jobling and David Crowley, *Graphic Design: Reproduction and Representation since 1800* (Manchester, 1996); Maurice Rickards and Michael Twyman, *The Encyclopedia of Ephemera: A guide to the fragmentary documents of everyday life for the collector, curator and historian* (London, 2000).

[90]   Michael Jubb, *Cocoa and Corsets: a selection of late Victorian and Edwardian posters and showcards from the Stationers' Company copyright records preserved in the Public Record Office* (London, 1984); Bodleian Library, *A Nation of Shopkeepers, Trade Ephemera from 1654 to the 1860s in the John Johnson Collection* (Oxford, 2001); Evanion Collection, http: //www.bl.uk/catalogues/evanion/ See Appendix 1.

[91]   Breward, *Hidden Consumer*; Laura Ugolini, 'Men, Masculinities and Menswear Advertising, c.1890–1914', in Benson and Ugolini, *Nation of Shopkeepers*, pp. 80–104.

[92]   Rob Schorman, *Selling Style: Clothing and Social Change at the Turn of the Century* (Philadelphia, 2003). Rickards identifies innovation in advertising with American firms and does not mention any British emulators; *Encyclopedia of Ephemera*, pp. 77–8.

[93]   Schorman, *Selling Style*, p. 130.

Consumption by and behalf of children raises particular issues in the theory of consumption, as Dan Cook has noted.[94] There have been some interesting studies of clothing consumption for contemporary British children which raise issues of peer group and familial identity which are echoed in my findings.[95] Cook's study of children's clothing in early twentieth-century America demonstrated the importance of this sector for both retailers and manufacturers.[96] This book will extend Cook's enquiry back into late nineteenth-century Britain, arguing for the importance of boys' clothing in the formation of British ready-to-wear.

Sources

In a special issue of *Fashion Theory* devoted to methodologies, the title of an article by John Styles summed up the state of the field: 'Reflections on a Contested Terrain'.[97] The variety of approaches currently being applied to the study of dress can be seen as appropriate to the 'multiple meanings and interpretations' of dress itself. It does, however, complicate the selection of an appropriate methodology for a cross-disciplinary research project. Three of the major sources used – surviving garments, photographs and consumption documents – each have their own literature and their own range of methodologies which will be summarised here; a detailed account of the methodologies used in this study can be found in Appendix 1.

Surviving Garments

Surviving garments, and the personal histories associated with them, offer the possibility of direct access to the lived experiences of non-elite social groups.[98]

---

[94]   Daniel Cook, 'The Missing Child in Consumption Theory', *Journal of Consumer Culture*, 8/2 (2008): 219–43.

[95]   Sharon Boden, Christopher Pole, Jane Pilcher, and Tim Edwards, 'New consumers? The social and cultural significance of children's fashion consumption', *Cultures of Consumption Working Papers*, 16 (2004), online at www.consume.bbk.ac.uk.

[96]   Daniel Cook, *The Commodification of Childhood: The Children's Clothing Industry and the Rise of the Child Consumer* (Durham, NC, 2004).

[97]   Styles, 'Dress in History'. See also Lou Taylor, 'Doing the Laundry? A Reassessment of Object-Based Dress History'; Christopher Breward, 'Cultures, Histories, Identities, Fashioning a Cultural Approach to Dress'; Valerie Steele, 'A Museum of Fashion is More than a Clothes Bag', all in *Fashion Theory*, 2/4 (1998).

[98]   Carol Tulloch, '"Out of Many, One People", The Relativity of Dress Race and Ethnicity to Jamaica, 1880–1907', *Fashion Theory*, 2/4 (1998): 359–82; *eadem* (ed.), *Black Style* (London, 2004); Angela Partington, 'Popular fashion and working class affluence', in Juliet Ash and Elizabeth Wilson, *Chic Thrills: a Fashion Reader* (London, 1992), pp. 145–61.

These enquiries are most easily focused on the twentieth century, for which the richest contextual material is available, but there have been important studies of earlier periods by Claudia Kidwell, Anne Buck, Jane Tozer and Sarah Levitt, Beverly Lemire, Elizabeth Wilson and Lou Taylor.[99] Surviving garments have been used as subjects for material culture studies for some time, as noted by Steele and by Severa and Horswill.[100] However, they present several methodological problems, notably how to relate the deductions made from individual examples to all garments of a similar category. Moreover, the link between surviving artefacts and past practice is not transparent: items in museums may have been selected for preservation by their original users, or by curators.[101] The basis for selection may be pragmatic, aesthetic, or shaped by personal interests.[102] This is a particularly important issue when applied to boys' clothing: the search of museum collections detailed in Appendix 1 revealed a strong bias against boys' suits and towards toddlers' dresses. This may have reflected curators' interest in fashionable female clothing, or pragmatic issues such as ease of display.[103] Although surviving boys' dresses may not be representative, they have been analysed qualitatively in Chapter 7 as exemplars of the contradictions inherent in designing dresses for male toddlers. Surviving boys' suits have provided invaluable information on the branding of clothing by retailers for discussion in Chapter 3.

---

[99]   Claudia Kidwell, 'Short Gowns', *Dress*, 4 (1978): 30–65; Anne Buck, *Dress in Eighteenth-Century England* (London, 1979); Jane Tozer and Sarah Levitt, *Fabric of Society: A Century of People and their Clothes 1770–1870* (Powys, 1983); Elizabeth Wilson and Lou Taylor, *Through the Looking Glass: A History of Dress from 1860 to the Present Day* (London, 1989).

[100]   Key texts for this approach include: E. McClung Fleming, 'Artifact Study: A Proposed Model', *Winterthur Portfolio*, 16 (1981): 153–73; Joan Severa and Merrill Horswill, 'Costume as Material Culture', *Dress*, 15 (1989): 51–64; Jules Prown, 'Mind in Matter, An Introduction to Material Culture Theory and Method', in Susan Pearce (ed.), *Interpreting Objects and Collections* (London, 1994), pp. 133–8; Nancy Rexford, 'Studying Garments for their Own Sake: Mapping the World of Costume Scholarship', *Dress*, 14 (1988): 68–75; Steele, 'Museum of Fashion'; Lou Taylor, *The Study of Dress History* (Manchester, 2002), esp. pp. 3–63. John Styles, *The Dress of the People: Everyday Fashion in Eighteenth Century England* (London, 2007), used samples of textiles left as tokens at the London Foundling Hospital, rather than garments, as evidence.

[101]   See Jane Tozer and Sarah Levitt, 'Cunnington's Attitude to Collecting', *Costume*, 20 (1986): 1–17, for a case study of an important collector.

[102]   'It is the best or better-than average that tend to be preserved, either as souvenir of some memorable event or because they were thought unsuitable to give to the poor after being outgrown'; Doris Langley Moore, *The Child in Fashion* (London, 1953), pp. 17–18.

[103]   For example, the founder of Bath Museum of Costume, Doris Langley Moore, had at least four nineteenth-century boys' suits in her collection when it was published as *The Child in Fashion*. When the collection was transferred to the Assembly Rooms Museum, Bath, only one of these suits was retained (BATH IV.24.2).

Pioneers in the study of surviving garments such as Phyllis Cunnington, Anne Buck and Elizabeth Ewing demonstrated how these can be interpreted as markers of age and status as well as items of consumption.[104] The bias towards upper-class practices inherent in the sources used has been justified by dress historians like Elizabeth Ewing by invoking a Veblenian model of 'emulation' in dress. This model is frequently invoked to explain the fashion for juvenile sailor suits after 1850; the evidence for this will be examined in Chapter 7.[105] My own previous study of children's clothes set out to unite the object-based model established by Buck with the close attention to gender shown by Jo Paoletti and Chris Breward.[106] It used largely unpublished museum collections throughout Britain to provide primary material.[107] The current study aims to use surviving garments as a form of evidence that is subject to the same level of scrutiny and analysis as other historical sources.

Photographs

Since the 1970s, photographs have increasingly been used as a source for historic research, yet the methodological and interpretative basis for their use is still highly contested. As John Berger noted, the principal difficulty is that of reconciling the 'ways of seeing' of photographer and viewer.[108] As photography has its own history, interpretation has to address the ways in which images have been used and viewed by successive audiences.[109] One way of avoiding these difficulties is to consider only formal and technical questions.[110]

Another approach is to treat photographs as transparent windows on the past; this is particularly tempting to dress historians, seeking otherwise unobtainable

---

[104]   Phillis Cunnington and Anne Buck, *Children's Costume in England 1300–1900* (London, 1965); Elizabeth Ewing, *History of Children's Costume* (London, 1977); Anne Buck, *Clothes and the Child:, A Handbook of Children's Dress in England 1500–1900* (Bedford, 1996).

[105]   Ewing, *History of Children's Costume*, pp. 83–7.

[106]   Clare Rose, *Children's Clothes Since 1750* (London, 1989).

[107]   The children's collections of the V&A Museum of Childhood, Bethnal Green, have only recently been published: Noreen Marshall, *A Dictionary of Children's Clothing* (London, 2008). A selection from the National Trust collections is included in Jane Ashelford, *The Art of Dress: Clothes and Society 1500–1914* (London, 1996), and items from the collections at Manchester and elsewhere were published by Anne Buck. A major European collection, at the Musée Galliera, Paris, was published as *La mode et l'enfant, 1780–2000* (Paris, 2001).

[108]   'Although every image embodies a way of seeing, our perception or appreciation of an image depends also upon our own way of seeing'; John Berger, *Ways of Seeing* (London, 1972), p. 10.

[109]   This is one of the themes of Anne Higonnet, *Pictures of Innocence: The History and Crisis of Ideal Childhood* (London, 1998).

[110]   See for example Helmut Gernsheim, *The History of Photography: From The Camera Obscura to the Beginning of the Modern Era* (London, 1969).

information about the ways in which clothing was worn.[111] This was the basis for Joan Severa's impressive photographic survey of clothing consumption in America.[112] However, in a field such as dress history where the chronology and nature of past practice is still being established, problems with the documentation and selection of images can undermine the validity of the findings.[113] This is an issue in the work of Audrey Linkman on the Documentary Photography Archive, Manchester, who highlights the use of photographs to mark rites of passage.[114] Dress historian Lou Taylor has explicitly confronted the problem of 'truth' in photography, and the ways in which they reveal the gap between the subjects' intentions and achievements.[115] This is the way in which family photographs have been used in this book, contributing to the discussion of consumption practices in Chapter 5.

An acknowledgement of the problematic relationship between intentions and effects in photography is the key to resolving the issues surrounding documentary photographs taken by nineteenth-century institutions. John Tagg has identified photographs taken by police, prisons, mental asylums and orphanages as part of a Foucauldian project to record and control their subjects.[116] Jennifer Green-Lewis has confirmed the links between institutional and criminal photography,[117] but highlighted the scientific and therapeutic uses of images of the mentally ill.[118] Photographs of the mentally ill were used not only for control, but to help patients to externalise their condition and as the 'voice of the voiceless' in funding appeals.[119] Lindsay Smith and

---

[111] See Alison Gernsheim, *Fashion and Reality* (London, 1963); Madeleine Ginsburg, *Victorian Dress in Photographs* (London, 1982); Miles Lambert, *Fashion in Photographs 1860–1880* (London, 1991); Averil Lansdell, *Fashion à la Carte 1860–1900: A Study of Fashion through cartes-de-visite* (Aylesbury, 1985).

[112] Joan Severa, *Dressed for the Photographer: Ordinary Americans and Fashion, 1840–1900* (Kent OH, 1995).

[113] Only 20 per cent of the photographs used by Severa had documented dates; the other 80 per cent had dates assigned by the author; ibid., p. xvii.

[114] Audrey Linkman, *The Victorians, Photographic Portraits* (London, 1993). See Appendix 1 for a discussion of this collection.

[115] 'Do [photographs] exaggerate, mock, deceive or manipulate and can they ever reflect the "truth"?'; see Taylor, *Study of Dress History*, p. 150; also figs. 29 and 39, pp. 172–3.

[116] John Tagg, *The Burden of Representation: Essays on Photographies and Histories* (Basingstoke, 1988), pp. 83–5.

[117] Criminal record photographs were used in Paris from 1851, in Bristol and Birmingham from 1854 and at Scotland Yard from 1868. Jennifer Green-Lewis, *Framing the Victorians: Photography and the Culture of Realism* (Ithaca, NY, 1996), p. 196.

[118] Inmate photographs by Dr H.W. Diamond, superintendent of the Surrey County Asylum and editor of the *Journal of the Photographic Society of London*, were published through the Royal Photographic Society in the 1850s; ibid., p. 146; pp. 176–7.

[119] This use was based ultimately on Lavater's theory of the face as a window on mental condition. Ibid., pp. 151–71.

Seth Koven have examined the ways in which publicity photographs were used by the child rescue charity Dr Barnardo's Homes between 1874 and 1877 to construct the child clients as 'street arabs' in need of rescuing from physical and moral danger by 'missionaries'.[120]

These critics have considered the Barnardo's photographs as paradigms for the institutional uses of photography, looking at their staged 'before and after' images of children shown first in rags and then in institutional uniforms. These were sold for 6d a pair as a way of raising publicity and funds. As Valerie Lloyd has noted, this was standard procedure for child rescue charities in the 1870s and afterwards.[121] In 1877, the mother of a 'rescued' child brought a court case against Barnardo's in which the 'before and after' photographs of her daughter formed part of the complaint. The court judgement prohibited the charity from selling any further images as having 'a tendency to destroy the better feelings of the children'.[122]

Yet the practice of institutional photography at Barnardo's Homes continued, with every child's picture taken on entry and exit. This policy produced up to 1,600 images a year and represented a heavy commitment for a charity that was constantly appealing for funds.[123] The reasons why the organisation took and archived these photographs is unclear: Barnardo himself stated in 1877 that their purpose was

> To obtain and retain an exact likeness, which being attached to a faithful record in our History Book of each individual case, shall enable us in future to trace every child's career, and to bring to remembrance minute circumstances which, without a photograph, would be impossible.[124]

They may also have been used in publications sold to supporters of the charity, such as the magazine *Night and Day*.[125]

---

[120] Lindsay Smith, *The Politics of Focus: Women, Children and Nineteenth-century Photography* (Manchester, 1998), pp. 125–30; Seth Koven, 'Dr Barnardo's 'Artistic Fictions': Photography, Sexuality, and the Ragged Child in Victorian London', *Radical History Review*, 69 (1997): 6–45; *idem, Slumming: Sexual and Social Politics in Victorian London* (Princeton, 2004). Interest in Barnardo's was stimulated by a centenary exhibition of their photographs at The National Portrait Gallery London: Valerie Lloyd, *The Camera and Dr Barnardo* (London, 1974).

[121] The images used by the Ragged School Union will be discussed further in Chapter 1. Lloyd postulates that the National Children's Home may have used the same photographer as Barnardo's; *The Camera and Dr Barnardo*, p. 13.

[122] Revd George Reynolds, 1876, cited in Lloyd, *The Camera and Dr Barnardo*, p. 12.

[123] The cost of photography (including images for sale) was £250 in 1874; Tagg, *Burden of Representation*, p. 83. These are held in the Barnardo's headquarters at Barkingside, London. See Appendix 1 for further details.

[124] Cited in Wagner, *Barnardo*, p 145. A selection of photographs was pasted into personal albums for use by Barnardo himself.

[125] Wagner, *Barnardo*, p. 159.

Whatever the rationale behind their production, the Barnardo's entry photographs represent an archive with immense potential for visual historians, containing in excess of 40,000 fully documented images up to 1900, and more thereafter. As yet there has been no systematic survey of the whole of this archive, but two historians have indicated ways that it might be used. Lydia Murdoch has exposed the ways in which a close examination of Barnardo's records can be used to correct their construction of client children as 'orphans' and 'waifs'. She has noted the ways in which the institution's use of visual conventions, such as the shift from a 'mug-shot' pose on entrance to a 'portrait' pose on exit, supports their claims to transform children's lives.[126] Caroline Bressey, mapping the presence of black women in nineteenth-century London institutions, has used the Barnardo's images to identify the presence of women whose ethnicity was not noted in paper records.[127] These readings of institutional documents against the purpose for which they were intended have served as a model for the use of the Barnardo's photographs in this book. Their validity as evidence will be examined in Chapter 1, and they will then be analysed for indications of families' clothing practices in Chapters 5 and 6.

Structure of the Book

This book is organised thematically, starting with a discussion of the key concepts of 'raggedness' and 'respectability', then moving on to look at the production and retailing of boys' clothes before considering how these clothes were consumed, and what they meant to their wearers and to those who saw them. It uses several large and unpublished sets of documents, with a brief overview of each set in the chapter where it is first discussed. Detailed accounts of the different archives and sampling methods used are placed in Appendix 1. Some of the datasets had more than 1,000 entries, and it has not been possible to reproduce them in full; the reader is referred to the appropriate tables in the author's PhD.[128] Appendix 2 presents a transcription of statements by manufacturers registering boys' clothing in the Board

---

[126]   Lydia Murdoch, Imagined Orphans: Poor Families, Child Welfare, and Contested Citizenship in London (New Brunswick NJ, 2006), esp. pp. 15–17 and 39. Murdoch also notes Barnardo's reliance on the conventions of melodrama, following Rohan McWilliam's seminal article, 'Melodrama and the historians', *Radical History Review*, 78 (2000): 59–62.

[127]   Caroline Bressey, 'Forgotten Geographies: Black Women, Victorian London and the Black Atlantic' (unpublished PhD dissertation, University College London, 2002); *eadem*, 'Forgotten Histories: Three Stories of Black Girls from Barnardo's Victorian Archive,' *Women's History Review*, 111/3 (2002): 351–74.

[128]   Clare Rose, 'Boyswear and the Formation of Gender and Class Identity in Urban England 1840–1900' (unpublished PhD thesis, University of Brighton, 2006).

of Trade archive between 1884 and 1887.[129] These have been included because of the light they throw on design processes.

Sources with evidence of the consumption of clothes – such as photographs – and sources concerned with production – such as manufacturers' copyrighted designs – will first be analysed separately. They will then be brought together to investigate how families selected from the goods available to them, and what their selections tell us about their concepts of boyhood and of masculinity. Quantitative visual analysis has been used to provide information about the scope and nature of manufacturers' and consumers' investment in boys' clothes. In addition, a qualitative analysis of surviving garments elucidates how abstract questions of meaning and value shaped the appearance of individuals.

Chapter 1 sets out the way in which 'raggedness' and 'respectability' were constructed as key terms in charitable discourse. It will examine representations of the 'street arab' in illustrated London papers to see how the meaning of this figure changed between 1870 and 1900. It will also examine the use of the pathetic 'waif' child for fundraising by Dr Barnardo and the Church of England. The preliminary analysis of a large sample of the Barnardo's entry photographs will show how it is possible to read through the rhetoric of 'waifdom' and gain a real understanding of clothing practice from these images.

Chapter 2 examines the evidence for the mass-production of boys' clothing in the Board of Trade archives at The National Archives. These show the importance of boys' garments to major manufacturers, and the use of minute changes in trimmings to vary their products. Chapter 3 investigates the documents used to sell boys' clothes, both catalogues from individual retailers and images for catalogues. The very large number of images of boys' clothing in the Stationers' Hall Archive raises important issues about the importance of this area for retailers.

Chapter 4 revisits the retailers' documents, using them to provide information on garment pricing. This is analysed to show pricing differentials between garments and between retailers and changes over time. Relating the prices to family budgets drawn from social surveys allows us to evaluate the real cost of boys' clothes and of specific garments. Chapter 5 examines the consumption of different garment types, using the Barnardo's entry photographs, school groups and family portraits. These show striking parallels as well as some expected differences. A case study of the presentation of cheaper and dearer versions of sailor suits in the Barnardo's photographs will illuminate how consumption decisions were shaped by factors other than cost.

Chapter 6 uses family and institutional photographs to assess age-related clothing practice. It examines how the popular understanding of 'boyhood' mapped onto legislative and educational age boundaries. It also investigates the tendency to dress boys to express family unity, which often overrode age conventions. Chapter 7 examines the ways that masculinity was expressed symbolically in boys'

---

[129] Transcribed from the registers of the Board of Trade volumes BT51/1–45 at The National Archives.

clothing, and particularly in the clothing of boy toddlers still in skirts. It examines two outfits based on military uniform, the sailor suit and the kilt, to see how advertisers and consumers perceived their patriotic overtones. Chapter 8 evaluates the findings of the book, and their implications for the study of childhood, for study of the clothing industry, and for dress history methodology. It also suggests some parallels from other disciplines and some directions for further study.

Chapter 1
Raggedness and Respectability

For mid-nineteenth-century writers, ragged clothing was often used as shorthand to indicate social status and more especially social need. In 1846 Charles Dickens wrote a letter to the London *Daily News* (reprinted in the *Illustrated London News*) in support of Ragged Schools:

> The name implies the purpose. They who are too ragged, wretched, filthy and forlorn, to enter any other place: who could gain admission into no charity-school, and who would be driven from any church-door: are invited to come in here.[1]

Nearly thirty years later, Dr Barnardo used raggedness as a key theme in the appeals for his Homes,[2] whose foundation he linked to an encounter with: 'eleven boys huddled together for warmth – no roof or covering of any kind was over them and the clothes they had were rags'.[3] The scanty clothing of poor children was implied in their characterisation as 'street arabs' or 'savages' in need of 'civilisation'.[4] By 1880 the discourse had shifted, and those who were denied the newly-identified 'right' of childhood because of poverty or family problems were presented as 'victims' or 'waifs'. The new concept was enshrined in the name of the Church of England Central Society for Providing Homes for Waifs and Strays (CEWSS), founded in 1881.[5] Once again, this state was represented through ragged clothing. The shift

---

[1]   Charles Dickens, 'Letter to the Daily News', quoted in the *Illustrated London News*, 11 April 1846.

[2]   Dr T.J. Barnardo founded and ran a number of residential institutions for children, notably Stepney Causeway Home for Boys (1870) and the Girls' Village Home Barkingside (1876); the umbrella organisation was called Dr Barnardo's Homes. See Lydia Murdoch, *Imagined Orphans: Poor Families, Child Welfare and Contested Citizenship in London* (New Brunswick, 2006), pp. 3–4.

[3]   Account published by Dr Barnardo in *The Christian*, 22 August 1872, cited in Gillian Wagner, *Barnardo* (London, 1979), p. 33.

[4]   Hugh Cunningham, *The Children of the Poor: Representations of Childhood since the Seventeenth Century* (Oxford, 1991), pp. 105–9.

[5]   Ibid., p. 136. The organisation's name was changed in 1893 to 'Church of England Incorporated Society for Providing Homes for Waifs and Strays' and by 1922 it was the 'Church of England Waifs and Strays Society'. In 1946 this was simplified to 'Church of England Children's Society', and since 1982 it has been known as 'The Children's Society'. See http://www.hiddenlives.org.uk/articles/history.html.

from threatening 'arab' to pathetic 'waif' took place in different media at different times, or co-existed, as Cunningham has shown in his analysis of 'street urchin' cartoons by Leech and May.[6] This complicates the interpretation of nineteenth-century texts and images.

This chapter will demonstrate how appearance, and particularly clothing, was used to reinforce social barriers from above and also to negotiate round them from below. It will start by examining definitions of respectable clothing for children, both as an abstract concept and then as applied to the practice of four major institutions: state-funded schools, Union Workhouses, Dr Barnardo's Homes and the CEWSS. A close analysis of texts and images from each type of institution shows that their different conceptualisations of 'respectable' clothing reflected very different views of 'their' children's future life paths. Yet the contrast between children in motley rags and children in neat, warm uniforms was a trope that each of them used to epitomise their work.[7] The emphasis on raggedness in charitable discourse, and the ways this shaped the presentation of poverty in publications like the *Illustrated London News* and the *Graphic*, will be the focus of the next section.

The final section of this chapter will evaluate the extent to which the polarised presentation of ragged street arabs and neatly dressed institutional inmates reflected reality, This will be done by quantifying the presence of key indicators of respectability (white collars) and of raggedness (obvious wear and tear) in photographs of boys entering Barnardo's and boys at Board Schools. Barnardo's entry photographs are a controversial source, seen by Tagg as an extension of Foucauldian systems of surveillance and control into charitable work.[8] It was assumed by Lindsay Smith that they served the charity's aims by 'dressing down' the children: 'we recognise the same pair of trousers, with the knees torn out, featuring time and time again on different boys.'[9] Caroline Bressey has accepted the entry photographs as an accurate representation of children, but only analysed a small sample.[10] Thus the potential seen by Valerie Lloyd in 1974 has not yet been realised: 'they are … a most staggering visual record of thousands of children, which would certainly repay statistical study.'[11] In this chapter a close examination

---

[6]   Ibid., pp. 113–22 and 155–62.

[7]   For Barnardo's use of clothing in his fundraising spectacles, see Murdoch, *Imagines Orphans*, pp. 36–42.

[8]   John Tagg, *The Burden of Representatio:, Essays on Photographies and Histories* (Basingstoke, 1988), pp. 83–102.

[9]   Lindsay Smith, *The Politics of Focus: Women, Children and Nineteenth-century Photography* (Manchester, 1998), p. 123.

[10]   Caroline Bressey in 'Forgotten Histories: three stories of black girls from Barnardo's Victorian archive', *Women's History Review*, 111/3 (2002), made systematic use of Barnardo's photographs of Black girls, but these are a small fraction of the total. Wagner reproduced a handful of images in *Barnado* to illustrate particular case studies.

[11]   Valerie Lloyd, *The Camera and Dr Barnardo* (London, 1974), p. 16.

of a sample of entry photographs from 1874–77 will determine their validity as evidence of clothing practice. The quantitative analysis of 1,800 Barnardo's photographs from 1874–99 will show how they can be used to critique the claims of the institution to transform 'raggedness' into 'respectability'. These images will allow us to read through the intentions of the institution to the rather different intentions of the sitters.

Defining the Respectable Boy

Establishing a normative experience of nineteenth-century boyhood is complicated by the fact that many of the sources were heavily influenced by the social position of the author. Nineteenth-century texts on child development can be divided between those written by the middle and upper classes for consumption by their peers (like those of Jane Emily Panton)[12] and those written by the middle classes for imposition on their social inferiors (like most school textbooks). Both sets of texts were prescriptive rather than descriptive, which increases the difficulty of interpretation. Even in the case of Board School textbooks, which set out a rigidly determined syllabus backed by the full weight of educational legislation, there were some areas that remained undetermined, for negotiation by the teachers involved. Chief among these was the standard of clothing required for school attendance. This is all the more surprising when improvement in standards of dress was seen as both an aim and an outcome of the civilising mission of state schooling.

The Respectable Schoolboy

The opposing concepts of 'raggedness' and 'respectability' were present from the origin of mass educational provision in Britain. The earliest nation-wide school organisations were the British Schools, set up by the Church of England, and the National Schools of the 'non-conformist' Protestant churches (Methodists and Presbyterians). From 1833 onwards these received some government funding but they were 'voluntary' in that churches were not obliged to provide them and children were not obliged to attend. Curriculum and levels of attainment were centrally determined and enforced by the Revised Code of 1862 that introduced the system of 'payment by results'.[13] 'Ragged Schools', mostly in large urban areas such as London, Liverpool, and Manchester, originated in the early nineteenth century and became more numerous and better regulated after the founding of

---

12   Jane Emily Panton, *The Way They Should Go*, (London, 1896); this is discussed extensively in Chapter 7.

13   Under this system, children were tested by government inspectors and the school only received funding for those who passed. Anne Digby and Peter Searby, *Children, School and Society in Nineteenth-Century England* (Basingstoke, 1981), p. 35.

the Ragged School Union in 1844.[14] Ragged Schools were run as charities, with no fees required, and often had a missionary or Evangelical Protestant flavour. Universal education was established by the 1870 Education Act, which required towns to provide schools if none were available, paying for them with local taxes controlled by a School Board, and by school fees (up to 9d per child per week) collected from parents. There were in addition numerous small independent schools charging low fees.[15] After 1891, fees for Board Schools were abolished, and they came to dominate educational provision, notwithstanding the distrust of some working-class parents.[16]

The workings of Board Schools are amply documented in textbooks and teaching manuals, which set out very detailed criteria for teaching (down to the number of stitches per inch in girls' sewing).[17] These might be expected to define such issues as the way that a boy's status as a schoolboy was reflected in his clothing. It was also expected that there would be a clear dividing line between the 'respectable' clothing which permitted attendance at Board Schools and the 'raggedness' which excluded.[18] However these concepts proved hard to define. Board School teachers' manuals revealed an awareness of the difficulties for families of providing adequate clothing for children, but no definition of what constituted 'adequacy' in clothing or footwear. In 1893 the London 'Rules for Teachers' stated that schools could not require pupils to wear shoes, and barefoot schoolchildren were common up to 1914.[19] Nor were there any official guidelines on age-related clothing, since many Infants' classes contained three-year-olds who were barely toilet-trained.[20]

Although clothing for schoolchildren was not formally prescribed, school attendance still presented an opportunity for raising standards of dress. This might

---

[14]   These were educating up to 23,000 children in London alone by 1870; Alan Kidd, *State, Society and the Poor in Nineteenth Century England* (Basingstoke, 1999), p. 87; see also Claire Seymour, *Ragged Schools, Ragged Children* (London, 1995), pp. 6–7.

[15]   Phil Gardner, *The Lost Elementary Schools of Victorian England: The People's Education* (Beckenham, 1984).

[16]   Digby and Searby, *Children, School and Society*, p. 31.

[17]   Ellen Rosevear, *A Text-Book of Needlework, Knitting and Cutting-Out with Methods of Teaching* (London, 1893), pp. 449–54, gives details of the precise tasks required of each level of children to a set standard in a set time.

[18]   The practice at Board Schools was for children to attend in their normal clothing; at this date uniforms were only required by a few private or grammar schools (notably Eton), and by 'Bluecoat' and 'Greycoat' charity schools where clothes followed rules laid down by founders in the sixteenth or seventeenth centuries. See Anne Buck, *Clothes and the Child: A Handbook of Children's Dress in England 1500–1900* (Bedford, 1996) pp. 218–19; Phillis Cunnington and Catherine Lucas, *Charity Costumes of Children, Scholars, Almsfolk, Pensioners* (London, 1978), pp. 103–5, 115–16.

[19]   Anna Davin, *Growing Up Poor: Home, School and Street in London, 1870–1914* (London, 1996), p. 137.

[20]   Ibid., p. 113.

be the result of direct intervention in needlework classes: 'The object of teaching needlework is to enable the girls to make and mend for themselves and their families ... The self-respect begotten of tidy clothes will find soap, a fireside, and an account at a penny bank.'[21] E.J. Urwick, writing in 1904, implied that school attendance per se raised clothing standards:

> Collars and ties are now almost as common as rags were a few years ago; the bare-footed ragamuffin of popular imagination figures still as the frontispiece to well-meaning philanthropic appeals, but is no longer a common object of the streets ... the civilising influence of the Board School has made him the exception instead of the rule.[22]

Picturing the Respectable Schoolchild

School children were presented to the public, and specifically the rate-paying middle classes, through articles in national newspapers. A survey of the *Illustrated London News* and the *Graphic* between 1870 and 1900 showed that these articles (and accompanying illustrations redrawn from photographs) served specific purposes. The first was to present schools as the solution to a pressing social problem: 'School or Gaol' was the title of an article in 1870.[23] Illustrations to articles on this theme showed the children as ragged, even if they were attending Board (not Ragged) Schools: for example, in an engraving based on a photograph published in 1886 four of the 30 boys were barefoot, five had no coats, and many looked ragged (Figure 1.1).[24] A smaller group of articles highlighted the power of the school system to transform ragged and wayward individuals into ordered classes, illustrated with groups engaged in 'drill' (physical or needlework).[25] In neither case was there an objective record of the actual appearance of schoolchildren.

More neutral images of schoolchildren might be found in group photographs taken at the instigation of schools. Many examples of these have been published, but the documentation of this material remains problematic. A sample of nineteen photographs with verified documentation of date and location and clearly legible content was sourced from national and regional archives (See Appendix 1

---

21   E.G. Jones, *A Manual of Plain Needlework and Cutting Out* (London, 1884), pp. 95–6.

22   E.J. Urwick, *Studies of Boy Life in Our Cities* (London, 1904), cited in Cunningham, *Children of the Poor*, p. 163.

23   The *Graphic*, 24 December 1870, p. 615. See also Michael Wolff and C. Fox, 'Pictures from the Magazines', in H.J. Dyos and Michael Wolff (eds), *The Victorian City: Images and Realities*, vol. 2 (London, 1973).

24   Murdoch, *Imagined Orphans*, pp. 27–35, discusses strategic exaggeration in drawings based on photographs.

25   'The School Board Drill Before the Prince of Wales', *Graphic*, 30 June 1883, p. 646; 'London Board Schools', ibid., 7 November 1885, pp. 517–20.

Figure 1.1   'Waifs and Strays of London: Raw Material for the School Board', *Illustrated London News*, 9 October 1886, p. 376. Courtesy of the NAL, Victoria and Albert Museum, London 2009.

for details). These were analysed to determine how many boys were wearing particular styles of garments, and how many showed evidence of 'raggedness' or 'respectability'. These categories were determined by the presence of visible holes and missing buttons on the one hand, and accessories such as stiff white collars on the other.[26] White collars would not have been appropriate with some types of suits worn by working-class boys, typically worn with a neckerchief or scarf tied at the neck to hide the top of the shirt.

Table 1.1 shows the incidence of these two indicators in the 19 school photographs dated between 1888 and 1900. The number of boys in white collars ranged from 16 out of 18 boys at Cotherstone in 1888 to 0 of 48 at Chaucer St. School, Southwark.[27] In some cases, as at Holden Street Infants, the lack of white collars is not a sign of lack of respectability, since all the boys wear sailor tops for which white collars were not needed.[28] There is, nonetheless, one boy in this group who wears a frilled collar of white embroidery over his sailor blouse (Figure 1.2). This anomalous combination can also be seen on two boys in Orange Street School.[29] Even more anomalous is the combination of garments worn by two boys at Elizabeth Street School in 1896 (Figure 1.3).[30] These two wear jackets with visible holes at the elbow and ragged cuffs, topped with stiff white collars and white ribbon bows. In this case it seems that someone has added the highly visible collar and bow to create the appearance of respectability for the photograph. Had the boys been positioned in the back row, with their ragged sleeves hidden, the illusion would have succeeded. This example highlights the way that the collar was understood as emblematic of respectability in the 1890s. It also clarifies the difficulty of gauging the state of boys' clothing from group pictures.

---

[26] Collars at this date were not sewn to the shirt, but detachable for ease of laundering and for economy. Thus a white collar might be purchased without a matching shirt, or a shirt without a collar. Shirts with separate collars were advertised as late as 1949 in the mail-order catalogue of Grattan Ltd, p. 109.

[27] London Metropolitan Archive (henceforth LMA), A4452.

[28] LMA N4287.

[29] LMA 4464.

[30] LMA A7395.

Table 1.1   Indicators of raggedness and respectability in school groups, 1880s–c.1900

Archive	School	Date	Ragged	Collars	Anomalous	Remainder	Total boys
Cotherstone 1888	Cotherstone	1888	0	16		2	18
Owslebury School	Owslebury	1880s	0	8		7	15
Owslebury School	Owslebury	1880s	3	3		5	11
Hants&IoW 68	Basingstoke	1889	0	10		1	11
BEA 44364	Kibblesworth	1890		20		6	26
BEA 44365	Kibblesworth	1890		8		4	12
LMA A4457	Snowsfields	1894	7	8		29	44
LMA A7393	Elizabeth Street	1894	0	31		11	42
BEA 44335	West Pelton	1894		3		0	3
LMA A4452	Chaucer Street	1895	7	0		41	48
LMA 80/1919	Southfields	1895	0	0		33	33
LMA A7394	Elizabeth Street	1896	0	21		7	28
LMA A7395	Elizabeth Street	1896		25	2	9	36
LMA A7396	Elizabeth Street	1896	0	12		13	25
Alresford no. 94	Cheriton	1896	0	9		7	16
Alresford no. 102	Ovington	1897	0	3		3	6
LMA N4287	Holden Street Infants	1897	0	1		15	16
Cotherstone 1898 II	Cotherstone	1898	0	8		7	15
Cotherstone 1898 III	Cotherstone	1898	0	16		4	20
LMA A4464	Orange Street Infants	1899	0	8		11	19
Hants&IoW 66	Meonstoke	1899	0	12		5	17
LMA A7397	Elizabeth Street	1900	0	26		5	31
BEA 43827	Scargill	c.1892		12		3	15
BEA 44277	Dudley	c.1900		23		5	28
			17	283		233	535

Sources: Alresford – E. Roberts, *In and Around Alresford in Old Photographs* (Alresford, 1975); BEA – North of England Open Air Museum, Beamish; Cotherstone – Cotherstone Wesleyan Methodist School, private collection; Hants & IoW – J. Norwood, *Victorian and Edwardian Hampshire & the Isle of Wight from Old Photographs* (London, 1973); LMA – London Metropolitan Archives; Owslebury – *Owslebury, A Village School: 150 Years 1840–1990* (1990).

Figure 1.2   Holden Street Infants School, London, 1897 [SC/PHL/02/N4287]. Courtesy of City of London, London Metropolitan Archives.

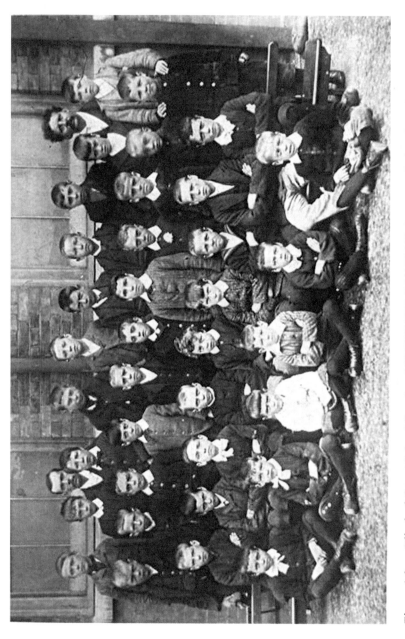

Figure 1.3   Elizabeth Street School, London, 1896 [SC/PHL/02/A7395]. Courtesy of City of London, London Metropolitan Archives.

Clothing as a Mark of Identity for Institutions

Clothing also acted as a mark of belonging for institutionalised children, and a sign of their separation from the outside world. Charities such as the Foundling Hospital in London had uniforms chosen by their founders in the seventeenth or eighteenth centuries that became increasingly distinctive and anachronistic with the passage of time. These uniforms formed part of the public spectacle at events like the Holy Thursday services in St Paul's, London for up to 6,000 'charity children'.[31] All clothing worn by institutionalised children was used both to express control and to advertise charitable actions, but the different forms that it took indicate important differences between institutions.[32]

After the introduction of the New Poor Law in 1834, workhouses became one of the major institutions providing for poor children, either on the main site or in separate District Schools.[33] Workhouse clothing was provided for all inmates, even those only resident for a short time, and shared many characteristics with prison clothing. It was designed to comply with the ruling of 'less eligibility', which ensured that workhouse accommodation would not attract the idle poor. Its uniformity and loose cut made it easier to distribute and helped to de-individualise the wearer. Its lack of references to current fashion made it highly distinctive, as was noted in 1913: 'Early Victorian patterns were for the most part used, and underneath the pleats and gathers the children looked swollen and shapeless.'[34] Workhouse clothing might also be stamped with the name of the institution to prevent inmates from absconding or from selling their clothes.[35]

We might expect to find some positive references in workhouse clothing to create an image of the ideal working-class child. However, it is hard even to

---

[31] As in the poem 'Holy Thursday' by William Blake, 1789; Hugh Cunningham and Michael Morpurgo, *The Invention of Childhood* (London, 2006), pp. 102–9.

[32] Cunnington and Lucas, *Charity Costumes*.

[33] Frank Crompton, *Workhouse Children: Infant and Child Paupers under the Worcestershire Poor Law, 1780–1871* (Stroud, 1997); Michael Crowther, *The Workhouse System 1834–1929: The History of an English Social Institution* (Athens, GA, 1981); Felix Driver, *Power and Pauperism: The Workhouse System, 1834–1884* (Cambridge, 1993); Simon Fowler, *Workhouse: The People, the Places, the Life behind Doors* (Kew, 2007); Norman Longmate, *The Workhouse* (London, 1974); Murdoch, *Imagined Orphans*, pp. 43–66.

[34] Margaret Bertha Synge, *Simple Garments for Children from Four to Fourteen* (London, 1913), p. xi.

[35] Ann Brogden, 'Clothing Provision by the Liverpool Workhouse', *Costume*, 36 (2002): 50–55; *eadem*, 'Clothing Provision by Liverpool's Other Poor Law Institution: Kirkdale Industrial Schools', *Costume*, 37 (2003): 71–4; David Englander, *Poverty and Poor Law Reform in Britain: From Chadwick to Booth, 1834–1914* (London, 1998); David Green, 'Pauper Protests: Power and Resistance in Early Nineteenth-century London Workhouses', *Social History*, 31/2 (2006), p. 148; Tina Vivienne Richmond, '"No finery": The Dress of the Poor in Nineteenth-century England' (unpublished PhD thesis, University of London, 2004), pp. 254–9.

know what was worn as workhouse clothing (unlike workhouse food) was not centrally regulated: each Union ordered sets of clothing from the contractor who submitted the cheapest bid.[36] Writers with direct experience of the workhouse refer only briefly to clothing, assuming that readers will know what it looks like: George Lansbury categorised it as 'the old, hideous Poor Law garb, corduroy and hard blue serge'.[37] Case studies of post-1834 workhouse clothing in Liverpool and London have been published by Anne Brogden and David Green, and Peter Jones has examined clothing given to paupers before 1834.[38] There is little material evidence for workhouse garments, with only one known survival from the nineteenth century.[39]

A single set of photographs of workhouse children survives in the Documentary Photography Archive, Manchester.[40] The images of Crumpsall workhouse, Manchester, taken in 1897, show a group of 23 boys; a mixed group of boys with two seated men; and a group of men with a single boy (Figure 1.4).[41] The latter group were dressed in light-coloured fabric, possibly cotton fustian. The men and boys in the other two groups were uniformly dressed in dark-coloured cotton corduroy.

The garments in this image are in many ways unexceptional as they are made from cheap but durable fabrics which were standard for working clothes, as Engels had noted in 1845:

> The men wear chiefly trousers of fustian or other heavy cotton goods, and jackets or coats of the same. Fustian has become the proverbial costume of the working-

---

[36]   These included major clothing manufacturers such as Coop of Wigan; Brogden, 'Clothing Provision', p. 53. Arthur Lynes of London claimed in 1870 to 'offer great advantages to Charitable Institutions'; *Smiles and Styles* (London, 1870), p. 125.

[37]   George Lansbury in Fowler, *Workhouse*, p. 138; see also George Haw, *From Workhouse to Westminster: The Life Story of Will Crooks, MP* (London, 1909), p. 113; Charlie Chaplin, *My Autobiography* (London, 1964), pp. 26–9.

[38]   Peter Jones, 'Clothing the Poor in Early Nineteen-Century England', *Textile History*, 37/1 (2006): 17–37.

[39]   A fustian jacket from Blaby Union, Leicestershire c.1840, Leicester Museums 1977.928; it is stamped on the back 'Blaby Union 45'. It is cut in a shape that was old-fashioned even in 1840, and extensively patched and darned. See Illustration 4.22, p. 268 in Clare Rose, 'Boyswear and the formation of gender and class identity in urban England, 1840–1900' (unpublished PhD thesis, University of Brighton, 2006). The Workhouse Museums at Southwell, Nottinghamshire and Ripon have not identified any nineteenth-century garments in their collections.

[40]   There is a set of photographs of interiors and inhabitants of Stockport Union Workhouse c.1895 at Stockport Local Studies Library, but these show only toddlers and adults, not schoolchildren.

[41]   In an album held as Documentary Photography Archive 2372/62.

Figure 1.4   Boys in Crumpsall Workhouse, Manchester 1897. Ref: 2372/113 from the Documentary Photographic Archive held by and reproduced courtesy of Greater Manchester County Record Office.

men, who are called 'Fustian Jackets' and call themselves so in contrast to the gentlemen who wear broadcloth.[42]

Both fustian and corduroy were standard choices for clothing in workhouses and industrial schools, as Brogden has shown for Liverpool.[43] Yet the groups show a troubling uniformity, with even the youngest boys dressed in long trousers and hobnailed boots. Thus the clothing was not stigmatising per se, but marked an institutional identity that overrode age identity.

Clothing and Dr Barnardo's Homes

Charities such as Dr Barnardo's Homes used clothing in a more nuanced way, to mark the social and moral transformation they offered to children. This was particularly noticeable in the staged 'before' and 'after' photographs sold by the charity between 1872 and 1877.[44] The 'before' pictures, given captions such as 'Raggedness, Necessity and Importunity' or 'Once a Little Vagrant', show boys dressed in clothing that is ragged or incomplete, with knees visible through gaping holes in the trousers, and the absence of hats, boots and jackets revealing matted hair, dirty feet and buttonless shirts. One distinctive pose, with a bare foot cradled in the opposite hand, seems designed to draw attention to the raggedness of the trousers.[45] The 'after' images show boys dressed in clothing that refer to the employment training they are receiving: workmen's cotton fustian overall jackets, mariners' jerseys or carpenter's aprons.[46]

After 1877, the nature of the photographs changed, as they were only used for internal records, and sometimes for Barnardo's publications such as *Night and Day*.[47] Interestingly, the policy on clothing boys seems to have changed as well. The evidence for this is derived from the individual 'exit' photographs that were taken of each child, and from occasional group photographs. An 1883 group of older boys preparing to emigrate to Canada were dressed in tailored three-piece suits with collars and ties. Thus their appearance was emphatically 'white-collar' even when

---

[42]   Engels, *The Condition of the Working Class in England in 1845*, cited in Sarah Levitt, 'Cheap Mass-produced Men's Clothing in the Nineteenth and Early Twentieth Centuries', *Textile History*, 22/2 (1991), p. 179.

[43]   Brogden, 'Clothing Provision', p. 71.

[44]   These were an effective fundraising device, selling at 6d each or twenty for 5s. These were substantial sums; 5s was a quarter of the weekly subsistence wage of £1. Lloyd, *Camera and Dr Barnado*, p. 12.

[45]   Card 27, illustrated in ibid., p. 20.

[46]   See images reproduced in Murdoch, *Imagined Orphans*, pp. 36–9; Wagner, *Barnardo*, pp. 144–5.

[47]   Wagner, *Barnardo*, p. 159.

they were destined for agricultural work.[48] The careful presentation of these boys may have been partly designed to counter Canadian or British opposition to child emigration.[49] However it would also have formed a deliberate contrast with the presentation of workhouse children as young labourers.

Younger boys were equally carefully presented on leaving, as can be seen from a sample page of exit photographs from 1891 (Figure 1.5). Each of these boys has the outward signs of respectability: a cap, a white collar and a ribbon bow. Each is carefully posed with one elbow on a pile of books, in an approximation of studio portraiture (although the rough blanket drapery is not of studio quality).[50] The suits they wear are of two kinds, either dark wool with groups of tucks down each front,

Figure 1.5   A group of young boys exiting Barnardo's in 1891. Courtesy of Barnardo's Archive.

or dark velveteen with plain fronts. These suits compare favourably with those worn by boys in school photographs, for example at Elizabeth Street School in 1896.

Indeed the smartness of the Barnardo's uniforms was a source of pride for the families of the wearers, as Arthur Harding found when he was taken out of Barnardo's for the day to visit his grandparents in the workhouse: 'My mother wanted to show me off in the uniform – it was a very smart uniform – and she took me there ... [Granny] said to me, "You look like a soldier".'[51]

---

[48]   Ibid., pp. 144–5; also image from Box 4 sheet 23, July 1883, Illustration 2.11, p. 72 in Rose, 'Boyswear'. For the practice of child emigration, see Gillian Wagner, *Children of the Empire* (London, 1982); Joy Parr, *Labouring Children* (London, 1980).

[49]   Wagner, *Barnardo*, pp. 245–9.

[50]   For the choice of bodily posture in 'after' photographs, see Murdoch, *Imagined Orphans*, pp. 27 and 39.

[51]   Raphael Samuel (ed.), *East End Underworld: Chapters in the life of Arthur Harding* (London, 1981), p. 12.

Waifs and Strays

The Church of England Central Society for Providing Homes for Waifs and Strays (CEWSS) was an organisation which had many of the same aims as Barnardo's Homes, but chose rather different means to achieve them. From 1882, they ran mostly 'scattered homes' each with up to 30 children in the care of 'house parents'.[52] This model of care was a development from the boarding-out policy adopted by some workhouse unions after 1869.[53] In setting up scattered homes the CEWSS rejected 'the huge mistake of great institutions, in which all training must be more or less mechanical, and all personal influence unknown'.[54] This criticism was directed at Workhouses and District Schools, but could also have applied to Barnardo's, whose Girls' Village Home housed more than 1,200.[55] It is somewhat disingenuous, as the CEWSS also ran larger institutions for older children along similar lines to the District Schools.[56]

Like Barnardo's, the CEWSS issued a monthly journal for supporters, *Our Waifs and Strays*, which presented their rationale both overtly and implicitly. Particularly helpful are illustrated articles describing visits to homes run by the Society, lists of donations received, and appeals for further help.[57] The published photographs of children in the homes show a more varied and individual range of garments than in Barnardo's images.[58] They point to the origins of the garments as donations from middle-class supporters, probably hand-me-downs. *Our Waifs and Strays* appealed for these in August 1884: 'may I suggest a destination for these discarded suits? There must be plenty just now, when the boys are trooping back from school.' A March 1887 article acknowledged that corduroy clothes were needed 'for common wear for the older boys', but also appealed for 'young

---

[52]   John Stroud, *Thirteen Penny Stamps: The Story of the Church of England Children's Society (Waifs and Strays) from 1881 to the 1970s* (London, 1971), pp. 93–107.

[53]   Francis Duke, 'Pauper Education', in Derek Fraser (ed.), *The New Poor Law in the Nineteenth Century* (Basingstoke, 1976), pp. 80–81.

[54]   Address by the Bishop of Bedford, *Our Waifs and Strays*, December 1887, p. 5.

[55]   Unease about some aspects of Barnardo's work was cited as one of the reasons for establishing the CEWSS; Stroud, *Thirteen Penny Stamps*, pp. 29–30. For the debate on the relative merits of 'barrack schools', village homes, and scattered homes, see Murdoch, *Imagined Orphans*, pp. 43–66.

[56]   Such as the Standon Farm Home, which trained boys in agriculture and tailoring, founded in 1885. See *Our Waifs and Strays*, July 1892, p. 9; Stroud, *Thirteen Penny Stamps*, pp. 97–8.

[57]   *Our Waifs and Strays*, Issue 1, October 1882, p. 3, has reports on the first homes opened, Clapton for boys and Dulwich for girls. Digitised copies of this and other CEWSS publications are available on http://www.hiddenlives.org.uk/publications/.

[58]   For example, group from Ashdon Home, *Our Waifs and Strays*, October 1900, p. 377; see Rose, 'Boyswear', Illustration 2.13, p. 74.

gentlemen's left-off suits'. The rationale behind the appeal for donated clothing formed a trenchant critique of workhouse policy:

> It is an undeniable fact that it does far more good, to both giver and receiver, to adopt an individual boy or girl to clothe than to send bundles of work to the Homes to be distributed to the children, as if they were mere machines. It is a great benefit, as well as a pleasure, to a child to have clothes that are *his own,* and not a *loan* to him from the Home. The want of personal possessions, in consequence of having everything in common, has been known to lead to dishonesty amongst workhouse children when they have gone out into service.[59]

Varied Forms of Respectability

Workhouses and charities such as Dr Barnardo's Homes and the CEWSS had the same aim, to reclaim the children of absent or failing parents and make them into useful citizens. State-funded schools were also expected to improve the behaviour and appearance of poor children. However, each type of institution had a different conception of the 'respectable' boy. For the workhouse system, 'respectability' in clothing could be defined in negative terms as the absence of nakedness, and of any disturbing individuality. These clothes also had to be cheaply made, extremely hard-wearing, and conform with the principle of 'less eligibility'. The garments themselves were based on those worn by adult labourers, with no concession made for the age of the boys.

For Dr Barnardo's Homes, 'respectable' clothing was an important part of the process of giving boys a new life in the physical and moral sense. The spectacles of child rescue that Barnardo staged in the 1880s and 1890s at venues like the Albert Hall derived much of their power from 'noisily smart and capitally drilled' groups.[60] The uniformity of the drilled groups was symptomatic of Dr Barnardo's view of the children in his care as belonging to him rather than to their birth families.[61] The uniformity of the clothing supplied by Barnardo's supported this group identity, and also reflected the corporate nature of the charity, with large homes run on a set plan. The homes included industrial workshops where the boys were taught to make clothing and shoes in order to gain employment skills and to reduce the costs of buying in goods.[62] Yet these workshops were apparently not very productive, and it seems likely that the clothing worn by boys in the exit

---

[59]   *Our Waifs and Strays,* March 1887, p. 2.

[60]   Murdoch, *Imagined Orphans,* pp. 36–42; for the effect of this on the child subjects, see June Rose, *For the Sake of the Children: Inside Dr Barnardo's, 120 years of caring for Children* (London, 1987), p. 66.

[61]   See Wagner, *Children of the Empire,* pp. 138–44.

[62]   Wagner, *Barnardo,* p. 83.

photographs was bought in from contractors.[63] The clothing worn in Barnardo's identified boys not only as members of the charity, but also as belonging to a particular age or occupational group, with older boys differentiated from younger, and future farmers from future seamen.[64] Dressing children to express the work they were being trained for had been a mainstay of charity work since the 1850s, as Vincent DiGirolamo has shown in his study of Bootblack Brigades.[65]

The clothing of boys by the CEWSS reflected a different ethos, with an emphasis in their publicity on their 'cottage homes' modelled on family groups and housed and clothed from middle-class donations. They seem to have encouraged emotional identification between patrons and clients as a means of increasing donations, and the gift of clothing was encouraged. However, it is worth noting that the charity also ran larger, more institutional units where special uniforms were worn, such as the 'farm school' at Standon.[66]

The sampled group photographs from Board Schools show a common understanding of 'respectability' in the presence of white collars and the absence of holes or patches. On some of the boys this has been over-stated by adding a redundant white frill to a sailor suit. In others the white collar has been added to a ragged suit as a pragmatic response to the need for smartness. It is not clear whether these collars were added by the boys' families or by the school; families' understanding of the symbolic importance of the white collar will be considered further in Chapter 6.

The Importance of Raggedness

As shown above, clothing was important in defining the position of the 'respectable' boy, whether at school or in an institution. The concept of 'raggedness' was even more important than 'respectability' for nineteenth-century educational discourse, as it defined a whole sector, that of the Ragged Schools. Raggedness was also seen as one of the defining characteristics of the poor children characterised as 'Street Arabs' or 'Waifs and Strays' who were the objects of attention from charities such as Barnardo's. As Cunningham has shown, ragged children were portrayed in a variety of ways from the 1840s onwards.[67] Raggedness was used not only as a tool to elicit sympathy from the viewer but also for its 'picturesque'

---

[63]   Murdoch, *Imagined Orphans*, pp. 125–8.

[64]   Shown in the 'before and after' cards, such as number 66 (naval recruit) and number 34 (brush-maker). Barnardo's Photographic Archive numbers ARC 0252, ARC 0250.

[65]   Vincent DiGirolamo, 'Redressing the Ragged Newsboy: Clothing, Character, and Coercion in Pre-World War I Britain', paper presented at the Warren I. Susman Memorial Graduate History Conference, Rutgers University, 1994 (text kindly supplied by Anna Davin).

[66]   Apparently some of the clothing was made in a tailoring workshop on the site. *Our Waifs and Strays*, April 1892, pp. 9–10; Stroud, *Thirteen Penny Stamps* p. 98.

[67]   Cunningham, *Children of the Poor*, pp. 114–22 and 155–63.

Figure 1.6   Street urchin confronted with ideal boy, Phil May, 1897. Courtesy of Anna Davin.

Figure 1.7   Street children as pathetic waifs, Dorothy Tennant, 1890. Courtesy
of Anna Davin.

qualities by cartoonists such as John Leech. The art critic John Ruskin was uneasy at the emotive use of raggedness, even when practised by esteemed artists such as Murillo: 'Are we the least bit more likely to take any interest in ragged schools, or to help the next pauper child that comes in our way, because the painter has chosen a cunning beggar feeding meanly?'[68]

The shift in characterisation of poor children towards 1900 can be tracked in popular images. Cunningham has highlighted Phil May's ambivalent attitude, as expressed in the introduction to *Gutter-snipes* in 1896: 'Children of the gutter roam about free and are often hungry but what would one give for such appetites? … Sometimes I wonder whether they don't lead the happier lives' (Figure 1.6).[69]

A similar intention was expressed by Dorothy Tennant (Mrs H.M. Stanley) in *London Street Arabs* (1890).[70] She explained her motivation thus:

> Most of the pictures I had seen of ragged life appeared to me false and made up.
> They were all so deplorably piteous – pale, whining children with sunken eyes
> … How was it, I asked myself, that the other side is so seldom represented? The
> merry, reckless, happy-go-lucky urchin …[71]

Tennant's style was based on fine artists like Murillo, while May's cartoons derived from humorous artists like Leech and Rowlandson, so that the two appeared very different (Figure 1.7). Yet both were mediated by the artistic skills which allowed them to present their work as art rather than as reportage, unlike the graphic renditions of photographs reproduced in illustrated newspapers.

'Ragged' Schools

The title of the Ragged Schools (grouped into a Union in 1844) has often been taken as summing up their activity, as in the Dickens quotation at the start of the chapter. In fact, it seems that 'raggedness' was more a metaphor than a condition of entrance. The founding document of the Ragged Schools Union set out thirteen categories of children they wished to serve, the eighth of which was: 'Children of honest parents too poor to pay for schooling or to clothe the children so as to enable them to attend an ordinary school.'[72] Yet ten of the remaining twelve categories referred to children who were either parentless or dependent on 'worthless drunken parents' and on the fringes of criminality. All of these situations might be reflected in 'ragged' clothing, but were not defined by it.

---

[68]   Ruskin on Murillo, cited in Cunningham, *Children of the Poor*, p. 159.

[69]   Phil May, *Guttersnipes* (London, 1896); see Cunningham, *Children of the Poor*, pp. 155–62, for examples.

[70]   Mrs H.M. Stanley (Dorothy Tennant), *London Street Arabs* (London, 1890); I am grateful to Anna Davin for the loan of this volume.

[71]   Ibid., p. 5.

[72]   Seymour, *Ragged Schools*, p. 5.

The 'raggedness' of the boys was as much moral as physical: 'thoroughly educated in all the sharpness and deceitfulness of vice … They take especial delight in the rudeness of their behaviour and the neglect of their persons.'[73] Those working directly with 'outcast' children were aware that their problems arose not only from absences – of food, clothing, and shelter – but from the *presence* of habits such as swearing, smoking and thieving. However, appeals for charitable donations stressed the lack of physical goods that well-wishers could supply. Of all these, the want of clothing was most easily conveyed and tended to stand as a metaphor for all other forms of 'raggedness'.

Improvement in the standard of clothing was taken as evidence of the moral reformation effected on Ragged School students: 'educate the mind, and it immediately revolts at the body being clothed in rags.'[74] After 1870, this connection was read in reverse, and children who were still visibly ragged were assumed by commentators to be those not yet receiving an education. An article in the *Graphic* of 1879 cited the assertion by head teachers that 'When a gutter-child comes to school he ceases to be a gutter-child'.[75] The writer then detailed the continuing phenomenon of 'gutter-children', identifiable by their ragged and dirty appearance, which he assumes would disqualify them from schooling. This assumption may have been valid for 1879, but ceased to be so after the enactment of compulsory attendance in 1883, as the 1886 image discussed above demonstrated.

Raggedness in Charitable Appeals

One reason for the stress on physical raggedness in the discussion of poor children was its visibility as an index of deprivation. For this reason, raggedness was a prominent feature of the images accompanying charitable appeals. After 1860 these images were often from photographic sources. The most famous such image, known variously as 'Poor Jo' (after a character in *Bleak House*) or 'Night in Town', was taken in 1860 by O.G. Rejlander.[76] The boy was posed in such a way that his ragged clothing and dirty hands were prominent but his face hidden, making him an anonymous body onto which the problems of particular children could be projected. An engraving based on this image was used on appeal literature by the Ragged School Union and its successor, the Shaftesbury Society, from at least 1870 to 1973.[77] The effectiveness of the Rejlander image was shown by Barnardo's imitation of it in an 1871 pamphlet.[78] Both the use of staged images,

---

[73]   Committee of Heyrod Street Ragged School, Manchester, 1862; cited in ibid., p. 19.

[74]   Revd Mr Ainslie, cited in the *Illustrated London News*, 11 April 1846, p. 237.

[75]   *Graphic*, 15 November 1879, p. 475.

[76]   Edgar Yoxall Jones, *Father of Art Photography, O.G. Rejlander, 1813–1875* (Newton Abbot, 1973), p. 27.

[77]   G. Franklin and D. Bailey, *The Shaftesbury Story* (London, 1979), p. 18; Jones, *Father*, fig.4 on p. 27.

[78]   Illustrated in Lloyd, *Camera and Dr Barnado*, p. 23.

and the borrowing of visual prototypes from competitors, was common practice for child rescue organisations in the 1870s. A wood engraving of a boy appealing to his Ragged School teacher, published by Barnardo in the *Children's Treasury* of 1874,[79] reappeared in a book by Alfred Alsop in 1881.[80] In each case the image was presented as recording an event that had happened to the author.

Barnardo's 'before' and 'after' cards represented standard practice for charities at this time. The American evangelist Dwight Moody had issued cards with 'before and after' photographs from 1862, and these may have been known to Barnardo after Moody's 1867 visit to England.[81] Alfred Alsop, the Manchester evangelist, began taking 'before and after' photographs in 1877, at the time when Barnardo was forced to cease.[82] The CEWSS regularly published illustrated case histories in *Our Waifs and Strays*. As late as 1900 they showed a ragged boy posed against a stone wall with the text: 'Raw Material: Entered Leicester Home, 1888, from immoral surroundings … [now] a respectable and respected young man.'[83] Although the photograph would have allowed the child to be recognised, the delay between photography and publication precluded this. In addition, the magazine was for subscribers to the charity only.

Barnardo's 'before' and 'after' pictures received wide publicity including reproduction in illustrated newspapers,[84] and seemed at first to have been accepted as representative of the changes effected by his organisation. However, in 1877 they were at the centre of a court case that questioned the validity of Barnardo's work and of his handling of donated funds. The case was instigated by a group which included a rival minister, representatives of the powerful Charity Organisation Society, and some dissatisfied parents of 'rescued' children. Their objections centred on the claims made by the photographs to be accurate accounts of the histories of individual children, rather than indications based on generalisations. As Koven has argued, there were two different concepts of 'truth' in photography at issue here.[85]

In his defence Barnardo cited the Ragged School Union's use of Rejlander's image, but this was not accepted as a relevant precedent, perhaps because of its anonymity. He might also have cited the 'before and after' photographs which Alfred Alsop was selling in Manchester.[86] Nonetheless, the Arbitration Court ruled against Barnardo's use of staged publicity photographs:

---

[79]   Illustrated in Wagner, *Barnardo*, p. 14.

[80]   'A Delver' (Alfred Alsop), *From Dark to Light; or, Voices from the Slums* (Manchester, 1881). For more examples of this literature, see Anna Davin, 'Waifs' Stories', *History Workshop Journal*, 52/2 (2001): 86–97.

[81]   Wagner, *Barnardo*, p. 44.

[82]   Cunningham, *Children of the Poor*, p. 142.

[83]   *Our Waifs and Strays*, December 1900, p. 404.

[84]   'Transformation Scenes in Real Life', *Graphic*, 16 January 1875.

[85]   Seth Koven, 'Dr Barnardo's "Artistic Fictions": Photography, Sexuality, and the Ragged Child in Victorian London', *Radical History Review*, 69 (1997), p. 29.

[86]   Cunningham, *Children of the Poor*, p. 142.

This use of artistic fiction to represent facts is, in our opinion, not only morally wrong as thus employed, but might in the absence of a very strict control, grow into a system of deception to the cause on behalf of which it is practised. [87]

This judgement did not affect the record photographs taken of children entering and leaving the Homes, which were not for sale.

The Reality of Raggedness

The charge of 'artistic fiction' was justified in the case of some if not all of the publicity photographs, (for example, those of the Holder sisters), as has been recognised by all critics.[88] What is less clear is its application to the tens of thousands of entry photographs taken after 1877. Before analysing the Barnardo's entry photographs in detail, it is necessary to refute the charge of 'artistic fiction' and to establish their validity as a historical source. This can be done in two ways: first, by examining the extent of 'dressing-down' in entry photographs taken between 1874 and 1877, when staged publicity photographs were still being produced, to see whether they record the clothing worn by individuals, or a set of ragged costumes loaned by the photographer. Secondly, the extent of 'raggedness' and 'respectability' in the entry photographs will be tabulated, and compared with the extent in school photographs. We would expect to see a clear distinction in levels of 'raggedness' between the children of families whose economic crisis had brought them to Barnardo's and children whose families were able to support them at home.

'Dressing-down' in Barnardo's Entry Photographs before 1877

All extant images in the Barnardo's archive taken between 1874 and 1877 were viewed. Staged representations of 'the street arab' were excluded: these were identified by the presence of backdrops (real or painted), the variety of postures, and the wide angle of vision. Identity shots of named individuals were analysed for evidence of clothing supplied by the photographer: these were identified by the lack of a backdrop, the standardised posture (face front) and the close cropping of the subject.[89]

The distinction between staged images and identity photographs can be seen in a series taken on 12 May 1875 (Figure 1.8). Photographs 275–281 are individual shots of seven boys from six families. Six of the boys had jackets that were visibly shabby and lacking in buttons;[90] each jacket was in a different style and material, and one boy had a distinctive checked shirt. However, the boy in photo 278 wore

---

[87]   Court of Arbitration, 1877, cited in Wagner, *Barnardo*, p. 159.

[88]   Ibid., pp. 140–41.

[89]   For the visual codes of the entry and exit photographs, see Murdoch, *Imagined Orphans*, pp. 37–9.

[90]   The boy in photo 280 had a sailor top with no buttons, worn like a jacket.

Figure 1.8   The promotion of raggedness in Barnado's photographs, May 1875
              [Barnardo's record photographs 281 and 282, and publicity groups
              283 and 284]. © Barnardo's Aftercare. A boy who has entered
              wearing a smart double-breasted jacket and cap is included in group
              283 (leaning against the wall) but omitted in group 284.

a neat double-breasted jacket, white collar and tie. In photo 283 the boys were grouped together, wearing the same garments as in the record shots. The boys with ragged clothes were shown seated, in postures that highlighted torn trousers and bare feet. The better-dressed boy was placed behind the other boys, but was still visibly incongruous. In photo 284 this boy was omitted and the group reads more convincingly as 'street arabs' in need of assistance.[91]

This sequence of images is interesting as it indicates that the transition from record shots to publicity photographs could be made through a change of location and posture, but without changing garments (although boots may have been removed from the two boys who are bare-footed in the group photograph). The better-dressed boy was not dressed in rags to complete the group, merely omitted. If dressing-down had been regularly practised, we might expect to have seen it here.

Another way of checking for the practice of 'dressing-down' is to compare garments to see if the same example was reused on different boys. One type of garment suitable for this purpose is the hand-knit sailors' jersey that would stretch to fit a variety of sizes. Four photographs from 1876 showed boys wearing such jerseys.[92] Two of these were so similar that they could possibly be the same

---

[91]   Interestingly, it was the first image (number 283) that was reproduced as an example of 'ragged boys' on the Barnardo's website www.barnardos.org (accessed 11 July 2005), and the photographic website www.topfoto.co.uk, image number 0205805 (accessed 20 September 2009).

[92]   Numbers 542, 596, 665, 940; numbers 596 and 665 were similar. See Rose, 'Boyswear', Illustrations 2.20–21, p. 91.

Figure 1.9   Barnardo's entrant 'respectably' dressed, 1877 [Barnado's 1001]. Courtesy of Barnardo's Archive.

garments, but the other two were visibly different. These two case studies indicate that, even when Barnardo was actively creating images for publication, the incidence of 'dressing-down' was less than might be expected. Indeed many of the entry photographs show boys who are far from ragged and could not be used to solicit donations (Figure 1.9).[93]

Comparing Raggedness: Barnardo's and Schools

The entry photographs in the Barnardo's archive were sampled using the methods described in Appendix 1. The initial case studies of entry portraits from the Barnardo's Archive indicated that some of the sitters wore garments that were ragged, with visible holes and missing buttons, and that others lacked the accessories necessary for 'respectability', especially the white collar. The presence of collars and scarves, and of visible raggedness, was tabulated in the two databases for all the Barnardo's entry photographs sampled.[94] These databases also noted the style of garment worn, and the length of the trousers, where visible; this data will be analysed in detail in Chapters 5 and 6. A summary of the data is given in Table 1.2. Of 1,874 boys in the sample, 371 (or 19 per cent) were visibly ragged. The close range of the Barnardo's images mean that signs of raggedness on jackets were easy to detect. However there may have been examples of ragged trousers that were not visible.

Table 1.2   Indicators of raggedness and respectability in Barnardo's, 1875–99

	Ragged	Collar	Scarf	Tie/bow	Unclear	Anomalous	Sailor	Jersey
Subtotals 1875–79 (79)	27	12	34	5	15	–	8	4
Subtotals 1880–84 (134)	28	42	43	15	28	2	9	5
Subtotals 1885–88 (110)	15	34	36	11	30	–	6	6
Subtotals 1888–89 (66)	8	18	22	8	15	–	9	1
Subtotals 1890–94 (797)	203	230	285	83	272	14	126	14
Subtotals 1895–99 (688)	90	232	228	107	180	5	143	14
Totals 1875–99 (1,874)	371	568	648	229	540	21	301	44
% of total (1,874)	19%	29%	33%	12%	27%	1%	16%	2%

---

93   See Clare Rose, 'In Search of Raggedness'/'Alla ricerca della cenciosita', in Tiziano Bonazzi (ed.), *Riconoscimento ed Esclusione* (Rome, 2003), pp. 156–80.

94   For complete dataset see Tables 2.2 and 2.3 in Rose, 'Boyswear'.

This analysis also showed that 568 (29 per cent) of the boys in the sample were wearing a white collar, and a further 648 (33 per cent) were wearing a scarf or neckerchief.[95] The number of white collars is remarkably high, especially if we consider that 345 of the boys were in sailor tops or jerseys with which collars were not strictly necessary. In fact, 58 boys wore white collars with their sailor tops, and 20 combined collars with ragged jackets (Figure 1.10).[96]

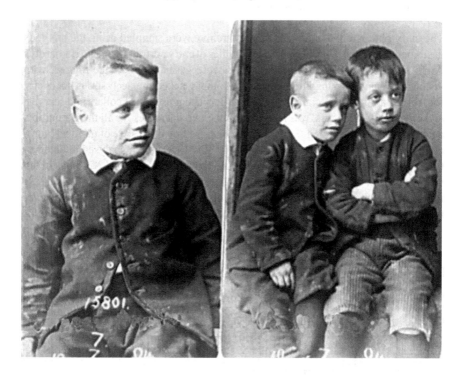

Figure 1.10   Barnardo's entrants numbers 15800–801, 1894. Courtesy of
               Barnardo's Archive.

The school group photographs in Table 1.1 contained 535 separate images of boys. Of these, 283 (53 per cent) were visibly wearing white collars and might be classed as 'respectable', and 17 (4 per cent) were visibly ragged. The remaining 231 (43 per cent) were not visibly ragged, and were not apparently wearing collars and have been classed as 'neutral'. This group includes over 90 boys who were wearing sailor suits or blouses, with which white collars would not normally be

[95]   Neckerchiefs could also be considered a sign of respectability. However, these have been excluded from this analysis in order to maintain parity with the school photographs.

[96]   See also Table 2.4 in Rose, 'Boyswear'.

worn. Two boys in school groups wearing white collars and ragged clothing were categorised as anomalous.

The figures for white collars in school photographs are likely to be accurate, as these are highly visible even on a reduced-scale image. The figures for raggedness are likely to be understated, as tears or worn areas are harder to recognise in a group photograph where the body is partly hidden. There may also have been other examples of boys with anomalous clothing that has not been recognised due to problems with the legibility of images.

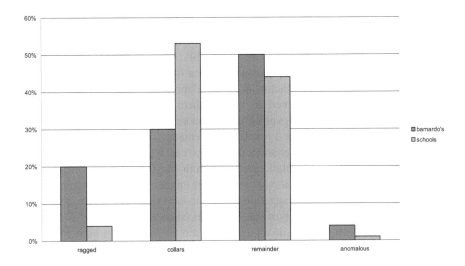

Figure 1.11   Raggedness, collars and anomalous clothing.

A comparison of the two sets of data shows that more of the Barnardo's entrants were visibly ragged, and fewer of the Barnardo's photographs showed white collars (Figure 1.11), making the boys living at home more 'respectable', as one might expect. Nonetheless, the proportion of boys wearing collars in the Barnardo's photos is surprisingly high, and the proportion of the visibly ragged is surprisingly low. The presence of anomalous combinations in both sets of data is also surprising. White collars placed over ragged jackets suggest optimism that the viewer would judge the intention (collar) rather than the execution (jacket). The addition of white collars to sailor tops, seen in both sets of data, underlines the importance of the white collar as a statement of respectability.

The Meanings of the Ragged Child

Ragged clothing was a key indicator of social deprivation in the nineteenth century, and images of ragged children were widely used for fundraising by charities, even after the court censure of Barnardo in 1877. The concept of raggedness was also used in a form of metonymy, as was shown by the regulations of the Ragged School Union, in which lack of clothing was only one of thirteen criteria for admission. The continuing power of raggedness as a metaphor was shown by the Shaftesbury Society's use of a logo based on Rejlander's ragged boy as late as 1973.[97]

While images of raggedness were consistently visible, their interpretation seems to have shifted over time. There was a minority view of street children as a source of humour from the 1840s onwards, seen in the work of Leech and Rejlander. However, the majority view at the start of the period, expressed in images and even more in texts, was of them as a threat to public order, in need of institutional discipline, whether that be 'school or gaol'. Even those who solicited sympathy for them did so by stressing the actual or potential threat they represented. The use of the term 'street arab' reinforced the view of them as a threat by aligning them with prevailing colonialist and evolutionary discourse.

By the 1890s both visual and textual representations of these children had a different focus. They were now characterised in texts as 'waifs', in need of guidance and protection. Visual representations ranged from May's humorous cartoons to the wistful prettification of Stanley. These gentler images were accompanied by a self-congratulatory sense that raggedness, and the behaviour that fostered it, was being eroded by the intervention of state agencies (such as schools) and charities.

However, the term 'waif', since it characterised the children as homeless and parentless, was not neutral in the same way that 'street arabs' had been. This was a key aspect of Barnardo's fundraising rhetoric, stressed in the titles of his publications: *Nobody's Children, Never Had a Home, Worse than Orphans*.[98] The concept of rescued children as homeless 'waifs' was also used to justify the institutional practices of the homes, including 'philanthropic abduction' of children to Canada.[99] As Lydia Murdoch's research on the Barnardo's case files has shown, these children were in fact members of family groups, and this status was demonstrated by the clothing they wore, as I will show in Chapter 6.

Definitions of Respectability

The idea of the 'respectable' boy was equally contested, even between charities. Barnardo's and the CEWSS had different organisational principles (one stressing institutional order, the other homeliness) and this was reflected in the clothing

---

[97]   Franklin and Bailey, *Shaftesbury Story*, p. 18; Jones, *Father*, fig 4 on p. 27.

[98]   Titles from Wagner, *Barnardo*, p. 333.

[99]   Wagner, *Children of the Empire*, p. 139. For the earlier history of child emigration, see Parr, *Labouring Children*, pp. 27–40.

worn by their inhabitants. However, both were equally concerned to distance themselves from the practices and ideologies of the workhouse. They did this by providing clothing that was seen as 'smart', and that was suited to the child's age and future employment, whether as an emigrant farmer, a merchant seaman, or a member of the shoe-black brigade. The clothing issued by workhouses fell short on both counts, with toddlers dressed the same as working men, and with all clothed as labourers, the lowest rung in the employment hierarchy. Charities' distancing of themselves from the workhouse seems to have been recognised even by poor families: Murdoch cites a case where a widowed mother secured places for her children in Barnardo's and then entered the workhouse herself.[100]

However, Barnardo's use of images and spectacles to present a polarised vision of the child 'before and after' belied a complex reality. A review of the entry photographs showed many boys in 'respectable' clothing. There was also a striking variety of garments, disproving the assumption by Smith that boys were dressed from a stock of ragged 'costumes'. Thus these images were not 'artistic fictions' and were legitimate sources for historical research. An analysis of the dataset of 1874 entry photographs showed that the level of raggedness in the clothing of the Barnardo's entrants (19 per cent) was exceeded by the level of 'respectability' as embodied by the white collar (29 per cent).

The statistical analysis of the school group photographs further narrowed the visual difference between boys whose families could support them and boys entering Barnardo's. The level of raggedness visible in the school groups was low but this almost certainly understated the total. The *Graphic* saw the legislation of compulsory school attendance in 1883 as breaking down the distinction between Ragged and Board School: 'at last "Jo", the unkempt little mendicant who makes pretence of sweeping crossings with worn-out broom, is to be swept into the School Board net.'[101] The ragged Board School group reproduced in 1886 supports this view.

What is most striking about the data from the Board School and Barnardo's photographs is the appearance in both of anomalous combinations of ragged jackets with white collars. These suggest that even families who lacked the money to renew ragged jackets understood the importance of the white collar in establishing 'respectability'. This should not have been an issue when entering Barnardo's, if the children were, as he claimed, 'Taken out of the Gutter'.[102] However, Murdoch has demonstrated that most children entering Barnardo's were not 'rescued' but taken there by parents who saw the charity as offering advantages in education and training as well as physical care.[103] In at least one documented case, a child was given new clothing by his mother's employer in order to make a good

---

[100]   Murdoch, *Imagined Orphans*, p. 86.

[101]   'Poor "Jo"', *Graphic*, 30 June 1883: 642.

[102]   Title of a leaflet by Dr Barnardo: *'Taken out of the Gutter.' A true incident of child life on the streets of London, etc.* (London, 1881).

[103]   Murdoch, *Imagined Orphans*, pp. 9, 84–91 and 125.

impression when entering Barnardo's.[104] The Barnardo's entry photographs reflect parents' awareness of the concepts of 'raggedness' and 'respectability' that shaped philanthropic discourse, and their concern to position themselves on the side of 'respectability'.

The findings from these photographs are important in several respects. They show how visual evidence can be used to undermine the purpose for which it was created. As Tagg and Murdoch recognised, the posture and composition of the entry photographs was modelled on criminal 'mug shots' to present the subjects as 'Nobody's Children'.[105] Yet by looking closely at the clothes they wear we can see the boys as members of families who were concerned to keep to socially accepted dress codes. The presence in the photos of distinctive garments like the braided suit offers a striking reminder that there was fashion for small boys, even if not all could afford it. The next chapter will investigate how boys' clothes were produced, Chapter 3 will look at how they were advertised, and Chapter 4 will analyse the prices for which they were sold. This will prepare the ground for a detailed analysis of family consumption patterns in Chapter 5, and evidence of age-related clothing practices in Chapter 6.

---

[104]   For example, a boy admitted to Barnardo's in 1888, his mother's 'employer having given the child a new suit for the occasion'. Wagner, *Barnardo*, p. 229.

[105]   Tagg, *Burden of Representation*, pp. 83–5; Murdoch, *Imagined Orphans*, pp. 26–39.

Chapter 2
Designing Boys' Clothes

In 1884 the manufacturers John Barran & Sons of Leeds registered a design for mass-produced clothing, depositing a photograph of the garment and a sample of fabric. They also made a statement clarifying the scope of the registration: 'A Pattern Consisting of two Silk Braids in close juxtaposition of different colours as shewn in specimen machine stitched in rows upon Boys' "Man O' War" or "Naval" Suits as shewn in photograph.'[1] Similar statements were repeated by manufacturers over the next three years, as they registered patterns of braid, tucks and cording intended for the front of little boys' jackets.[2] This emphasis on decoration is not what we would expect from mass manufacturers at a time of rapid expansion.[3] We would expect them to be targeting the families shown in the Barnardo's entry photographs, who needed 'respectable' clothing but might not be able to afford fancy styles.

The analysis of the different forms taken by 'respectable' clothing in institutions and in schools in the previous chapter showed that this was defined partly by negatives: not ragged, or the wrong size. The preliminary analysis of the Barnardo's entry photographs indicated that by the 1870s even impoverished children were wearing a wide variety of clothing styles, not just generic rags. Wearing newly fashionable styles demonstrated that the family was aware of clothing trends, and could afford to follow them.

This chapter will examine the element of fashion in the making of boys' clothing. This will be done through the analyses of sets of visual documents from mass manufacturers, bespoke tailors, and female dressmakers. The focus on visual documents is partly pragmatic, as some of the archives contained only images with little accompanying text. These provided evidence of the level of stylistic differentiation in mass-produced boys' clothing in this period. Comparing and tracking the appearance of different types of garments in different sources gives us an insight into the development of specialisation within different branches of the clothing industry. It indicates how manufacturers selected and directed current trends in order to maximise their own profit margins and market shares.

---

[1] Design: Board of Trade (BT) 50/396; Register entry: BT51/9 (1884), both The National Archives (TNA).

[2] The statements are only present in Registers BT51/1 to BT51/45, 1884–87. See Appendix 2 for transcription.

[3] The number of clothing workers in Leeds doubled in the 1860s and again in the 1870s, then trebled in the 1880s. Katrina Honeyman, *Well Suited: A History of the Leeds Clothing Industry, 1850–1990* (Oxford, 2000), p. 29.

As the review of the literature on the clothing industry indicated, there is a prevailing view that male ready-to-wear clothing at this time was characterised by 'style monotony' and that this was beneficial to manufacturers.[4] Christopher Breward has argued strongly for the centrality of fashion in creating male identities, and Laura Ugolini noted the importance of fashion for youths and boys.[5] This divergence is partly due to the different sources used: Godley and Honeyman consulted the records of mass manufacturers, which concentrate on issues of production, while Breward prioritised the *Tailor and Cutter*, a fashion journal for bespoke tailors. Ugolini and Breward also used advertising material, but as Schorman demonstrated this often blurs the distinctions between value and fashion.[6] Sarah Levitt's work on registered designs for garments opened up a new source of information on clothing manufacturers, which will prove crucial to a re-evaluation of the role of design in boyswear, and the role of boyswear in the clothing industry.[7]

This chapter will evaluate these views by investigating each of the main forms of clothing provision in turn. Large numbers of designs for mass production were registered in the Board of Trade archive, and these will be considered in the first section. As the records are in several non-continuous series, each set will be analysed separately before the findings from all Board of Trade documents are discussed. The second section will examine the contribution of bespoke tailors to clothing provision for boys, using the *Tailor and Cutter* and a manual on boys' clothing by the same publisher. In the third section the practice of dressmakers will be evaluated by examining dressmaking patterns for boys sold by Butterick & Company and by *Myra's Journal*. This section will also discuss the limitations of the dressmaking skills taught in Board Schools.

Each of these sources includes patterns and images of garments, which together indicate the importance of style changes, and indeed of fashion, in boys' clothing.

---

[4]   Ben Fine and Ellen Leopold, *The World of Consumption* (London, 1993); Andrew Godley, 'The Development of the UK Clothing Industry, 1850–1950: Output and Productivity Growth,' *Business History*, 37/4 (1995): 46–63; *idem*, 'The Emergence of Mass Production in the UK Clothing Industry', in Ian Taplin and Jonathan Winterton (eds), *Restructuring within a Labour Intensive Industry: The UK Clothing Industry in Transition* (Aldershot, 1996), pp.8–23; Katrina Honeyman, 'Style Monotony and the Business of Fashion: The Marketing of Menswear in Inter-war England', *Textile History*, 34/2 (2003): 171–91.

[5]   Christopher Breward, *The Hidden Consumer: Masculinities, Fashion and City Life, 1860–1914* (Manchester, 1999); Laura Ugolini, *Men and Menswear: Sartorial Consumption in Britain, 1880–1939* (Aldershot, 2007).

[6]   Rob Schorman, *Selling Style: Clothing and Social Change at the Turn of the Century* (Philadelphia, 2003). Farid Chenoune and Phillipe Perrot have recognised the interdependence of the bespoke and ready-to-wear trades, and of French and British producers: Farid Chenoune, *A History of Men's Fashion* (Paris, 1993), pp. 66–8; Phillipe Perrot, *Fashioning the Bourgeoisie: A History of Fashion in the Nineteenth Century* (Princeton, 1994).

[7]   Sarah Levitt, *The Victorians Unbuttoned* (London, 1986), esp. Chapters 1 and 10, and the index to designs on pp. 227–8.

The fourth section will examine the genesis of new styles like the sailor suit in order to clarify which branch of the clothing trade was most innovative, and which was investing most in design. This will feed into the examination of the marketing of boys' garments in Chapter 3, and the analysis of the cost of clothes in Chapter 4. Data on the production of specific garment types in this chapter will also form the basis for the analysis of consumption patterns in Chapter 5.

Mass-produced Designs for Boys' Clothes in the Board of Trade Registrations

Overwhelming evidence for the importance of design in mass-produced boys' garments can be found in the designs for manufactured goods registered under the terms of copyright acts between 1842 and 1900. The procedure for the registration of designs was established by an Act of Parliament in 1842 and administered by the Patent Office, under the jurisdiction of the Board of Trade, so that documents are filed with the prefix 'BT' (Board of Trade). Sarah Levitt's work on the BT archives had established their importance as a source for the study of mass-produced clothing, and had indicated the sections of the archive likely to be most helpful as BT43, BT45 and BT50.

Board of Trade Documents 1870–83: BT43 and BT45

Because of the overlaps and discontinuities between the different series, BT43, BT45 and BT50 were searched and analysed separately, using the methods described in Appendix 1. BT 43 (Ornamental Designs) was divided into thirteen Classes, and both Class 12 (Textiles) and Class 13 (Lace and Miscellaneous) contained designs for garments. Class 12 contained some 15,000 designs: textiles and small items were represented by samples, and garments by sketches, engravings or photographs. While registrations began in 1842, there was only one boy's suit registered before 1870 (Figure 2.1).[8]

In Class 12 between 1870 and 1883 there were only 50 designs for outer garments (dresses, jackets, trousers, suits, coats, jerseys) but 28 of these were for boys, compared to 13 for men, 24 for women, and one for a girl.[9] There were three surprising points in this data, the first being the high proportion of designs for boys compared to women, when we would expect that women's clothes would be more subject to fashionable change, and more worthy of copyright protection. The second notable point was the way in which registrations were grouped, with all but five in sets of two or more similar garments rather than single items. The third was

---

[8]   A boy's tunic, registered by J. Robinson of Commercial Road London, BT43/12 38244 (1846).

[9]   For full dataset, see Table 3.1 in Clare Rose, 'Boyswear and the Formation of Gender and Class Identity in Urban England 1840–1900' (unpublished PhD Dissertation, University of Brighton, 2006).

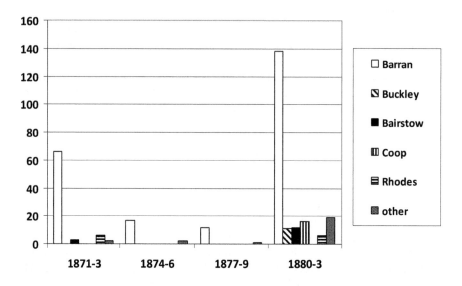

Figure 2.1   Manufacturers registering boys' garments in BT43 Classes 12 and
13.

the presence of many firms not known from the work of Honeyman, Chapman and
others, and the absence of well-known names such as E. Moses & Son.[10] Of the
nine manufacturers of boys' clothing represented in BT43/12, six were previously
unpublished, including one from Leeds.[11]

BT43 Class 13 (Lace and Miscellaneous) ran concurrently with Class 12, and
there were 329 garments registered in this category from 1870. Of these, 290
were for boys as against 37 for women, two for men and four for infants.[12] Of
the boys' designs, 256 were registered by manufacturers from Leeds, and 248
of these were from John Barran & Sons. In 1873, 1876 and 1879, Barran made
groups of registrations, 95 in all: this may reflect the three-year validity of each
registration.[13] The volume and tempo of Barran's registrations increased sharply
from 1880, with 138 designs in only three years. These were registered in batches

---

[10]   For example, Bairstow Sons & Co. of Huddersfield registered BT43/12/360153–
7, BT43/12/360391 and BT43/12/360944–5 in 1880. Samuel Brothers was the only
London manufacturer in this section (BT43/12/292866, 1874; BT43/12/293202, 1874;
BT43/12/374951, 1881).

[11]   Robinson, London; S. & J. Curtis, Birmingham; T. Kellam, Leicester; Bairstow
Sons & Co., Huddersfield; J. Jackson & Co., Leeds; R. Walker & Sons, Leicester.

[12]   Over the period 1843–69 there were a further 62 registrations for women, 8 for
men, and 2 for boys: H.J. Nicoll, BT 43/13 159544 and 204499, both 1866. For the full
dataset, see Table 3.2 in Rose, 'Boyswear'.

[13]   Levitt, *Victorians Unbuttoned*, p. 3.

in the summer and winter of each year, suggesting new ranges prepared for each season.[14] The second most prolific registrant was Coop & Co. of Wigan, with 16 designs. The remaining 26 registrations were made by eight other firms, five of whom were previously unknown from published sources.[15] Altogether, eleven of the eighteen firms registering boys' clothes in BT43 were not known from the work of Honeyman and Chapman, and several were in locations such as Walsall and Wigan, not previously recognised as major centres for clothing manufacture.[16]

The series of 'Useful' designs, BT 45, ran in parallel with the 'Ornamental' designs in BT43 between 1842 and 1883.[17] This category contained 6,740 designs arranged in numeric order in 30 volumes, but yielded only 21 garment designs between 1870 and 1883. The greatest number of registrations from a single manufacturer was 15 from H J Nicoll, and these were placed singly between 1845 and 1883.[18] There were some repeat registrations by firms around 1850, but the only firm that registered more than one design in BT45 after 1870 was H.J. Nicoll.[19] Most of the firms that used BT43 did not appear in BT45, and those that did were represented by single designs rather than the groups registered in BT43. For example, Corah Sons & Cooper of Leicester registered a group of thirteen designs in BT43/12, but only one in BT45.[20] In the 1850s and 1860s, users of BT45 had been mostly based in London, and in areas associated with elite tailoring and

---

[14] The evidence for seasonal ranges will be discussed further in Chapter 3.

[15] Bairstow & Oates, Huddersfield, BT43/13/273703–5 (1873); Buckley & Sons, Leeds, BT43/13/352969–74 (1880), BT43/13/389293 and BT43/13/389388 (1882), and BT43/13/399131 and BT43/13/400487 (1883); W. Dixon & Co., Nottingham, BT43/13/335496–7 and BT43/13/355567–70 (1880); Genese & Young, London, BT43/13/407621 (1883); Grocott & Kitching, London, BT43/13/338663 (1880); George Macbeth, Manchester, BT43/13/277147 (1873), BT43/13/312461 (1877), BT43/13/339153 (1880) and BT43/13/367545 (1881); Taylor Tucker & Co., Bristol, BT43/13/353660 (1880).

[16] Dixon, Grocott, Taylor Tucker, and Genese & Young were not mentioned by Stanley Chapman, *Merchant Enterprise in Britain from the Industrial Revolution to World War I* (Cambridge, 1992); *idem*, 'The Innovating Entrepreneurs in the British Ready-made Clothing Industry', *Textile History*, 24/1 (1993): 5–25.

[17] Levitt, *Victorians Unbuttoned*, p. 4.

[18] The first design registered by Nicoll was BT45/0393 (1845), with eleven more up to BT45/5105 (1869). After 1870, they registered BT45/5265 (1871); BT45/5343 (1872); BT45/5552 (1873).

[19] Firms registering three designs were: Welch Margetson, London, BT45/1618 (1848), BT45/1826 (1849) and BT45/2159 (1850); and J. Swain & Co., London, BT45/1195 (1847) and BT45/2416–7 (1850). Firms registering two designs included Elias Moses, BT45/1718 (1848), BT45/3042 (1851). Moses' BT45/1718, the 'Duplex waistcoat', was highlighted by Levitt in *Victorians Unbuttoned*, p. 100, in such as way as to give a misleading impression of this firm's presence in this archive.

[20] Corah, BT45/6241 (1881).

retailing such as Bond Street and Regent Street.[21] The 1870s registrants included three firms from Manchester and two from Leicester, both centres for the garment industry, but none from Leeds.[22] The only firms in BT45 known to have been manufacturing on a large scale were Corah, and H.J. & D. Nicoll, and the Nicoll brothers were also retailers.

Whether or not the designs in BT 45 were for mass production they were united by their novelty of cut and construction. The sole design for boys' clothing in this class was described on the form as for 'the cutting and making of boys short trousers', and showed a diagram for an unusual cloverleaf cut with sharply sloped side seams.[23] This formed a complete contrast with the 36 designs for boys' trousers in BT43 which were for applied decoration on garments of unspecified cut. Thus it seems that the choice of registration in BT 43 'Ornamental' or BT 45 'Useful' was based on a distinction between novelty of decoration and novelty of cut or construction.

Design in BT registrations 1870–83

The garments registered for boys in BT 43/12 were mainly suits with ornamented jackets and short trousers. Eighteen of the jackets registered relied for their effect on panels of narrow braid in interlaced patterns or tabs made from strips of wider braid. This was especially noticeable in the twelve designs from Bairstow Sons & Co. of Huddersfield, registered as outline drawings.[24] It was evident from these that the surface patterning, not the cut of the garment, was the object of interest. Other manufacturers such as Rhodes & Co. and Jackson & Co. of Leeds used photographs of garments that were harder to interpret.[25] Nineteen of the designs registered (those by Bairstow, Rhodes and Buckley & Sons, Leeds) were suits with short trousers trimmed to match the jackets.[26] Eight designs were for jackets or

---

[21]   1850s registrants in BT45 included Doudney, Fletcher, Geoghan, Guthrie, Haldane, Reynolds & Tillock and Roe, all based in London's Bond Street and Jermyn Street, sites of the elite bespoke tailoring trade.

[22]   C. Fleet, 20 High Street, Shrewsbury, BT45/5299 (1871); Barmer & Henton, Leicester, BT 45/5370 (1872); Beaty Bros, Royal Exchange Manchester, BT45/5378 (1872); D. Moseley, Manchester, BT 45/5449 (1873); Chiswell & Co., St Ann's Square, Manchester, BT45/5507 (1873); R. Hastie, Gloucester, BT45/5956 (1878).

[23]   BT 45/6271 (1879), T. Knight, 3–4 Aldermanbury, London.

[24]   Bairstow as note 8, and BT43/12/374758–61 (1881); see Illustration 3.1, p. 102 in Rose, 'Boyswear'.

[25]   Rhodes, BT43/12/352933–7 (1880) and BT43/12/352975 (1880); Jackson, BT43/12/361061–2 (1880).

[26]   Rhodes as note 11; Bairstow as notes 8 and 10; Buckley, BT43/12/317683 (1880).

knitted sailor tops registered without matching trousers.[27] The remaining garments were two jacket and skirt ensembles of a type worn by young boys.[28]

As in Class 12, the designs for boys' garments registered in Class 13 were principally patterns for applying braid or other trim. The 84 designs registered by Barran between 1872 and 1879 appeared in the registers as tissue-paper patterns stamped with interlaced motifs probably taken from stamps used to mark garment pieces for decoration (Figure 2.2).[29] Sometimes the intended placement of this motif was indicated by the outline of a garment piece.[30] In other cases the purpose of the design was indicated by Barran's annotation: the manufacturers' inscription, 'Designs for braiding for little boys suits'.[31] From 1879 onwards, the 138 garments Barran registered were jackets trimmed with braid or textured embroidery, represented through photographs of actual garments or garment pieces (Figure 2.3).[32] Jackets with braid trimming were also the focus of the registrations made by Coop & Co., presented as full-sized patterns for jacket fronts trimmed with braid (Figure 2.4).[33] These too may have been reproduced from patterns used in the workshop. Buckley & Sons of Leeds presented their designs through photographs of finished garments on a living model (Figure 2.5).[34] Annotations on the photographs specified that the registration was not for the whole suit, nor even for the whole jacket, but only for the applied decoration: 'Class XIII, Braiding Pattern'.[35]

The basis on which designs were allocated to BT43 Class 12 or Class 13 was not clear. Two firms, Buckley of Leeds and Bairstow of Huddersfield, registered

---

[27] S. & J. Curtis, Birmingham, BT43/12/262497 (1874); Jackson & Co., BT43/12/361061–2 (1880); T. Kellam, Leicester, sailor jersey, BT43/12/353422 (1880); Samuel Bros, BT43/12/374951 (1881); R. Walker & Sons, Leicester, Sailor jerseys, BT43/12/407626–8 (1883).

[28] Samuel Bros, BT43/12/ 293202 and BT43/12/ 292866 (1874).

[29] See Illustration 3.2, p. 103 in Rose, 'Boyswear'. Levitt in *Victorians Unbuttoned*, p. 103, interpreted these patterns as 'rubbings taken with crayon over paper', but they are in ink, not crayon, and in continuous lines, not sketched.

[30] For example Barran's BT43/13/ 268775–8 (1872).

[31] Barran, BT43/13/268946 (1873).

[32] For Barran registrations BT43/13/390813–31 (1882), see Figure 3, p. 6 in Clare Rose '"The novelty consists in the ornamental design": Design innovation in mass-produced boys' clothing, 1840–1900', *Textile History*, 38/1 (2007): 1–24,

[33] For example, BT43/13/ 373190 (1881), Illustration 3.3, p. 104 in Rose, 'Boyswear'.

[34] Buckley & Sons, BT 43/13/389293 (1882); Illustration 3.4, p. 105 in Rose, 'Boyswear'.

[35] Buckley BT43/13/389389; the trousers in the photograph had been crossed out with pen strokes. These photographs might have been intended for publicity purposes, but no advertising images from Buckley have yet been found.

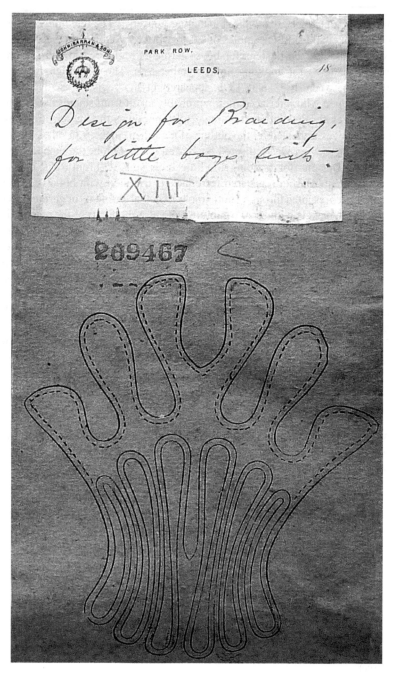

Figure 2.2   'Design for Braiding for little boys' suits', Barran, 1873
               [BT43/13, 269467]. Courtesy of The National Archives, Kew.

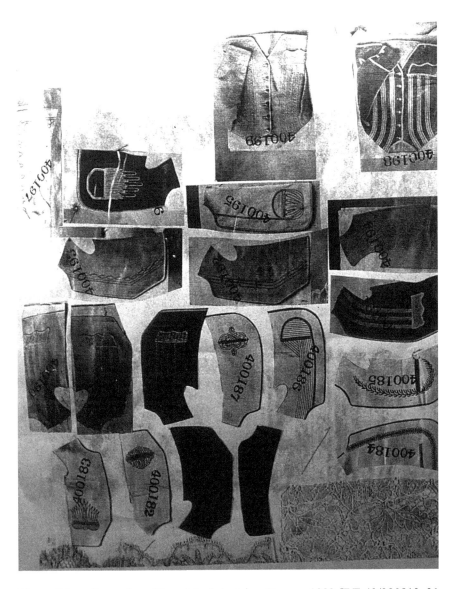

Figure 2.3   Examples of boys' jacket styles, Barran, 1882 [BT 43/390813–31 1882]. Courtesy of The National Archives, Kew.

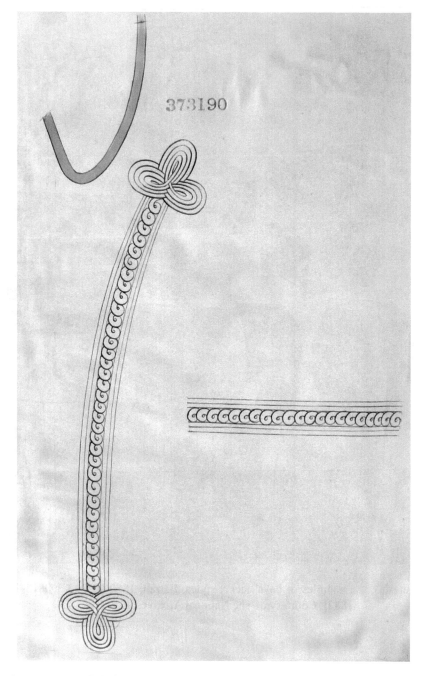

Figure 2.4   A full-size braiding pattern for a boy's jacket, Coop, 1881 [BT 43/13 373190]. Courtesy of The National Archives, Kew.

Figure 2.5   Registration with a modelled photograph, Buckley, 1882 [BT 43/13 389293]. Courtesy of The National Archives, Kew.

designs in both.[36] In the case of Buckley in particular, the alternation between registrations in Class 13 and Class 12 suggests that there was little perceived difference between them. There was no instance of a design being registered in both categories. There was, however, a difference in the scope of the designs for boys' clothing in Class 12 and Class 13. In Class 12, 23 out of 30 registrations were for complete suits of jacket and short trousers, but in Class 13 only 18 of the 292 designs were for suits. Of the 292 Class 13 designs, 263 were braided patterns, shown either as isolated motifs or worked on garment pieces (Figure 2.6).

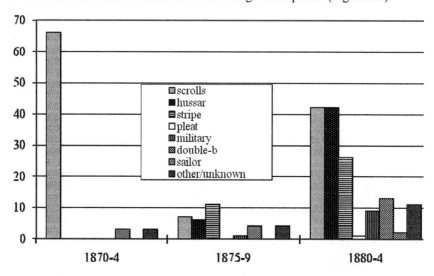

Figure 2.6   Styles of jackets registered in BT43 Class 12 and Class 13, 1870–83.

The designs showed striking similarities between manufacturers and between Classes.[37] Suits by Bairstow and by Rhodes & Co. in Class 12 had lines of interlaced braid either side of the jacket opening which could have been taken from Barran's interlaced patterns in Class 13.[38] Most of these designs shared the

---

[36]   Buckley, BT43/12/317683 (1880), BT43/13/352969–74 (1880), BT 43/13/389293 (1882), BT43/13/389388 (1882), BT43/13/399131 (1883); Bairstow, BT43/13/273703–5 (1873), BT43/12/360153–7 (1880), BT43/12/360944–5 (1880), BT43/12/375758–61 (1881).

[37]   Even an unusual design such as Buckley's BT43/12/317683 (1880), was copied by Barran's BT43/13/390820 (1882).

[38]   Bairstow BT43/12/360153–7; Rhodes & Co., BT43/12/352933–7; Barran BT43/13/297847–9. Designs with braid or a line of tucks up the front of the jackets were also registered by Macbeth, BT43/13/277147 (1873), BT43/13/339153 (1879), BT43/13/367545 (1881); Buckley, BT43/13/352969–74 (1880), BT43/13/389293 (1882), BT43/13/389388 (1882); W. Dixon & Co., BT43/13/335496–7 (1880), BT43/13/355570 (1880); Grocott & Kitching, BT43/13/338663 (1879); Taylor Tucker & Co., BT43/13/353660 (1880).

same basic jacket cut, single-breasted and collarless, with the front corners cut away or rounded off below the waist. This provided a large flat surface to be decorated with braid, pleats, pocket flaps and fancy lapels. The designs could be divided into seven subtypes according to the arrangement of the applied features.[39] The commonest were the 'scroll' with braid applied in a curve from hip or waist to shoulder,[40] and the 'hussar' where braid was applied in horizontal strips or knots across the chest.[41] By 1883 jackets with braid or pleats applied in narrow vertical bands were the third major subtype.[42] Less common types trimmed with braid were the 'military' (based on eighteenth-century military uniform), the 'double-breasted', with a braid-trimmed front panel, and 'other' (see Figure 2.2).[43] The only type of jacket not defined by applied decoration was the sailor top, with a broad collar open at the neck to show a contrasting panel. There were five designs for these, all made from machine-knitted wool.[44]

While these categories are in some senses arbitrary, they are nonetheless indicative of the strong consensus between manufacturers about the target age range, about design trends and about manufacturing processes.[45] In the period 1870–83, novelty in boys' clothes was understood by manufacturers as novel decoration rather than cut, as seen from their use of BT43, 'Ornamental', to register boys' clothing designs, while men's and women's clothing were also registered in BT45, 'Useful'. In spite of some variations in cut, including the introduction of sailor blouses,[46] the main focus in the registrations was in patterns of applied braid applied to standard jacket shapes. The implication is that manufacturers saw slight variations in trim as providing an effective and profitable way to increase sales.

---

[39]   These categories were selected and named based on the designs, as the accompanying documentation does not give them names.

[40]   See Barran, BT43/13/268775–9 (1872).

[41]   See Buckley, BT43/12/317683 (1880). References to hussar uniforms were common in small boys' suits from the 1770s onwards, and in women's jackets in the 1820s and periodically thereafter. See Clare Rose, *Children's Clothes Since 1750* (London, 1989), pp. 94 and 100; Alison Matthews David, 'Decorated Men: Fashioning the French Soldier, 1852–1914', *Fashion Theory*, 7/1 (2003): 3–38.

[42]   For 'stripe', see Bairstow's BT43/12/360945 (1880); for 'pleat', see Barran's BT43/13/390817 (1882).

[43]   For 'military', see Bairstow's B43/12/360391 (1880); for 'double-breasted', see Barran's BT43/13/374329 (1881); for 'other' see Jackson & Co.'s BT43/12/361061–2 (1880).

[44]   Sailor tops: BT43/12/353422 (T. Kellam, Leicester, 1880; BT43/12/ 407626–8 (R. Walker & Sons, Leicester, 1883); BT43/13/ 407621 (Genese & Young, London, 1883).

[45]   Age-related dress codes will be discussed in more detail in Chapter 6, but the prevalence of short trousers (shown in 36 designs) indicates a young age group. There was also a skirted outfit for even younger boys, BT43/12/292866 (Samuel Bros, 1874), identified as such in the Registration documents.

[46]   Designs for sailor jerseys were registered by T. Kellam, Leicester, sailor jersey, BT43/12/353422 (1880); R. Walker & Sons, Leicester, BT43/12/407626–8 (1883); Genese & Young, London, BT43 13/407621 (1883).

Registered Designs 1883–1900: BT50

After 1883, the classification system for registered Designs changed and they were entered into a single series of 367,200 of designs in 408 volumes of Representations, catalogued as BT50. Of the 355 designs for garments found during the search described in the Appendix, 18 were for men, 75 for women, and 262 for boys. However, this does not necessarily reflect the proportion of garment designs in the whole series. The 262 designs for boys' clothing in BT50 were distributed over the period 1883–1900.[47] The designs were registered by 47 different manufacturers; as in BT43, the largest single registrant was John Barran & Sons with 129 entries. The next most frequent were Coop of Wigan with 31 and Buckley of Leeds with 20. Bairstow & Sons, Schofield & Parkinson and Rhodes registered six designs, and Rhodes & Clay and Ernest Marsden registered four designs each. The remaining 38 manufacturers registered one or two designs each, to a total of 56.

A comparison between the names of manufacturers in BT50 and those from BT43 showed substantial continuity across the period 1870–86 (Figure 2.7). Barran was the most frequent and most copious registrant, with 363 designs in total. The second largest number of registrations during the whole period (47) came from Coop, but these all appeared between 1883 and 1885. The third most prolific registrant was Buckley with 31 designs, entered up to six at a time between 1880 and 1892. Bairstow of Huddersfield followed a similar pattern but ceased registering after 1886.

There was less of a distinct pattern in the timing of registrations in BT50 than in BT43. The bulk of the designs for boys' garments were registered between 1883 and 1892, with 224 before 1893 and 39 after. The decline in registrations over time is even more marked if we look at individual firms. Even Barran cut down after 1892, from a maximum of 55 designs per annum to a minimum of eight. Their registration of large groups of designs in 1884, 1888, 1889, 1890 and 1891 did not fall into the three-year pattern seen in BT43.

Some of the decline in registrations could be explained as the result of changes in practice by particular businesses or even by individual managers. For example, Ernest Marsden appeared in the Registers for the first time in 1898 (BT50/327180) with the phrase 'late of Coop & Co.' suggesting that he was setting up a new business. Coop & Co. did not register any designs between 1886 and 1898, although they expanded their manufacturing premises twice in the period, suggesting a shift from design to production as a driver in the business.[48] Barran also experienced a changeover in management in the late 1880s, as the founder's two elder sons stepped down as Partners in 1886 and 1888, and two younger sons replaced them in 1882 and 1886.[49] However, these structural changes within firms did not coincide exactly with changes in the frequency and number of their registrations,

---

[47]   The whole dataset is given as Table 3.3 in Rose, 'Boyswear'.

[48]   John Hannavy and Chris Ryan, *Working in Wigan Mills* (Wigan, 1987), p. 78.

[49]   David Ryott, *John Barran's of Leeds, 1851–1951* (Leeds, 1951), pp. 25–6.

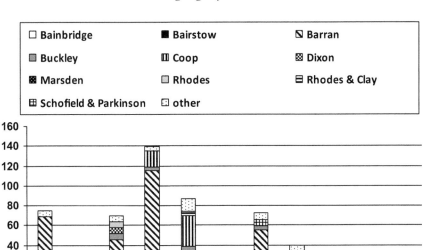

Figure 2.7   Manufacturers registering boys' garments in BT43 and BT50, 1870–1900.

so we should not overstate their importance. As the number of registrations by all firms declined after 1892, it is likely that there were causes common to all manufacturers. One of these may have been a change in the types of boys' clothes being manufactured, and this will be examined below. A further factor that should be considered is the type of competition between firms – if manufacturers began to compete by price rather than by design we would expect Registrations to decline. This hypothesis will be examined in the discussion of retailing in Chapter 3 and of garment pricing in Chapter 4.

Garment Designs in BT50

The majority of the garment designs in BT50 were shown in formats established in BT43: as a photograph of a garment piece, a finished garment laid flat, or a complete outfit on a live model. There were also some designs represented by line or wash drawings showing the positioning of trimmings on a garment.[50] No manufacturers registered designs by means of the stamped patterns that had been used earlier.[51] However, some registrations with photographs were now accompanied by a sample of fabric and trimming, as seen in 72 of Barran's 130 Registrations in

---

[50]   For example, BT50/39759–68, Coop (1884).
[51]   For example, BT43/13/ 268775–80, Barran (1872).

BT50.[52] This was not completely new, as accessory manufacturers had submitted actual examples of socks, gloves, collars and even hats for Registrations from the 1840s.[53] Samples of decorated fabric intended for clothing had also been registered in earlier series.[54]

Barran's use of textile samples from 1883 onwards focussed not on the fabric itself but on decoration with pleating, tucking, and applied braid.[55] This is clarified by the inscriptions that appear next to some trimmed swatches: 'section showing essential feature of design'.[56] The primacy of the decoration is highlighted by the use of different fabrics in the photographs and swatches of the same designs. For example, the photograph in one registration photograph shows a sailor blouse made from dark coloured velvet, but the accompanying sample is worked on navy wool serge.[57] This disparity indicates that these styles were available in different fabrics, and this will be considered further in Chapter 3.

The primacy of trimming over fabric choice or even cut in determining the 'design' of a garment is clarified by manufacturers' statements in the Registers for BT 50 up to 1887 (see Appendix 2). Of the 35 statements relating to boys' clothing, only 5 mention the cut or shape of the garment, and this is in conjunction with a decorative trimming: 'Applicable to Braided pattern on, and shape of, Jacket'.[58] All the other statements are quite clear that it is the surface decoration rather than the cut of the garment which forms the 'design': 'It is the pattern that we desire to register.'[59]

An analysis of garment types in the BT50 registrations is shown in Figure 2.8. There was one newly introduced style, the 'Norfolk' jacket with broad pleats in the jacket fabric held in place by a belt.[60] It is noticeable that the sailor jacket, which barely figured in BT43, was the single commonest style in BT50 with 77 out of 262 registrations. Jackets with 'stripe' trimming were also common (11 per cent), but jackets with braid applied in scrolls or frogging, which dominated BT43, made up only 5 per cent each of the total. There were also a substantial number (33 per cent)

---

[52]   For example, BT50/226873, Barran (1894); Illustration 3.8, p. 121 in Rose, 'Boyswear'.

[53]   For example, BT 43/13/7368, 1843, a woman's bonnet in silk-covered wire.

[54]   For example, BT43/13/274376–8 (1873), wool fabrics with braided patterns for women's skirts.

[55]   Pleats, BT50/ 134, (Barran, 1883); braid, BT50/18253 (Barran, 1884).

[56]   Barran BT50/194760 (1892). See Figure 1, p. 4 in Rose, 'The novelty consists'.

[57]   Ibid.

[58]   BT50/18889, Buckley (1884). Other examples are BT50/1469–70 (Hepworth, 1884); BT50/3651 (Macbeth, 1884); BT50/9167 (Barran, 1884).

[59]   See Appendix 2 for full texts.

[60]   For example, BT50/89766 (E. Marsden, Wigan, 1898); Illustration 3.10, p. 124 in Rose, 'Boyswear'.

of hybrid designs combining elements from two styles – often Norfolk pleats with sailor collars.[61] The Norfolk jacket proper was seen in only eight designs.[62]

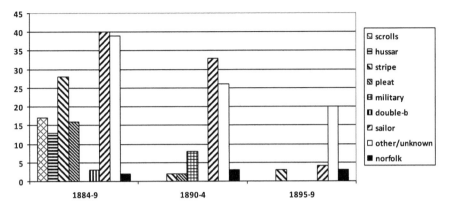

Figure 2.8   Styles of boys' jackets registered in BT50, 1883–1900.

Summary of Findings from Registered Designs, 1870–1900

The examination of the BT43 and BT50 archives of clothing designs revealed the importance of this sector in the trade of major Leeds manufacturers such as Barran and Buckley. The activities of lesser-known manufacturers such as Coop of Wigan were also highlighted. Between 1870 and 1883 all designs were examined, making it possible to quantify the proportion of designs for boys to those for men. In BT43, 'Ornamental', the proportion of boys' designs was surprisingly high: 318 out of 379, or 84 per cent of all garments. Conversely, men's garments dominated the designs in BT45, 'Useful', with 13 out of 21 registrations in the latter. As the number of designs for clothing in BT45 was smaller, boys' garments still formed the dominant category in clothing registrations between 1870 and 1883, with 326 designs out of the total of 633 (51 per cent) as against 21 per cent for women and 19 per cent for men.

After 1883, changes in the registration procedure meant that the whole series could not be viewed, and a variety of filtering strategies were used to select designs for boys' garments. As a result, a further 262 designs for boys, 81 for women and 19 for men were identified. While the references were selected with a strong bias towards known manufacturers of boys' clothing, it is worth noting that manufacturers registering designs for boys did not register designs for men at the same time. Even when manufacturers were producing clothing for both age groups, as did Barran and Coop, these were registered separately.

---

[61]   For example, BT50/74707 and BT50/74711 (Rhodes, 1887); BT50/214983 (J Harding, Manchester, 1893); BT50/268984 (W. & R. Cook, Tiverton, 1896).

[62]   The earliest of these was BT 50/89766 (J. May & Sons, Leeds, 1887).

The falling off in the frequency and volume of registrations for boys after 1886 was surprising, as the new procedures gave a longer period of protection and a higher fine for infringement, leading to an increase in registrations in general.[63] Given that only ten firms registered four or more designs over the whole period, and only five of these firms registered designs more than twice, internal changes in each company may be sufficient explanation. The typological analysis of the designs registered adds to the picture of an industry in flux after 1885. By 1890 not only was the volume of registrations reduced, but the variety of designs was less, with most garments either sailor jackets or sailor hybrids. There was a crossover point around 1884, when the registration of jackets with scrolls of braid declined sharply (ceasing altogether by 1890) and the registration of sailor suits rose. Another point of transition occurred in 1889, when the registration of designs using applied patterns of braid ('scroll', 'hussar' and 'stripe') came to an end.

It would be tempting to explain this with reference to changes in the cost of materials or of the skilled labour required for this work. However the designs for sailor suits registered after 1889 all included novel braid trims, so the shift in design types is likely to relate to changes in fashion rather than changes in manufacturing practice. Both Godley and Honeyman note that up to 1900 the standard practice in Leeds was to subcontract out the more technically demanding parts of garments, especially jackets, so changes in the costs of subcontracting may be relevant here.[64] Chapter 3 will provide a quantitative analysis of marketing images to see whether the change in dominant styles seen in BT43 and BT50 reflects a change in the styles on offer to consumers, or indeed a reduction in the number of different styles available. The next section will examine designs for boys' clothes from tailors to see how they correspond with the trends identified in the BT documents.

Boys' Clothes Made by Tailors

The importance of bespoke tailoring as an innovator of male styles is contested; Breward saw the *Tailor and Cutter* as the 'authoritative voice of the trade press for men's clothing', while Chenoune saw innovations proceeding from the ready-to-wear trade.[65] This section will use tailors' publications to evaluate the provision of boys' clothing from 1870 onwards, using quantitative visual analysis to produce data for comparison with that for ready-to-wear clothing. The text of these

---

[63]   The registration period was lengthened to five years, and the fine was raised from £5 to £50. The £5 stamp duty on each design was also abolished. Levitt, *Victorians Unbuttoned*, p. 5.

[64]   Honeyman, *Well Suited*, p. 22; Godley, 'Development of the UK Clothing Industry', p. 57.

[65]   Breward, *The Hidden Consumer*, p. 25; Chenoune, *A History of Men's Fashion*, pp. 66–9.

publications also provides material for qualitative analysis. Some of this deals with the relations between the bespoke and mass trade, and will be discussed here. Tailors' publications also contained information about the age ranges for particular styles, and this will be taken forward for examination in Chapter 6.

Tailoring publications often included patterns for cutting particular garments, presented in the form of highly reduced diagrams which needed to be scaled up for use. These patterns were given in one size only, and resized by the tailor to suit the needs of his clients.[66] While designs were often accompanied by detailed descriptions of fabric and trim, these were also open to negotiation, making it difficult to compare the styles given for tailors with those in manufacturers' sources of the same period.

The best source for tailoring practice between 1870 and 1900 was the *Tailor and Cutter* and associated books and fashion plates published by the John Williamson Company.[67] The *Tailor and Cutter* claimed to be the leading trade journal in both London and New York, and many of its designs were registered in the Copy 1 archive.[68] Other tailoring publishers were represented by fashion plates in the same archive, and these have been included in the analysis. Copies of the *Tailor and Cutter* between 1868 and 1888 contained 123 different outfits for boys. The 14 outfits presented up to the end of 1870 appeared as pattern diagrams with a grid of measurements, and there were also sketches of the finished outfits included in some plates. From 1872 the practice of the magazine changed, and only 13 of the 109 styles featured were given as pattern diagrams. The others were illustrated in drawings that could be discussed with clients; it is not clear how tailors gained the knowledge needed to cut them. Williamson also published large format posters for tailors to display; some of these were found in Copy 1 and will be discussed in Chapter 3.

Of the 124 garments illustrated, 38 were for older boys and 85 for younger boys, including two for boys not yet in breeches. Some of the styles shown were unlike anything seen in other sources; this was particularly true of some tweed kilt variants published in 1875–77. The commonest boys' style in the *Tailor and Cutter* 1868–88 was the short sailor suit, with twenty designs, followed by lounge suits with long trousers (seventeen) and short suits with scrolling braid trim (ten). Interestingly, designs for boys' Norfolk and short lounge suits, which might be considered as core aspects of tailors' trade, were less numerous than suits with fancy applied trim (seventeen examples).

In addition to magazines and fashion plates, Williamson also published texts such as *The Cutter's Practical Guide to Cutting every Kind of Garment Made by*

---

[66]　*Gentleman's Magazine of Fashion*, January 1862, Plate the Fourth (n.p.). Access to graduated measures, and knowledge of how to use them, are likely to have been restricted to professional tailors.

[67]　Breward, *Hidden Consumer*, p. 25.

[68]　Based on the holdings of the National Art Library, which holds volumes from 1868–77, 1881, 1886 and 1892; and images registered in the Copy 1 archives at TNA.

Tailors (1890).[69] This appeared in twelve volumes, one of which, *Juvenile, Youths', and Young Men's Garments* illustrated twenty different suits, three coats and three waistcoats.[70] All of the suits were included in the Copy 1 plates and had also been published in the magazine. The book added pattern diagrams, instructions for cutting and making up, and comments on the appropriateness of each outfit.

The commentary on the different suits is helpful in distinguishing between those seen as standard and those which were novelties. For older boys, the Eton suit was 'the garment above all others the high-class tailor is called upon to make',[71] followed by Norfolk suits: 'no garment of a fancy kind has remained so long in favour as this, and it is worn by boys, youths and men, in almost the same style.'[72] For younger boys:

> Of all the styles adopted for juvenile wear there are probably none in such universal favour as the sailor suit ... thus, when the little one is first put into suits he generally has the sailor blouse and a kilt, then he comes to wear knickers, and then very soon the regular Jack-tar trousers.[73]

There were a number of further styles recommended for young boys, all of which depended for their effect on applied frogs or scrolls of braid (Figure 2.9).

Between 1870 and 1900 the styles recommended for boys by tailors shifted, but some of the underlying attitudes remained the same. There was greater latitude in fabrics and trimmings for young boys than there was in clothing for older males. Even when the braided trimmings on young boys' jackets were based on military dress uniforms there was a degree of fantasy unconstrained by uniform regulations.[74] The opportunity for invention in boys' clothes was recognised by the *Tailor and Cutter*: 'A really artistic juvenile garment, which I need scarcely say affords much more scope for novelty and originality than the slight variations which are allowed in clothing for adults.'[75] This emphasis on novelty of design and particularly of trimming also had drawbacks which will be discussed at the end of this chapter.

---

[69] William D.F. Vincent, *The Cutter's Practical Guide: Part I, Juvenile, Youths and Young Men* (London, 1890).

[70] See Illustrations 3.25–3.28 in Rose, 'Boyswear'.

[71] Vincent, *Cutter's Practical Guide*, p. 15.

[72] Ibid., p. 13.

[73] Ibid., p. 64.

[74] See Figure 9 in Clare Rose, 'The novelty consists'.

[75] *Tailor and Cutter*, 17 June 1880.

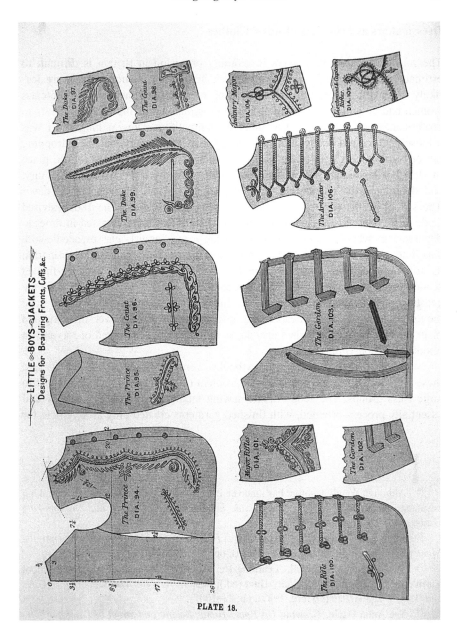

Figure 2.9   Boys' suits with braided trimming to be made by tailors, 1890. Courtesy of the NAL, Victoria and Albert Museum, London 2009.

Dressmakers as Providers of Boys' Clothes

The role of female dressmakers in clothing provision in Britain is difficult to estimate as they typically worked alone or in small workshops, and were less likely to leave a 'paper trail' of advertising or other documents.[76] Middle-class women had an ambiguous relationship to dressmaking, acting both as clients to professional dressmakers and as amateur competitors. Dressmaking itself was a loosely structured occupation, with many girls apprenticed but then dropping out or combining it with other work.[77] Needlework teaching had a central place in British educational policy from the 1840s into the early twentieth century, and dominated the curriculum for girls, taking up half of each school day.[78] The school needlework syllabus was minutely prescribed by the 1862 Revised Code of Regulations for Board Schools, in which pupils were assessed in order to determine the school's funding for the following year.[79] For girls' classes, needlework was 'one of the failing subjects ... it secures as many marks at an examination as arithmetic and school management'.[80] Needlework manuals for state-funded schools concentrated on teaching basic stitches and assembly processes through the construction and mending of underwear. This was partly a pragmatic decision, since the materials needed were cheaper than for outer garments. However, mending and plain sewing also served a class agenda, as they were skills required of servants in middle-class households.[81]

Surprisingly few needlework textbooks were published in the 1870s and these were largely concerned with the problem of teaching a practical subject to large class groups. The scope of the sewing taught was extremely narrow and essentially process-oriented, with finished garments created only as a vehicle for

---

[76]   Although Wendy Gamber has made an exemplary study of American dressmaking businesses using credit records; *The Female Economy: The Millinery and Dressmaking Trades, 1860–1930* (Urbana, 1997).

[77]   Ibid., pp. 134–6; also Beth Harris (ed.) *Famine and Fashion: Needlewomen in the Nineteenth Century* (Aldershot, 2005), Part II, pp. 141–228.

[78]   See Annemarie Turnbull, 'Learning Her Womanly Work: the Elementary School Curriculum, 1870–1914', in Felicity Hunt (ed.), *Lessons for Life: The Schooling of Girls and Women, 1850–1950* (Oxford, 1987), pp. 83–100.

[79]   See Anna Davin, *Growing Up Poor: Home, School and Street in London 1870–1914* (London: Rivers Oram, 1996), pp. 144–5.

[80]   Amy K Smith, *Needlework for student teachers: intended for the use of pupil teachers, scholarship candidates and certificate students (1st and 2nd year)*, 4th edn (London, 1897), p. 3

[81]   An 1850 textbook included sections explicitly directed at the needs of employers, such as instructions for marking family crests on household linen. Lady E. Finch, *The Sampler; or, A System of teaching plain needlework in schools* (London, 1850, 1855).

demonstrating the correct use of stitches.[82] When needlework textbooks gave explicit instructions for making outer garments, it was because the books were also aimed at individual women working at home. For instance, the sixth edition (1885) of *The Standard Needlework Book* had instructions and diagrams for a toddler's frock, a girl's jacket, a boy's plain shorts suit and a sailor suit. These were contained in an appendix not present in earlier editions, 'Dressmaking and Tailoring for the People', and the change of audience was reflected in a new subtitle 'for use in schools and families' and a lower cover price (1s 6d not 2s).[83]

The large gaps left by school instruction on dressmaking were partly filled by the other sources of information that proliferated between 1870 and 1900. The arrival of Butterick's pattern company in London in 1873 seems to have been a watershed moment, making paper patterns more affordable and more available to home dressmakers.[84] The demand for dressmaking information resulted in an explosion of British pattern publications after 1873, including *Myra's Journal of Dress and Fashion* (from 1875), *Myra's Mid-Monthly Journal and Children's Dress* (1877–82), *Mrs Schild's Monthly Journal of Parisian Dress Patterns and Needlework* (1879), *Schild's Mother's Help and Little Dressmaker* (1878), *Weldon's Illustrated Dressmaker* (1880) and *Mrs Leach's Children's and Young Ladies' Dressmaker* (1882). Each issue contained an illustrated catalogue of up to 100 patterns, and fashion and lifestyle advice. Butterick also published *Metropolitan Fashions*, a monthly update of their illustrated catalogue, in a joint British and American edition. The expansion of dressmaking practice was reflected in the sales of sewing machines: Singer alone sold 60,000 in the UK in 1879.[85] While Godley points out that some of these machines may have been used by dressmakers or outworkers,[86] the middle-class amateur was important enough as a market to warrant decorative 'parlour' sewing machines.[87]

---

[82] For example, Smith's *Needlework for student teachers* had 100 pages devoted to methods of teaching correct stitching technique, but no practical applications for them other than patching (16 pages) and darning (54 pages). This textbook had sold 20,000 copies by 1897.

[83] T.H.P., *The Standard Needlework Book, a System for graduated instruction in plain Needlework in which arithmetic is brought to bear practically. Arranged in six standards each distinguished by its colours, containing also plans on a reduced scale, by inch or metric measure, and knitting rules. For use in schools and families, and as a handbook for inspectors*; sixth edition, enlarged and revised (London, 1885).

[84] See Kevin Seligman, 'Dressmakers' Patterns: The English Commercial Paper Pattern Industry, 1878–1950', *Costume*, 37 (2003): 95–113; Joy Emery, 'Dreams on Paper: A Story of the Commercial Pattern Industry', in Barbara Burman (ed.), *The Culture of Sewing: Gender, Consumption and Home Dressmaking* (Oxford, 1999), pp. 235–54.

[85] Andrew Godley, 'Homeworking and the Sewing Machine in the British Clothing Industry 1850–1905', in Burman, *Culture of Sewing*, pp. 255–68.

[86] Godley, 'Homeworking', p. 262. See also Sarah Levitt, 'Clothing Production and the Sewing Machine', *Textile Society Journal*, 9 (1988): 179–92.

[87] Adrian Forty, *Objects of Desire: Design and Society 1750–1980* (London, 1986), pp. 95–9. In Burman, *Culture of Sewing*, see: Nicholas Oddy, 'A Beautiful Ornament in

Styles for Boys in Dressmaking Sources 1870–1900

The limits to amateur dressmaking activity are suggested by the content of the 36 dressmaking manuals first published between 1870 and 1900. These texts concentrated on ladies' dresses, the garments which were most expensive to purchase and which attracted most attention, and only five contained any information on making children's clothes.[88] The best source for information on home dressmaking for boys around 1870 was *Cassell's Household Guide: Being a complete encyclopaedia of domestic and social economy, etc.*, published as a part work during 1869–71.[89] This gave sketches and instructions for standard garments for boys up to age 12, including suits with short trousers for boys aged eight and over.[90] These suits were to be made of tweed, currently fashionable for middle-class women's ensembles, and trimmed with interlaced braid.[91]

The Butterick pattern catalogue, even in 1873, showed a more nuanced understanding of clothing for boys, and much greater attention to seasonal trends for summer and winter of each year. By 1882 the date of first publication for each pattern was given, to enable customers to distinguish between newer and older styles. In their summer 1873 catalogue, Butterick offered 456 patterns, 193 of which were for women, 162 for misses and girls, 43 for infants and children, 52 for boys up to age 15, and 6 for men (underwear and overalls).[92] Of the 52 patterns for boys, 37 were for jackets, coats or waistcoats, 8 for kilts or trousers, and 7 for underwear and accessories.[93] The sizing of the patterns for tunics or kilts showed a substantial overlap with patterns for short trousers. Kilts were available for ages two to six, short trousers for ages three to ten, and long trousers for ages three to ten or seven to 15. The implications of these overlapping age ranges will be discussed in Chapter 6.

---

the Parlour or Boudoir: The Domestication of the Sewing Machine', pp. 285–302; Tim Putnam, 'The Sewing Machine Comes Home', pp. 269–84; Nancy Page Fernandez, 'Creating Consumers: Gender, Class and the Family Sewing Machine', pp. 157–68.

[88] F. White, *Easy Dressmaking. Containing diagrams, etc* (London, 1892); Mrs L.E. Smith, *Practical Dressmaking* (London, 1895); H. Green, *Dressmaking Simplified. Simple rules for measuring, marking, and cutting out a dress, etc.* (Walsall, 1895); Mrs A. Platts, *Hints on Practical Dressmaking, etc.* (Leeds, 1898); Anon., *Dressmaking for All: A handbook of dress and dressmaking* (London, 1900).

[89] *Cassell's Household Guide: Being a complete encyclopaedia of domestic and social economy, etc.* (London, 1871). The copy seen at York Castle Museum had belonged to a young woman married in 1870.

[90] Ibid., vol. I, pp. 177 and 332; vol. IV, pp. 60–61.

[91] Ibid., vol. IV, p. 68.

[92] Dressmaking patterns and pattern catalogues have not been systematically collected by British libraries and archives, and pre-1900 holdings are extremely patchy, so a facsimile edition was used: Nancy V. Bryk, *American Dress Pattern Catalogs, 1873–1909* (New York, 1988).

[93] Ibid., pp. 29–32.

The separation of sets of clothes into upper- and lower-body garments and the emphasis on upper-body garments (jackets or bodices) can be explained either in terms of the convenience of the pattern company (sell two patterns to make up one outfit) or in terms of the convenience of the home dressmaker (update a plain skirt with a novel bodice). Boys' patterns had a relatively high proportion of kilts and trousers to jackets (10 out of 58). This may be because dressmakers were relatively unfamiliar with these male garments, or because trousers required a greater degree of fit and more careful sizing than jackets.

In the summer 1882 Butterick catalogue there were 85 patterns for boys, 29 for men, 134 for infants, 226 for girls and 384 for women.[94] However, a large number of these patterns were for underwear or accessories, with only 49 for main garments. Butterick's *Metropolitan Fashions* for August 1886 published 740 patterns, 66 of which were for boys aged two to fifteen and 29 for men.[95] However only 38 of the boys' patterns were for main garments, and once again the majority of these (24) were jackets or other tops, with only six styles of trousers or knickerbockers, and eight kilts or tunics for the youngest boys (Figure 2.10).[96]

A representative British source for dressmaking patterns at this date is *Myra's Journal of Dress and Fashion*, which began in 1875 and continued until 1912.[97] *Myra's Journal* was mainly interested in women's clothes but also published a total of 141 patterns for boys between 1875–77 and 1883–99.[98] The sister publication *Myra's Mid-Monthly Journal and Children's Dress* (1877–82) published 120 patterns for boys over the five years of its existence. The patterns offered by both *Myra's* publications were accompanied by technical notes giving the age and gender of the intended wearer and suggesting fabrics for making up. These notes were important in distinguishing boys' tunics and blouses from girls' dresses.[99] There was a second edition of *Cassell's Household Guide* in 1884, with updated patterns for women's and girls' clothes. However, the sections on boys' clothing were reprinted unchanged from 1870, although fashions for boys had changed noticeably.[100] This confirms the key role of pattern publishing companies after 1873.

---

[94]   Ibid., pp. 62–4.

[95]   *Metropolitan Fashions for Autumn and Winter, 1886–87,* vol. XXIV no. 1, number F.8.35 in the National Art Library. See Appendix 1.

[96]   The menswear section of the catalogue contained underwear, shirts, overalls, a Norfolk jacket and knickerbockers that could be worn for sports such as cycling, but no office clothing such as lounge suits.

[97]   For the readership of *Myra's Journal of Dress and Fashion*, see Christopher Breward, 'Patterns of Respectability: Publishing, Home Sewing and the Dynamics of Class and Gender 1870–1914', in Burman, *Culture of Sewing*, pp. 21–31.

[98]   For a further breakdown of pattern types, see Table 3.12 in Rose, 'Boyswear'.

[99]   See Chapter 7 for more on gender distinctions in young boys' dresses.

[100]   *Cassell's Household Guide: being a complete encyclopaedia of domestic and social economy, etc.*, 2nd edn (London, 1884), vol. II, pp. 361–2; vol. IV, pp. 8–10, 20–21, 59–62, 68–9.

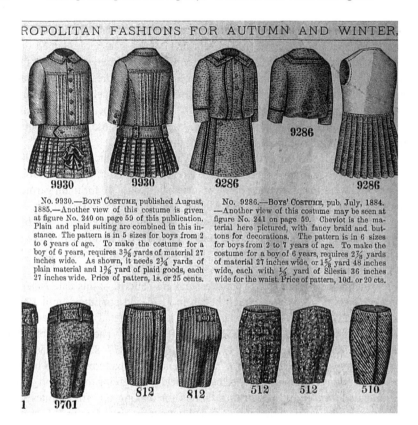

ROPOLITAN FASHIONS FOR AUTUMN AND WINTER.

No. 9930.—BOYS' COSTUME, published August, 1885.—Another view of this costume is given at figure No. 240 on page 59 of this publication. Plain and plaid suiting are combined in this instance. The pattern is in 5 sizes for boys from 2 to 6 years of age. To make the costume for a boy of 6 years, requires 3⅜ yards of material 27 inches wide. As shown, it needs 2¼ yards of plain material and 1⅜ yard of plaid goods, each 27 inches wide. Price of pattern, 1s. or 25 cents.

No. 9286.—BOYS' COSTUME, pub. July, 1884.—Another view of this costume may be seen at figure No. 241 on page 59. Cheviot is the material here pictured, with fancy braid and buttons for decorations. The pattern is in 6 sizes for boys from 2 to 7 years of age. To make the costume for a boy of 6 years, requires 2⅞ yards of material 27 inches wide, or 1⅝ yard 48 inches wide, each with ¼ yard of Silesia 36 inches wide for the waist. Price of pattern, 10d. or 20 cts.

Figure 2.10   Patterns for boys' jackets, kilts and trousers by Butterick, 1886. Courtesy of the NAL, Victoria and Albert Museum, London 2009.

Altogether 393 garments or outfits for boys were identified in pattern catalogues and magazines from 1873 to 1900.[101] Of these, 224 were for boys in the middle age-range, wearing short trousers; 149 for the youngest boys wearing kilts and tunics, and only 14 for older boys wearing long trousers.[102] The single commonest garment featured in dressmakers' documents was the dress-like tunic, in 121 versions.[103] As tunics were the boys' garments that were closest to women's' dresses in cut, trim and fabric, they would be well within the core competences of the dressmaker. The next commonest garments were blouses, to be worn with short trousers, in 36 versions, followed by sailor tops (32) and lounge jackets (23) (Figure 2.11).

---

[101]   See Table 3.11 in Rose, 'Boyswear'.

[102]   Where jackets alone were illustrated, these were assigned to knickerbockers or trouser suits based on comparisons with suits seen in manufacturers' and retailers' sources.

[103]   See Figure 3.18, p. 195 in Rose, 'Boyswear'.

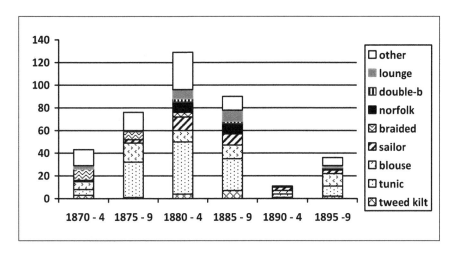

Figure 2.11   Styles for boys in dressmakers' patterns, 1870–99.

There was, however, a significant difference between the numbers of patterns for different types of clothes in different sources. In *Myra's Mid-Monthly* 50 per cent of boys' patterns were for tunics, 20 per cent for transitional tunic and shorts outfits, 29 per cent for short trouser suits, and 2 per cent for suits with long trousers. In *Myra's Journal*, 43 per cent of the boys' patterns were for tunics, 17 per cent for tunics worn with shorts, 37 per cent for short trouser suits and 1 per cent for long trouser suits. In the three Butterick catalogues, patterns for short trouser suits dominated at 69 per cent, with 8 per cent for long trouser suits, and 16 per cent for tunics and 7 per cent for tunics and shorts. Butterick's greater emphasis on patterns for older boys and adult males may reflect differences in consumer preferences between the US and British markets. It may also indicate a less strongly gendered practice of clothing provision in the USA, with the division between tailor and dressmaker less strongly marked. Or it may reflect lesser availability of male clothing, making home production more important. These national differences await further study.

Competition between Providers of Boys' Clothing

The previous sections have laid out the findings on types of boys' clothing available from mass manufacturers, bespoke tailors, and female dressmakers (professional and amateur). There were some surprising points of agreement, notably the wish to present a range of different boys' styles at the same time, the use of applied trimmings rather than cut to define these styles, and a concentration on clothing for younger boys. There are also differences between the documents which make them hard to compare.

It is particularly difficult to compare photographs or drawings of actual garments registered by manufacturers in BT43 and BT50 with patterns of potential garments published for tailors and dressmakers. Both tailors and dressmakers offered bespoke services in which the pattern was only the starting point for negotiations with the client over cut and trimming. In contrast, the images in the registration documents were accurate representations of the finished item, as registration would be invalidated by any changes. Legal judgements on infringement of copyright might turn on minute details of design, as Welch Margetson found when they challenged an imitator in 1846.[104] There were also important differences between patterns for tailors and for dressmakers. Tailors' professional training would give them the skills to create a pattern for any size from a single diagram, while dressmakers were more likely to use full-sized patterns made in set sizes. Moreover, access to tailors' patterns was deliberately restricted: the *Tailor and Cutter* was only available on subscription to professional tailors, and a complete set of *The Cutter's Practical Guide* cost £7 10s in 1890. Dressmaking patterns, in contrast, were available to both amateurs and professionals for as little as 3d each.[105] One way of evaluating the competing claims of dressmakers, tailors and mass manufacturers as the originators of clothing for young boys is by comparing their designs with the clothing advertised for sale in shop catalogues. This will be done in Chapter 3.

When examined closely, the texts that accompany plates or registration documents in the different sources for boys' clothes can tell us a great deal about competition between the different branches of the clothing trade. They indicate that boys' clothing was hotly contested by amateur dressmakers, professional dressmakers, bespoke tailors and mass manufacturers. There appear to have been several factors which intensified this competition. One was the closeness between young boys' tunics and women's dresses, which made them a legitimate part of the repertoire of dressmakers. The availability of boys' garment patterns to female dressmakers may have encouraged them to expand into young boys' suits.[106]

It seems that mothers expected to be involved in the ordering of young boys' clothing and sometimes made contradictory demands of tailors: 'Ladies have generally the ordering of these garments, and they seldom forget to tell us to make them to fit nicely and to be sure and make them large enough for their growth.'[107] Even more problematic was female clients' expectations of pricing, based on

[104]   Sarah Levitt, 'Clothing', in Mary Rose (ed.), *The Lancashire Cotton Industry, A History Since 1700* (Lancaster, 1996), pp. 154–86.

[105]   For the effect of commercial patterns on relations between amateurs and professionals see Gamber, *Female Economy*, pp. 151–5.

[106]   The increasing use of 'tailored' effects in women's dresses from the 1870s onwards may also have blurred the boundary between dressmaking and tailoring practice. Lou Taylor, 'Wool Cloth and Gender: The Use of Woollen Cloth in Women's Dress in Britain, 1865–85', in Amy de la Haye and Elizabeth Wilson (eds), *Defining Dress: Dress as Object, Meaning and Identity* (Manchester, 1999), pp. 30–47.

[107]   *Tailor and Cutter*, 17 October 1868.

their experiences with female dressmakers who were not bound by the 'log' that determined professional tailors' pay. This was particularly noticeable in boys' clothing, where the finishing processes were more important than the cut and fit. The *Tailor and Cutter* warned in 1868 that:

> Boys' and youths' clothing form a difficult branch of our profession: the difficulty does not exist so much in the cutting and fitting as in the style and trimming ... Boys of so small a stature are generally covered, and occasionally beautifully dressed, by tailoresses with whom the higher class of legitimate clothiers have no chance to compete successfully, owing to the fantastic manner in which the garments are trimmed, the cost of making, if paid for according to the 'log', and the general desire of mammas to have their children neatly and nicely clothed for as little money as possible.[108]

Boys' clothing was also contested between bespoke tailors and mass manufacturers. Throughout the 1870s and 1880s subscribers to the *Tailor and Cutter* were warned of the threat to their business posed by the wholesale trade. Manufacturers were able to undercut the bespoke trade in price, which was seen as the main selling point for boys' clothes:

> The work does not pay, there being nearly as much work to be done as for a man's garment, and the whole price of the youngsters is not expected to be more than the cost of making for an adults, at least such is paterfamilias' view of the case. The natural consequence of such a state of things is, that the tailor avoids these jobs as much as possible, whilst on the other side the parent is inclined to buy at the cheapest market, and consequently buys at the ready made establishment where goods are got up by female labour at the lowest possible rates ... and thus the hard working tailor allows branch after branch of his legitimate business to slip out of his hands.[109]

The fashion for extensive trimming on boys' clothing also worked to the advantage of mass manufacturers. After devoting five pages to variants on braided boys' suits, Vincent admitted that:

> Some of our readers may possibly experience difficulty in doing this braiding, and it might be of great service to them to know the name and address of a firm who do all kinds of braiding for the trade. Messes Lyons of 66 and 67, Milton Street, London, make this branch of business a speciality, and do a large trade in

---

[108]   Ibid.

[109]   *Tailor and Cutter*, June 1877, p. 236. French tailors had acknowledged the effects of competition from ready-to-wear clothes as early as 1851; Perrot, *Fashioning the Bourgeoisie*, p. 54.

it both for the wholesale and retail trades. There is still another plan which will help the tailor over the difficulty, viz., to use Mr Briggs' transfer papers.[110]

The *Tailor and Cutter* also acknowledged specialist manufacturers' expertise in design. In 1880, an article on 'the artistically designed, and luxuriantly trimmed garments which are the ordinary clothing of the children of the middle, as well as of the upper, classes of the present day' cited the manufacturers George Macbeth & Sons of Manchester as a source for 'some of the best styles which are now being introduced'.[111] Taken together, these texts show that by 1890 bespoke tailors saw the provision of boys' clothing as dominated by mass manufacturers, who had the advantage in design, in trimming, and most of all in price:

> Owing to the keen competition brought to bear by the ready-made houses, the prices are necessarily kept low ... so that it will be necessary for those who aspire to clothe the coming race to be very expert in the matter of economy in every detail. ... Nonetheless, although the immediate profit may not be large, yet this branch is well worth the attention of every tailor desirous of building up a LASTING connection.[112]

We might expect price competition between tailors and mass manufacturers to lead to a simplification of clothing styles, but this was not the case, as was shown by the hundreds of designs registered in the BT archives. This was partly due to the economies of scale in mass production. While there are no figures available for the volume of boys' clothing produced in Leeds and Manchester, it is indicated by the size of the specialist producers. In 1880 Macbeth of Manchester had more than 90 employees in their boys' clothes department,[113] and Barran of Leeds had 2,000 employees by 1904.[114] Another way that manufacturers could keep prices competitive while maintaining variety in design was to make minor changes in fabric and trimming on a standard shape. This would fit with the subcontracting practised by firms like Barran, whose jackets were cut out in a highly mechanised factory and assembled in a lower-paid workshop. The emphasis on trimmings and on seasonal changes in late nineteenth-century boys' clothing undermines Fine and Leopold's dichotomy between male and female clothing by aligning boys with the 'feminine', high-fashion model.[115] To fully understand the interaction

---

[110]   Vincent, *Cutter's Practical Guide*, p. 60. Godley suggests that this method was also followed by Barran, who subcontracted out the jackets on which trimming was concentrated, while making the accompanying plain trousers themselves; 'Development of the UK Clothing Industry', p. 57.

[111]   *Tailor and Cutter*, 17 June 1880, p. 219.

[112]   Vincent, *Cutter's Practical Guide*, p. 1.

[113]   *Tailor and Cutter*, 17 June 1880, p. 222.

[114]   Honeyman, *Well Suited*, p. 261.

[115]   Fine and Leopold, *World of Consumption*, p. 236.

between price and design in the production of boys' clothing we need to examine the ways in which the garments were marketed, and this will be the focus of Chapter 3.

Chapter 3
Advertising Boys' Clothes

In October 1895, the tailors Grainger & Bliss of Weymouth issued an illustrated flyer announcing: 'a splendid assortment of new tweeds, worsted, serges, west of England and Scotch suitings … in the latest patterns, unrivalled for style and finish … Boys', youths' and men's ready-made clothing of the newest and most stylish designs.'[1] This sales flyer, found in the Stationers' Hall Archive, was copyrighted by a commercial printer. A stamp in the corner indicates that it was a standard sheet, available for personalisation by retailers at prices from 33s for 100 up to 86s 6d for 5,000.

The late nineteenth century has been described as the period of the 'great expansion' for advertising and it is known that some of the biggest advertisers were clothing manufacturers such as H.J. & D. Nicoll.[2] Examining the extent of advertisements for boys' clothing will clarify how important it was to the expanding clothing trade. Chapter 2 showed that mass manufacturers, bespoke tailors, and female dressmakers were competing to provide boys' clothing, and were doing so through design: we would expect this to be reflected in advertising. Schorman found that in America advertising was one of the main weapons in the rivalry between tailors and manufacturers, with mass-produced clothes promoted like bespoke.[3] Ugolini and Breward have uncovered the complexity of menswear retailing, and the interdependence of different types of providers.[4] Analysing the ways the boys' clothes were presented will help us to understand how different providers competed with each other. It will also help us to understand how consumers discriminated between equivalent garments.

This chapter will analyse documents produced by manufacturers, tailors, commercial printers and retailers. The images in these documents were qualitatively

[1]   Clements Newling of Cheapside, London; Stationers' Hall Archive, Copy 1 121/307 (1895), The National Archives (henceforth TNA).

[2]   T.R. Nevett, *Advertising in Britain: A History* (London, 1982), p. 67; Andrew Godley, 'The Development of the Clothing Industry: Technology and Fashion', *Textile History*, 28/1 (1997), p. 6.

[3]   Rob Schorman, *Selling Style: Clothing and Social Change at the Turn of the Century* (Philadelphia, 2003), p. 18.

[4]   Christopher Breward, *The Hidden Consumer: Masculinities, Fashion and City Life, 1860–1914* (Manchester, 1999); Laura Ugolini, 'Men, Masculinities and Menswear Advertising, c.1890–1914', in John Benson and Laura Ugolini (eds), *A Nation of Shopkeepers, Five Centuries of British Retailing* (London, 2003); *eadem, Men and Menswear: Sartorial Consumption in Britain 1880–1939* (Aldershot, 2007).

different from the photographs and drawings registered by manufacturers, as they illustrated not actual garments but garment types. Images in the registration documents had to be an accurate representation of the finished item, since any variation would invalidate the registration.[5] Advertising images, in contrast, might be reused over a number of years to represent garments for different retailers and for different manufacturers. The repeated use of these images helps us to understand the nature of the market for boys' clothing, and the interaction between manufacturers, retailers and consumers. The first two sections of this chapter will discuss this interaction.

The visual qualities of advertising images could also add value to the garments they represented. Many of the documents selling boys' clothing were carefully designed in themselves, with full colour images and texts designed to appeal to children as well as parents. They have important implications for our understanding of the ways in which clothing was sold and consumed before 1900. Most of the documents analysed in this chapter are visual: many, indeed, are images of garments with little or no accompanying text. In the third section of this chapter this material has been analysed quantitatively to determine which garment types were promoted by which retailers and advertising agents at which date. This will illuminate the degree of consensus, and of specialisation, between different firms and between competing sectors, notably tailors and retailers.

In the fourth section of the chapter the analysis of particular garment types will underpin a discussion of the role of innovation, and indeed fashion, in the boys' clothing trade. This will be followed by an evaluation of the ways that the labelling of boys' clothing at the point of sale reflects on the role of manufacturers. Understanding which garments were promoted – and therefore available- at a given date will also help us to evaluate the consumption patterns which will be discussed in Chapter 5.

Sources for the Advertising of Boys' Clothes

Evidence for the ways in which boys' clothes were advertised was found in archives containing retailers' catalogues, sales sheets and posters. These archives (discussed in full in Appendix 1) varied in size and scope. The House of Fraser archive contained catalogues from the retailers in the group, including important early examples from the Army and Navy Stores, London. The John Johnson archive at the Bodleian Library was the work of an individual who collected

---

[5]   Clothing manufacturers intended registration to provide legal protection for their designs, as was shown by a court case brought by Welch Margetson for infringement of copyright in 1846; Sarah Levitt, 'Clothing', in Mary Rose (ed.), *The Lancashire Cotton Industry: A History Since 1700* (Lancaster, 1996), pp. 154–86.

retailing and other ephemera from the eighteenth to the twentieth centuries.[6] Many of the holdings are unique to this archive, but not all are dated. The Evanion collection at the British Library is a smaller personal collection, made in London from 1880 onwards, and most of its holdings are dated. Each of these archives held complete retailers' catalogues. The Copy 1 (Stationers' Hall) collection at The National Archives holds documents registered for copyright between 1842 and 1912. These are very well documented but incomplete, many being represented only by their covers or by single pages.[7] This archive contained approximately 86,000 advertising documents dated 1870–1900, from price tickets to large wall posters.

The Copy 1 registrations had been made by different types of persons: commercial printers or publishers, retailers, wholesalers, manufacturers, and even commercial artists. In some cases the business of the registrant was hard to determine, and their status was clarified by cross-checking in London directories.[8] In some cases sequences of documents in Copy 1 proved to be the pages of a catalogue prepared for a specific retailer. There were also many images in Copy 1 that were intended for use in retail catalogues, but registered by commercial printers. These present important evidence for the workings of the advertising industry, and the place of boys' clothing within it, and will be considered separately.[9]

Complete retailers' catalogues represented only a small proportion of the documents advertising boys' clothing in the Copy 1 archives. Of the approximately 86,800 commercial documents registered in Copy 1 (Paintings, Drawings and Photographs) between 1870 and 1900, 2,635 were for use in the sale of clothing. Of these, 60 per cent concerned garments for women, 24 per cent for men, 14 per cent for boys and 2 percent for girls, with some overlaps. However, these figures were swayed by the presence of 980 separate registrations by Alfred Stedall, each representing a single woman's garment. Stedall, whose name was not known from published sources, described themselves as 'Wholesale and Export Manufacturers', based in Cannon Street, London.[10] H.J. Nicoll, a manufacturer and retailer based

---

[6] For a selection from the John Johnson Collection, see Michael Turner and David Vaisey, *Oxford Shops and Shopping: A Pictorial Survey from Victorian and Edwardian Times* (Oxford, 1972). A larger selection has now been digitised; see http://johnjohnson. chadwyck.co.uk/marketing.do.

[7] See Appendix 1. A selection was published in Michael Jubb, *Cocoa and Corsets: A Selection of Late Victorian and Edwardian Posters and Showcards from the Stationers' Company Copyright Records Preserved in the Public Record Office* (London, 1984). See also Clare Rose, 'Advertising Ready-Made Style: The Evidence of the Stationers' Hall Archive', *Textile History*, 40/2 (2009): 185–201.

[8] See Appendix 1.

[9] I would like to thank Hugh Alexander, in the Image Library at the Public Record Office, for introducing me to this archive and for encouraging my work on Copy 1.

[10] This document is from the Books Commercial (BC) series of Copy 1: BC 972/17696 (1899). See Appendix 1 for details.

in Regent Street, registered 254 images of clothes for women, boys and girls. John Williamson, publishers of the *Tailor and Cutter*, were also well represented in Copy 1, with 132 posters, fashion plates and single images of men's, women's and boys' clothing.

Boys' Clothes in Retailers' Catalogues

The 285 documents attributable to specific retailers included 40 whole or part catalogues showing boys' clothing.[11] Some of these gave an overview of their entire stock, in which boys' garments played a minor role. Other catalogues were designed specifically to sell boys' clothing, as with the twenty-five documents registered by Barkers of Kensington in 1888.[12]

There were also catalogues from retailers who specialised in clothing for men and boys. An early innovator in this area was Arthur Lynes, who published twice-yearly volumes which combined children's stories and a catalogue of boys' and men's clothing.[13] The presentation of the volumes highlighted their claims as literature, with titles such as *Fiction and Fashion* and eighty pages of stories preceding sixteen of clothing (Figure 3.1).This may have been a ploy to claim cheaper postal rates, or it may have reflected Lynes' literary ambitions, as each volume contained a story by him alongside professional writers such as Henry Mayhew. The Lynes volumes represent a development from the catalogues of 1840s retailers such as E. Moses & Son, who had used doggerel verses in their publicity.

> It has been the custom of our firm, since its establishment twenty-six years ago, to publish half-yearly an amusing Book, which we intended to be not only a catalogue of our prices and a manifesto of our intentions, but a *brochure* containing some novelty entirely distinct from the business portion of the work.[14]

---

[11]   For a complete listing of the documents showing boys' clothing in Copy 1, House of Fraser and John Johnson archives, see Tables 3.5–3.7 in Clare Rose, 'Boyswear and the Formation of Gender and Class Identity in Urban England, 1840–1900' (unpublished PhD Dissertation, University of Brighton, 2006).

[12]   Copy 1 083/161–85, 1888, Barkers of Kensington. This firm had a reputation as a specialist in drapery; Alison Adburgham, *Shops and Shopping 1800–1914* (London, 1989), p. 164.

[13]   Lewis of Liverpool issued booklets of *Penny Readings* from 1882, but it is not clear whether these contained advertisements; Nevett, *Advertising in Britain*, p. 97.

[14]   Arthur Lynes & Son, *Smiles and Styles* (London, 1871), p. 115.

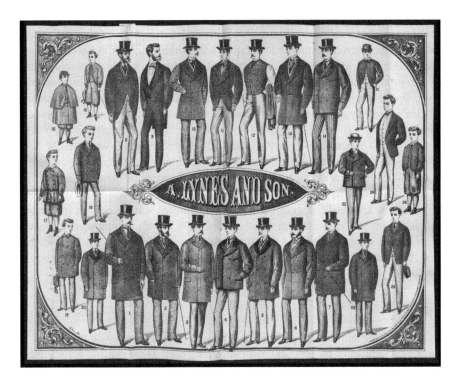

Figure 3.1   Boys' and men's clothes in a mail-order catalogue by Arthur Lynes, 1871 [Shelfmark: JJ MC 4(16), p. 128 (plate)]. Courtesy of the Bodleian Library, University of Oxford

Unfortunately Lynes' works were not recognised as literature by the copyright libraries and only a few examples survive from the period 1870–76.[15] They seem to have divided their trade between boys and adult men, selling retail, mail-order and in bulk to institutions and wholesalers, and providing both ready-to-wear and made-to-measure garments.[16]

Lynes may have been one of the first firms to concentrate on boys' clothing, but they were soon copied. In 1878, W. & G. Sampson registered a series of twenty

---

[15]   The British Library holds eight Lynes publications: *New Winter Magazine (*1870); *Summer Journal*, 1870; *Smiles and Styles* (1871); *Wit and Wear* (1871); *Mirth and Modes* (1872); *Fiction and Fashion* (1872); *Stories and Styles* (1873); *Novelettes and Novelties* (1873). Cambridge University Library holds the third, fifth, sixth and seventh of these. The John Johnson Collection at the Bodleian holds the third, fifth and eighth of the British Library series and three others, *Twice a Year* (1875), *Romance and Reality* (1876) and *Merriment and Models* (1876).

[16]   Arthur Lynes & Son, *Merriment and Modes* (London, 1876), John Johnson (JJ) Men's Clothing (MC) Box 4/19, p. 96.

drawings of boys' clothes, presumably intended for a sales catalogue.[17] They seem to have been an established retailer, with three branches in Oxford Street and another in Leicester Square at this period.[18] In the early 1880s, Charles Baker & Co. established a retailing chain based on the sale of clothing for men and boys. One of their newspaper advertisements from 1886 showed equal numbers of men's and boys' styles,[19] but most of their flyers and catalogues emphasised boys' clothing.[20] In 1897, Baker & Co. took over another retailer, Fred Watts & Co. of 136 Tottenham Court Road and 256 Edgware Road. Watts & Co. had registered a fully illustrated catalogue of boys' clothing in 1895, and at the point of the takeover the catalogue was re-registered in the name of Baker.[21] Each of the eighteen pages of the catalogue was individually signed over to Baker & Co. by Mrs Watts as executrix, suggesting that this document was seen as an important part of the operation of the firm. By the late 1890s, boys' clothing seems to have been highly contested, with Our Boys Clothing Company (London) and the Don Association of Woollen Manufacturers (Manchester) both registering boys' catalogues in 1896.[22]

Advertising Posters and Fashion Plates

As well as the multi-page catalogues and leaflets, the Copy 1 archive held a surprising number of posters advertising boys' clothes. These showed between ten and thirty boys in different suits, set out in rows or arranged in a landscape, often with a title such as 'new styles for 1895'. Produced in full colour lithography and in sizes from 60cm × 40cm up to 160cm × 100cm or larger, these were clearly intended to attract customers.[23] However, the relationship between the businesses displaying the posters, the companies registering them, and the garments themselves was surprisingly hard to define. Some of the posters in Copy 1 were registered by manufacturers who had used BT43 and BT50, such as Barran of Leeds, Coop of Wigan, and W. Shannon & Son of Walsall.[24] Another poster was from Hart &

[17]   Sampson, Copy 1 41/200–219 (1878).
[18]   *Kelly's Directory* (London, 1889), p. 1288.
[19]   C. Baker & Co., *The Graphic* Christmas Number (1886), n.p.
[20]   C. Baker & Co. catalogue, Copy 1 65/92 (1884).
[21]   Watts & Co., Copy 1 120/27–33 (1895); Mrs Watts and Baker, Copy 1 134/214–230 (1897).
[22]   Our Boys Clothing Company, Copy 1 127/535; Don Association, Copy 1 127/574–8, Copy 1 127/638–50 (1896).
[23]   One exception was a black-and-white 'style plate' registered by John Barran & Sons as Copy 1 98/354 (1891). This had 91 outline drawings of garments, each numbered, and text giving options for cutting and finishing. The implication is that these are styles to be made to order, unlike the ready-made boys' jackets registered in the Board of Trade BT43 and BT50 documents discussed in Chapter 2.
[24]   W. Shannon, BT50/89372 (1887).

Figure 3.2   A poster selling boys' clothes copyrighted by R.H. Parnall in 1886
[Copy 1 74/355]. Courtesy of The National Archives, Kew. The
thirty different styles are all numbered and would probably refer to
a pricelist for ordering.

Levy of Leicester, who Stanley Chapman identified as moving from second-hand
dealing into manufacturing and retailing.[25] .R & H. Parnall of Bishopsgate Street,
who registered six posters between 1880 and 1889,[26] were described in *Kelly's
Directory* from 1870 to 1899 as 'wholesale clothiers, shirt-makers and outfitters',
with a manufacturing branch in Chessington, Surrey (Figure 3.2).[27] Four further
posters for boys' clothing were registered by the printer Wesley Petty of Leeds,
who placed many documents in Copy 1.[28] Another firm who registered eight
posters for boys' clothes between 1888 and 1894 was AJW Pewtress of Newstead
Road London, listed in *Kelly's Directory* for 1878 under printers.[29]

The manufacturers, wholesalers, and retailers who registered posters for boys'
clothing seem to have specialised in this area, with boys' styles present in each
document. This was not the case in the posters and fashion plates for use by
bespoke tailors. Out of 218 such documents registered in Copy 1 by publishers

---

[25]   Stanley Chapman, 'The Innovating Entrepreneurs in the British Ready-made Clothing
Industry', *Textile History*, 24/1 (1993), p. 22.

[26]   Parnall: Copy 1 50/300 (1880); Copy 1 054/466 (1881); Copy 1 062/137 (1883);
Copy 1 070/084 (1885); Copy 1 074/355 (1886); Copy 1 085/508 (1889).

[27]   *Kelly's Directory* (London, 1870), p. 1127; they were still listed in the 1899 edition,
p. 1929.

[28]   Petty posters: Copy 1 80/569 (1887); Copy 1 116/66 (1895); Copy 1 144/294
(1898); Copy 1 148/451 (1899).

[29]   Pewtress posters: Copy 1 83/128 (1888); Copy 1 089A/030 (1890); Copy
1 089A/031 (1890); Copy 1 095/145 (1891); Copy 1 095/146 (1891); Copy 1 112/205
(1894).

for bespoke tailoring, only eight showed boys' clothes.[30] This is surprising, since tailors' fashion plates showed styles for women alongside men.[31] The separation between men's and boys' clothing in tailors' fashion plates may imply that the two were seen as separate specialisations, or that they sold to different customer bases.

While the posters and fashion plates in the Copy 1 archive came from different branches of the clothing trade, they shared a common visual language. They showed up to forty male figures in a variety of postures, but usually standing and frontal, set against a plain background or in a park landscape. Even when they were placed in a scenic setting the figures were carefully spaced out, which destroyed the natural effect but ensured the garments were legible. Each figure was identified with a style name or number, for reference to a stock list or price sheet. Some of the scenic plates incorporated images of landmark buildings in the background.[32] Both scenic and plain plates had elaborate graphic frames, often incorporating a title and a date, and sometimes a monogram or other logo of the company. Names of manufacturers and retailers were either absent or printed in small type. For example the posters registered by Coop had their logo, with the motto 'Forma et Utilitas' (shape and usefulness) and a small image of their factory (Figure 3.3).[33] This reticence was apparently against the interest of the manufacturer, but would allow retailers to claim the goods shown as theirs exclusively.[34]

Labels in Surviving Boys' Clothes

The covering up of the mass origins of boys' clothing is also apparent in surviving garments, even those produced by manufacturers like Barran who had invested heavily in design. An extensive investigation of museum collections throughout Britain revealed 43 surviving boys' suits thought to date from 1870–1900 (dating was complicated by a prevailing lack of documentation).[35] This sample was problematic as an indicator of consumption, since it included no everyday serge

---

[30]   Copy 1 62/277 (1883), Edmé Guichard; Copy 1 86/526 (1889), Copy1 89a/156 (1890), Copy 1 89b/26 (1890), Copy 1 89b/159 (1890) Copy 1 109/52 (1893) Copy 1 119/401 (1895) all by John Williamson & Co.; Copy 1 120/367 (1895), F.T. Prewett.

[31]   Copy 1 89b/153 (1890), West End Plate.

[32]   Windsor Castle, Copy 1 77/25 (1887), J.W. Porter; Manchester Town Hall, Copy 1 56/57 (1882), J. Hammond & Co., Manchester.

[33]   Copy 1052/152 (1881); 067/133 (1884); 092/049 (1890); 107a/185 (1893); 110b/093 (1893); 115a/119 (1894); 131/282 (1897); 161/299 (1900).

[34]   Jefferys states that this was still standard practice in the early twentieth century. James Jefferys, *Retail Trading in Britain 1850–1950: A Study of Trends in Retailing with Special Reference to the Development of Co-operative, Multiple Shop and Department Store Methods of Trading* (Cambridge, 1954), p. 304.

[35]   For example, only four of the ten sailor suits found were securely dated.

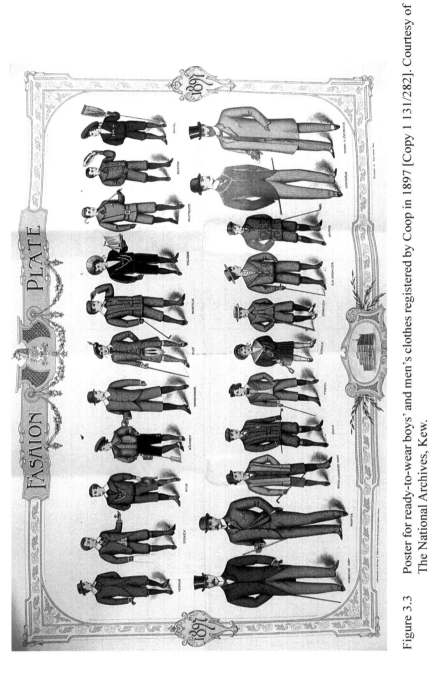

Figure 3.3   Poster for ready-to-wear boys' and men's clothes registered by Coop in 1897 [Copy 1 131/282]. Courtesy of The National Archives, Kew.

Table 3.1　Boys' suits in museum collections with manufacturers' labels

Museum no.*	Date	Jacket cut	Fabric	Trousers	Manufacturer/Retailer
VAMC 1961.T137	c.1875	sailor blouse	navy velvet	short	Clack, Ludgate Hill
BATH IV.24.8	1880s	sailor	cotton	long	made on board RN ship
VAMC 1930.T186	1880s	court	navy velvet	short	Samuel Bros, Sydenham House
VAMC 1974.T519	c.1880c	18th C style	navy velvet	short	Samuel Bros, Sydenham House
VAMC 1974.T518	1887	fauntleroy	purple velvet	short	Eldridge & Young, Salisbury
VAMC 1963.T161	c.1890	court	black velvet	short	H.J. Nicoll, 114 Regent St and Paris
VAMC 1970.T83	c.1890	sailor tunic	linen	long sailor	Rowe of Gosport, 106 New Bond St
GCM 1978.184	c.1890	sailor	navy velvet	short	Kempton & Co., 32 Argyll St
WOR 1962.3537	c.1890	fauntleroy blouse	navy velvet	short	Whiteley's front
BATH IV.24.10	1890s		purple velveteen	short	Swears & Wells
LON1979.396/5	1890s	fauntleroy	peacock velvet	short	Peter Robinson
GCM 1966.93	1897	evening	black wool	short	Macbeth, Liverpool and Manchester
GCM 1954.951	1898	hussar	navy and blue wool	short	Barran?
GCM 1954.952	1898	db sailor	navy wool	short	Barran regd 331385
GCM 1954.953	1898	sailor	white cotton	long	Barran?
GCM 1954.950	1898	blouse suit	brown velvet	short	Barran?
BATH IV.24.11	c.1900		burgundy wool	short	Peter Robinson
HCMS 1976.31.757	c.1900	rugby	diagonal tweed	short	Abbey Gate
HCMS CRH 1969.102a	c.1900	sailor	white cotton	short	Bon Marché, Brixton
HCMS CRH 1969.102c	c.1900	sailor	white cotton	long	Peter Robinson

Sources: BATH – Museum of Costume, Bath; GCM – Gallery of Costume, Manchester; HCMS - Hampshire County Museums Service; LEIC – Leicester City Museums; MOL – Museum of London; VAMC – V&A Museum of Childhood; WOR – Worthing Museums.

sailor suits, but several versions in silk velvet.[36] What it did indicate was the complexity of the relationship between manufacturers and retailers (Table 3.1).

Only twenty surviving suits had any information about their makers; in one case the donors provided this information, and the remainder were identified by means of manufacturers' or retailers' marks. Fourteen suits had tapes woven with the name of a firm, and one suit had metal buttons stamped with a name.[37] The presence of retailers' name tapes in 1880s boys' garments is somewhat surprising, as these are more usually found in ladies' made-to-measure dresses.[38] Their use by retailers of ready-to-wear children's clothes suggests that these firms saw their reputation as valuable.

Three of the firms represented were London department stores – Whiteley of Bayswater, Peter Robinson, Bon Marché Brixton – who may have had garments made by in-house workshops or by outside contractors.[39] Another four were firms who were both manufacturers and retailers – George Macbeth of Manchester, H.J. Nicoll, Samuel Brothers, Rowe of Gosport. Nicoll was a large-scale manufacturer (Mayhew estimated that they employed up to 1,200 outworkers) selling through their own stores in London, Manchester, Liverpool and Paris.[40] The large number of commercial images they registered in Copy 1 may indicate a mail-order business as well. Macbeth was noted in the *Tailor and Cutter* in 1880 as a major manufacturer of boys' clothes, with their own retail outlets and mail-order business.[41]

Two further surviving garments had card tickets printed with the name and trademark of a manufacturer stitched onto them: Bullock & Sons (Macclesfield) and Abbey Gate (Leeds).[42] These labels would be removed when the garment was first worn, so they only survive on unworn items. Yet another type of manufacturers' mark was the stamped inscription 'Rd. No. 331385' found on the

---

[36]   For example, the only surviving example of a Norfolk suit found in a museum collection has an associated date of 1910 (information from Rachel Boak, Bath Museum of Costume (BMC), 13 April 2004).

[37]   Eldridge & Young, Salisbury: V&A Museum of Childhood 1974.T518.

[38]   Lou Taylor, *The Study of Dress History* (Manchester, 2002), p. 14. Jane Ashelford, *The Art of Dress: Clothes and Society, 1500–1914* (London, 1996), pp. 257–9; Edwina Ehrman, 'Clothing a world city: 1830–60' in Christopher Breward, Edwina Ehrman and Caroline Evans, The London Look, Fashion from Street to Catwalk (London, 2004), p. 38.

[39]   Ashelford, *The Art of Dress*, pp. 257–9.

[40]   Cited in David Green, *From Artisans to Paupers* (Aldershot, 1995), p 163. Nicoll registered a total of 22 designs between 1842 and 1900 in BT43, 45 and 50: fifteen for men, six for boys and one for a woman.

[41]   *Tailor and Cutter*, 17 June 1880. This article states that Macbeth's designs for boys' clothing were protected by registration, but only one was found, BT 43/13/339153, (1880).

[42]   A kilt suit, Gallery of Costume, Manchester, 1951.317, 'Bullock & Sons, Woollen merchant and Clothing Manufacturer, Macclesfield, 14s 6d'; and a tweed 'Rugby' suit, Hampshire County Museums Service 1976.31.757, 'The Abbey Gate, Superior Manufacture, Made in England'.

back of a cotton waistcoat (Figure 3.4).[43] This corresponded to a design registered in BT50 by Barran of Leeds in 1898 (Figure 3.5). This waistcoat was part of a group of four suits, all unworn, acquired from the same source, and it is thought by the curators responsible that they were all from Barran, although the others are

Figure 3.4   A blue cotton waistcoat, part of a sailor suit [1954.952].
© Manchester City Galleries.

---

[43]   Gallery of Costume, Manchester, 1954.952.

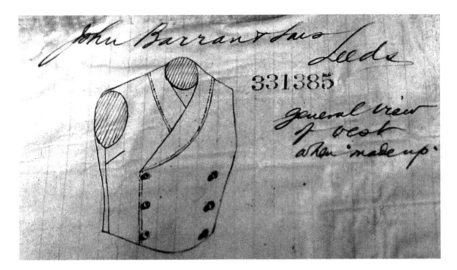

Figure 3.5   Registered design for the same waistcoat by Barran, Leeds, 1898 [BT 50/33185]. Courtesy of The National Archives, Kew.

unmarked.[44] The lack of permanent labels on garments from a manufacturer as keen to protect his designs as Barran is surprising, but indicates the extent to which retailers controlled the interface with consumers.

Advertising Documents Registered by Printers

The Copy 1 advertising documents also included many from commercial printers: 265 from Richard Taylor & Co. (17 New Bridge Street, London), 94 from Julian Green (Whitehall Road, Leeds), 71 from Clements Newling (96 Wood Street, London) and 63 from Wesley Petty (Whitehall Printeries, Leeds). The status of the firms was clarified by pricelists for ordering multiple copies stamped on some documents. A substantial proportion of their advertising images were for boys' clothes: 138 from Taylor, 47 from Petty and 33 from Green.

   Some of the documents registered by Petty were advertising novelties in the form of half-length figures with mottoes, lithographed in colour and die cut to shape. The coloured figures took various forms: a lady in evening dress ('Yes! It's just lovely'), a seashell painted with a seaside scene ('What are the wild waves saying?'), a boy on a seaside donkey ('Hold fast'), a boy with a telescope ('You can see it with one eye'), a boy reading ('Learn this lesson well' – Figure 3.6).[45] On the

---

[44]   A further suit by Barran has been identified in the collections of Leeds Industrial Museum; Sarah Levitt, *The Victorians Unbuttoned* (London, 1986), p. 100, fig.11.

[45]   It's just lovely, Copy 1 111/380 (1894); Wild waves, Copy 1 116/111 (1895); Hold fast, Copy 1 116/120 (1895); see it with one eye, Copy 1 116/122 (1895); Learn this lesson, Copy 1 131a/115 (1897); all registered by Wesley Petty, Leeds.

Figure 3.6   Advertising novelty registered by Wesley Petty of Leeds, 1897
               [Copy 1 131a/115, 1897]. Courtesy of The National Archives,
               Kew.

reverse was information about a retailer, with text that referred to the catchphrase
on the front: 'Hold fast to good old-fashioned Square Deals'. Interestingly, some of
the retailers featured on these die-cut novelties, with addresses from Perth, Leeds,
Dewsbury and Cardiff, identified themselves as specialists in boys' clothing. Two
of them gave prices starting from 3s 11d for boys and 21s for men, suggesting that
they were aiming at value-conscious consumers.[46] The combination of attractive
presentation and low prices has implications for the pricing of boys' clothes: these
will be examined in Chapter 4.

Other images registered by printers in Copy 1 corresponded to those in retail
catalogues preserved in the John Johnson and Evanion archives. Identifying
these made it possible to date some sales documents: for example, a flyer for
the Capital and Labour Clothing Stores of 376–80 Holloway Road, London,
included an image registered by Richard Taylor in 1896.[47] It also clarified how
retailers adjusted the images in their catalogues over a number of years. A series
of catalogues produced by Richard Taylor and Co. for Marychurch & Blackler
of Oxford contained garment images registered between 1896 and 1900.[48] Some
of these were highlighted as novelties: 'Beaufort Suit, A perfectly New Style for

---

46   Masters, Cardiff, on Copy 1 116/111; Jameson's, Perth, on Copy 1 111/380.
47   Capital and Labour Clothing Stores, JJ MC 1/23; Copy 1 127/217 (1896).
48   JJ Oxford Trades (OT) Box 13/12–14; Box 14/3–8.

6. QUEEN STREET, OXFORD.

The Clifford Suit,
For Boys of 3 to 9 years of age.
In a variety of Tweeds,
Velvets, etc.
From **8/9** to **21/-**

The Parisian Suit.
For Boys of 5 to 12 years of age.
STILL THE MOST POPULAR SUIT.
In Neat Pattern Tweeds, also fine Black
and Blue Serges.
8/11 11/6 13/6 15/11 18/6
*Length of Tweed with all Suits,
at 8/11 and over.*

The Eton Suit.
Made from Fine Serges, Vicunas
and Worsteds.
Eton Jacket and Vest,
16/11 19/6 23/6 28/6
Eton Suit, **22/6 29/6 37/6**
Grey Hairline Trousers,
6/6 7/11 9/6 12/6

Figure 3.7   Page from a catalogue for Marychurch & Blackler of Oxford
[Shelfmark: JJ OT 14(8a), p. 7]. Courtesy of the Bodleian Library,
University of Oxford.

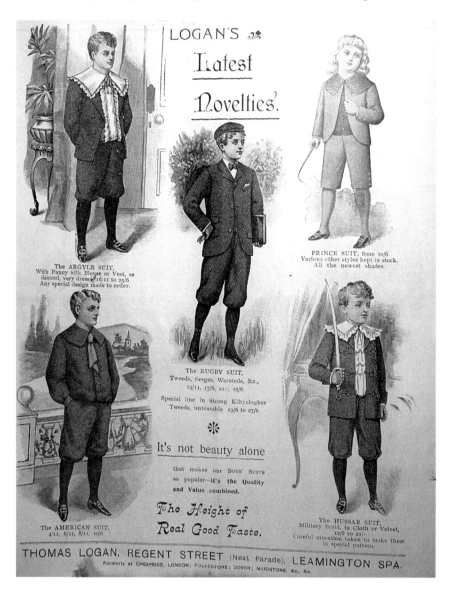

Figure 3.8   Catalogue page for Logan, registered by Wesley Petty, 1900 [Copy 1 B C 975/18747]. Courtesy of The National Archives, Kew.

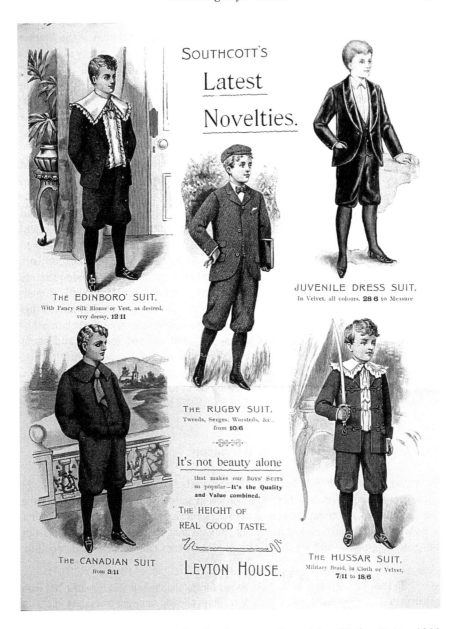

Figure 3.9   Catalogue page for Southcott, registered by Wesley Petty, 1900 [Copy 1 BC.974/18528]. Courtesy of The National Archives, Kew.

Spring' or 'The Conway Suit, This Style is a modern development of the Marine Suit'. Other images were repeated from a previous year, but with minor alterations such as the style of collar, or the same style was illustrated with a different drawing.[49] There were some garments that were sold using the same image from year to year, with text such as 'The Parisian Suit … Still the Most Popular Suit' or 'The Norfolk Suit, This Suit is still largely in demand' (Figure 3.7).[50] Thus Marychurch & Blackler were using Taylor's stock images to show both standard and novel styles of garments.

More problematic was the reuse of images in two catalogues registered in Copy 1 by Petty for C.G. Southcott of Hull and Thomas Logan of Leamington Spa.[51] These were handsomely produced, with fourteen pages of black and white illustrations wrapped in full colour covers on coated stock. The covers had different images and letterpress, but some of the internal pages were identical in image and layout (Figures 3.8 and 3.9). As Southcott was a Leeds-based manufacturer who had a chain of tied retailers, we might assume that the garments shown represent goods made by Southcott and perhaps supplied to independents such as Logan.[52] However, the fact that the images used were not specially drawn, but taken from the stock which Petty made available to any retailer, makes this supposition problematic.[53] These documents raise questions about the relationship between catalogue images and the actual garments offered for sale, and about the relationship between catalogue publishers and manufacturers in originating, selecting and publicising new styles. Some answers to these questions can be obtained by a comparison of the garment types in retailing and in manufacturing documents.

Boys' Garment Types in Retailing Documents

As stated above, the retailing documents varied in format from multi-page catalogues to single images. They also varied in status from catalogues linked to a specific retailer's or manufacturer's stock to generic images for use by a number of retailers. The analysis of catalogues showed that these were composed from the generic images, and so these sets of documents can be analysed together.

---

[49]   In Box 14/7 and Box 14/8, the drawing for the lounge suit was repeated, but with a change in the collar; the 'Clifford' suits were shown in the same cut and fabric, but with two different drawings.

[50]   See Illustrations 3.14 and 3.15, pp. 144–5 in Rose, 'Boyswear'.

[51]   Petty for C.G. Southcott of Hull, Copy 1 BC 974/18528 (1900); Petty for T. Logan of Leamington Spa, Copy 1 BC 975/18747 (1900), TNA.

[52]   Katrina Honeyman *Well Suited: A History of the Leeds Clothing Industry, 1850–1990* (Oxford, 2000), p. 298. By the 1930s they were struggling to compete with larger firms; Ugolini, *Men and Menswear*, pp. 183–4.

[53]   These images will be discussed further in Chapter 7.

Documents produced by manufacturers such as Coop and by tailoring publishers will be analysed separately in order to show up differences with documents for retailers.

The 436 retailing documents in the Copy 1 archives contained 914 images of boys' garments, and the 59 unregistered catalogues in the John Johnson and other archives added another 305 giving 1,219 in total. These were sorted into categories based on those used for garments in the Board of Trade archives. Suits for young boys with short trousers or kilts dominated, in 985 (or 81 per cent) of the images. The commonest younger boys' style was the sailor suit with short trousers in 208 images (17 per cent of the total) (Figure 3.10). This was followed in popularity by the Norfolk suit (128 images) and the Rugby (lounge suit with short trousers – 117), and the 'stripe'/Greenwich styles (80). The most popular suit with long trousers was the lounge, with 86 representations, followed by the Eton suit (64) and the sailor suit with long trousers (41). There were also a number of less common styles, seen in a total of 397 images. There was a shift in the dominant styles after 1895, with the introduction of suits with blouses for young boys, which formed 15 per cent of all designs for that period, equalling the number of sailor suits. The shift from sailor suits to blouses has implications for the way we interpret their meanings which will be discussed in Chapter 7.

In addition to these images in documents produced for retailers and retailing manufacturers by catalogue publishers, the thirteen sales documents produced by manufacturers (Coop, Barran, Shannon and others) contained 176 images of boys' garments. Of these 176 designs, 164 were for suits with short trousers, the remainder being divided between styles for older boys in long trousers and for toddlers in skirts. We would expect the distribution of garment styles in the Copy 1 manufacturers' documents to be very close to that in the BT45 and BT50 registrations, as the posters registered by Coop represent the sales tools for the garments registered in the BT series. In both sets of documents, the commonest style overall was the sailor suit, and the introduction of the blouse suit in 1894 coincided with disappearance of the 'stripe' suit that was seen frequently during the 1880s. But there were some noticeable differences between the manufacturers' documents in the Copy 1 and BT series which are important for what they tell us about these two sources.

The manufacturers' advertising sheets had a wider age range, from adults down to young boys in kilts and tunics. They also showed a different range of styles: 15 per cent of the boys' suits depicted were plain lounge suits (not present in the BT registrations), and 8 per cent were Norfolk suits (2 per cent in the BT documents). This suggests that the advertising sheets represented the whole range of clothing made, while the BT archives represented more highly decorated garments whose design was worth protecting by registration. There were also some garments present in manufacturers' BT registrations but not visible in their Copy 1 documents, such as jackets with braid trimming in a 'frogged' pattern. This may be a result of a lack of differentiation between different subtypes of braid trimmings. It may also reflect the different priorities of two different manufacturers, as the BT designs in

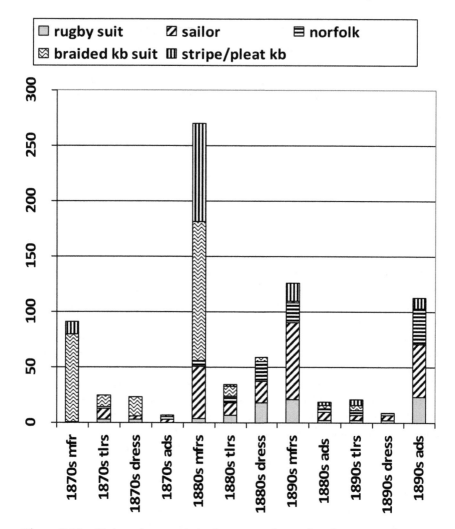

Figure 3.10   Styles of garments in documents from advertisers, manufacturers, tailors and dressmakers, 1870s–1890s.

the 1880s were dominated by Barran, while the Copy 1 posters were mainly from Coop.

Of the 218 tailors' documents registered in Copy 1, eight contained images of boys' clothing; six of these eight were published by Williamson.[54] In these eight documents there were 53 images, 33 (or 63 per cent) of which were for

    [54]   Copy 1 062/277, Edmé Guichard (1883); Copy 1 086/526, John Williamson & Co. (1889); Copy 1 89a/156, John Williamson & Co. (1890); Copy 1 89b/026, John Williamson & Co. (1890); Copy 1 89b/159, John Williamson & Co. (1890); Copy 1 109/052, John

shorts suits, 16 (or 30 per cent) for long suits and 8 per cent for tunics and kilts, including a sailor kilt ensemble.[55] This is very similar to the proportions of designs for each age group in the *Tailor and Cutter*. However, the boys' styles featured most frequently in tailors' magazines, sailor and lounge suits, were less dominant in the posters.

Fashion Innovation by Different Types of Garment Producers

Examining the representation of particular styles in different sources clarified how different types of clothing providers followed fashion cycles, and where new fashions originated. Figure 3.10 shows the incidence of the leading styles in different sources and in different decades. From this we can see that the single most common type of boys' outfit in all the sources studied was the braided short suit, followed by short sailor suits, 'stripe' suits, and Norfolk and Rugby suits. It is evident that the manufacturers' registrations in the BT series are far more numerous than other categories of documents, particularly before 1890. Even so, the dominance of braided suits in the 1870s is striking. The 1870s dressmakers' documents (pattern books and magazines) were also dominated by braided suits. In the 1880s, braided suits again dominated manufacturers' documents, with the 'stripe' suit coming second. However, the other sources showed a more even distribution of styles in the 1880s and in dressmakers' patterns the 'stripe' and braided suits were the least common. This discrepancy may partly be explained by the clustering of manufacturers' documents (both BT and Copy 1) in the first half of the decade, when these styles were more common in all sources. By the 1890s the braided suit was almost absent from all sources, being replaced by the sailor suit in manufacturers' and advertisers' documents. Again, tailors' and dressmakers' documents showed less domination by any one style.

A detailed investigation of the different garment sources indicated that design innovation, as well as design proliferation, typically originated with manufacturers rather than bespoke tailors. For instance, sailor suits were introduced as a new style for boys in the mid-1860s, apparently made by naval outfitters.[56] Their first appearance in clothing industry sources was in 1870, when a version was registered by the manufacturer and retailer Donald Nicoll & Co.[57] In the same year

---

Williamson & Co. (1893); Copy 1 119/401, John Williamson & Co. (1895); Copy 1 120/367, F.T. Prewett (1895), all TNA.

[55]   Copy 1 89b/159, John Williamson & Co. (1890), TNA.

[56]   The earliest recorded instance of a boy dressed in a sailor suit is the 1846 portrayal of Edward, Prince of Wales, by Winterhalter. The second known example of a boy's sailor suit dates from 1855, but was made to wear on a long sea voyage (Museum of London 1942.20). The first portrait showing sailor suits worn in everyday life dates from 1865. This chronology will be discussed in detail in Chapter 7.

[57]   BT43/13/ 238638, D. Nicoll, 1870. Illustrated in Levitt, *Victorians Unbuttoned*, p. 98, fig. 9.

a dressmakers' pattern for a boy's sailor suit was published in the *Young Ladies' Journal*.[58] The first tailoring pattern for a sailor suit appeared in the *Tailor and Cutter* only in 1873, and was mentioned with a concern that 'the making of these things will pass out of the tailor's hands'.[59] Other boys' styles that were important for manufacturers and retailers were ignored by tailors. The 'stripe' suit, trimmed with strips of braid or pleated fabric, was the third most numerous style in the documents studied but did not appear in any of the tailoring sources. This finding supports Chenoune's view that mass manufacturers were innovating, and doing so in ways that suited their manufacturing processes.[60]

Conclusions

As the preceding analysis has shown, there was a broad agreement in the publicity documents produced by clothing retailers, mass manufacturers and bespoke tailors as to the scope, nature and styles of garments offered for boys. The publicity documents showed clothing for boys from toddler to near-adult, but the largest numbers of images, and the greatest range of styles, were for boys in short trousers. The surviving garments with retailers' labels found in museums were also short suits. This suggests that retailers were focusing their efforts on this age range, rather than on older or younger boys. This is surprising as we might expect there to be a greater variety of clothing either for toddlers in skirts, dressed with reference to feminine fashions, or for adolescents whose entry to the workplace would give them access to greater funds for distinctive clothing. It was also noticeable that many of the finished catalogues and posters were designed to sell mostly or exclusively clothing for boys, suggesting that this was a market worth cultivating. The implications of these findings for our understanding of clothing consumption will be examined further in Chapters 4 and 5.

The large number of designs for boys' garments registered in the BT and Copy 1 archives indicated that they were economically important to both manufacturers and retailers. Their designs were highly differentiated, subject to fashionable change, and worth protecting by copyright. However, the role of mass manufacturers in the democratisation of clothing styles has been obscured by the anonymity of their products at the point of sale. Neither publicity materials nor the garments themselves identified the name of the manufacturer, only that of the retailer. Retailers specialising in boys' clothes were often large-scale businesses, such as John Lewis of Liverpool who claimed to sell 50,000 boys' suits in 1859 alone.[61]

---

[58]   *Young Ladies' Journal* pattern exhibited in 'Sailor Chic' at the National Maritime Museum, Greenwich, October 2000.

[59]   *Tailor and Cutter*, March 1875, p. 105.

[60]   Farid Chenoune, *A History of Men's Fashion* (Paris, 1993), p. 66.

[61]   Asa Briggs, *Friends of the People: The Centenary History of Lewis's* (London, 1956), p. 33.

The commercial importance of the trade by the 1890s is confirmed by the fact that retailers were willing to pay for dedicated catalogues of boys' clothing, with lithographic illustrations printed on expensive coated stock. The 1870s catalogues from Lynes demonstrate that boys' clothing was also a focus of the pioneers of ready-to-wear and mail-order retailing.[62]

The John Johnson collection and the Copy 1 archives show that boys' clothing was also important in the development of advertising material, especially after 1890. Each advertising flyer registered at the Stationers' Hall represented an investment in design that had to be recouped by multiple sales, with personalised documents produced in batches of 500 to 3,000. Moreover, the business practice of Richard Taylor, Wesley Petty and other advertising publishers was based on adapting the same material for different retailers, as was seen in the matching catalogues for Southcott and Logan registered by Petty in 1900. Thus each advertising image in the Copy 1 archive would have been printed hundreds of times and associated with retailers throughout Britain. Multiple reproductions of advertising images may have helped to create a shared conception of the 'norm' for boys' clothing, even among those unable to purchase it.[63] The degree of consensus in clothing practice for boys across social classes will be examined further in Chapter 5.

The sales posters by Coop preserved in Copy 1 were a particularly valuable source for examining manufacturers' design strategies, and the interaction between manufacturers and retailers. The large number of subtly differentiated styles for boys and the changes from year to year show that fashion was important to sales. The large size and full colour lithography of the posters implies a wish to control the way that goods were presented by the retailer. However, the lack of any overt reference to the producers of the clothing, either on the posters or on the garments themselves, indicates the complexity of late nineteenth-century consumer attitudes towards mass-produced goods. This echoes what Schorman has observed in America, where a retailer stated: 'I will not use electros [images] … which advertise a manufacturer's product too obviously. I can't afford to have people think I am cheap.'[64]

The importance of design in both manufacturing and selling boys' clothing has important implications for our understanding of the garment trade. It undermines Fine and Leopold's dichotomy between men's clothing and women's fashion by aligning boys with the 'feminine', high-fashion model. The multiple variants of standard styles, in manufacturers' designs and in advertising images, should also cause us to re-examine the ways in which clothing was used to form and express boys' class and gender identity. Did the availability of ready-made garments foreclose mothers' decisions on the clothing appropriate to a particular age group,

---

[62]   E. Moses & Son had been selling ready-to-wear garments for both working-class and middle-class boys in the 1850s. See Rose, 'Boyswear', pp. 139, 150 and 234–9.

[63]   For the effect of mass reproduction of advertising images, see Schorman, *Selling Style*, p. 26.

[64]   *Printers' Ink*, 26 November 1914, cited in ibid., p. 148.

or did it increase their choices? Did the mass marketing of particular styles erode their status value, or was this maintained through the use of exclusive detailing? What patriotic intention can we attribute to the choice of a sailor suit when it forms one of the dominant clothing styles? These issues will be examined in the following chapters.

Chapter 4
Affording Boys' Clothes

In 1893, Charles Baker & Co. issued an illustrated price list detailing the clothes for boys and men available from their four London branches or by mail order (carriage paid, with full money-back guarantee).[1] They repeated a claim they had been making since the early 1880s: 'Opened to keep pace with the Civil Service Stores … 25 per cent under usual London prices.' This suggests a highly price-conscious clientele, yet the styles on offer included middle-class formal wear, Eton suits for boys and morning coats for men. Moreover, each outfit was available in several different qualities, so that a youth's tweed suit might cost as little as 9s or as much as 25s 9d for the smallest size. This document indicates both the importance of pricing to ready-to-wear retailers, and the difficulty of abstracting trends and policies from the wealth of detail available. Yet knowing what garments cost is essential to understanding their social meanings.

This chapter will examine the costs of clothes, both in cash terms and in terms of family budgets. In doing this it will join the ongoing debate on the cost of living conducted by economic and social historians.[2] It would seem on the face of it that the growth of clothing advertising described in Chapter 3 implies increased consumption and that this in turn implies an improvement in living standards.[3] This was the deduction made by Asa Briggs in his study of Lewis's of Liverpool from the 1850s onwards.[4] This picture of a generally rising standard of living up to 1900 is supported by economic historians such as William Hamish Fraser and Harold Perkin.[5] They have tended to use data on expenditure from censuses or social

---

[1]   John Johnson Collection (JJ) Men's Clothing (MC) 1/5.

[2]   See the discussion on methodology in Peter Scholliers (ed.), *Real Wages in 19th and 20th Century Europe: Historical and Comparative Perspectives* (New York, 1989).

[3]   Although mass consumption of clothing existed prior to industrialisation: see Ben Fine and Ellen Leopold, *The World of Consumption* (London, 1993); Beverly Lemire, *Dress, Culture and Commerce: The English Clothing Trade before the Factory, 1660–1800* (Basingstoke, 1997).

[4]   Lewis's success was founded on the sale of men's and boys' ready-to-wear; by 1859 they were selling 50,000 boys' suits a year, and further expansion was linked by Briggs to a rise in living standards of living, for the upper working and lower middle classes. Asa Briggs, *Friends of the People: The Centenary History of Lewis's* (London, 1956), pp. 30–33, 119 and 128.

[5]   William Hamish Fraser, *The Coming of the Mass Market, 1850–1914* (Basingstoke, 1981), pp. 58–9. Harold Perkin discusses the limits of this improvement in *The Rise of Professional Society: England since 1880* (London, 1989), pp. 36–40.

surveys, rather than tracking the cost of particular items over time. Andrew Godley examined changes in clothing expenditure as a tool for estimating productivity in the garment industry, and came to the conclusion that it remained steady at about 7 per cent of median family budgets over a long period.[6] Laura Ugolini's work on men's clothing consumption, which draws on both consumer and industry sources, suggests that clothing prices were relatively stable until 1900, but that there was a perception of a rise in the cost of living between 1900 and 1914.[7]

An opposing view is presented by many nineteenth-century accounts such as those in the *Cornhill Magazine* which emphasise the high cost of clothing, and the difficulties many families faced in affording it. But when these texts contrast garments made at home by the 'deft fingers' of the mother with those made by sweated labour for a 'slop shop' or purchased from a disease-ridden second-hand stall, they reveal the preconceptions of the author as much as actual practice. Much nineteenth-century writing on family budgets (including the surveys of Booth and Rowntree) was allied to campaigns to ameliorate social conditions, which would encourage an emphasis on the gap between incomes and the cost of living. Even autobiographies may have been shaped by the wish of writers to emphasise the poverty of their childhood as a marker of the distance travelled. A further problem was caused by the inequitable division of resources within working-class families. As Ellen Ross revealed, male heads of households tended to claim a disproportionate share of family expenditure.[8] This elision between the expenditure of the family unit and the expenditure of individual members has been difficult for later researchers such as Benson, Treble and Johnson to unpick.[9]

This chapter will make a detailed analysis of typical boys' garment prices, both in cash terms and as a percentage of family incomes, to clarify how they relate to changes in the cost of living. The first section sets out the available information on family budgets for clothing in the period 1870–90 and in the 1890s. This is drawn from census data and from the social surveys of Booth and Rowntree, which are not without inconsistencies. The second section gives prices of typical sets of boys' clothes 1870–1900, selected from the retailing documents discussed in Chapter 3. These show variations over time, between retailers, and between garment types and subtypes so that we need to consider price ranges as well as

---

[6]   Andrew Godley, 'The Development of the UK Clothing Industry, 1850–1950: Output and Productivity Growth', *Business History*, 37/4 (1995): 46–63.

[7]   Laura Ugolini, *Men and Menswear: Sartorial Consumption in Britain, 1880–1939* (Aldershot, 2007), pp. 54–6.

[8]   Ellen Ross, *Love and Toil: Motherhood in Outcast London 1870–1918* (Oxford: 1993); *eadem*, '"Fierce Questions and Taunts": Married Life in Working-class London, 1870–1914', *Feminist Studies*, 8/3 (1982): 575–602.

[9]   John Benson, *Production, Consumption and History: The British Working Class* (Wolverhampton, 1994); James H. Treble, *Urban Poverty in Britain 1830–1914* (London, 1979); Paul Johnson, *Saving and Spending: The Working-Class Economy in Britain, 1870–1939* (Oxford, 1985).

absolute prices. The third section brings together these two sets of data to consider changes in the cost of boys' clothes as a proportion of family budgets over the period. The fourth section considers alternative ways of budgeting for clothing: second-hand purchases, clothing clubs and home sewing. Understanding the costs of clothing is the key to interpreting the data on clothing consumption that will be discussed in Chapter 5. It will also help us to evaluate the novel designs from manufacturers and retailers examined in Chapters 2 and 3, and to clarify how these affected pricing.

The Real Costs of Boys' Clothes

Family Budgets 1870–1890

The sources used for this chapter were those based on census data or on extensive social surveys. These have some flaws, but present information on family incomes in a format that can be compared across time. Family clothing budgets at the beginning of this period have been derived from Robert Dudley Baxter's *National Income: the United Kingdom,* (1868) and Leone Levi's *Wages and Earnings of the working classes: with some facts illustrative of their economic condition, drawn from authentic and official sources* (1867), both based on the 1861 Census data.[10] Levi calculated that the average male wage across all occupations was 22s per week, and the average wage for all workers (men, women and children) was 15s. Baxter refined Levi's calculations by allowing for enforced idleness (seasonal, structural or personal), which reduced nominal wages by as much as 20 per cent over the year.[11] He showed that 70 per cent of the working population was in occupations where the male average wage was between £10 10s and £52 a year, with women's and children's wages a fraction of this.[12] Ten per cent of the population were 'higher skilled labour' with a male wage between £50 and £73 pa, and a further 11 per cent were 'middle class' but with a wage under £100 pa. These sums are equivalent to an average weekly wage of 4s–20s for unskilled men, 19s 4d–28s for skilled workers, and up to 38s 6d for the lower middle class (see Table 4.1).

Family incomes were not strictly equivalent to male wages: Levi calculated the average family income as 31s, based on the equivalent of two workers per family.[13] Baxter stated 'in the great majority of occupations the average wages of a boy, a woman, and a girl, added together, amount to those of a man', so

---

[10]   Leone Levi, *Wages and Earnings of the working classes: with some facts illustrative of their economic condition, drawn from authentic and official sources* (London, 1867); Robert Dudley Baxter, *National Income: The United Kingdom* (London, 1868).

[11]   Baxter, *National Income,* p. 47.

[12]   Overall incomes, ibid., p. 64; women's and children's wages, pp. 88–95.

[13]   Levi, *Wages and Earnings,* p. 9.

that total family income might be double that of the male breadwinner.[14] Fraser departed from Baxter and Levi in giving a multiplier of 1.4 between breadwinner and family income, which seems more realistic.[15] The number of family members available to work in each household would be different at different stages in the life cycle, and would be lowest when there were dependent children present.

Levi and Baxter do not give details of expenditure, but these can be found in Miranda Hill's detailed case study of an artisan family with an income of 30s in 1888.[16] Of this, 1s was allocated for clothing the husband, 2s for clothing the wife and children, and a further 1s 8d for boots, giving a total of 4s 8d.[17] This is higher than the calculations of clothing expenditure in 1880 made by Miss Mackenzie in the 1920s. Mackenzie allocated a clothing budget of 1s per week from a labourers' income of 17s, 2s per week from an artisans' income of 22s 6d, and 2s 6d from a lower middle-class income of 32s.[18]

Family Budgets after 1890

From 1890 onwards it is much easier to find information on family budgets and estimates of typical expenditure on clothing. Charles Booth's *Life and Labour of the People in London* (1892–97) and Seebohm Rowntree's *Poverty, a Study of Town Life* (1901) were based on social surveys in London and York respectively.[19] Booth estimated expenditure on clothing for a sample of thirty households, six of whom he categorized as 'class B', ten as 'class C & D' and fourteen as 'class E & F'.[20] Booth based his budgets on the needs of a male adult, 'allowing three-fourths for a woman and in proportion for children', and his estimate for a typical family with children was equivalent to that for three men.[21] Thus in 'class B' a single male with a budget of 5s 11d would spend a minimal 1d a week on clothes, and the family budget would be 15s per week, of which 3d would be allowed for clothes. In classes C and D (still below the 'poverty line'), the clothing expenditure would be 4d per week for a man or 1s for a family, from a family budget of 22s 6d. Over the 'poverty line' the allowance for clothing increased dramatically to 1s 1d for a man

[14]   Ibid., p. 49.

[15]   Fraser, *Coming of the Mass Market* , p. 22.

[16]   Miranda Hill, 'Life on Thirty Shillings a Week', *Nineteenth Century*, 23 (1888): 458–63.

[17]   Ibid., p. 462.

[18]   Cited in Fraser, *Coming of the Mass Market* , p. 58.

[19]   Charles Booth (ed.), *Life and Labour of the People in London, Series I: Poverty, Series II, Industry* (London, 1892–97); B. Seebohm Rowntree, *Poverty, A Study of Town Life* (London, 1901).

[20]   Booth, *Life and Labour* vol. I (1892), p. 44.

[21]   As the most generous estimate for family incomes was only twice that of a single man, this suggests that children acted as a drain on resources for this category.

or 3s 3d for a family, from a total family budget of 30s.[22] The data presented by Booth is extremely detailed and convincing, but it is important not to over-interpret it. Booth's category of 'clothes etc' covered medicine and household goods as well, and he admitted that for the poorest 'It is only by evading the payment of rent, or going short of food, that clothes or household things can be bought.'[23]

Rowntree's research in 1890s York used the 'class' framework of Booth, but paid more attention to individual variations. The population in York was apparently more prosperous than that of London, with only 9 per cent around the 'poverty line' and 52 per cent with family incomes of 31s or over. [24] Based on his interviews, Rowntree estimated the sums needed to clothe adults and children adequately as 26s a year for adults and from 17s to 27s for children.[25] This averages out at between 4d and 6d per family member per week. However, we need to bear in mind the unequal pattern of income distribution noted by Ross, and recognised by Booth. Booth's original guidelines for male respondents stated: 'the clothing should be adequate to keep the man in health, and should not be so shabby as to injure his chances of obtaining respectable employment.'[26] When clothing was linked so intimately to wage-earning capacity, the clothing of the breadwinner was likely to be prioritised over that of women and children.

Another problem with Rowntree's family budgets is that boots and shoes were included in the sums for clothing. Scrutiny of the individual budgets shows that expenditure on footwear was usually equal to or greater than expenditure on other garments. For instance, in Budget No.1, a family with an income of 17s 6d per week and four dependent children spent 26s on boots and only 11s 4d on clothing over a period of 26 weeks. This averages out to a family expenditure of 1s on boots and 5d on clothes per week, in spite of the fact that 'the father mends the children's boots himself in the evening, thus effecting a considerable saving'.[27] This compared with another labourers' family with only one child and an income of 24s a week, who spent an average of 10d on boots and 5d on clothes.[28] A third family with an income of 25s a week and three children spent only 7½ d per week on boots but 14d on clothing (total 1s 9½ d).[29]

Thus, from incomes between 17s 6d and 25s a week, the working-class York families interviewed by Rowntree spent between 15d (1s 3d) and 21d (1s 9d) each week on clothing and boots together. The division between the two types of expenditure varied, with some families spending more on garments and others on boots. These variations may relate to slight differences in occupation. Wear

---

22   Booth, *Life and Labour*, vol. I (1892), p. 44.
23   Ibid., p. 45.
24   Rowntree, *Poverty*, p. 56.
25   Ibid., p. 141.
26   Ibid., p. 140.
27   Ibid., p. 311.
28   Ibid., Budget No. 11, pp. 329–31.
29   Ibid., Budget No. 8, pp. 326–7.

Table 4.1   Family incomes and clothing budgets, calculated weekly, 1870–1900

Date	Source	Labourers			Artisans			Lower middle-class wage	Middle-class family clothes	Upper middle-class wage
		Male wage	Family income	Family clothes	Male wage	Family income	Family clothes			
1860	Mackenzie		13s	9d		20s 6d	1s 6d	27s 6d	2s	
1860s	Baxter	4s–20s	8s–40s		20s–28s	40s–56s		38s		38s–114s
1880	Mackenzie		17s	1s		22s 6d	2s	32s	2s 6d	
1890s	Booth	22s 6d		1s	30s		3s 3d	49s 6d	6s 6d	
1890s	Rowntree	15s	17s 6d	1s 6d	25s	25s	1s 10d	52s 0d	2s 6d	
1890s	Layard							57s 6d	7s 6d	

Sources: R.D. Baxter, *National Income: The United Kingdom* (London, 1868); C. Booth (ed.), *Life and Labour of the People in London, Series I: Poverty; Series II, Industry* (London, 1892–97); G.S. Layard, 'How to Live on £150 a Year', *Cornhill Magazine*, May 1901; Miss Mackenzie, cited in W.H. Fraser, *The Coming of the Mass Market, 1850–1914* (Basingstoke, 1981); B.S. Rowntree, *Poverty, A Study of Town Life* (London, 1901).

on boots would also be directly related to the distance walked to and from work or school each day. The variations may also reflect the short time span of the specimen budgets; over a period of a month or less, a single purchase of clothing or boots would alter the balance noticeably. As there is no clear pattern, it is safest to assume that expenditure on clothing as a whole was equally divided between garments and boots. In this case, from Rowntree's minimum clothing budget of 5d per person per week, only 2½d would be available for garments as opposed to boots (Table 4.1).

Families above the 'poverty line' have been less intensively studied, but indications of their budgets are given in the 1901 *Cornhill Magazine* articles discussed above. In the article 'How to Live on 30s a Week', Arthur Morrison allocated 2s a week for clothing both parents and two or three children.[30] G.S. Layard suggested that professional and clerical families on £150 would spend £6 a year on shoes for the family, £6 on clothing for the wage-earner, and £13 on clothing for the wife and children. This equates to 7s 6d per week: 2s 3½ d for the husband, and 5s 3d for the other three persons from a weekly income of 57s 6d.[31]

Looking at Table 4.1, we can see that there were marked differences between the clothing budgets derived from different authorities. For instance, Booth's labourer with an income of 22s 6d allowed 1s for clothes, while Rowntree's family on 17s 6d a week allowed 1s 6d for clothes. In Rowntree's data, an increased family income of 25s (40 per cent higher) was linked to a modest increase in the clothing budget from 1s 6d to 1s 10d. However, in Booth's data the increase in the clothing budget was much steeper, from 1s at 22s 6d to 3s 3d at 30s. This suggests a different conception of 'adequate' clothing between the two groups, perhaps hinging on the provision of additional clothes for leisure wear. In the circumstances it is hard to know whether the London or York data are more representative. In the case of Rowntree's budget for a lower middle-class family the sum spent on clothing is clearly anomalous; Booth gives a weekly budget of 6s 6d for a family at this level, while Layard allows 7s 6d. Rowntree's very low sum of 2s 6d may relate to the specific economies practised by his family No. 18 rather than to general patterns of consumption. In this sense Rowntree's detailed examination of particular cases may be a weakness as well as a strength.

Clothing Prices 1870–1900

In order to understand how and why consumers purchased particular garment types at particular dates it is necessary to establish their costs, both in cash terms and as a proportion of family budgets. While it may not be possible to re-create

---

[30] Arthur Morrison, 'How to Live on 30s a Week', *Cornhill Magazine*, May 1901, in Edgar Royston Pike (ed.), *Human Documents of the Age of the Forsytes* (London: 1969), p. 159.

[31] George S Layard, 'How to Live on £150 a Year', *Cornhill Magazine*, May 1901, cited in Pike, *Human Documents*, pp. 161–5.

the whole range of choices available to past consumers, it is possible to gauge this by using data from ready-to-wear retailers. Chapter showed the variety of ready-to-wear boys' garments offered in retailers' catalogues by the 1870s. These offered detailed information on the operations of particular retailers, but were uneven in their survival and in the extent to which they represent clothing retailing in general. Documents from the periods 1870–89 and 1890–1900 will be analysed in groups in order to highlight any inconsistencies before the groups are compared to show changes over time.

For the period 1870–89 there were eighteen documents with prices, from ten retailers based in London (with some mail-order sales) and two from Oxford. Most of these retailers were advertising primarily to the middle classes: Arthur Lynes also offered contract clothing for 'Charitable Institutions' but no details of this trade survive.[32] The presentation of Lynes' catalogues as illustrated children's albums in itself implies high profit margins and high costs. The newspaper advertisements were more modest, but their middle-class audience was implied by their presentation in publications such as *The Graphic*.

The prices for the smallest and cheapest suits for young boys (with short trousers) and for older boys (with long trousers) were extracted and tabulated in Table 4.2. These showed a degree of consensus between retailers. From 1870 to January 1881, the lowest price for young boys' suits was between 8s 6d and 25s, with a mode of 10s 6d. This price was found in documents from five different retailers. Prices for young boys in the Lynes catalogues started at 12s 6d in 1870 and dropped to 10s 6d by 1876. Not all of the documents from 1870 to 1881 gave prices for older boys, but those that did had prices between 14s 6d and 29s. Prices for older boys varied between retailers and between catalogues from the same retailer. This may reflect differences in sizing or in the complexity of the cut.

Table 4.2   Lowest prices for boys' suits from retailers' catalogues, 1870–89

Retailer	City	Source	Date	Short suit	Long suit
Nicholson's	London	MOL	1870	10s 6d	
A. Lynes & Sons, *Smiles & Styles*	London	JJ MC 4/16	1871	12s 6d	14s 6d
A. Lynes & Sons, *Merriment & Modes*	London	JJ MC 4/19	1872	10s 6d	25s
A. Lynes & Sons, *Novelettes & Novelties*	London	JJ MC 4/17	1873	8s 6d	16s
C. Lyons	London	MOL 97.81/5	1874	10s 6d	21s
A. Lynes & Son, *Twice a year*	London	JJ MC 4/20	1875	8s 6d	14s 6d

---

32   Arthur Lynes & Son, *Smiles and Styles* (London, 1870), p. 115; JJ MC Box 4/16.

A. Lynes & Son, *Romance & Reality*	London	JJ MC 4/18	1876	10s 6d	20s
B. Isaacson	London	MOL 97.81/5	1878	10s 6d	
Samuel Bros	London	JJ MC 2/51	1879	14s	29s
Samuel Bros	London	*Graphic* 1-1-81	1881	10s 6d	
Woolf Bros	London	Evan 4708	1881	2s 11d	9s 11d
C. Baker & Co.	London	Evan 5192	1883	2s 11d	8s 11d
C. Baker & Co.	London	Copy 1 65/92	1884	3s 6d	8s 11d
Army & Navy	London	HF6/22/8	1886	9s	
C. Baker & Co., Xmas display ad	London	*Graphic* 25-12-86	1886	2s 11d	
C. Baker & Co., *ABC Guide to London*	London	JJ MC 3/2	1887	2s 11d	8s 11d
Universal Clothing Co.	Oxford	JJ OT 13/41	1887	2s 6d	working 3s 11d , older 8s 11d
Jackson & Co.	Oxford	JJ OT 12/91	1889	2s 6d	8s 11d

Sources: Copy 1 – Stationers' Hall Archive, The National Archives; Evan – Evanion Collection, the British Library; HF – House of Fraser Collection, Scottish Business Archive, University of Glasgow Archives; JJ – John Johnson Collection, Bodleian Library, MC – Men's Clothing, OT – Oxford Trades; MOL – Museum of London Archive.

For the period 1881–89 there were documents from a wider range of retailers in the John Johnson, Copy 1 and other archives. Some of the catalogues were undated but have been given approximate dates by matching the images used with those registered in Copy 1. The unregistered documents are particularly important for the period 1884–95. For 1896–1900 there is a significant overlap between registered and unregistered sources, particularly with material from Watts and Baker. The documents from late 1881 to 1889 showed an even stronger consensus over pricing, and these prices were noticeably lower than previously (Table 4.3). The prices for young boys' suits were between 2s 6d and 3s 6s in six out of the seven documents. The prices in the Army and Navy Stores catalogue (1886) were anomalous, starting at 9s in the seventh. Older boys' suits were only listed in five of these documents, and were priced at 8s 11d or 9s 11d. There were three Oxford stores that offered suits for working men, and one of these also advertised suits for working boys, listed in an 1887 document at 3s 11d.[33]

---

[33] Universal Clothing Co.; other stores selling working clothes were Jackson & Co. and Marychurch & Blackler, all from Oxford and held in JJ Oxford Trades (OT) 7.

Table 4.3   Lowest prices for boys' suits from retailers' catalogues, 1891–1900

Name	City	Source	Date	Knicker-bocker suit	Long suit
Marychurch & Blackler	Oxford	JJ OT 14/3	1892	2s 6d	8s 11d
Inge Edwin	London	JJ MC 1/66	1893	2s 11d	8s 11d
C. Baker & Co.	London	JJ MC 1/5	1893	3s 11d	10s 9d
Army & Navy Stores	London	HF6/22/9	1894	5s	24s 9d
Harrod's	London	reprint	1895	4s 9d	21s 6d
Fred Watts & Co.	London	JJ MC 2/81	1895	2s 6d	6s 11d
Crisp & Co.	London	JJ Win Bills VII	1896	1s 6d SALE	
Knowlman Bros	London	JJ MC 1/70	1896	2s 11d	10s 11d
C. Baker & Co.	London	JJ MC 1/7	1896	2s 11d	10s 9d
Capital & Labour Clothing Stores	London	JJ MC 1/23	1897	4s 6d	13s 6d
C.How	Wimbledon	JJ MC 1/64	1897	1s 11d SALE	10s 6d
Fred Watts & Co.	London	JJ MC 2/82	1897	2s 6d	6s 11d
Marychurch & Blackler	Oxford	JJ OT 14/7	1899	3s 11d	7s 11d
Allen Foster & Co.	London	Copy 1 972/17775	1899	3s 11d	
Marychurch & Blackler	Oxford	JJ OT 14/8a	1900	8s 6d	
C.G. Southcott	Hull	Copy 1 974/18528	1900	4s 11d	
R. Needham & Sons	Brighton	Copy 1 975/18706	1900	15s 6d	29s 6d
C. Baker & Co.	London	Copy 1 975/18721	1900	4s 11	10s 9d
T. Logan	Leamington Spa	Copy 1 975/18747	1900	5s 11d	21s
Sword & Robb	Birmingham	Copy 1 977/19478	1900	3s 11d	14s 6d

Sources: Copy 1 – Stationers' Hall Archive, The National Archives; Evan – Evanion Collection, the British Library; HF – House of Fraser Collection, Scottish Business Archive, University of Glasgow Archives; JJ – John Johnson Collection, Bodleian Library, MC – Men's Clothing, OT – Oxford Trades, Win Bills – Window Bills; MOL – Museum of London Archive; reprint – Alison Adburgham, *Victorian Shopping: Harrod's Catalogue, 1895* (Newton Abbot, 1972).

From 1890 to 1900 a sample of twenty dated retailers' documents gave prices starting from 1s 6d for a young boy's suit.[34] The lowest prices were found in documents advertising annual sales and may not represent normal practice.[35] The pricing structure was complex, with garment types offered in a range of fabrics, each with a different price scale (Figure 4.1).[36] Each of these variants was available in five or six sizes, but it is not clear whether the size ranges for each were the same.[37] Leaving these considerations aside, the starting prices for young boys' suits ranged from 2s 6d to 15s 6d. The prices were clustered around three modal points: 2s 11d (three examples), 3s 11d (four examples) and 4s 11d (three examples). Prices for older boys' suits (excluding sale prices) ranged from 6s 11d up to 29s. They were grouped in four price bands: 6s 11d to 8s 11d (five examples); 10s 6d to 10s 11d (five examples); 13s 6d to 14s 6d (two examples) and 21s up to 29s 6d (four examples).

There are several points of interest in this data. The clusters of prices, especially at the lower end of the scale, suggest that retailers had common price points for particular groups of garments. There was a consistent price differentiation between different garment types, with plain or Greenwich suits the cheapest, followed by sailor, then Norfolk and Rugby lounge suits.[38] The high price of lounge suits with short trousers may relate to their more detailed cut and finishing, and to the fact that they were often sold with waistcoats. They may also have been confined to the upper end of the age range and hence have needed more fabric than styles worn only by the youngest boys. This is borne out by the closeness in the starting prices between lounge suits with short and long trousers.[39] Finally, the consensus over sale prices suggests that the supply of garments in the 1890s was controlled by large-scale manufacturers and wholesalers with similar operating costs.

Clothing Prices in Terms of Family Budgets

If we examine the garment prices from advertisements in terms of the typical incomes discussed above, we see that the modal price for young boys from 1870–81, 10s 6d, represented 26 per cent of a lower middle-class weekly income of

---

[34]   Three catalogues for Fred Watts & Co. of Tottenham Court Road were registered as separate pages in 1895–97, but are here counted as three documents.

[35]   1s 6d from Crisp & Co., 67 Seven Sisters Road, London 1896 (JJ Window Bills VII); 1s 11d from Charles How, 1 Wimbledon Broadway, 1897 (JJ MC 1/63).

[36]   For instance, Baker & Co. offered three versions of the 'sultan' suit in 1887, at prices starting from 2s 11d, 6s 11d, or 9s 11d; *ABC Guide to London*, 1887 (JJ MC 3/2).

[37]   The relationship between size and age-ranges for particular styles and conceptions of masculinity will be examined in Chapter 6.

[38]   This discrepancy explains the anomalous pricing between the Marychurch & Blackler documents of 1899 and 1900; the 3s 11d suit from 1899 is a 'blouse' set for a young boy, and the 8s 6d garment is a Norfolk suit for an older boy.

[39]   7s 11d as opposed to 6s 11d in Watts 1895 and Inge 1894.

38s 6d (Table 4.4).[40] An older boys' suit at 14s 6d represented 37 per cent of such an income, or six weeks of the 2s 6d middle-class clothing budget given by Mackenzie.[41] Between 1881 and 1890 the drop in prices for young boys' suits brought them down to 7 per cent of the same weekly income, or just over one week's 2s 6d clothing budget. The price drop for older boys' suits to 8s 11d brought them down to 23 per cent of the total weekly income, or three and a half weeks' clothing budget. Suits for working boys at 3s 11d would represent 13 per cent of an artisan's weekly income of 30s, or just over one week of Mackenzie's estimated 3s 3d clothing budget.

Table 4.4   Wages and garment costs compared, 1870–1900

	1860–70 Mackenzie /Baxter	1870 Clothing costs	1890s Booth/ Rowntree/ Layard	1890 Clothing costs
Labourer wage low	13s		15s	
Labourer wage high	20s		22s 6d	
Suit cost low				2s 6d
Suit cost high				7s 6d
Artisan wage low	20s		25s	
Artisan wage high	28s		30s	
Clerical wage low	28s		50s	
Clerical wage high	38s		57s 6d	
Suit cost low		10s 6d		3s
Suit cost high		21s		25s

Sources: R.D. Baxter, *National Income: The United Kingdom* (London, 1868); C. Booth (ed.), *Life and Labour of the People in London, Series I: Poverty, Series II, Industry* (London, 1892–97); G.S Layard, 'How to Live on £150 a Year', *Cornhill Magazine*, May 1901; Miss Mackenzie, cited in W.H. Fraser, *The Coming of the Mass Market, 1850–1914* (Basingstoke, 1981); B.S. Rowntree, *Poverty, A Study of Town Life* (London, 1901).

In the 1890s, there were no suits sold specifically for working-class boys, but the three retailers whose advertisements targeted a working-class clientele (Jackson, Universal and Marychurch) offered young boys' suits from 2s 6d. This 2s 6d suit represented 14 per cent of a labourer's weekly wage of 18s, or two weeks of the family clothing budget of 1s to 1s 6d given by Rowntree and Booth. For an artisan

---

[40]   Data from Baxter, *National Income*, p. 47.

[41]   Fraser, *Coming of the Mass Market*, p. 58.

Figure 4.1   Part of a coloured flyer for Baker & Co., 1883 [Evanion 5192].

with wages of 25s (Rowntree) or 30s (Booth), the 2s 6d suit represented between 8 per cent and 10 per cent of a week's earnings, and for middle-class clerks it was 5 per cent of a 50s wage. Long suits for older boys, at 6s 11d, represented 14 per cent of a 50s middle-class wage, and 28 per cent of an artisan's 25s.

It is important not to overstate the decline in clothing costs, particularly when the sums involved (2s 6d=12.5p) seem so trifling to modern eyes. Fraser stated that the family clothing budget was typically 6 per cent to 8 per cent of annual income across this period but it is not clear whether this is based on low or high income levels.[42] Rowntree gave 5d per week as the minimum needed to clothe a child; this works out at less than 3 per cent of a family income of 17s 6d.[43] The cheapest 2s 6d suit for a small boy would represent six weeks of this notional clothing allowance, or 14 per cent of the family's income for a single week. This is not a negligible cost.

These findings could be criticised on the grounds that the information on retailers before 1880 is very patchy and that the surviving documents are mainly from an elite who could afford to publish illustrated catalogues. This may be the case for Lynes, whose catalogues are far from mere functional selling tools. Yet it is worth noting the downwards trend in Lynes' prices for young boys' suits over the period 1870–76, from 12s 6d to 8s 6d. After 1881, the documents show a gap between the consensus price for young boys (2s 6d–2s 11d) and the higher price asked by the Army and Navy Stores (9s).

The size of the gap between prices suggests that these establishments were targeting different sets of consumers. The Army and Navy Stores at this time was a co-operative whose membership was limited to serving military and naval officers, who would be solidly middle-class. This suggests that lower-priced retailers were targeting families with lower middle-class or even artisan income levels. This is borne out by the advertisements for working men's clothes in documents by Jackson, The Universal Clothing Co. and Marychurch & Blackler in the 1890s.

By 1894 the starting price for a young boy's suit from the Army and Navy Stores had dropped sharply to 5s, which was a pricing point shared by other retailers including Harrods. This may represent a change in the quality of the goods stocked, or a change in sales policy to respond to increased competition. Large retailers may have priced particular garments as 'loss leaders', offset by increased prices on other items. This practice is suggested by the very wide range of prices in the Army and Navy 1894 catalogue: from 5s to 21s 6d for the smallest size of sailor suit, depending on fabric.[44] It may be significant in this connection that the highest starting prices in the 1890s were charged by smaller firms, Logan of Leamington Spa and Needham of Brighton.

---

[42]   Ibid., p. 38. See also Godley, 'The Development of the UK Clothing Industry'.

[43]   Fraser, *Coming of the Mass Market*, p. 59.

[44]   Army and Navy Stores catalogue (1894), House of Fraser Collection HF6/22/9, p. 1064, Scottish Business Archive, University of Glasgow Archives.

The high prices of the elite traders are all the more noticeable when set against the decline of clothing costs in both real and absolute terms between 1870 and 1900. The sharp step downward is particularly noticeable in young boy's suits after 1881. This may have been linked to manufacturers' development of mass-production methods for boys' suits, as seen in the BT registers. By 1900 the cheapest advertised suit cost 2s 6d. This price drop is even more striking when we consider that in 1850 the cheapest working suit for boys advertised by E. Moses & Son had cost 3s 6d, a third of a labourers' weekly wage of about 10s.[45] By 1900, labourer's wages had risen to about 18s, and a third of this, 6s, would buy one of the cheapest suits from Harrods, or two from Baker & Co. Without denying the real insufficiency of some working-class incomes at this time, it is clear from these figures that clothing was becoming relatively more affordable for all but the poorest. The fall in clothing prices would allow consumers to increase the quantity or the quality of their purchases. With standard styles cheaply available, and retailers competing on price, there was less need for special 'working-class' garments.

Alternative Sources of Clothing

Credit Clubs

There were of course many families in which any purchase requiring a lump sum of cash, however small, remained problematic. Many households had a low overall income that required weekly budgets calculated in fractions of pence. In other households, the income was sufficient but inequitably distributed, with the personal spending by the male breadwinner leaving an inadequate amount for the wife and children. This category included not only the working-class households of Bethnal Green described by Ellen Ross,[46] but middle-class suburban families such as that of V.S. Pritchett.[47] In these situations families would look for ways to facilitate clothing acquisition either by buying on credit, by buying second-hand, or by making at home. Market traders are another possible source of clothing, but their activities are hard to evaluate from existing sources.

---

[45]   Eric Hobsbawm, *Labouring Men: Studies in the History of Labour* (London, 1964) , p. 81, based on data from Leeds, 1838; David Green, *From Artisans to Pauper: Economic Change and Poverty in London, 1790–1870* (Aldershot, 1995), p. 142, based on data from St George-in-the-East, London in 1845.

[46]   Ellen Ross: 'Survival Networks: Women's Neighbourhood Sharing in London Before World War I', *History Workshop Journal*, 15 (1983): 4–28; *eadem, Love and Toil.*

[47]   Mr Pritchett bought for his office 'many articles of silver and china, far superior to those we had in our house', while Mrs Pritchett 'had a hard time making both ends meet'. V.S. Pritchett, *A Cab at the Door* (Harmondsworth, 1974; 1980 reprint), pp. 90 and 126.

Credit clubs were not strictly speaking a source of clothing, but a source of credit that facilitated clothing purchases. There were commercial versions operated by 'check trading' companies which sold credit notes entitling the holder to buy a suit from a number of participating retailers.[48] Sean O'Connell and Chris Reid have shown how they facilitated working-class consumption before 1914. One of the largest, the Provident Clothing and Supply Co. Ltd, had 300 agents in 1890, and 3,000 by 1908.[49] Their attraction may have rested as much on their convenience as on their value for money, as Maud Pember Reeves observed in 1913: 'So much a week regularly paid has a great attraction for them. If the club will, in addition to small regular payments, send someone to call for the amount, the transaction leaves nothing to be desired.'[50] The system required payments by both consumers and retailers to cover the cost of credit and of administration by the check company, leading the Board of Trade to denounce the 'wickedness of check trading' in the 1940s.[51]

Savings clubs tied to specific retailers offered less flexibility, but had fewer administrative costs, and may have been better value in some cases. For example the clothier L. Falle of Leeds ran a savings scheme offering a man's suit worth 21s for a down payment of 7s and six 1s vouchers.[52] There were also independent clothing 'clubs', which have been seen as an important factor in improving women's access to credit and their ability to purchase goods including clothing.[53] A Women's Co-operative Guild survey in 1901 stated: 'practically every poor person we spoke to, bought boots, drapery and furniture through these clubs.'[54] It is likely that these schemes were used primarily for expensive adult clothing, but it is possible that they were also used to clothe boys.

Another way of defraying the cost of major purchases of clothing was through membership in a Co-Operative Store, which paid a dividend based on the customer's spending in the previous quarter. In 1896, the *Co-Operative News* instituted a discussion of good uses for the 'divi' and several of the published responses mentioned clothing: 'I have known the dividend come as a godsend to some poor anxious mother waiting to provide for her little ones some very necessary clothing, which otherwise she might have gone into debt for.'[55] Co-operative stores were supplied by the central Co-Operative Wholesale Society, benefiting from its ability to manufacture and purchase in bulk. This should have

---

[48]   Johnson, *Saving and Spending*, p. 152.

[49]   Sean O'Connell and Chris Reid, 'Working-class Consumer Credit in the UK, 1925–60: The Role of the Check Trader', *Economic History Review*, 58/2 (2005), p. 383.

[50]   Maud Pember Reeves, *Round About a Pound a Week* (London: 1913), p. 63, cited in Johnson, *Saving and Spending*, p. 149.

[51]   Cited in O'Connell and Reid, 'Working-class Consumer Credit', p. 397.

[52]   Copy 1 BC 972/17534 (1899).

[53]   Treble, *Urban Poverty*, pp. 135 and 182.

[54]   Cited in Johnson, *Saving and Spending*, p. 152.

[55]   Mrs Hindle of Bury, in *Co-Operative News*, 2 April 1898.

led to lower prices for goods including clothing, but this is hard to quantify as price lists were not found in the Co-Operative archives.[56] One surviving document from 1902 gave indicative prices of 3s 6d for a boy's sailor suit, 10s 6d for a middling boy's suit, and 18s for a youth's.[57] These prices were lower than those given by other retailers in 1900, and the rebate from the dividend would make them lower still to member households.[58] Vivienne Richmond has noted that some independent traders adopted the term 'co-operative' for their clothing clubs, suggesting that the Co-Operative stores were seen as a benchmark for good value.[59]

There were also charitable or semi-charitable clothing schemes, some of which added value through donations from local philanthropists. One London parish clothing club cited by Johnson added 1d to every 1s saved in this way.[60] Clothing clubs making bulk purchases on behalf of members were offered discounts from retailers, including the Brixton Bon Marché department store.[61] However, some charitable clubs had regulations restricting the type of goods that could be ordered, which limited their usefulness.[62] Concern over the standard of pupils' clothing led some schools to run clothing or boot clubs for pupils and their families.[63] Schools also held sales of garments made in needlework classes, though this was prompted as much by the need to cover costs as by charitable concerns: 'It has long been the custom in voluntary and Board schools to sell the garments made by the scholars at a little over the first cost of the materials.'[64] These sales were restricted to the items on the syllabus, principally underwear, but savings on these items might allow for greater expenditure on other purchases. Even so, in poorer areas such sales were not successful, 'the parents being too poor to purchase'.[65]

Second-hand Clothes

Schools and church groups were also involved in the sale of second-hand clothing through the jumble sales which were a new development in the 1880s. These served the dual purposes of making clothing available at low cost and raising funds for the organisers. Goods for jumble sales were often donated by middle-

---

[56]   Visited in 2000 when it was at the Co-Operative College, Stanford Hall, Loughborough; it has since been moved to Manchester.

[57]   *Manchester and Salford Co-Operative Herald*, October 1902, p. 168.

[58]   Johnson, *Saving and Spending*, pp. 126–43.

[59]   Tina Vivienne Richmond, '"No Finery": the Dress of the poor in Nineteenth-Century England' (unpublished PhD thesis, University of London, 2004), p. 199.

[60]   Johnson, *Saving and Spending*, p. 151.

[61]   Richmond, 'No Finery', p. 197.

[62]   Ibid., p. 188.

[63]   Ibid., p. 189.

[64]   Ellen Rosevear, *A Text-Book of Needlework, Knitting and Cutting-Out with Methods of Teaching* (London: 1893), pp. 2–3.

[65]   Ibid.

class well-wishers, and were supposedly of better quality than those available new to working-class consumers.[66] Garments from middle-class families were also solicited by charities such as the CEWSS. Donated garments not only saved money for the charity, but created a physical bond between donor and recipient.[67] Clothing donation through personal patronage networks was also practised. Rowntree saw donated middle-class clothing as better than new, both in price and in quality: 'the family get a good many old clothes given to them, which are carefully repaired, and then probably wear longer than cheap new ones would do'.[68] However, donated clothing might also act as a visual marker of the subordinate social and financial status of the recipients. A gold velvet suit passed on from a richer family caused Edward Brown (b. 1880) 'a good deal of mortification ... it stood out against the drab cloth suits of my associates in quite a startling way'.[69]

While charitable redistribution of clothing was seen by middle-class commentators as a social good, the commercial resale of clothing was generally discussed as in pejorative terms. Margaret Synge wrote in 1913 that 'too many garments are bought from second-hand clothing shops, which have increased rapidly during the last few years'.[70] Pawning clothes with no intention of redeeming them was a strategy practised by families in economic crisis, like that of Jack Lanigan (born in Salford in 1890): 'Brother and I did have a new suit for father's funeral (purchased on tick), blue serge, short trousers, and a stiff peak cap ... We never saw those suits again ... into the pawnshop they both went.'[71] However, while up to 50 per cent of all items pledged were clothing the rate of non-redemption was low at about 5 per cent, so sales from pawn may not have been a major source.[72]

There were also second-hand dealers who were not pawnbrokers, who may have been particularly common in urban areas with large working-class populations. When Jack Lanigan was job-hunting in 1900 his mother bought him an outfit from 'a very well known second-hand clothes shop in Salford, Hertzog by name' for a total cost of 4s 6d including shoes and socks.[73] For more respectable families, buying (or selling) second-hand clothing was a practice not admitted to in memoirs. Middle-class women's magazines acted as a forum for the sale or exchange of clothing, but this was usually cloaked by the use of pseudonyms

---

[66]   Richmond, 'No Finery', pp. 222–47.

[67]   *Our Waifs and Strays*, March 1887, p. 2.

[68]   Budget No. 1 in Rowntree, *Poverty*, p. 311.

[69]   Edward Brown (b. 1880), in John Burnett, *Destiny Obscure: Autobiographies of Childhood, Education and Family from the 1820s to the 1920s* (London, 1982), p. 152.

[70]   Margaret Synge, *Simple Garments for Children (from 4 to 14)* (London: 1913), p. xiii.

[71]   Jack Lanigan in Burnett, *Destiny Obscure*, p. 87.

[72]   Johnson, *Saving and Spending*, pp. 168 and 173.

[73]   Lanigan in Burnett, *Destiny Obscure*, p. 90.

or box numbers.[74] Discretion was key to the practice of second-hand dealers in respectable suburbs, such as Mrs Howe Dickens of Holland Park, whose publicity card stated: 'she has no shop, therefore no goods are exposed ... Goods are sent to the Colonies direct.'[75]

Home Sewing

If second-hand clothing purchase was under-reported because of its negative connotations, home clothing production may have been over-reported due to its positive associations. Autobiographers often mentioned home sewing as an indication of the devotion and industriousness of the mother of a poor family: 'everything depended on the skill and character of the mother. Nothing ready-made could be purchased, not even a shirt.'[76] Will Crooks, the paradigmatic working-class boy made good, stated that 'the children could not remember the time when she [the mother] did not make all their clothes'.[77] A set of articles on the cost of living published in *The Cornhill Magazine* in 1901 assumed that home sewing was essential on economic grounds. Discussing working-class families with a total income of 30s a week, Herbert Morrison stated: 'Some children's clothes are bought at the slop-shop, but more are made at home from father's and mother's cast-offs ... some women are very neat with joins and patches, while others cobble miserably, or not at all.'[78] Even in a lower middle-class family with an income of £150 a year, G.S. Layard felt that: 'the wife must of course be her own and her children's dressmaker .. This applies more particularly to the children's clothing ... The father's discarded waistcoats and trousers will be metamorphosed by her deft fingers into second-best suits for the boys.'[79]

On closer examination these assertions reveal some unanswered questions. The first is how women filled the gap between the limited processes taught in the Board School needlework syllabus and the skills needed to make – or remake – outer garments. In spite of claims that needlework classes would empower working-class mothers to make and mend for their families, the approved syllabus dealt only with underwear, blouses and baby items made from light cotton.[80] Cutting down or refurbishing men's clothing made from heavy cotton or wool required different stitches (preferably a sewing machine) and an understanding of male garment shaping. These were skills that were hard for women to acquire unless they worked

---

[74] Margaret Beetham, *A Magazine of her Own? Domesticity and Desire in the Woman's Magazine, 1800–1914* (London, 1996), p. 149.

[75] Copy 1 BC 971/17327 (1900).

[76] Alfred Ireson (b. 1856), in Burnett, *Destiny Obscure*, p. 72.

[77] George Haw, *From Workhouse to Westminster: The Life Story of Will Crooks, MP* (London, 1909), p. 6.

[78] Morrison, 'How to live on 30s a week', p. 159.

[79] Layard, 'How to Live on £150 a Year', p. 163.

[80] See 'Dressmakers as Providers of Boys' Clothes' in Chapter 2.

in the garment industry. The gap between mothers' intentions and their skills is highlighted by autobiographical accounts of home sewing projects. Laura Ugolini cites several instances where boys were embarrassed by having to wear home-made garments whose status was obvious to all observers. The embarrassment seems to have been twofold: firstly at having clothes that were less well made than their peers', and secondly at the implication that the family was too poor to buy new.[81] V.S. Pritchett describes several instances of his mother's over-ambitious home sewing, as when she cut down her husband's suit trousers for her sons.[82] On another occasion she sent her sons to visit relatives wearing trousers made from a chair cover.[83] Mrs Pritchett's home sewing seems to have been conducted not as self-effacing thrift but as a public campaign to shame her husband into providing adequate housekeeping expenses. It drew on both the official view of home sewing as a sign of a conscientious mother, and the understanding that home-made clothes were a source of social embarrassment and shame, to be avoided at all costs.

Conclusions

The analysis of clothing costs in terms of typical wages has shown that boys' clothing became much cheaper in real terms between 1870 and 1900. The documents used were biased towards the upper end of the market, and it is likely that even lower prices were available from undocumented sources such as market stalls. This fall in price gave poorer families access to a wider choice of garments from a wider range of retailers. By 1900, the sharp distinction between clothes for working boys, and clothes for young gentlemen seen in 1850s catalogues had been elided. Retailers sold low-priced and high-priced garments from the same catalogue page, and popular styles such as sailor suits were offered in multiple versions with fine price gradations.

The fall in prices lessened the need for home production of clothing, but may have increased supply to the second-hand market, by encouraging prosperous consumers to replace and sell on partially worn garments. Or it may have removed the need for second-hand purchase, as Phillipe Perrot has seen in France at this time.[84] It is difficult to gain an objective view of the extent of second-hand clothing purchasing, as it was strongly associated with poverty and may have been understated in sources such as autobiographies. Conversely, the extent of home

---

[81]   Several examples and a cartoon on this theme are reproduced in Ugolini, *Men and Menswear*, pp. 208–11 and 217.

[82]   Pritchett, *A Cab at the Door*, pp. 90–91.

[83]   Ibid., p. 29.

[84]   Phillipe Perrot, *Fashioning the Bourgeoisie: A History of Clothing in the Nineteenth Century* (Princeton, 1994), pp. 70–71.

sewing may have been overstated by autobiographers as it reflected well on 'the skill and character of the mother.'[85]

The *Cornhill Magazine* articles, while claiming to present an objective picture of family budgets, also use emotive terms that reveal the writers' preconceptions. Morrison emphasises the desirability of home sewing by contrasting it with purchase from 'slop-shops', a pejorative term referring to firms that produced shoddy goods by exploitative means.[86] Layard compared home production for children with the purchase of the husband's suits from a 'tailor', a term implying bespoke production.[87] These two commentators agreed in seeing a gulf between high-priced and high-quality bespoke and low-priced and low-quality ready-to-wear that could only be bridged by home sewing. This polarisation reflects a view of the clothing industry based on a model from the 1850s, but belied by the variety and volume of ready-to-wear garments offered in shop catalogues in 1899. Accounts from Pritchett and other autobiographers make it clear that by this date purchased clothing was the norm, and home-made clothing an inadequate substitute that acted as a visible marker of relative poverty.[88]

Visual sources such as photographs of school groups and Barnardo's entrants offer another way of evaluating consumption practices in terms of the types of garments chosen, and their suitability to both the wearer and the occasion. In some cases we can infer the origins of the garments from their appearance: for example, a boy photographed in 1896 wearing clothes that are not only shabby and badly fitting but visibly mismatched, may be wearing second-hand garments.[89] The Barnardo's entry images give evidence of clothing practices in a large sample of the population. They can be analysed to show how the styles promoted by manufacturers and retailers were received by consumers. They also allow us to evaluate how changes in the cost of clothing affected consumption: did poor families buy the cheapest garments, and use the money thus saved on other goods? Or did lower prices lead to more frequent or more specialised purchases? How did the availability of the same style at a range of prices affect consumer choice? These questions will be examined in the next chapter.

---

[85]   Alfred Ireson (b. 1856), in Burnett, *Destiny Obscure*, p. 72.

[86]   Elizabeth Wilson and Lou Taylor, *Through the Looking Glass: A History of Dress from 1860 to the Present Day* (London, 1989), p. 33.

[87]   Layard, 'How to Live on £150 a Year', p. 164.

[88]   See also an anecdote from Ernest Barker (1887), cited in Ugolini, *Men and Menswear*, p. 50.

[89]   The jacket is of a type normally worn as part of a Highland kilt ensemble; Barnardo 18800 (1896).

Chapter 5
Consuming Boys' Clothes

In 1910, the schoolboys of Finsbury Park presented a remarkably consistent appearance, as recollected by C.H. Rolph:

> At this period the boys' outfitters' shops, Isaac Walton, John Baker, Man and Boy, etc., sold little suits which, among those whose parents could afford them, amounted to a uniform and probably represented the last dying kick from the days when all children were got up as diminutive adults. A tweed or serge Norfolk jacket buttoning right up to the throat, surmounted by a huge white Eton collar (celluloid for week-days, starched linen for Sundays) … The boys who didn't have Norfolk jackets usually had coloured blouses, plus jerseys in the winter. Such boys, generally speaking, wore shorts, as distinct from the button-up knee breeches that went with the Norfolk jacket.[1]

Rolph's account establishes the purchase of boys clothing as a normative practice, involving specific retailers and specific goods. Differences in the material of a collar or the construction of a pair of short trousers reflected distinctions of time, place, and family income within the overall consistency. Yet evidence for these distinctions is hard to find in nineteenth-century texts, which tend to present clothing choices in morally loaded terms. For example, descriptions of East End 'monkey parades' placed working-class youths as ethnographic 'others' and distanced them from middle-class readers.[2]

As the manufacturers' and retailers' documents discussed in Chapter 3 showed, the appearance of clothing was very important to its commercial success. We would expect the multiple options offered by retailers to encourage consumers to make fine distinctions between styles. Establishing the consumption rates of different garment types will allow us to evaluate the effects of manufacturers' and retailers' investment in producing and promoting varied ranges of garments. Looking at the diffusion of novel styles will clarify whether lower prices led to homogenisation or differentiation of clothing practices. It will also clarify the importance of fashion in shaping the clothing practice of a broad sample of boys.

Unmediated evidence of clothing practice might be sought in material sources such as surviving garments; but an extensive survey of museum collections showed that these were strongly biased in age and class terms, with a predominance of

---

[1]   C.H. Rolph, *London Particulars* (Oxford, 1980), pp. 62–3.

[2]   Several accounts of these are given in Christopher Breward, *The Hidden Consumer: Masculinities, Fashion and City Life, 1860–1914* (Manchester, 1999), pp. 206–15.

toddlers' tunics from elite families.[3] Another likely source for clothing practice was photographs from the Board Schools which were a key site for defining childrearing practices.[4] However, it proved difficult to find well-documented school group photographs, and those that were identified were difficult to read. Family portrait photographs were easier to read, but surviving examples with precise documentation were scarce, and from a narrow range of elite families.[5] By contrast, the Barnardo's entry photographs were copious in number, carefully documented and (as demonstrated in Chapter 1) valid as historical evidence.

Taken together, these sets of photographs offered a large sample of boys wearing the standard styles for which prices are known, and allow us to examine the ways in which consumers discriminated between different goods of equivalent price. In the first part of this chapter each source will be analysed separately in order to consider the biases inherent in the data, before they are compared to give general conclusions about consumption practices. In the second section the data on consumption derived from all the photographs will then be compared with the advertising data discussed in Chapter 3. This will allow us to evaluate how consumers reacted to retailers' promotion of particular styles. We would expect cost to be one of the main factors affecting consumption decisions, and changes in the pricing differentials between styles will also be considered.

As already established, one of the commonest styles was the sailor suit, sold in different versions for different prices. The third section of the chapter will present a detailed case study of the consumption of different types of sailor suits. This will clarify to what extent consumer choices were affected by price, and to what extent they were influenced by perceptions of value. In the final section, autobiographies will be used to illuminate the ways in which boys themselves understood clothing consumption. This will prepare the way for the discussion in Chapters 6 and 7 of the ways in which particular clothing styles were used to construct social identities.

Evidence for Consumption Practice: Photographs

A search of archives, publications, and online collections revealed 80 dated portrait photographs of non-royal boys and a further 11 images of royal princes from the period 1870–1900.[6] This sample included twelve sets of siblings and eight sets showing a single sitter over a number of years (some of these sets overlapped). The ways in which these sets presented age-related codes of masculinity will be discussed in detail in Chapter 6. As Table 5.1 shows, there were 24 photographs

---

[3]   See Appendix 1.

[4]   Anna Davin, *Growing Up Poor: Home, School and Street in London, 1870–1914* (London, 1996).

[5]   See Appendix 1.

[6]   See Appendix 1 for details. Royal children were excluded as not necessarily typical of general practice.

from the 1870s, 19 from the 1880s, and 37 from the 1890s. The drop in numbers for the 1880s reflects the vagaries of preservation for this material. While the total number of images is small, it is possible to see some trends in garment consumption.

Table 5.1   Documented portrait photographs of boys, 1870–1900

Source	Name	Date	Birth	Age	Notes
WOR 62/513	Ernest	1870	1868	2	white dress braided
WOR 62/512	Lionel	1870	1868	2	white dress braided
WIN 3213	Alex Baring	1871	1869	2	white dress
WIN 3214	Francis Baring	1871	1866	5	sailor long white top
WIN 3214	Fred Baring	1871	1867	4	sailor long white top
NPG Ax46295	M.J. Mostyn	1872	1870	2	white dress
WOR 62/2026	H. Foster	1873	1868	5	short tunic velvet
DPA 2043/5	E.T.W. Patterson	1873	1869	4	dress
DPA 2043/5	T.J. Patterson	1873	1871	2	dress
NPG Ax128329	Hollyer	1874	1870	4	sailor braid
WOR 62/521	A. Kettlewell	1874	1864	10	sailor suit
Lambert 155	H. Aldis	1875	1870	5	double-breasted short
NPG Ax128307	Hollyer	1875	1870	5	sailor bound
NPG Ax128346	Hollyer	1875	1870	5	double-breasted short
NPG Ax128353	Hollyer	1875	1870	5	sailor bound
DPA 2043/3	E.T.W. Patterson	1875	1869	6	short open jacket
DPA 2043/4	T.J. Patterson	1875	1871	4	short suit
WOR 62/530	?	1877	1867	10	sailor long
DPA 1427/87	D.M. Watson	1877	1874	3	sailor short
DPA 0613/23	A.E. Kent	1878	1876	2	dress
NPG Ax128300	Mason	1879	1877	2	white dress
NPG x13860	Lytton Strachey	1879	1874	5	tunic + coat
NPG x13861	Lytton Strachey	1879	1874	5	tunic velvet revers kilt skirt
NPG x13893	Lytton Strachey	1879	1874	5	tunic + coat hobbyhorse

DPA 1857/13a	H.E. Blackaby	1880	1878	2	dress
DPA 2005/6	A.W. Turner	1881	1879	2	dark dress
WOR 67/1067	A. Evans	1882	1878	4	tunic, brown velvet
WOR 67/1067	C. Evans	1882	1878	4	tunic, brown velvet
VAMC 82.27-1995	J. Laczkovic	1883	1875	8	kilt
NPG Ax128360	McDonald	c.1883	1873	c.10	jersey shorts seaside
DPA 1068/10	E. Henriques	1883	1879	4	sailor short
DPA 2005/13	G.M. Turner	1883	1881	2	dress
DPA 1985/10	L. Hilton	1884	1882	2	dress
DPA 1953/67	h. Birchall	1885	1880	5	sailor short
WOR 62/569	Jackie	1885	1883	2	tunic, braided
DPA 2005/11	F.E. Turner	1885	1870	15	long suit
DPA 1766/25	H.H. Venables	1885	1882	3	kilt tunic
NPG x126443	H. Granville Barker	c.1885	1877	c.8	sailor long white top
DPA 1858/4	C. Meredith	1886	1884	2	dress
Leicester 11	H.O. Wilshere	1886	1884	2	sailor short white top
DPA 1263/1	H. Salisbury	1887	1883	4	kilt sailor
DPA 1263/1	L. Salisbury	1887	1885	2	dress
DPA 2005/4	A.W. Turner	1889	1879	10	Rugby short
WOR 61/541/5	?	1890	1886	4	kilt sailor
DPA 1264/8	R.D. Horner	1890	1875	15	Rugby short
DPA 1858/5	C. Meredith	1890	1884	6	short sailor
NPG x21467	L. Myers	1890	1881	9	sailor top dark
DPA 1823/5	M. Witte	1890	1888	2	dress
WOR 61/541/6	?	1891	1886	5	sailor short
NPG Ax68413	Myers b	c.1891	1886	c.5	tunic + coat
NPG Ax68416	Myers b	c.1891	1886	c.5	tunic + coat
DPA 884/7	Billie	1892	1889	3	tunic
WOR 62/1470	W. Smith	1892	1888	4	sailor short
DPA 1823/6	M. Witte	1892	1888	4	kilt sailor
Wilshere 8	H.O. Wilshere	1893	1884	9	short sailor suit tweed
WOR 62/1803	A. Norris	1894	1884	10	sailor short

WOR 62/1803	H.W. Norris	1894	1886	6	sailor short
DPA 1823/7	M. Witte	1894	1888	6	sailor short
NPG x13135	Duncan Grant	1895	1885	10	Eton longs
DPA 1276/2	E. Jones	1895	1885	10	Norfolk short
DPA 1276/2	T. Jones	1895	1886	9	Norfolk short
NPG x3690	Mackail	1895	1892	3	tunic w Burne Jones
BEA 44425	Manners family	1895			sailor
BEA 44425	Manners family	1895			Norfolk
DPA 1305/2	H. May	1895	1886	9	Rugby short
DPA 1305/2	R. May	1895	1891	4	sailor short
WOR P3231	Walker, ?	1895	1888	7	hussar short
Wilshere 12	H.O. Wilshere	1895	1884	11	long? 3pce
Wilshere 12	R.G. Wilshere	1895	1893	2	kilt sailor, white
NPG Ax68329	Myers b	c.1895	1886	c.9	Fauntleroy w lace
DPA 0447/10	Arthur	1896	1886	10	Norfolk short
DPA 1823/8	M. Witte	1896	1888	8	Rugby short
WOR 62/1798	E.L. Sturdee	1897	1891	6	sailor tweed
WOR P6886	E. Petty	1898	1893	5	short blouse
Wilshere 22	H.R. Pochin	1899	1893		short blouse + bow
Wilshere 22	R.E. Pochin	1899	1892		short blouse + bow
DPA 2083/30	O. Entwistle	1900	1896	4	sailor short
BEA 44428	Manners family	1900			suit long 3pce
BEA 44428	Manners family	1900			suit long 3pce
DPA 1976/7	J. Monaghan	1900	1898	2	tunic short

Sources: BEA – North of England Open Air Museum, Beamish; DPA – Documentary Photography Archive, Manchester; Lambert – M. Lambert, *Fashion in Photographs 1860–1880* (London, 1991); LMA – London Metropolitan Archives; NPG – National Portrait Gallery, London; VAMC – V&A Museum of Childhood; Wilshere – J. Wilshere, *Leicester Portrait Photographers before 1900* (Leicester, 1988); WIN – Winchester City Museum; WOR – Worthing Museum.

The photographs were analysed using the same categories as was used for the manufacturers' and retailers' documents in Chapters 2 and 3. As most of the manufacturers' designs presented only a jacket, these categories are based on jacket styles. The single commonest garment in family portraits was the sailor top: fourteen were worn with short trousers, four with long trousers and five with a skirt or indeterminate lower garment. Tracking these over time showed that the proportion of sailor tops in portraits fell from 1870 to 1880 then rose in the 1890s. However, as the numbers of images are small the findings may not be statistically significant.

A more representative sample of images was obtained from twenty-five school group photographs.[7] These showed a wider range of children, including some whose families might not have been able to afford individual portraits.[8] Unfortunately, 182 of the 541 individuals in these groups were illegible, either because the boy's body was obscured or because the photograph was fuzzy. For most boys only the neck and shoulders were visible; fortunately this was enough to distinguish some of the main jacket types, and the materials of which they were made (dark wool, textured corduroy or crumpled cotton).

The largest category of recognisable garments in school photographs was the lounge suit with 143 examples (40 per cent of 359 visible) (Table 5.2). Of styles designed for boys, the commonest was the sailor suit, seen in 65 examples (18 per cent of visible). Norfolk and 'stripe' suits were less common in these photographs, with 40 and 31 examples respectively. The school photographs covered a shorter timespan than the portraits, 1888–1900. There was also a variable rate of legibility, with the images from the late 1890s being most legible. Nevertheless, there were some shifts in the predominance of particular styles over time, with sailor suits most common in the early 1890s, and lounge jackets most common in the late 1890s.

---

[7]   For details of the archive search, see Appendix 1.

[8]   The cost of studio portraits prevented many families from acquiring photographs. This encouraged some photographers to set up an itinerant service photographing families or groups outside their houses. These have unfortunately not been systematically collected or published. Rebecca Preston of Kingston University presented a paper on 'The Face of Home in British Domestic "Real Photo" Postcards, 1902–1918' at the Design History Society Conference, September 2007.

Table 5.2   Clothes in school photographs, 1888–1900

Archive	Date	Tunic	Blouse	Sailor	Pleats	Norfolk	Lounge	Other	Total Boys	Unclear
Owslebury School				3				2	15	10
Owslebury School					1			3	11	7
Cotherstone	1888			2		3			18	13
Hants & IoW 68 Basingstoke	1889			1		5	5		11	
BEA 44364 Kibblesworth	1890			7			9		26	10
BEA 44365 Kibblesworth	1890			5					12	7
BEA 43827 Scargill	1892			4	1	1			15	9
BEA 44335 West Pelton	1894			1		1			3	1
LMA A4457 Snowsfields	1894		1	4	6	2	19	6	44	6
LMA A7393 Elizabeth St	1894			7	7	1	2	7	42	18
LMA 80/1919 Southfields	1895					1	32		33	
LMA A7394 Elizabeth St	1896			2	3	4	5	4	28	10
LMA A7395 Elizabeth St	1896			2	5	2	11	5	36	11
LMA A7396 Elizabeth St	1896			2	1	2	19	1	25	0
Alresford no 94 Cheriton	1896			6		1			16	9
Alresford no 102 Ovington	1897			2					6	4
LMA N4287 Holden St Infants	1897		12	4					16	
LMA A4452 Chaucer St	1898		1	2		2	22	8	48	13
Cotherstone II	1898	2	1	9		1	1		15	1
Cotherstone III	1898		1	2		5	7		20	5
LMA A4464 Orange St	1899			7	1		4	3	19	4
Hants & IoW 66 Meonstoke	1899		1	4					17	12
LMA A7397 Elizabeth St	1900			5	6	4	4	6	31	6
BEA 6426 Sacriston Sunday	1900					3	3		6	0
BEA 44277 Dudley	1900					2			28	26

Sources: Alresford – E. Roberts, *In and Around Alresford in Old Photographs* (Alresford, 1975); BEA – North of England Open Air Museum, Beamish; Cotherstone – Cotherstone Wesleyan Methodist School, private collection; Hants & IoW – J. Norwood, *Victorian and Edwardian Hampshire & the Isle of Wight from Old Photographs* (London, 1973); LMA – London Metropolitan Archives; Owslebury – *Owslebury, A Village School: 150 Years 1840–1990* (1990).

Barnardo's Entry Photographs

In the first section of the Barnardo's archive, dated 1875–88, 323 images of boys wearing suits with shorts or trousers were sampled (Table 5.3).[9] Of these, 73 had a jacket that was indeterminate or illegible in the photograph, and a further 4 had no jacket; this left 246 images for analysis. The commonest jacket style was the lounge, seen on 127 boys. The remaining 123 images were divided between sailor tops, 'stripe' jackets, jerseys, braided jackets, and other styles.

Table 5.3   Clothes worn by Barnardo's entrants, 1875–99

	Tunic/dress	Blouse	Sailor	'Stripe'	Norfolk	Lounge	Jersey	Other	Unclear	No jacket	Legible
Subtotals 1875–79 (79)	3	3	8	2	0	26	4	22	15	3	61
Subtotals 1880–84 (134)	0	1	9	4	1	66	5	22	28	1	105
Subtotals 1885–88 (110)	7	4	6	14	1	35	6	5	30	0	80
Subtotals 1888–89 (66)	0	0	9	13	0	28	1	2	15	0	51
Subtotals 1890–94 (797)	10	5	128	117	24	238	18	12	272	6	519
Subtotals 1895–99 (688)	20	44	146	77	89	183	14	20	180	6	502
Totals 1875–99 (1,983)	40	57	306	227	115	576	48	83	540	16	1,318
%	3%	4%	23%	17%	9%	44%	4%	6%			

In the second set of Barnardo's data, 1888–99, there were 1,551 images of individual boys, 467 of which were illegible, and 12 of which showed no jacket, leaving 1,072 to be analysed.[10] Of these, 449 showed boys in lounge jackets (42 per cent of legible images). The next commonest garment type was the sailor top (26 per cent), followed by the 'stripe' jacket (19 per cent) and the Norfolk jacket (10 per cent). Blouses and jerseys were much less common, each worn in only 3 per cent of images. This data is interesting as it shows clear preferences for

---

[9]   The complete dataset is Table 2.2 in Clare Rose, 'Boyswear and the Formation of Gender and Class Identity in urban England, 1840–1900' (unpublished PhD thesis, University of Brighton, 2006).

[10]   As many of the photographs analysed showed more than one boy, the number of images of boys is greater than the number of photographs. See Rose, 'Boyswear', Tables 4.5 and 4.6 for full datasets.

different garment types. The degree to which these preferences were age-related will be considered in Chapter 6.

Taken together, the two sets of Barnardo's data show that the garment most frequently worn by boys was the adult-style lounge jacket. This was used as part of working-class ensembles, with a collarless shirt and neckerchief, or in a middle-class suit with a matching waistcoat, a white collar and a tie. The lounge jackets used in these different ensembles probably differed in fabric and finish, but this information was not discernible in the images. There is also a possibility that some lounge jackets may have passed from middle-class to working-class owners through the second-hand market. This flexibility may account for its dominance in the data.

However, the prevalence of the lounge jacket decreased over the period, the bulk of the difference being made up by an increase in specifically boyish styles. This substitution was particularly noticeable over the period 1880–89: in 1880–84, lounge jackets formed 63 per cent of legible garments, and 'stripe' jackets 4 per cent. By 1885–89 the proportion of lounge jackets had dropped to 48 per cent, while the 'stripe' jackets increased to 21 per cent in a striking correlation.

Consumption Practice in All Photographs

The photographs of families, school groups and Barnardo's entrants provided a large sample for determining the consumption of garment types. Comparing the distribution of garment types in these three datasets will allow us to evaluate how the garments in retailers' catalogues were consumed by boys from a range of social backgrounds. The number of images in each dataset differed, as did the number of images that were legible enough to be analysed. This was a particular problem with school group photographs. The data has been expressed in percentages and arranged by five-year periods from 1875–1900 in order to facilitate comparison (Table 5.4).

In this table we see that the data from family portraits is anomalous in two ways: it is derived from a small dataset, with as few as nine examples of boys aged three to sixteen over a five-year period, and it includes a large number of young boys wearing tunics or dresses. The data from schools and from Barnardo's is more closely comparable both in terms of the size of the datasets and the results. The first period for which all three sets of data are available is 1885–89. Only 45 per cent of the images in school photographs from these dates were legible; in these, the Norfolk jacket was the most frequently visible, followed by sailor and then lounge types. Of the Barnardo's images from this period, 74 per cent were legible, and they were dominated by lounge jackets, which were over twice as common as the next most frequent, the 'stripe', and three times as common as sailor jackets. Norfolk jackets were very uncommon in the Barnardo's images at this date. In 1890–94, 55 per cent of the images from schools were legible, compared to 66 per cent of Barnardo's. The same jacket types were dominant in both: lounge, followed by sailor, 'stripe' and Norfolk, but the dominance of lounge jackets was much more marked in the Barnardo's images. In the final period, 71 per cent of the school images were legible as against 74 per cent of Barnardo's. The two datasets agreed in the ranking of the three main garment types (lounge, sailor, Norfolk). Portraits showed a narrower range of garments in each period before 1895–99.

Table 5.4   Consumption of garment types compared, 1875–1900

	Tunic	Blouse	Sailor	'Stripe'	Norfolk	Lounge	Jersey	Other	Legible	Total	Illegible
1875–79 portrait	38%		31%					31%	13	13	
1875–79 Barnardo	5%	5%	13%	3%	0%	43%	7%	36%	61	79	23%
1880–84 portrait	66%		11%				11%	12%	9	9	
1880–84 Barnardo	0%	1%	9%	4%	1%	63%	5%	21%	105	134	22%
1885–89 portrait	40%		30%	0%		20%		10%	10	10	
1885–89 school		0%	24%	4%	32%	20%		20%	25	55	55%
1885–89 Barnardo	5%	3%	12%	21%	1%	48%	5%	5%	131	176	26%
1890–94 portrait	27%		66%			7%		0%	15	15	
1890–94 school		1%	31%	15%	6%	33%	0%	14%	91	142	45%
1890–94 Barnardo	2%	1%	24%	22%	5%	45%	3%	2%	525	797	34%
1895–99 portrait	9%	14%	23%		14%	18%		22%	22	22	
1895–1900 school	1%	7%	19%	7%	11%	44%		11%	243	344	29%
1895–99 Barnardo	4%	9%	29%	15%	18%	36%	3%	4%	508	688	26%

It is evident from this analysis that there are some problems in comparing these datasets. The first is that of differential survival; the number of documented family portraits for this period was remarkably small. Secondly, the circumstances in which some photographs were taken limited their use as evidence; this was particularly noticeable with the school groups. The third problem is that of intrinsic bias; families who could afford portraits of their children would probably be wealthier than some of the families represented in school groups, and this might affect their choice of clothing styles.[11] The cost differentials between the most frequently worn styles will be examined in the next section. Finally, the school groups represent a narrower age range than the other datasets. The implications of this will be discussed further in Chapter 6.

---

[11]   Audrey Linkman, *The Victorians: Photographic Portraits* (London, 1993), pp. 130–33.

Advertising and Consumption

At first sight, the data comparing consumption and advertising patterns is remarkable for the lack of consistency and even contradiction between advertisers and consumer behaviour (Table 5.5). For instance, while the proportion of images advertising lounge jackets rose from 7 per cent to 19 per cent between 1875 and 1899, the proportion of lounge jackets in the Barnardo's images ranged from 43 per cent in 1875–79 to 63 per cent in 1880–84 and back to 36 per cent in 1895–99. We would expect there to be a high proportion of lounge jackets, a more adult style, among Barnardo's entrants, many of whom were of an age to leave school and start work. (The association of specific garments with particular age ranges will be considered in more detail in Chapter 6.) However, the fluctuation within this group suggests that there may have been other factors involved.

The case of the 'stripe' suit is more suggestive. This style first appeared in advertising images in 1880,[12] and was moderately common in retail documents up to 1890 (15 per cent of all styles) followed by a sharp decline in 1895–99, to 3 per cent. The same style first appeared in the Barnardo's entry photos in 1875, but in very small numbers.[13] In the entry photos, 'stripe' jackets were common between 1885–94, at 21 per cent of the total, and only started to decline in 1895–99. The presentation of this style in school photographs peaked in 1890–94, then declined, but was never at the same level as in Barnardo's images. The data from schools may be slanted by the difficulty in identifying the narrow strips of trimming that characterise the style in group photographs. Interestingly, although present in school photographs, 'stripe' jackets were totally absent from the sample of family portraits.

The consumption pattern for Norfolk suits was different again. These were available from retailers from 1872,[14] and formed 6 per cent of advertising images across the period 1875–89, rising to 12 per cent in 1890–99. They were first seen in the Barnardo's portraits in 1884 and in the sample of portraits only in 1895.[15] In school photographs from the late 1880s, Norfolk suits were the dominant identifiable style (32 per cent), but in school groups from the 1890s they were much less common. This discrepancy may be attributed to the small size of these samples; the data for the 1880s is derived from four photographs of three schools. Leaving aside this anomalous set of data, the picture for Norfolk suits is of a low but steady level of both advertising and consumption up to 1889. An increase in

---

[12] In a large style sheet registered by Thomas Way, Stationers' Hall Archive, Copy 1 51/396, TNA.

[13] A 'stripe' jacket was worn by Barnardo's entrant number 268, in 1875; 1157, in 1877; 1906, in 1881.

[14] Arthur Lynes, *Merriment and Modes* (London, 1872), p. 93, no. 226; John Johnson Collection (JJ), Men's Clothing (MC) 4/19.

[15] Barnardo's 4265 (1884); Documentary Photography Archive (DPA) 1276/2 (1895).

advertisements for Norfolk suits in 1890–94 was followed by an increase in the number of boys wearing them in both school and Barnardo's photographs after 1895.

Table 5.5   Prevalence of specific garment types in advertisements and in consumption data, 1875–99

	Blouse	Sailor	'Stripe'	Norfolk	Lounge	Jersey	Other	Illegible	Total visible	Total	Percentage legible
1875–79 portrait		31%					31%	0	13	13	100%
1875–79 school											
1875–79 Barnardo	5%	13%	3%	0%	43%	7%	36%	18	61	79	77%
1875–79 ads		16%	0%	7%	7%		70%	0	44	44	100%
1880–84 portrait		11%				11%		0	9	9	100%
1880–84 school											
1880–84 Barnardo	1%	9%	4%	1%	63%	5%	21%	29	105	134	78%
1880–84 ads	3%	14%	15%	6%	14%	7%	41%	0	105	105	100%
1885–89 portrait		30%			20%		10%	0	10	10	100%
1885–89 school	0%	24%	4%	32%	20%	0%	20%	30	25	55	45%
1885–89 Barnardo	3%	12%	21%	1%	48%	5%	5%	45	131	176	74%
1885–89 ads	1%	27%	14%	5%	12%	1%	39%	0	179	179	100%
1890–94 portrait		66%			7%			0	15	15	100%
1890–94 school	1%	31%	15%	6%	33%	0%	14%	51	91	142	64%
1890–94 Barnardo	1%	24%	22%	5%	45%	3%	2%	272	525	797	66%
1890–94 ads	1%	24%	9%	12%	17%	0%	38%	0	234	234	100%
1895–99 portrait	14%	23%	0%	14%	18%	0%	22%	0	22	22	100%
1895–99 school	7%	19%	7%	11%	44%	0%	11%	101	243	344	71%
1895–99 Barnardo	9%	29%	15%	18%	36%	3%	4%	180	508	688	74%
1895–99 ads	15%	19%	3%	13%	19%	1%	30%	0	617	617	100%

The data for sailor suits was more consistent across all sources. This style was also easier to identify, even in school photographs, due to its distinctive collar. Sailor suits were common in advertising documents in 1885–89 (26 per cent), declining slightly in 1890–94 and 1895–99. In school photographs, sailor suits represented 24 per cent of identifiable jackets in 1885–89, 31 per cent in 1890–94, and 19 per cent in 1895–99. In the Barnardo's photographs, sailor suits were noticeably less common than in school groups in 1885–89 (12 per cent), then increased sharply in 1890–94 (22 per cent), and again in 1895–99 (29 per cent).

In all these examples the prevalence of a particular style in consumer data lagged several years behind its prevalence in advertising images. In the case of the sailor suit there was a double delay – between advertising documents and school groups, and between school groups and Barnardo's entrants. This could be explained in terms of a Veblenian trickle-down of styles from the comfortably-off patrons of retailers with illustrated catalogues, to economically mixed families attending Board Schools, to the economically insecure whose children entered Barnardo's. It might also indicate changes in retailing practice so that the number of advertisements for a particular style was not directly related to the number of examples sold. This may have been caused by pricing differentials for particular boys' garments, with advertisements highlighting more expensive styles with a higher profit margin.

Pricing and Consumption

The analysis of retail catalogues in Chapter 4 indicated that these documents contain information on pricing differentials between styles over time. However, many retail documents (especially single-sheet flyers) only mentioned one or two styles, or did not indicate styles beyond the generic 'suits for boys and youths'. Few retailers were represented over the whole period, with the exception of Baker & Co. of London.[16] It would be possible to track changes in pricing through Baker's documents, but doing so would privilege the pricing practice of one retailer. I have therefore based my analysis on an average of prices from all retailers, omitting two documents where prices were anomalously high.[17] The availability of standard styles like sailor suits in different fabrics at different prices and for different age ranges also complicates comparisons.[18] In order to compare garments with similar

[16] With sales documents dated 1883, 1884, 1887, 1896 and 1900; see Tables 4.2 and 4.3.

[17] Army and Navy Stores (1886), House of Fraser (HF) 6/22/8, Scottish Business Archive, University of Glasgow Archives; Needham of Brighton (1900), Copy 1 Books Commercial (BC) 975/18706. An 1894 Army and Navy Stores catalogue (HF 6/22/9) gave prices that were high, but matched by Harrod's.

[18] Not all sales documents provide information on age ranges, so it was not possible to factor this in to the comparison of prices.

levels of warmth and durability, only versions in wool (not cotton, linen or silk) will be used for this analysis. The price differentials between sailor suits in different fabrics will be examined in the next section.

Tracking the prices of three of the most commonly worn styles over the period 1880–1900 gives results that are hard to reconcile with data on consumption. The typical cost of a wool sailor suit in the sample of retailers' catalogues rose over this period from 3s 6d to 4s 10d; yet at the same time its incidence in Barnardo's entrants increased, while its incidence in school groups increased before dropping off after 1895. The average cost of a Norfolk jacket dropped sharply after 1885, from 8s 11d to as low as 4s 11d; this may be one reason why its incidence increased sharply in the Barnardo's photographs at this time.[19] School photographs showed a distinct drop in numbers of Norfolk suits between 1885 and 1895, but this is based on a small sample and may not be representative.

The average price of suits with lounge jackets and short trousers seems to have remained remarkably constant in cash terms, from 9s 11d in 1880 to 10s 2d in 1900. As typical wages rose slightly over the period, lounge suits were cheaper in real terms by 1900; yet at the same time the number of lounge suits worn by Barnardo's entrants dropped from 63 per cent to 36 per cent. The rise in the incidence of Norfolk suits on Barnardo's entrants suggests that this style was substituted for lounge jackets, as a cheaper alternative. However, changes in costs, and in pricing differentials, do not seem to have affected the uptake of sailor suits. These increased in price over the period, but also increased sharply in the Barnardo's images. This suggests that consumption patterns were not determined by cost alone.

The analysis of the clothing advertisements in Chapter 3 indicated that different styles dominated at different times. If retailers were promoting particular styles very strongly, this may have affected consumer perception of the value that they represented. After 1890, Norfolk suits were promoted through advertisements and through competitive pricing. The effects of this may be seen in the sharp increase in the number of Norfolk suits on Barnardo's entrants from 1895. However, the number of sailor suits in Barnardo's photographs after 1895 also increased, even though this style was less widely advertised and less competitively priced. The opposite was true of lounge suits, which were widely advertised while remaining stable in price, but which were markedly less common in the Barnardo's photos by 1900. This suggests that there may have been other factors affecting the choice of particular garment types.

---

[19]   The only price found for a Norfolk suit in 1885–89 was 5s 11d; prices in 1890–94 ranged from 5s 11d to 14s 6d, and in 1895–1900 from 4s 11d to 10s 6d. The lowest price was given by the Capital and Labour Clothing Stores, Holloway Road, London; JJ MC 1/23 (1897).

Price and Value: A Case Study of Sailor Suits

Sailor suits were sold in different fabrics for different prices in the same document, and offer a case study that will illuminate the rationale for consumer choices. By the 1890s sailor suits were among the cheapest and the most expensive standard styles available for young boys.[20] In 1895, Baker & Co. sold versions in white cotton drill for 4s 5d; in striped cotton for 4s 11d; in blue serge for 4s 11d; and in velvet for 13s 9d. In the same year, Harrod's sailor suits were available in unbleached linen, bleached drill, striped cotton, wool serge, cotton velveteen or silk velvet, at prices from 4s 9d to 94s (£4 14s) for age seven.[21] Cotton or linen sailor suits were not only cheap, but also washable, unlike versions made of wool or velvet. We would expect this double advantage to make cotton sailor suits more popular than wool ones: this preference was apparently confirmed by the dominance of cotton sailor suits in museum collections in Britain.[22]

However, a close analysis of the photographic evidence contradicts this preference. While sailor suits were one of the most easily identifiable garments in all school groups, only one of the 81 examples seen was made of light-coloured cotton.[23] They were also prominent in family photographs, worn by 28 of the 80 boys in the sample: but only 5 of these had light tops.[24] The absence of light-coloured sailor suits was even more noticeable in the Barnardo's images, where only 22 of the 306 sailor suits identified were made of light-coloured cotton. This is all the more surprising when we consider that white or pale blue cotton is easy to distinguish from navy blue serge in photographs. As the photographic sources all agree, we must conclude that light cotton sailor suits were not as popular as the number of survivals would indicate.

One reason for this is suggested by the Barnardo's entry photographs, where ten of the twenty-two light cotton sailor suits were visibly in need of laundering.[25] This was particularly noticeable in comparison with siblings wearing dark wool

---

[20]   Full Highland dress suits with kilt, velvet jacket, plaid and sporran were even more expensive at about 20s for the set; C. Baker (1895), JJ MC 1/6. However, these were never so widely worn as sailor suits. The meanings attached to Highland dress will be discussed in Chapter 7.

[21]   Not all variants were available in the smallest sizes. Alison Adburgham, *Victorian Shopping: Harrod's Catalogue, 1895* (Newton Abbot, 1972), p. 980.

[22]   Thirteen cotton or linen sailor suits dated 1870–1900 and three wool ones were found in the survey of museums detailed in Appendix 1. There were further examples of cotton sailor suits that were not securely dated and were not included in the survey.

[23]   Elizabeth Street School, 1896, London Metropolitan Archives (LMA) A7375.

[24]   F. & F. Baring (1871), Winchester City Museum; H.O. Wilshere (1886) and R.G. Wilshere (1895) in John Wilshere, *Leicester Portrait Photographers before 1900* (Leicester, 1988), pp. 11–12; Harley Granville Barker c.1885, National Portrait Gallery x126443.

[25]   Barnardo's numbers 8799 (1889), 8853–4 (1889), 13031 (1892), 14703–4 (1893), 19491 (1897), 19596 (1897), 19599 (1897), 20806 (1898).

jackets, as in Figure 5.1.[26] In each case the brothers' clothes were presumably subject to the same type and extent of wear, but the evidence of this is much more visible on the light cotton tops. In these two instances we can see that the cotton sailor top had a hidden price in terms of the upkeep needed to keep it looking good.

The other factor which was noticeable in the Barnardo's photographs with summer sailor suits was their seasonality. All were taken in summer months (June– September) when a light cotton garment might be appropriate. However, in several cases the sailor tops were worn layered over wool waistcoats.[27] This highlights the second disadvantage of the cotton sailor jackets, their lack of warmth as outer garments. The status of cotton sailor jackets as seasonal rather than year-round wear can also be seen in two examples where the garments worn were visibly too small (Figure 5.2). These could be interpreted as clothing that was bought the previous year and has been outgrown. Purchasing clothing for a particular season implied an extended wardrobe and hence an increased budget, even if the additional outlay was small. Thus it seems that the cotton sailor suit was perceived as less useful than the same style in dark wool, which would be suitable for wear year-round, and would not require frequent laundering. This calculation of utility in terms of value rather than price seems to have been clearly understood by the families of boys represented in the Barnardo's entry photographs.

It is, however, important to recognise that, while the quantitative analysis shows Barnardo's entrants as slow to follow fashionable trends, qualitative data presents a slightly different picture. Individual Barnardo's entrants wore suits that were highly fashionable, and likely to be costly. A boy entering in 1876 wore a velvet sailor suit with braid edging and short trousers, an outfit similar to those sold for 14s by Lynes in 1873.[28] In 1876, an entrant wore a suit trimmed with braid motifs on cuff and knee, strikingly similar to a suit illustrated in Lynes' 1875 catalogue for 8s 6d (Figure 5.3).[29] The fashionable nature of this suit is confirmed by the closeness of its trimming to the braid motifs registered in great numbers by manufacturers between 1872 and 1876.[30] These examples indicate that at least some of the families using Barnardo's were able to purchase novel and fashionable garments. This belies the tendency of Barnardo's and other charities to present their clients as outside the norms of middle-class practice.[31]

---

[26]   Barnardo's numbers 15647–9, ages six, eight and ten (1889).

[27]   Barnardo's numbers 8853; 13031; 19596.

[28]   Barnardo's number 897 (1876); Arthur Lynes, *Novelettes and Novelties* (London, 1873), JJ MC 4/17, p. 118, velveteen sailor suit.

[29]   Barnardo's number 1001 (1877); Arthur Lynes, *Twice a Year* (London, 1875), JJ MC 4/20, fig. 216, braid trimmed suit.

[30]   Barran & Sons alone registered 83 braid motifs in the Board of Trade documents at The National Archives: BT 43/13/268775–80 (1872); BT43/13/268946–75 (1873); BT43/13/274126–39 (1873); BT43/13/278300–14 (1873); BT43/13/297846–62 (1876).

[31]   It may also indicate that places in Barnardo's were being taken up by middle-class families who had suffered financial reverses, like the examples cited in Harold Perkin, *The Rise of Professional Society: England Since 1880* (London, 1989), pp. 95–6.

The Meanings of Consumption in Autobiographies

The choice of clothing for boys may have been determined not only by pragmatic factors such as availability, cost, and ease of upkeep, but by the more nebulous concept of suitability. The notion of suitability rests on the way in which clothing fits the wearer into society. As autobiographies often deal with the subject's emergence from a specific social context, we would expect them to be rich sources of information on the social meanings of clothing and the 'feelings, desires, and expectations' of their wearers.[32]

There were, however, problems in using autobiographies as sources for the consumption of boys' clothing.[33] References to clothing acquisition by boys were surprisingly rare; this may reflect the lack of children's involvement in clothing choice.[34] Gwen Raverat attributed her lack of interest in clothes as an adult to the fact that as children 'our clothes were imposed on us from above, without even the power of veto'.[35] Some autobiographies highlighted parents' utilitarian view of children's clothes as a family resource that could be converted to cash when needed, like Jack Lanigan's funeral suit.[36] George Acorn related how this attitude persisted even when he was a working youth, with his mother appropriating first the sum he saved for a suit, and later the suit itself, to help household expenses.[37] Acorn is unusual in detailing the actual prices of the clothes in question: 8s for his first working suit as a school-leaver, and 15s for the suit he bought himself.[38]

Another major theme in autobiographies was the importance of clothing in creating social identities. This was often addressed in a negative form, when children were excluded from activities for lack of appropriate clothing: 'Matt and I never went to Sunday School because we never had any decent clothes to go in.'[39] Autobiographers also recalled occasions when wearing clothing different from their

---

[32]   Laura Ugolini, *Men and Menswear, Sartorial Consumption in Britain, 1880–1939* (Aldershot, 2007), p. 7.

[33]   See Appendix 1 for autobiographical sources consulted.

[34]   See Ugolini, *Men and Menswear*, pp. 60–63.

[35]   Gwen Raverat, *Period Piece* (Cambridge, 1952), pp. 253 and 256. Laura Ugolini's intensive research on autobiographies confirms the lack of choice by children; *Men and Menswear*, pp. 60–61.

[36]   Jack Lanigan in John Burnett (ed.), *Destiny Obscure: Autobiographies of Childhood, Education and Family from the 1820s to the 1920s* (London, 1982), p. 87.

[37]   George Acorn, *One of the Multitude: an Autobiography of a Resident of Bethnal Green* (London, 1911), p. 187. The father of the autobiographer Albert Goodwin had faced a similar problem; Goodwin in Burnett, *Destiny Obscure*, p. 298.

[38]   Lanigan in Burnett, *Destiny Obscure*, p. 90; Acorn, *One of the Multitude*, pp. 119 and 136.

[39]   Lanigan in Burnett, *Destiny Obscure*, p. 88.

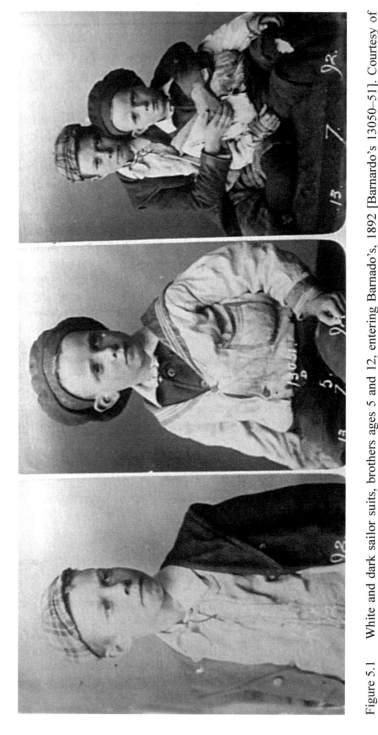

Figure 5.1   White and dark sailor suits, brothers ages 5 and 12, entering Barnardo's, 1892 [Barnardo's 13050–51]. Courtesy of Barnardo's Archive.

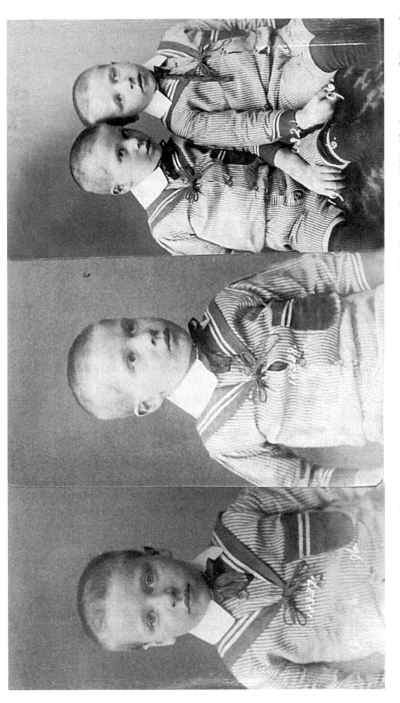

Figure 5.2   Two brothers in sailor suits, ages 5 and 7, entering Barnado's 1898 [Barnardo's 18337–8]. Courtesy of Barnardo's Archive.

peers made them the target of scorn.[40] The positive side of social conformity through clothing is less often described, which makes Rolph's account quoted above even more valuable. Frederick Willis, at school in south London in the 1890s, confirms that his school clothing was 'a tweed Norfolk suit which I very well remember being bought at a large shop in London for 8s 11d'.[41]

These passages are interesting in presenting normative rather than exceptional clothing practice, and in identifying the role of multiple retailers in facilitating clothing conformity. The price of 8s 11d cited by Willis is surprisingly high, when major retailers such as Baker were offering Norfolk suits for as little as 5s 11d.[42] This may indicate that the cheapest available version was not necessarily the best value for money, as with sailor suits.[43] Or it may indicate a desire on the part of the family to express social distinction by purchasing clothing above the minimum level. The two standard outfits in Rolph's memoir – Norfolk jacket and breeches, or jersey and shorts – probably corresponded to different purchase prices and hence different levels of family income.

Evaluating Consumption Practice

The analyses in this chapter have shown the complexity of consumption behaviour in the late nineteenth century, and the importance of visual evidence in providing data not available in texts. The comparison of advertising documents and photographs of consumers showed that retailers' promotion of different garment types did result in increases in consumption, but with a time-lag of up to five years. It also suggested that the families represented in school photographs responded more quickly to advertising campaigns than did the families represented in Barnardo's. This is what we would expect: that new clothing styles would be taken up first by wealthier families, and more slowly by poorer ones.

Yet an examination of consumption patterns for particular garments in terms of their prices showed that cost was not the only determinant for consumption. This was confirmed by the detailed case study of different types of sailor suits in the Barnardo's archive. The cheapest form of sailor suits, made from white cotton, were surprisingly absent from these photographs, which were dominated by mid-priced versions in dark wool. This is all the more surprising as cotton sailor tops were washable, which might also be thought to make them more practical than wool.[44] However, a close examination of photos showing both types showed that

---

[40]   As with Edward Brown's gold velvet suit, in Burnett, *Destiny Obscure*, p. 152. Further examples are given by Ugolini, *Men and Menswear*, pp. 50–52.

[41]   Frederick Willis, *A Book of London Yesterdays* (London, 1960), p. 42.

[42]   Copy 1 BC 975/18721 (1900).

[43]   The quoted price may also have been misremembered.

[44]   Wool garments (other than underwear made of loosely woven flannel or knitted jersey) were not considered washable at this period. Cleanliness was maintained by using removable cotton linings: 'many mothers prefer to have a loose [cotton] lining ... because

Figure 5.3   Barnardo's entrant in velvet sailor suit, 1876 [Barnardo's 897].
               Courtesy of Barnardo's Archive.

washability was not necessarily a benefit for poorer families, as it would add to the labour and cost of maintaining the garment. Moreover, the layering of light cotton tops over heavy wool waistcoats and vests in some photos (Figure 5.1) implies that lightweight fabrics were seen as insufficiently warm, and hence less useful than wool. Cotton sailor suits may also have been more closely associated with seaside holidays and therefore seen as less suitable for everyday wear. The associations and symbolism of sailor suits will be examined more closely in Chapter 7.

The autobiographies quoted acknowledge the importance of clothing in creating and maintaining social identities. Personal texts reveal that clothing consumption by pre-adolescents was determined as much by family budgets and concerns as by the needs of the individual. But they also show that boys were very aware of the local norms of age-and activity-appropriate clothing, and very sensitive to any transgression of these. Photographs from schools and from Barnardo's also reveal the importance of clothing in locating boys both in an age group and in a family group and these will be examined in more detail in Chapter 6.

---

it can be readily washed, and frequently changed', *Cassell's Book of the Household, A Work of Reference on Domestic Economy* (London, 1889), p. 152.

Chapter 6
Age, Employment and Boys' Clothes

In 1900, ten-year-old Jack Lanigan passed the School Leaving Examination and entered a new stage of life:

> I went accompanied by Mother to a very well-known second-hand clothes shop in Salford, Hertzog by name. I was fitted out with coat, trousers, shirt, stockings and shoes for the sum of four shillings and sixpence, which was a lot of money in those days ... The following Monday morning my mother accompanied me 'looking for work' and we were not long in finding it.[1]

The importance of clothes in marking the transition from toddler at home, to schoolboy, to working lad, was recognised in nineteenth century autobiographies and social surveys. Yet the choice of garments appropriate to each stage or position in life was far from straightforward. Retailers offered numerous choices for each age range, not all of which would have been affordable or available to all consumers. There would also have been local clothing practices and occupational conventions for boys in work.

This chapter will examine the ways in which clothing expressed a boy's social position in terms of age, family membership and employment status, using documented portraits, school photographs and Barnardo's entry images. As the analysis of clothing designs in the previous chapters indicated, different clothing types were available for different age groups, and progress from a toddler's tunic to a youth's suit marked the stages of a boy's development. We would expect these stages to be related to the ages at which boys moved through state schools and on to full-time employment, and this correlation will be examined here. However, most boys were not only members of age groups but also of sibling groups, and this created a tension between expressing membership of an age cohort and a family group. In choosing clothing, families also had to balance pragmatic considerations of cost and availability against social conventions. This balancing led at times to anomalous combinations such as the white collars on ragged jackets seen in the Barnardo's entry images in Chapter 1.

The first and second sections of this chapter will outline the legal and biological definition of childhood in the late nineteenth century. Mass-production processes relied on a standardisation of the sizes in which particular styles were made, and these will be examined in the third section. This will focus on dresses, shorts and

[1]   Jack Lanigan in John Burnett (ed.), *Destiny Obscure: Autobiographies of Childhood, Education and Family from the 1820s to the 1920s* (London, 1982), p. 90.

long trousers, the garments associated with the life stages of infancy, boyhood and youth. We might expect some resistance to manufacturers' and retailers' attempts to define the ages at which certain types of clothing were available for boys. In the fourth section, consumers' attitudes will be evaluated through advice literature, tailoring and dressmaking magazines, which guided mothers (especially) in the selection of socially appropriate clothing.

The following sections examine the actual practices of age-related clothing, starting with school photographs, which will indicate how the three life stages intersected with the age divisions between Infants and Junior Schools. In the sixth section the whole sample of Barnardo's entry photos will be analysed to see how the wearing of short and long trousers, and of sailor tops and lounge jackets, correlates to the wearers' ages. These images contain many sibling pairs, which can be used to show how families dressed boys of different ages, both in terms of the garments chosen and in terms of their newness and state of repair. The following sections will examine in turn photographs of siblings with ragged, respectable and mixed clothing, to see how the state of boys' clothing relates to their age. There will be a close focus on boys around the age for entering full-time employment, which we would expect to lead to higher family income and hence to better clothing. Taken together, these separate analyses will show how families balanced the wish to represent their boys' age, family and employment status with pragmatic factors of availability and cost.

Legal Definitions of Childhood

Legal Definitions

The statutory definition of childhood has evident importance in defining the meanings of boys' clothing. Discussions of boyhood in the nineteenth century were framed by legislation that drew increasingly fine distinctions between the expectations and entitlements of different age groups. The Education Act of 1876 made it illegal to employ children under the age of ten, and in 1878 children aged ten to thirteen were officially restricted to half-time work in factories and workshops. In 1891, the legal minimum age for working was raised to eleven (half-time only up to thirteen) and in 1899 it was raised again to twelve.[2] These restrictions were challenged by contemporaries who saw them as both too loose and too stringent, and evaded by families who needed additional income.[3] In 1897 Sydney and Beatrice Webb were arguing for a minimum working age of

---

[2]   Hugh Cunningham, *The Children of the Poor: Representations of Childhood since the Seventeenth Century* (Oxford, 1991), p. 176.

[3]   For children's work in two contrasting districts, see Anna Davin, *Growing Up Poor: Home, School and Street in London, 1870–1914* (London, 1996), pp. 157–98; Barbara Copeland and Gavin Thompson, 'The 'Boy Labour Problem' in Lancashire', in Michael

fourteen (legislated in 1918), while a 1901 inter-Departmental Committee on the Employment of School Children found that 'all children should have liberty to work as much and in such ways as is good for them'.[4] Debates on the training of older boys continued into the early twentieth century, when it was felt that: 'at the age of fourteen, as a general rule, the control of school and home end together. The lad goes to bed a boy; he wakes as a man.'[5] This passage reflects anxieties that social controls through education might cease just at the onset of the dangerous state of puberty.[6]

Legislation also defined the beginning of childhood as distinct from 'infancy'. This was intimately related to the structure of Board Schools, which from the outset were classified into 'infant schools, for children below seven years of age; junior schools, for children between seven and ten years of age; and senior schools, for older children'.[7] While the original provision was intended for age five and upwards, the needs of working mothers led many schools to admit children aged two or three. In London in 1904 these 'under-age' children formed up to 10 per cent of the total school population and sometimes warranted a separate 'Babies' Room'.[8] Infants' and babies' departments of schools were mixed, but children over eight were segregated by sex and by ability, with progression through the 'standards' dependent on performance in examinations. This segregation was more noticeable for boys, as they moved from female teachers in the Infants' department to male teachers in the Juniors'.[9] The gendering of the Elementary School affected every aspect of the child's experience, from the entry through separate doors to the separate classrooms and syllabuses and the segregated boys' and girls' playgrounds. Such a powerful and widespread enforcement of age and gender divisions might well shape the popular understanding of this issue.

Winstanley (ed.), *Working Children in Nineteenth-Century Lancashire* (Lancaster, 1995), pp. 93–114.

[4] Cunningham, *The Children of the Poor*, pp. 183 and 181.

[5] R.A. Bray, *Boy Labour and Apprenticeship* (1911), cited in Cunningham, *The Children of the Poor*, p. 185. See also Ennis Richmond, *Through Boyhood to Manhood: A Plea for Ideals* (London, 1899); C.E.B Russell, *Manchester Boys: Sketches of Manchester Lads at Work and Play* (Manchester, 1905).

[6] Harry Hendrick, Images of Youth: Age, Class and the Male Youth Problem, 1880–1920 (Oxford, 1990).

[7] *Minutes of School Board for London* I. 156 (1871); cited in the *Oxford English Dictionary*, 2nd edn (Oxford, 1989), vol.VIII, p. 314, 'Junior' 5.

[8] Ellen Ross, *Love and Toil: Motherhood in Outcast London, 1870–1918* (Oxford, 1993), p. 148; Davin, *Growing Up Poor,* pp. 113–14.

[9] Davin, *Growing Up Poor*, p. 121.

Physiology and Boys' Clothing

Throughout the nineteenth century and into the twentieth, the clothing worn by boys provided a staged transition from the dresses worn by infants of both sexes to the suits with long trousers that denoted an adult male.[10] The term 'breeching' was often applied to the first step, when dresses gave way to an outfit with trousers. However, in the period 1870–1900 there were several subsequent stages, when the first outfit (often a hip-length blouse with shorts or knickerbockers) gave way to a jacket and shorts and finally to adult-styled suits with long trousers. The use of short trousers to denote the middle stage of boyhood was new in the 1870s, and was blurred by the adoption of knickerbockers for sportswear by men.[11] Although there was wide agreement on the staged progress of 'breeching', there was considerable divergence in the suggested ages for transition, across texts and across the period.

The change from infant's dresses to boy's trousers was limited by the earliest age at which a boy was toilet-trained and could be trusted in non-washable wool trousers rather than washable cotton petticoats. Current paediatric advice places this between the ages of 24 and 36 months. This first change seems to have had symbolic as well as practical importance, and was described as a rite of passage by early twentieth-century autobiographers such as C.H. Rolph: 'Breeching ... had almost the status of a domestic crisis, with neighbours popping in to admire the emancipated victim and the new clothes in which he was being emancipated.'[12] When school attendance became the norm after 1870, we might expect breeching to be identified with the transition from home to school. Yet, as Rolph observed when he started school in 1904:

> Among the smaller scholars there were several in this epicene [skirted] state, their mothers' reluctance to 'breech' (or britch) them persisting even into their school days. But these were the boys who went to school at the age of two and a half and, even so, could not yet be regarded as 'house-trained.'[13]

Thus the lowest age of breeching was determined by physiology rather than by social conventions.

The age for changing from boys' to men's clothes might be linked to the biological changes of puberty, but this is hard to define in age terms. Two nineteenth-century sources placed the age of puberty for boys between thirteen

---

[10]   Anne Buck, *Clothes and the Child: A Handbook of Children's Dress in England 1500–1900* (Bedford, 1996), pp. 150–53.

[11]   See Jo Paoletti. and Carol Kregloh, 'The Children's Department', in Claudia Kidwell and Valerie Steele (eds), *Men and Women, Dressing the Part* (London, 1989), p. 38.

[12]   C.H. Rolph, *London Particulars* (Oxford, 1980), p. 27.

[13]   Ibid, p. 26.

and sixteen but it is not clear whether they referred to a middle-class segment or to the whole population.[14] R.A. Bray, writing soon after recruiting drives for the Boer War had revealed the poor physical condition of working-class men, was concerned about the developmental gap between middle-class and working-class boys of the same age: 'In the industrial and reformatory schools [for homeless and delinquents] we are told that the boys at the age of thirteen average four inches less in height and a stone less in weight than the ordinary public [fee-paying] school boy at that age.'[15]

This gap is borne out by Floud's analysis of data on middle-class and upper-class boys, which indicates a gap of about 5 inches in height at age fifteen in 1900.[16] Even within the working class there were developmental differences related to nutrition, with a study of York schoolboys showing a variation of 3½ inches in height and 5½ lb in weight at age thirteen.[17] Another study that found that only 15 per cent of working-class boys would reach the physical standards required for joining the navy by the age of 15 ¼.[18] Some of this difference might be based on differences in the onset of puberty, which in itself would be affected by nutrition.

Retailers' Age Ranges for Clothing

We would expect standard sizing to be a key factor in the spread of mass-produced children's clothing. Early catalogues from Moses, Lynes and others did not give any indication of size ranges, relying on the client's self-measurement form. This may indicate that garments were only made in one or two sizes, although that seems unlikely. Later catalogues indicated the range of sizes available, but these were not always related to age. For instance, the Army and Navy Stores catalogue of 1886 offered young boys' outfits in sizes from 'X' to '4'.[19] The practice of giving age equivalents alongside stock size numbers seems to have become common only

---

[14]   1871 Census Report; J.C. Browne, 'Education and the Nervous System', in M.A. Morris, *The Book of Health* (London, 1883). Cited in Davin, *Growing Up Poor*, p. 4, n.1.

[15]   R.A. Bray, 'The Boy and the Family', in E.J. Urwick, *Studies of Boy Life in Our Cities* (London, 1904), p. 259. Michael Childs cites a weight difference of 28lb or two stone in *Labour's Apprentices: Working-Class Lads in Late Victorian and Edwardian England* (Montreal, 1992), p. 8.

[16]   Roderick Floud, Kenneth Wachter and Annabel Gregory, *Height, Health and History: Nutritional status in the United Kingdom, 1750–1980* (Cambridge, 1990), p. 185.

[17]   Bray, 'The Boy and the Family', p. 260.

[18]   Ibid., p. 259.

[19]   Army and Navy Stores catalogue 1886, HF6/22/8, p. 1316 and p. 1319. On the importance of standardized sizing, see Andrew Godley, 'Comparative Labour Productivity in the British and American Clothing Industries, 1850–1950', *Textile History*, 28/1 (1997), pp. 70–71.

in the 1890s.[20] These age sizes give a strong indication of the expected relationship between age and garments worn, even if this was not always accurate.

Information on age ranges in retail catalogues is given in Table 6.1, with the earliest and the youngest age selected to give an age bracket for each category of garments. These show a substantial overlap between stages. Suits with short trousers were available for ages two to fourteen and with long trousers for age ten upwards. [21] However this is blurred by the association of particular styles with either short or long trousers: Eton suits (always with long trousers), were used for formal wear from age eight, and Norfolk suits (always with knickerbockers) were used for outdoor pursuits up to adulthood. Sailor suits were particularly anomalous, available in versions with either short or long trousers for ages four to eleven.[22]

Table 6.1   Ages advised for wearing dresses, shorts and long trousers in all sources

Source	Period	Dress		Tunic + shorts		Shorts		Long	
		min	max	min	max	min	max	min	max
Dressmaking	1870–90	2	7	3	6	3	10	7	15
Tailors	1870–85					7	11	13	18
Shops	1870–90					2	10		
Dressmaking	1890–1900	2	4			3	13		
Tailors	1888							10	16
Shops	1890–1900			2	7	2	16	10	18

Some of this confusion can be resolved by looking at *The Boy and How to Suit Him* (Figure 6.1). While written in the form of an advice guide presenting normative middle-class practice to parents,[23] it was published by Richard Taylor and Co. for distribution by retailers and was actually a form of advertising. The text suggests that kilts would be worn by the youngest, with short trousers starting from age four.[24] From ages seven to nine the boy was to wear short trousers only, but from age ten he might wear long trousers in a formal Eton suit, or an everyday lounge suit.[25] By age fourteen, 'we are now coming dangerously near the border line when the "boy" (or youth as we perhaps ought to call him) likes to be thought

---

[20]   Age ranges for boys' clothes are given in the Army and Navy Stores catalogue of 1894, although girls' and infants' clothes have size numbers; HF6/22/9, pp. 1061–8.

[21]   Fred Watts 1895, Harrod's 1895, Marychurch & Blackler 1899.

[22]   Army and Navy Stores 1894, HF 6/22/9.

[23]   Richard Taylor & Co., *The Boy and How to Suit Him* (London, 1899); Copy 1 BC 971/17475.

[24]   Ibid., p. 6.

[25]   Ibid., p 9.

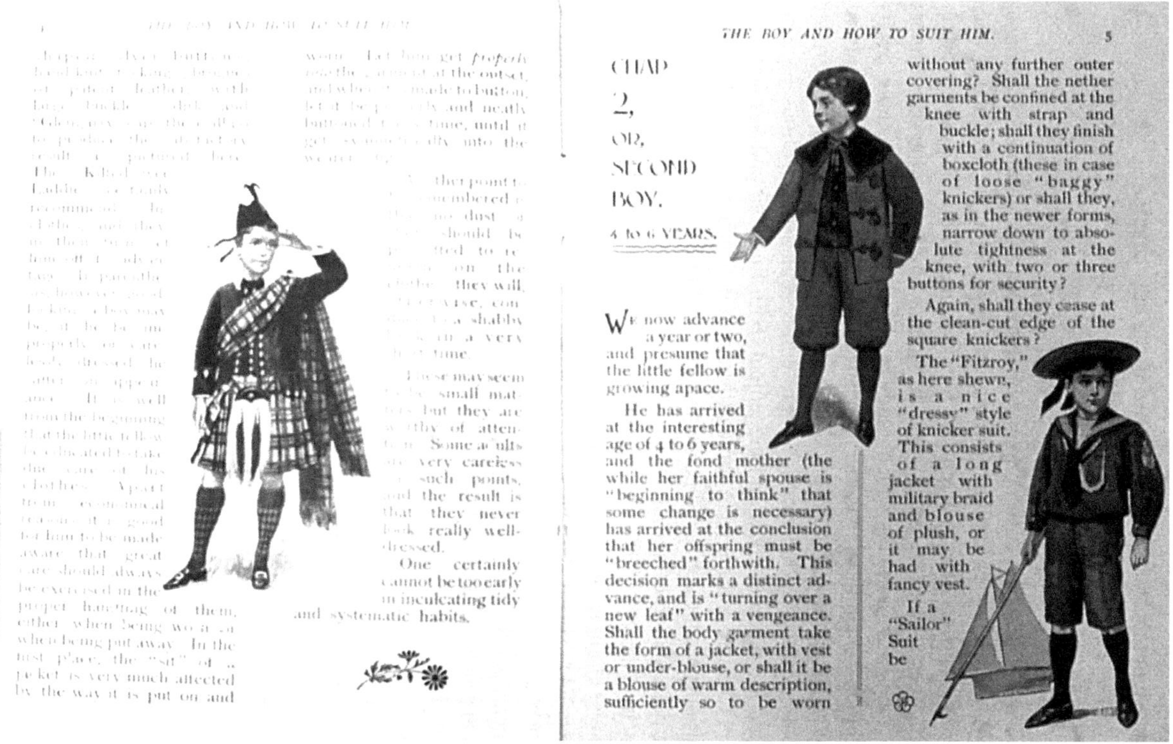

THE BOY AND HOW TO SUIT HIM. 5

One certainly cannot be too early in inculcating tidy and systematic habits.

CHAP 2, OR, SECOND BOY.

4 to 6 YEARS.

We now advance a year or two, and presume that the little fellow is growing apace.

He has arrived at the interesting age of 4 to 6 years, and the fond mother (the while her faithful spouse is "beginning to think" that some change is necessary) has arrived at the conclusion that her offspring must be "breeched" forthwith. This decision marks a distinct advance, and is "turning over a new leaf" with a vengeance. Shall the body garment take the form of a jacket, with vest or under-blouse, or shall it be a blouse of warm description, sufficiently so to be worn without any further outer covering? Shall the nether garments be confined at the knee with strap and buckle; shall they finish with a continuation of boxcloth (these in case of loose "baggy" knickers) or shall they, as in the newer forms, narrow down to absolute tightness at the knee, with two or three buttons for security?

Again, shall they cease at the clean-cut edge of the square knickers?

The "Fitzroy," as here shewn, is a nice "dressy" style of knicker suit. This consists of a long jacket with military braid and blouse of plush, or it may be had with fancy vest.

If a "Sailor" Suit be

Figure 6.1 *The Boy and How to Suit Him*, R. Taylor & Co., 1899 [Copy 1 BC 971/17475]. Courtesy of The National Archives, Kew.

a man'.[26] This text is interesting for the way in which it acknowledges a range of clothing practices and preferences in individual families. It also demonstrates the complex process of representing age, in which trouser length was only one factor. Its positioning of the patriotic styles of sailor and 'Highland' suits in the lowest age range is a point that will be re-examined in the next chapter.

Advice on Age-appropriate Clothing

Variations in boys' physical development, both between and within social groups, fed parental uncertainty as to what clothing was appropriate at a particular age. Texts aimed at families offer rich sources for studying the anxieties surrounding clothing practices.[27] They present a world in which women were the sole arbiters of family appearance, and in which ready-made clothing was notable by its absence. Guides for mothers, whether published as books or in magazines, have several points in common. One is a focus on clothes for young boys, in skirts or short trousers. Another is that clothing is presented as an aspect of housekeeping that reflected the mother's skill and judgement, both financial and aesthetic. As discussed in Chapter 2, there were some differences between dressmaking books, which dealt only with established garment types, and magazines whose rationale lay in their presentation of new styles.

We saw in Chapter 2 that dressmaking books for amateurs devoted very little space to boys' clothing, with the fullest treatment found in *Cassell's Household Guide* (1869–71). This text suggested that the breeching process should start at six, with the transitional tunic and short worn up to eight.[28] The 1884 second edition reprinted unchanged the patterns and text published in 1870, with no acknowledgement of changes in practice.[29] Magazines, with their detailed description of patterns and advice pages for anxious mothers, were better sources for evaluating the practice of age-related dress codes for boys. Three publications discussed in Chapter 2 have been used here: *Myra's Mid Monthly Journal and Children's Dress* (1877–82), *Myra's Journal of Dress and Fashion* (1870–1900) and London editions of Butterick's *Metropolitan Catalogue of Fashions* for 1873, 1882 and 1886. Editorial text in the *Tailor and Cutter* also advised on the garments suitable for different ages, even though tailors were able to adjust patterns to fit older or younger sizes. Table 6.1 presents the age ranges advised for boys' garments in these sources. There were some surprising contradictions, particularly around the ages for going

---

[26]   Ibid., p. 11.

[27]   See Christina Bates, 'How to dress the Children? A Comparison of Prescription and Practice in Late-Nineteenth-Century North America', *Dress*, 24 (1997), pp. 46–7.

[28]   *Cassell's Household Guide* (London, 1869–71), vol. I, p. 370; vol. II, p. 361.

[29]   *Cassell's Household Guide: being a complete encyclopaedia of domestic and social economy, etc.*, 2nd edn (London, 1885), vol. II, pp. 361–2; vol. IV, pp. 8–10, 20–21, 59–62, 68–9.

into long trousers: dressmaking patterns were presenting these from age seven, but tailors only from age thirteen.

Some of these differences may be nationally based, as Butterick's patterns were produced initially for an American market. Some may be the result of individual preferences, as *Myra's* publications were directed by the eponymous editor.[30] Some may reflect changes in the clothing trade: in the 1890s, the perceived threat from ready-to-wear manufacturers (as discussed in Chapter 2) may have encouraged tailors to be more flexible in their attitudes to age-specific clothing. Nonetheless, the data suggests a consensus by 1900 over a younger age for wearing long trousers, and a truncating of the intermediate stages of breeching. This is visible even within the same publication: in 1877 *Myra* gave patterns for boys' tunics up to age six, and for suits with shorts from age four, but by 1897 the same publication advised tunics up to age four, and shorts suits from age three.

Age Distinctions in Practice

School Photographs

The texts from tailors, dressmakers, and retailers all advise on clothing practice, but to understand how this was carried out we need to examine photographs. A sample of family portraits of boys with documented dates and ages was first studied: this indicated a range of acceptable practice.[31] There was no discernible trend in the lower age for wearing trousers, seen on a boy of three in 1877 and on a boy aged two in 1886. Of the twenty documented portraits found, nine showed boys (aged between two and ten) in sailor suits. The implications of this will be considered in more detail in the next chapter.

The ages of the boys in the school group photographs analysed earlier were not recorded, but could be deduced from a division into Infant and Junior groups. This is seen in two groups from London Infant Schools (Figures 1.2 and 6.2)[32] and in groups of older and younger pupils from Cotherstone Wesleyan School, County Durham. The arrangement of these groups meant that it was not possible to determine how many boys in each group were wearing short or long trousers. But the jackets were legible, and showed the operation of age distinctions. 'Holden Street Infants' were all dressed in sailor tops or blouses with short trousers. In the

---

[30]   'Myra' was the pseudonym of Mrs. Mathilda Browne, who provided fashion advice and an editorial column for the *Englishwoman's Domestic Magazine* from 1865 to 1875, before setting up the *Myra's* publications. See Margaret Beetham, *A Magazine of Her Own? Domesticity and Desire in the Woman's Magazine, 1800–1914* (London, 1996), pp. 79–81.

[31]   For the sources of family photographs consulted, and the problems in obtaining a representative sample, see Appendix 1.

[32]   Holden Street Infants, LMA N4287 (1897); Orange Street Infants, LMA A4464 (1899).

Orange Street Infants group, seven of the eleven boys with identifiable jackets were wearing sailor tops. In a pair of photographs from Cotherstone School, sailor or blouse tops were worn by 12 out of 17 boys in the Infants but only 2 of the 20 Juniors.[33] The data from Cotherstone is particularly interesting as it shows a clear division of garment types corresponding to the divisions within the school.

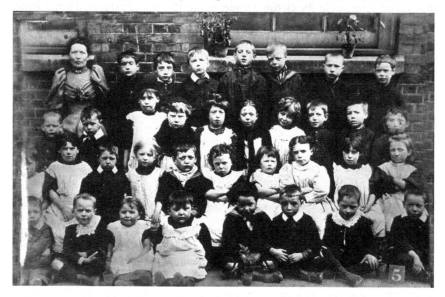

Figure 6.2   Infants' class at Orange Street School, London, 1899 [SC/PHL/02/ A4464]. Courtesy of City of London, London Metropolitan Archives.

There do not appear to have been any formal regulations governing clothing at Board Schools in this period, so these results suggest that the age distinction between 'infants' and 'boys' had been internalised by pupils and their families. The operation of age-specific dress codes in Board Schools is referred to by two autobiographers. Frederick Willis picked a fight with a boy who 'wore a sailor suit and hat suitable for a boy two or three years his junior'.[34] C.H. Rolph remembered a distinction between clothes worn by younger and older schoolboys, though he was unclear about the clothing worn by younger ones.[35]

---

[33]   Cotherstone Wesleyan School, private collection, 1898; see Clare Rose, 'Boyswear and the Formation of Gender and Class Identity in Urban England 1840–1900' (unpublished PhD Dissertation, University of Brighton, 2006), pp. 296, 341.

[34]   Frederick Willis, *A Book of London Yesterdays* (London, 1960), p. 54.

[35]   Rolph, *London Particulars*, p. 63.

Age Distinctions in Barnardo's entry Photographs

The largest set of data for age-specific clothing practice was found in the Barnardo's archive. From 1886 onwards, Barnardo's entry photographs were marked with the child's age in addition to the name, date and record number (names have been omitted here in accordance with Barnardo's data protection policy). Leaving aside the photographs where the age was either missing or illegible, the sample included 1,508 boys aged two to sixteen taken between 1888 and 1899. Each image was analysed to determine the type of jacket and of lower garment (skirt/short trousers/long trousers).

An analysis of jacket types worn by Barnardo's entrants with known ages (Table 6.2) showed that the three commonest types of jackets over all ages were the lounge (36 per cent) and the sailor (30 per cent), and the 'stripe' or 'Greenwich' (19 per cent). However the distribution of these showed distinct age profiles. In the Barnardo's sample the proportion wearing sailor jackets peaked at ages three and four (70 per cent) and continued high (43 per cent to 53 per cent) from ages five to nine. The number of 'stripe' jackets was between 20 per cent and 25 per cent from ages five to nine, then increased sharply at age ten. Age ten marked a watershed, with fewer entrants in sailor tops and more wearing both 'stripe' jackets and lounge jackets; by age twelve 73 per cent were in lounge jackets, 16 per cent in 'stripe' jackets, and only 3 per cent in sailor tops.

Table 6.2   Jacket types worn by Barnardo's entrants with known ages, 1888–99

	Blouse		Sailor		'Greenwich'		Norfolk		Lounge		Total	
Age (yrs)	no.	%	no.	%	no.	%	no.	%	no.	%	no.	%
2	1	33%	2	66%							3	100%
3	1	9%	8	72%	2	18%					11	
4	4	9%	33	70%	6	13%	2	4%	2	4%	47	
5	5	9%	29	53%	14	25%	3	5%	4	7%	55	
6	6	6%	43	46%	23	24%	11	12%	11	12%	94	
7	7	7%	44	44%	21	21%	18	18%	10	10%	100	
8	9	8%	52	46%	28	25%	13	11%	12	11%	114	
9	7	4%	83	52%	33	20%	19	12%	19	12%	161	
10	4	4%	12	11%	35	32%	19	18%	41	37%	111	
11	2	3%	9	11%	15	19%	12	15%	41	52%	79	
12	2	2%	3	3%	15	16%	6	6%	70	73%	96	
13	0		1	2%	2	3%	4	7%	52	88%	59	
14			1	2%	4	10%	0		35	78%	40	
15					1	3%	1	3%	34	94%	36	
16			1	2%	1	2%			59	96%	61	
	48		321		200		108		390		1067	100%
		4%		30%		19%		10%		36%		

The analysis of the wearing of skirts, shorts and long trousers was restricted to 812 of the 1508 images in the original dataset, as the lower body was hidden in the remainder.[36] This particularly affected older boys, who were often placed at the back of sibling groups. Table 6.3 shows the results of this analysis, with a tapered change from dresses to short trousers and then to longs. At age two, only 10 per cent of the (small) sample wore short trousers. At age three, 36 per cent wore short trousers while 64 per cent were in skirts, but at age four the proportions were reversed with 83 per cent in short trousers and only 15 per cent still in skirts. Between ages five and seven the number of boys in skirts was negligible, with only one or two examples. Long trousers were seen in single examples on boys aged four and five, on 7 per cent of boys aged six, and on 10 per cent of boys aged eight. The number wearing long trousers jumped up to 28 per cent at age ten, to 50 per cent at age 12, and 76 per cent by age 13.

Table 6.3   Progression from skirts to shorts to long trousers by age in Barnardo's entrants, 1888–99 (percentages of visible images)

Age (yrs)	Total	Legible	Skirt		Short		Long		Unclear	
			no.	%	no.	%	no.	%	no.	%
2	21	21	19	90%	2	10%	0		0	
3	30	28	18	64%	10	36%	0		2	7%
4	79	59	9	15%	49	83%	1	2%	20	25%
5	82	61	1	1%	59	97%	1	2%	21	26%
6	138	89	2	2%	81	91%	6	7%	49	35%
7	154	105	1	1%	97	92%	7	6%	49	32%
8	161	95	0		86	90%	9	10%	66	41%
9	169	93	0		85	91%	8	9%	76	47%
10	182	106			76	72%	30	28%	76	42%
11	125	58			40	69%	18	31%	67	54%
12	117	51			26	51%	25	49%	66	56%
13	73	30			7	24%	23	76%	43	59%
14	55	20			4	20%	16	80%	35	64%
15	50	7			1	14%	6	86%	43	86%
16	72	10			0		10	100%	62	86%
TOTALS	1,508	812								

---

[36]   The proportion of images in which the lower body is not visible rises steadily with age, from 25 per cent at age four to 86 per cent at age fifteen. This is caused by the way that the photographs were posed, with older siblings placed at the back of family groups.

This data shows that, while there was a certain degree of flexibility in the ages at which actual boys progressed through the different stages of clothing, there was a clear consensus about the upper limit for each stage. Nearly all boys were in short trousers at four, and long trousers at thirteen. This is particularly interesting when we consider that families in economic crisis are likely to have deferred or minimised clothing purchases, so that progress to the next stage of clothing may also have been deferred. The data for both jacket and trouser types indicates that ten was a watershed age for clothing practice in families whose boys entered Barnardo's. As ten was the official age for leaving school and starting full-time employment in the 1890s, we need next to consider the relationship between clothing and employment.

Employment Status and Clothing in Barnardo's Family Groups

Clothing was seen by late nineteenth-century commentators as one of the key determinants of boys' employment destinations. C.E.B. Russell stated in *Manchester Boys* (1905): 'even if he be a smart, bright youngster it is almost hopeless for him to attempt to obtain work in an office in the city, or in any of the many warehouses without decent clothes.'[37] This view is confirmed by Jack Lanigan's account of being bought a (second-hand) suit for job-seeking which was pawned once the job was secured.[38] Once a boy was earning, the added income could mean an increased standard of clothing either for the individual or for the family as a whole.

The Barnardo's entry photographs from 1886 to 1899 can be used to examine the link between employment status, family incomes, and clothing practice by comparing sets of brothers. Families who gave up their boys to Barnardo's were by definition in a state of economic crisis, but the preliminary analysis of the photographs in Chapter 1 suggested that this destination had been reached by a number of routes. Some boys showed evidence of prolonged financial hardship in their poor-quality and ragged clothing while others were respectably presented suggesting that their families had previously been relatively prosperous. There were also families with a mixture of these qualities. The latter are particularly interesting as they show evidence of Campbell's gap between intentions and actions.[39]

Analysing each group of families in turn illuminates how poverty affected families' adherence to the norms of clothing practice established above. Poorer families might delay boys' progress to the next clothing stage (because of lack of

---

[37]   Russell, *Manchester Boys*, p. 13.

[38]   Lanigan in Burnett, *Destiny Obscure*, p. 90.

[39]   Colin Campbell, 'The Meaning of Objects and the Meaning of Actions, a Critical Note on the Sociology of Consumption and Theories of Clothing', *Journal of Material Culture*, 1/1 (1996): 93–105.

funds) or hasten it (in order to speed entry to school and then employment). Or they might disregard clothing conventions entirely, dressing boys in any available garments. More prosperous families might speed boys' progression through stages of clothing to demonstrate that the availability of funds, or delay it in order to emphasise boys' status as dependants rather than workers. In some families, there is a marked difference in the type or quality of clothing between brothers below and above the minimum working age. These allow us to examine how clothing expenditure was allocated within families. Looking at the differences within as well as between families will help to illuminate the scope and the limitations of clothing as an indicator of economic status.

Sorting Barnardo's Sibling Group Photos

As explained in Appendix 1, the sample of images from the Barnardo's archive was selected by taking all sibling groups and some control groups. Omitting siblings whose age was not recorded (including all before 1886) gave a sample of 895 brothers.[40] Family groups were then sorted into 'ragged' (if all members showed signs of raggedness), 'respectable' (if all members had white collars and/ or ties) and mixed (if 'raggedness' and white collars were both present). Boys who showed neither signs of raggedness nor white collars were categorised as 'neutral'. By this definition, 258 of the brothers were 'respectable', 190 'ragged', 193 'mixed' and 259 'neutral'.

The 259 'neutral' brothers were in 137 family groups, some with wide age ranges and some very close including three sets of twins.[41] At age four, 81 per cent were in short trousers, the remainder in skirts. At age ten, 88 per cent of those whose legs were visible were in short trousers. Long trousers were seen on 35 per cent of eleven-year-olds, but only 50 per cent of twelve- and thirteen-year-olds. The data for the thirteen-year-olds may be skewed by the small size of the cohort, reduced to seven legible images by the arrangement of the subjects with older boys standing behind younger siblings.

The jacket types worn by these brothers showed clear age-related preferences. Of the 67 sailor tops in this group, only five were worn by boys aged nine and over; the mode ages being six and seven. Norfolk jackets were less common (23 examples) but showed an older age profile, commonest at ages nine, ten and eleven. Lounge jackets were worn by boys from age five upwards, but were commonest on boys aged twelve and over. The tendency to dress brothers alike was stronger in this group, seen in 44 of the 137 families. This produced some contraventions of age-appropriate practice, such as brothers aged nine and twelve dressed in

---

40   The full set of data is given as Table 5.7 in Rose, 'Boyswear'.

41   Numbers 7456–7 (1888), aged two; 18474–5 (1893), aged eleven; 19237–8 (1897), aged six. Names of children have been suppressed in accordance with Barnardo's Data Protection regulations.

Figure 6.3   Brothers, ages 10, 8 and 16, entering Barnardo's 1889 [Barnardo's 8916–18]. Courtesy of Barnardo's Archive.

matching 'stripe' jackets and short trousers,[42] or brothers aged six, seven and eleven dressed in matching sailor tops and long trousers.[43]

'Ragged' Brothers in Barnardo's Photographs

In the set of 'ragged' brothers there was only one in a skirt, an infant less than a year old.[44] All boys between age two and age six were in short trousers. Long trousers were seen from the age of seven (three examples). At age ten almost as many of these boys wore long and short trousers, and by age eleven long trousers dominated. There were, however, one or two examples of boys in short trousers up to the age of fourteen. Compared to the data in Table 6.3 the 'ragged' brothers were progressing through the clothing stages earlier than the whole cohort. In several 'ragged' families the change had taken place between the ages of nine and eleven.[45] In two, there was a change between brothers aged ten and eleven.[46] Thus it seems that eleven was an accepted age for going into long trousers in these families.

However, there were also some 'ragged' families where younger brothers had progressed to long trousers at ten (Figure 6.3),[47] or even at age seven.[48] Conversely, there were some families where older brothers were still in short trousers aged twelve,[49] or even fourteen.[50] This levelling-up and levelling-down may have been caused by external factors such as the availability or cost of short or long trousers, or it may demonstrate a wish to present brothers in the same way.

The commonest jacket types worn in these families were the lounge jacket and the sailor top in almost equal numbers (42 and 37), followed by the 'stripe' jacket with narrow strips of trimming (23). Sailor and 'stripe' jackets dominated the 'ragged' subset up to the age of eight but were seen in only one or two examples at ages nine and over. Lounge jackets were seen in few examples before the age of ten, but dominated from eleven upwards. Examining jackets and trousers together showed that in 36 out of 42 examples the lounge jacket was worn with long trousers, even by boys as young as seven years old.[51] Conversely, in 34 out of 37

---

[42]   Numbers 12120–22, ages 12 and 9, 1891.

[43]   The sailor trousers match each other, but not the sailor tops, suggesting that they were bought at different times; numbers 13103–5 (1892).

[44]   This data is Table 5.8 in Rose, 'Boyswear'.

[45]   Numbers 11387–8 (1891); 11801–2 (1891); 14452 (1893).

[46]   Numbers 13629–30 (1892); 14771–2 (1893).

[47]   Numbers 7878 (1888); 8917 (1889); 10443 (1890); 13195 (1892); 15698 (1894); 16572 (1895).

[48]   Numbers 11524 (1891); 18914 (1896).

[49]   Numbers 15502 (1894); 16288 (1894); 19030 (1897).

[50]   Number 37401 (1899).

[51]   Number 16569 (1895).

instances the sailor top was worn with short trousers, even on a boy of eleven.[52] It is noteworthy that the association of particular jacket types with particular ages should be seen so clearly even on boys whose clothes show signs of poverty. It is also noteworthy that in 25 of the 88 families in this sample two brothers wore the same jacket type, including five where both brothers wore the less common 'stripe' jacket.[53]

'Respectable' Brothers

The 260 brothers entering Barnardo's defined as wearing 'respectable' clothing showed some clear differences from the 'ragged' and 'neutral' brothers.[54] Five of the 'respectable' boys were in skirts, and two of these were three and four years old. Apart from these two exceptions, all the boys aged three to six were in short trousers. There was one seven-year-old in long trousers, all eight-year-olds wore short trousers, and only two nine-year-olds wore long trousers. Of the 34 ten-year-olds in this group 24 were still in short trousers and only 7 in long (three not visible). At age eleven, only one of 19 boys was visibly in longs. At age twelve, 9 out of 22 boys were still in short trousers and 7 in longs, and of the handful of boys aged thirteen and over two were still in short trousers. Thus in this group the mode age for entering long trousers was twelve. If we look at pairs of 'respectable' brothers with one in short and one in long trousers, the picture is less clear. In four of the long/short pairs the brother in long trousers was aged ten and the brother in short trousers was aged seven.[55] However, there was also a long/short pair of brothers aged ten and twelve, [56] and another with brothers aged twelve and fourteen. [57]

The inconsistency in the age of progression to long trousers can be explained by the strong tendency of families in this sample to dress both brothers alike, even when there was a gap of three years in age. So some ten-year-olds were assimilated to seven-year-old juniors,[58] and some to thirteen-year-old elders.[59] Out of 125 families in this sample, 74 had two or more brothers wearing jackets in the same style and often in the same fabric, even when there was a gap or four or five years in age (Figure 6.4).[60]

---

[52] Number 1404 (1888).

[53] Numbers 11276–7 (1891), Illustration 5.6, p. 307 in Rose, 'Boyswear'; numbers 10380–81(1890); 13629–30 (1892); 14706–7 (1893); 15502–3 (1894).

[54] See Table 5.9 in Rose, 'Boyswear'.

[55] Numbers 10794–5 (1891); 11734–5 (1891); 13707–8 (1892); 15299–15300 (1894).

[56] Numbers 15182–3 (1894).

[57] Numbers 11744–5 (1891).

[58] Numbers 21322–3 (1899).

[59] Numbers 14509–10 (1893).

[60] Brothers aged 9 and 13, numbers 16991–2 (1895); aged 8 and 11, 17322–3 (1895); aged 5 and 10, 18461–2 (1896).

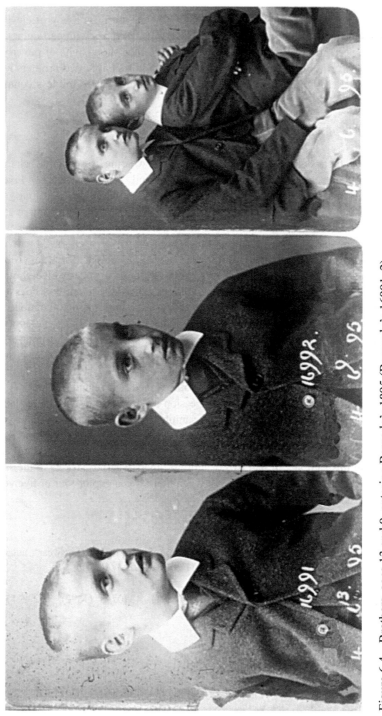

Figure 6.4 Brothers, ages 13 and 9, entering Barnado's 1895 (Barnardo's 16991–2).

'Mixed' Brothers

Boys were attributed to the 'mixed' group either because there were differences in levels of clothing between brothers (one 'ragged' and one 'respectable') or because the clothing of individuals had anomalies such as a white collar on a ragged jacket. These two categories will be analysed separately as they require different explanations. There are 76 brothers in the sample with inconsistencies in their clothing.[61] Some of these are minor, such as three-piece suits worn with collar and tie but crumpled,[62] or clothes which are clean and pressed, but obviously too small. This can be seen on a pair of brothers whose summer sailor suits are so small that the buttons gape across their stomachs, although they are worn with immaculate collars and ribbon bows (see Figure 5.2).[63] This suggests that the family saw the garments as conveying a meaning that was independent of the quality of fit. Otherwise, the too-small garments could have been sold or pawned and replaced by better-fitting substitutes.

A more striking inconsistency is the wearing of a white collar with ragged clothing. This pairing, visible in some of the school photographs discussed in Chapter 1, can be seen on five families (see Figures 1.3 and 1.9).[64] In some of these examples the wear on the clothing is relatively minor,[65] or the worn areas are limited and might have occurred immediately before entry.[66] But in other cases a white collar was added to clothes that had clearly been worn out for some time, as evidenced by patches or large holes.[67] These cases can be understood as embodiments of Campbell's separation of the intention (of respectable dressing) and execution of consumption, pushed apart by the lack of economic means. They may also represent attempts to establish the family's class status as 'white collar' workers as distinct from its economic position.[68]

Standards of dress could also be inconsistent within families, and 113 boys in 55 families showed a difference in levels of 'raggedness' and 'respectability' from their brothers.[69] This might be seen in one wearing a collar and the other not, or one having torn clothes and not the other, or in radically different types of clothing. Looking at the way these differences relate to the boys' ages will help to clarify how changing family circumstances affected clothing. Where funds

---

[61]   See Table 5.10 in Rose, 'Boyswear'.

[62]   For example, numbers 16345–7 (1894).

[63]   Numbers 18337–8 (1896).

[64]   Numbers 11552–3 (1891); 15400–401 (1894); 17106–7 (1895); 18664–5 (1896); 18951–2 (1896).

[65]   For example, numbers 11552–3; see Illustration 5.9, p. 310 in Rose, 'Boyswear'.

[66]   For example, number 15400 has torn trouser knees.

[67]   As in numbers 18664–5 (1896).

[68]   Information on family occupations is held in Barnardo's files which were closed to me under Data Protection regulations.

[69]   Table 5.11 in Rose, 'Boyswear'.

for clothing were limited, we might expect to see a greater expenditure on boys over the minimum age for employment (ten) to reflect their increased capacity for earnings. We might also expect to see elder brothers dressed in newer clothes while younger brothers had hand-me-downs showing more signs of wear.

In fact, the evidence on this is equivocal: in 28 family groups, the older brother was better dressed than the younger, and in 24 the younger was better dressed. There were 14 examples where the older brother had a collar and the younger did not; and 8 of the boys with collars were ten, just at the school leaving age. However there were also 7 families where the older brother, aged between ten and thirteen, did not wear a collar but the younger brother did. So any connection between the age of starting employment and increased 'respectability' in clothing is weak. This connection is further undermined by the distribution of 'raggedness' in this sample. Of 29 ragged boys in this sample, 16 were older brothers and 15 were aged ten or over.

In a few of the families in this sample, there was a difference between the clothes of older and younger siblings that suggests downward mobility. In families like the one in Figure 6.5 the older boy, aged eleven, wore a coarse wool or corduroy jacket in the adult 'lounge' shape with a neckerchief and the younger, aged nine, had a jacket in an age-specific shape with a white collar.[70] These outfits are differenced both by age and by class, with the older brothers lacking the 'white collar' status of the younger ones.[71] It is noteworthy that this change took place at the age for leaving school and starting employment. In these cases, we seem to see the triumph of economic reality over family aspirations.

Evaluating Age, Employment and Boys' Clothes

As discussed in Chapter , the concept of childhood in nineteenth-century England was not only gendered but also classed. Anna Davin has shown how 'the conflict between middle-class ideals and working-class realities of childhood led to increasing regulation of the conditions of children's lives'.[72] In particular, the structures, timetables, and demands of the Board School system intimately affected every aspect of working-class family life, from food and hygiene to earnings.[73] E.J. Urwick, writing in 1904, saw the influence of Board Schools as beneficial in

---

[70] Numbers 21816–8 (1899), Illustration 5.10, p. 310 in Rose, 'Boyswear'. See also numbers 16056–7 (1894); 16247–8 (1894); 19432–3 (1897); 21793–4 (1899).

[71] The older brother number 16247 did wear a white collar, but his jacket was of the heavy corduroy of working men's clothes. This combination was worn by George Acorn, which led to accusations of pretentiousness from his father. *One of the Multitude: An Autobiography of a Resident of Bethnl Green* (London, 1911), p. 117.

[72] Anna Davin, 'When is a Child not a Child?', in Helen Corr and Lynn Jamieson (eds), *The Politics of Everyday Life* (London, 1990), p. 37.

[73] Davin, *Growing Up Poor*, esp. Chapter 8.

Figure 6.5   Brothers, ages 11 and 9, entering Barnardo's 1894 [Barnardo's 16247–8]. Courtesy of Barnardo's Archive.

reforming the habits and clothing of the poor: 'Collars and ties are now almost as common as rags were a few years ago.'[74] Texts such as these had the effect of emphasising the gulf between respectability and raggedness, even as they claimed to see it overcome. They also ignored the economic and practical constraints on poor boys' access to clothing.

Both the images and texts analysed in this chapter indicate that age-related clothing practices for younger boys were aligned to the age divisions between Infant and Elementary Schools. This is unsurprising when we consider the ways in which schools acted as a common forum in which norms of behaviour were both created and enforced.[75] What is surprising is that these clothing practices were enacted by families rather than enforced by educational authorities, and were visible in photographs of boys taken outside the school setting as well as in class groups.

The analysis of the Barnardo's entry photographs showed that Campbell's distinction between consumers' intentions and behaviour was a key one for poor nineteenth-century families.[76] They demonstrated their *intention* of 'respectability' through dressing boys under twelve in age-specific clothing styles which were broadly similar to those worn in middle-class families. The use of white collars on visibly ragged jackets also appears to have been a deliberate statement demonstrating an understanding of the conventions of respectability. This knowledge can be seen as a form of 'cultural capital' that might be especially important in defining the identity of families lacking in financial capital.

These photographs also show how consumers used their knowledge of clothing conventions to select clothing from the range of styles and sizes offered by retailers. For example, while short trousers were available in size two, 15 per cent of the Barnardo's entrants were still in skirts at four. Long trousers were available from size ten, but twelve-year-old Barnardo's entrants were evenly divided between shorts and longs. Retailers who specialised in shorts suits for boys would have a vested interest in extending the age at which their products were worn; but their extended age ranges were not necessarily accepted by consumers. The interaction between the availability of clothing, advice to consumers, and consumer practices problematises the links made by Paoletti, Helvenston and Tosh between clothing and attitudes to masculinity. There does seem to have been a lowering of the age of transition from dresses to short trousers over the period 1870–1900, but it is not clear whether this reflected a wish to 'declare his sex by his garments at as early a period as possible'.[77] If so, we would expect a concomitant lowering of the age for progressing to the long trousers associated with adulthood, but this did not occur.

---

[74]   Urwick *Studies of Boy Life*, p. xi.

[75]   Corresponding to Pierre Bourdieu's definition of the habitus; *The Logic of Practice* (Cambridge, 1990), pp. 55–6.

[76]   Campbell, 'The Meaning of Objects', pp. 98–100.

[77]   *Harper's Bazaar*, 1893, cited in Sally Helvenston, 'Advice to American Mothers on the Subject of Children's Dress, 1800–1920', *Dress*, 7 (1981), p 40.

The Barnardo's entry photographs also show that the relationship between expenditure on clothing and entry to work was not so clear-cut as might be expected. We might presume boys at the age for seeking work to be better dressed, following the observations of C.E.B. Russell and the reminiscences of Lanigan. In fact, there were several examples in the Barnardo's entry photos where school-age younger brothers were better dressed than working-age elder ones. These examples show the families' understanding of the different conventions governing clothing in the workplace and in schools. They also suggest that the schoolboy was potentially, if not actually, of higher social status than the young worker. The gap between the age of entering employment and the age of putting on adult clothing may also constitute a claim that these individuals were still children, even when economically active. This would extend the 'prolonging of material dependence on adults' identified by Tosh in middle-class families to more general practice.[78] Treating young wage-earners as dependent children might have been influenced by economic motives, such as parents' wish to maintain control over their sons' wage packets.[79] But there were also campaigns in the labour movement at this time to prolong childhood by raising the minimum age of employment.[80] These photographs may indicate families' resistance to the necessity of children leaving school aged eleven.

The other major finding from the Barnardo's data was the preference for dressing siblings in matching jackets. In the 'respectable' group there were 75 pairs of brothers dressed alike, even when one of them was unusually old or unusually young in terms of the norms of practice. Even in the sibling groups classed as 'ragged' 25 out of 88 wore matching jackets. This data is remarkable when we consider that families entering Barnardo's were by definition facing severe economic hardship. This finding is not adequately explained by factors such as the availability of cheap garments, as in some cases boys wore garments of the same type but in different fabrics and possibly from different sources.[81] The presence of pairs of brothers in matching short or long trousers when one is an inappropriate age strengthens the likelihood that this matching represents a deliberate choice.

The practice of dressing siblings to match was uneconomic, as it required that two or more outfits were purchased together, and that old clothes were discarded rather than being handed down. Arthur Morrison assumed that in working-class families 'clothes descend in the same way from the biggest to the smallest, being

---

[78]   John Tosh, *A Man's Place: Masculinity and the Middle-Class Home in Victorian England* (New Haven, 1999), p. 150.

[79]   For families' dependence on the earnings of young workers, and tendency to appropriate their possessions, see Acorn, *One of the Multitude*, pp. 136 and 187; also Ross, *Love and Toil*, pp. 159–61.

[80]   Cunningham, *Children of the Poor*, p. 177.

[81]   See Illustration 5.6, p. 307 in Rose, 'Boyswear'.

shortened and "taken in" for each successive wearer'.[82] Handing down was presented as normative practice in autobiographies,[83] and matching outfits were only mentioned in the context of special occasions such as weddings.[84] Thus this practice has been written out of the historic record and was only identifiable in the Barnardo's images.

Dressing siblings as a harmonious group was a particularly loaded practice as it was associated with elite social groups, from the Royal family to the middle classes (Figure 6.6). Sets of matching garments preserved in museum collections reinforce these elite associations.[85] A set worn by sons of the first Lord Swaythling (born between 1869 and 1879)[86] is particularly interesting as it straddles the divide of 'breeching' but the two outfits express visual harmony through fabric, trimming and cut.[87] The practice of dressing siblings in harmony was condemned as an extravagance even for middle-class families. The author of *How to Dress on £15 a Year, as a Lady* (1873) stated:

> Dressing children all alike is expensive, or even in twos and twos, nice as it may be to see it, for obviously it must occasion a waste of old clothes, which is all very well when it can be afforded, but under our economical *regime*, they must all descend from the one to the other, without regard for appearances.[88]

---

[82]   Arthur Morrison, 'How to Live on 30s a Week', *Cornhill Magazine*, May 1901, in E. Royston Pike (ed), *Human Documents of the Age of the Forsytes* (London, 1969), p. 159.

[83]   Laura Ugolini, *Men and Menswear: Sartorial Consumption in Britain 1880–1939 (Aldershot: Ashgate, 2007)*, pp. 207–8; Tina Vivienne Richmond, '"No Finery": the Dress of the poor in Nineteenth-Century England' (unpublished PhD thesis, University of London, 2004)., pp. 69–70, cites several examples.

[84]   Two examples of matching bridesmaids' outfits are given by Richmond, 'No Finery', pp. 112–13. Richmond also cites (p. 77) an example of young men wearing matching neckerchiefs as a sign of group identity, but matching suits for brothers are not mentioned here or elsewhere.

[85]   Worthing Museum has a single example (1967.1023) from a pair of identical brown velvet dresses worn by twin brothers for a photograph in 1882; Illustration 5.33, p. 344 in Rose, 'Boyswear'. Another pair of similar tunics worn by brothers c.1868 is in the V&A Museum of Childhood, 1968.T221 & 222; see Clare Rose, *Children's Clothes since 1750* London, 1989), Plate 5.

[86]   *Debrett's Peerage and Baronetage* (2000), www.xreferplus.com (accessed 5 June 2006).

[87]   The first suit consists of a dress and open-fronted jacket and the second of a wide-cut tunic and short trousers; both are made of black cotton velvet trimmed with interlaced lines of braid. Museum of London 1970.119/1&2; see Illustrations 5.34–5.35, p. 345 in Rose, 'Boyswear'.

[88]   A Lady [Mrs Millicent Whiteside Cook], *How to Dress on £15 a Year, as a Lady* (London, 1873), p. 99.

Figure 6.6   A middle-class family c.1894: boys aged 10 and 8 [62/1803].
Courtesy of Worthing Museum.

This makes it all the more interesting to see this practice on Barnardo's entrants.

It may be argued that the Barnardo's entrants are not typical of working-class practice. However they are likely to have been more affected by financial constraints than boys whose families were able to support them at home. Hence the adherence to social conventions seen in this sample is likely to have been even stronger in more prosperous sections of the working-class. The findings from these images overturn our expectation that working-class boys would have a shorter period of boyhood to correspond with earlier economic activity, and undermine the rhetoric of difference seen in contemporary writers on nineteenth-century working-class life such as Bray. The groups of siblings in the Barnardo's entry photographs showed the complex way in which clothes were related to boys' age and family status. In these groups there was a clear progression from sailor or 'stripe' jackets and shorts for younger boys to lounge jackets and long trousers for older boys, evident even in 'ragged' families where clothing purchase was infrequent. Yet this was counteracted by the strong preference for dressing brothers alike, or even keeping brothers in matching but too-small outfits. There were families where the older brother of working age was worse dressed than a schoolboy sibling, a combination that strongly suggests the social descent of a family.[89] There were families where the reality of ragged jackets was overlaid with the respectable veneer of a clean white collar. All of these examples suggest that even the poorest families were aware of the meanings of clothing, not just in terms of 'raggedness' and 'respectability', but as nuanced markers of the familial and social position of the wearer. The extent to which clothing carried symbolic, as well as social, meanings will be examined in the next chapter.

---

[89]   For the economic insecurity of the lower middle classes, see Harold Perkin, *The Rise of Professional Society: England since 1880* (London, 1989), p. 95.

Chapter 7
Masculine Symbolism in Boys' Clothes

In 1896, Jane Emily Panton published a book for socially anxious middle-class mothers, *The Way They Should Go*. She included advice on clothing young boys:

> Of course it is ridiculous of parents without a drop of Scotch blood in their veins to adopt a tartan, and those who do so are most deservedly laughed at; but one can procure simple tweed kilts which anyone can wear, and which are to be preferred in every way to the odious common sailor suit; for kilts are dear to buy, and so can never become really common, though they wear out so many ordinary suits they cannot be considered really expensive … Of course when school-time comes the kilt must go.[1]

This passage is unusually frank in its acknowledgement of the relationship between clothing and social status. What is particularly interesting is that the two outfits discussed, the Highland kilt and the sailor suit, are not seen in terms of any masculine, patriotic, or imperial references. This is surprising, as they are both derived from military uniform. John Mackenzie has shown how Imperialism permeated all levels of British society, from school textbooks to boys' comics.[2] Civilian identification with the armed forces was encouraged by groups such as the Navy League, founded in 1895, which had 100,000 members by 1914.[3] The Highland soldier, as Heather Streets has pointed out, had a particularly privileged position in late nineteenth-century imperial ideology as a representative of a 'martial race'.[4] Graham Dawson sees Imperial figures as shaping the whole notion of heroism, and of masculine identity, in the late nineteenth century.[5] The popular culture of Imperialism was highly visual, and we would expect its images to be reflected in the marketing of boys' sailor and Highland suits.

This chapter will analyse the expression of masculinity and patriotism in young boys' clothing, focusing on three main areas: sailor suits and Highland kilts for boys

---

[1]   Jane Emily Panton, *The Way They Should Go* (London, 1896), p. 98.

[2]   John Mackenzie, *Propaganda and Empire: The Manipulation of British Public Opinion, 1880–1960* (Manchester, 1984); *idem* (ed.), *Imperialism and Popular Culture* (Manchester, 1986).

[3]   Mackenzie, *Propaganda and Empire*, p. 154.

[4]   Heather Streets, *Martial Races: The Military, Race and Masculinity in British Imperial Culture, 1857–1914* (Manchester, 2004).

[5]   Graham Dawson, *Soldier Heroes: British Adventure, Empire, and the Imagining of Masculinity* (London, 1994).

aged roughly three to ten years old, and dresses for male toddlers. The first section will set out the context of late nineteenth-century Imperialism and the ways that this was brought to bear on boys' education and leisure pursuits. The second will set out the royal precedents for boys dressed in sailor suits and kilts, which might be expected to exert a powerful influence on consumption. In the third section, a close examination of the chronology of sailor and kilt wearing will allow us to question its links to royal influence. The fourth section will analyse how they were presented to consumers in advertising images, examining the changes produced by the onset of the Boer War in 1899. The fifth will examine the ways that sailor and Highland suits were modulated to reflect distinctions of status and age as well as gender, using texts from women's magazines, tailors' and dressmakers' manuals. In the sixth section, an analysis of surviving examples of sailor suits will help to clarify how the themes highlighted in texts and images were put into practice. Masculine symbolism was needed in very young boys' clothing in order to create a visible difference from young girls or from undifferentiated infants. The final section of this chapter will analyse surviving young boys' dresses to clarify the specific design features used to create a masculine identity.

Taken together, this material will clarify the complex ways in which masculinity was embodied in clothing for boys. The evidence suggests that in clothing masculinity was not polarised against femininity, but modulated by the wearer's age and class status. The presentation of boys' garments was also permeated by an element of play or fantasy that was not permitted for older boys and young men. This playfulness is the key to the interpretation of these garments, and undermines any attempt at a simple interpretation of masculinity in this material.

Imperialism and Masculinity

John Mackenzie has argued that an Imperial and militaristic ethos surrounded children in the late nineteenth century, both at school and in their leisure hours. The history and geography taught in state schools aimed at the 'inculcation of patriotism and good citizenship' and the key dates and personages were those of military and naval campaigns.[6] The prize books given away by schools and churches were drawn from sets featuring military or missionary heroes, with competing titles on the most approved figures.[7] Imperial themes were also prevalent in boys' leisure reading, typified by magazines like the *Boys' Own Paper* and the novels of G.A. Henty, which mixed adventure, patriotism and Imperialism.[8] John Springhall has analysed the ways in which this body of writing promoted 'a spirit of manliness,

---

6   Mackenzie, *Propaganda and Empire*, p. 177.

7   Ibid., p. 214.

8   Ibid., pp. 203–5. See also Kelly Boyd, 'Knowing Your Place: The Tensions of Manliness in Boys' Story Papers, 1918–39', in Michael Roper and John Tosh (eds), *Manful Assertions: Masculinities in Britain Since 1800* (London, 1991), pp. 145–67; Helen Kanitkar, '"Real true

of steadfastness and of courage' through tales of Imperial adventures, military campaigns, and righteous conflicts.[9] One of the main publishers for young people went so far as to claim Imperial motives for their productions: 'the boys' papers of the Amalgamated Press have done more to provide recruits for our Navy and Army and to keep up the esteem of the sister services than anything else'.[10] The use of Imperial rhetoric to support pragmatic aims may in fact have been the default position, as Andrew Thompson and Bernard Porter have shown in their analysis of children's reaction to initiatives such as Empire Day.[11]

A similar mixture of institutional and personal motives can be seen in the many late nineteenth-century organisations promoting naval activities for boys. These had stated aims that ranged from training and recruitment, to fostering financial and political support of the armed forces, to recreation. The encouragement of good-quality naval recruits had been a matter of official concern before the time of Nelson, and after 1855 the Royal Navy established training ships as centres for recruitment and training. By 1896 there were four ships with 4,000 places available for boys aged sixteen. However, these places were apparently oversubscribed by a factor of ten, swelled by applicants from the numerous naval training schools for boys aged between eleven and fourteen.[12] The earliest of the schools were set up by charities: the Training Ship *Chichester* was established in 1867 by Lord Shaftesbury, the philanthropic founder of the Ragged Schools. These were followed by state-funded examples run as residential Poor Law Schools, starting with TS *Goliath* in 1870.[13] By 1884, 25 per cent of all boys leaving London Poor Law Schools were enlisting as sailors in the Royal or Merchant Navy, and another 20 per cent enlisted as naval or military bandsmen.[14] This was in spite of a prevailing

---

boys": Moulding the Cadets of Imperialism', in Andrea Cornwall and Nancy Lindisfarne (eds), *Dislocating Masculinity: Comparative Ethnographies* (London: 1994).

[9]   John Springhall, 'Building Character in the British Boy: The Attempt to Extend Christian Manliness to Working-class Adolescents, 1880–1914', in Michael Roper and John Tosh (eds), *Manful Assertions: Masculinities in Britain Since 1800* (London: Routledge, 1991), pp. 52–74.

[10]   Cited in Mackenzie, *Propaganda and Empire*, p. 205.

[11]   Andrew Thompson, *The Empire Strikes Back? The Impact of Imperialism on Britain from the Mid-Nineteenth Century* (Harlow, 2005), esp. Chapter 4; Bernard Porter, *The Absent-Minded Imperialists: Empire, Society and Culture in Britain* (Oxford, 2004), esp. Chapter 9. See also Clare Rose, 'The Meanings of the Late Victorian Sailor Suit', *Journal of Maritime Research*, http://www.jmr.nmm.ac.uk/server/show/ConJmrArticle.270/, online September 2009.

[12]   Archibald S. Hurd, 'How Blue Jackets are Trained', *The Windsor Magazine*, 1896, p. 322.

[13]   Lydia Murdoch, *Imagined Orphans: Poor Families, Child Welfare and Contested Citizenship in London* (New Brunswick, 2006), p. 120.

[14]   Ibid., p. 137.

reluctance on the part of the boys' families to give the permission needed for a lengthy period of enlistment.[15]

There were many middle-class supporters for the work of the training ships. In October 1871, *The Times* stated that their benefits both to individuals and to the nation as a whole 'are gains worth purchasing at a higher price than a few out-of-date wooden men-of-war'.[16] Florence Nightingale sent a personal donation for the rebuilding of the *Goliath* after a fire, feeling that 'Every so trained, and so depauperised boy, is a bequest to England worth making'.[17] When Dr Barnardo's Homes established a naval training school in 1901, they described it as a 'Handy-man's factory' in which 'smart little Jack Tars are evolved and drafted into the sea services of the Empire'.[18] Several of these ships were moored in central London, where they were visible to passers-by, and they were also used as components of spectacular fundraising or ceremonial events such as the Lord Mayor's Show. In 1872, the *Chichester* boys and their bands paraded through the streets of London in naval uniforms to give displays in front of the Lord Mayor, an event described as 'as fine a spectacle of seamanlike promise as any we could hope to see'.[19]

In addition to the residential training ships there were further organisations that provided naval training to boys living at home. The earliest of these was the Naval Lads' Brigades, founded in 1856 by acting seamen with the express purpose of encouraging naval recruitment, and continuing today under the name of Sea Cadets.[20] From 1890 onwards, there were also groups with the more general aim of increasing public support and understanding of naval life, rather than recruitment per se. These organised spectacular exhibitions, displays and lectures, funded by individual subscriptions. The Navy League alone had 100,000 individual members by 1914, their loyalty rewarded by specially designed magazines and collectables such as cigarette cards.[21] George Orwell was a juvenile member in 1910: 'at seven years old I was a member of the Navy League and wore a sailor suit with *HMS Invincible* on my cap'.[22] The continuing demand for naval leisure activities is typified by the expansion of the Boys Scouts into Sea Scouts within a year of their foundation in 1907.[23] As Hugh Cunningham and Michael Morpurgo point out, the high membership of voluntary organisations indicates a level of popular support for their aims.[24] Thus the Royal Navy provided careers for both paupers

---

[15]   Ibid., p. 138.

[16]   Ibid., p. 120.

[17]   Ibid., p. 120.

[18]   Ibid., p. 135.

[19]   *The Graphic*, 13 January 1872, p. 23.

[20]   www.seacadets.org.uk (accessed 4 April 2007).

[21]   Mackenzie, *Propaganda and Empire*, p. 154.

[22]   Ibid., p. 255.

[23]   Ibid., pp. 241–3.

[24]   Hugh Cunningham and Michael Morpurgo, *The Invention of Childhood* (London, 2006), p. 209.

and princes, and received support from civilians through membership of voluntary groups and attendance at spectacles.

Kilt-wearing Highland soldiers were also key figures in the national imagery of late nineteenth-century Britain. As early as the 1780s the 'clearance' of crofters from the land and the lack of alternative employment had made the army an important destination for young Scots men. Seen as naturally warlike, brave and loyal, Highland soldiers were singled out for praise in the Crimean War of 1853–56.[25] Their popular reputation was confirmed when a Highland regiment was responsible for the relief of a besieged British garrison at Lucknow during the Indian Mutiny of 1857.[26] Within a year, this thrilling event had been written up by the popular press, re-enacted in popular theatre, and memorialised in Royal Academy paintings and cheap ceramic figurines.[27] This led to a heightened public awareness of these regiments: by the 1870s, Cockney army recruits frequently expressed a preference for serving in Highland regiments, which by then were largely composed of non-Highlanders.[28] The trustworthy figure of the Highlander was also used to sell a range of consumer goods including coffee essence.[29] The distinctive appearance of these regiments was an important part of their appeal to recruits and to the public, and meant that the kilt was retained for active duty as late as the trenches of World War I, in spite of its many inconveniences.[30]

Princes in Kilts and Sailor Suits

The period from 1860 onwards was one in which Britain's navy and army were at the centre of national consciousness, defending both Imperial outposts and trading networks. Their work was endorsed at the highest level of British society, with royal princes dressed for public appearances in miniature uniforms that prefigured their future roles as military and naval commanders. Queen Victoria had dressed her heir in a sailor suit for a state visit in 1846, and in a Highland outfit for the opening ceremony of the Great Exhibition in 1851; both these outfits were commemorated in images that were widely reproduced.[31] As Christopher Breward

---

[25] Streets, *Martial Races*, p. 56.

[26] Ibid., pp. 53–62.

[27] The play *Jessie Brown* by Dion Boucicaut, and the painting *In Memoriam* by Sir Joseph Noel Paton, RA. See Streets, *Martial Races*, pp. 61–2.

[28] Ibid., pp. 176–81.

[29] The original label for Camp Coffee Essence, marketed from 1885, showed a soldier from the Gordon Highlanders waited on by a Sikh servant; this label was redesigned in 2006 following protests against its perpetuation of colonial stereotypes, http://news.bbc.co.uk/2/hi/uk_news/409264.stm (accessed 1 August 1999).

[30] See the official website of the Argyll and Sutherland Highlanders: www.argylls. co.uk.

[31] The portrait of the prince in a sailor suit by F.X. Winterhalter was engraved for sale in 1848; Richard Ormond and Caroline Blackett-Ord, *Franz Xaver Winterhalter and the Courts of*

points out, 'The propaganda value of uniform, having been established in the late eighteenth century, was one that continued to underpin the presentation of the aristocratic self throughout the nineteenth'.[32]

The association of royal princes with naval uniforms was more than symbolic, as many of them went through a period of naval training. Victoria's second son, Alfred Duke of Edinburgh, was enlisted as a midshipman at the age of fourteen in 1858 and continued to serve as a naval officer throughout his life.[33] The two elder sons of the Prince of Wales, Princes Albert Victor and George, were enlisted for five years of naval training in 1877, aged thirteen and twelve. Prince George remained a naval officer until the death of his elder brother in 1892 made him heir to the throne.[34] In the next generation two sons of George V, Princes Edward (VIII) and Albert (George VI), were enrolled for naval training at Osborne naval College in 1907, and Dartmouth in 1907, Albert continuing in the navy throughout World War I.[35] The royal children were also dressed in sailor suits for leisure activities. In 1875, the five children of the Prince of Wales were photographed by Bassano dressed in sailor suits.[36] Princes Albert Victor and George (aged eleven and ten) wore 'correct' sailor suits with white cotton tops and dark wool bell-bottom trousers while their three sisters (aged from six to eight) had sailor-styled dresses of dark cotton. These images, available for sale to the general public, might be expected to have a direct influence on the fashion for juvenile sailor suits.

The royal association with Highland dress was less purely militaristic, tempered by Queen Victoria's love of her Scottish holiday home at Balmoral, purchased in 1842.[37] Her enthusiasm for Scotland was given public expression in her 1868 publication of *Leaves from the Journal of our Life in the Highlands*.[38]

Europe, 1830–1870 (London, 1987), p. 192. The opening of the Great Exhibition was recorded by H.C. Selous in a painting now at the Victoria and Albert Museum (no. 329-1889).

[32]   Christopher Breward, *The Hidden Consumer: Masculinities, Fashion and City Life, 1860–1914* (Manchester, 1999), p. 67.

[33]   John Van der Kiste, 'Alfred, Prince, Duke of Edinburgh', in *Dictionary of National Biography* (Oxford, 2007), vol.1, p. 725.

[34]   Henry Matthew, 'George V, King of Great Britain', in *Dictionary of National Biography* (Oxford, 2007), vol. 21, p. 864.

[35]   Prince Edward: H.C.G. Matthew, 'Edward VIII [*later* Prince Edward, duke of Windsor] (1894–1972)', in *Oxford Dictionary of National Biography* (Oxford, 2004), online edn http://www.oxforddnb.com/view/article/31061 (accessed 17 June 2008)]. Prince Albert: H.C.G. Matthew, 'George VI (1895–1952)', in *Oxford Dictionary of National Biography* (Oxford, 2004), online edn http://www.oxforddnb.com/view/article/33370 (accessed 17 June 2008).

[36]   A series of photographs, National Portrait Gallery London (NPG) x96023, x96034–6.

[37]   Streets, *Martial Races*, p. 59.

[38]   Queen Victoria, *Leaves from the Journal of our Life in the Highlands, from 1848 to 1861. To which are prefixed and added, extracts from the same journal, giving an account of earlier visits to Scotland, and tours in England and Ireland, and yachting excursions*, ed. Sir Arthur Helps (London, 1868). For the influence of 'balmoralmania' on design, see Michael

Even the German Prince Albert was portrayed in a kilt in a Highland setting.[39] Royal children were dressed in kilts both for state occasions like the opening of the Crystal Palace and for leisure pursuits. In 1849, Victoria commissioned two portraits of her children wearing Highland dress and posed against a backdrop of Scottish moorland. In these images the kilt is linked to hunting and outdoor pursuits, rather than to military uniform.[40]

Sailor and Highland Suits for Boys

Military references in young boys' clothing were an established convention by the mid-nineteenth century. In the 1820s, one of the first outfits designed specifically for young boys was known as a 'hussar' suit, linking it to an elite cavalry regiment.[41] This identification was based on the use of horizontal lines of braid across the chest, a detail that was also taken up by fashionable women's clothing in the 1820s.[42] In the 1890s, braided trimmings continued to carry military associations: the *Cutter's Practical Guide* illustrated eight braid-trimmed styles, four with military names (Rifle, Artilleur, Lancer, Gordon), and four with aristocratic titles (Prince, Regent, Duke, Count) (see Figure 2.9).[43] In the 1770s, some of the earliest suits designed for young boys rather than men had had long trousers like a sailor's instead of the knee-breeches worn by adults; this was called a 'sailor' ensemble in Europe but not in Britain. As long trousers became conventional for men and boys in the 1820s, the association of this ensemble with sailors was lost.[44]

As the analysis of clothing styles in Chapter 2 showed, references to military uniform in boys' clothing were far outnumbered by styles derived from sailors and kilted Highlanders (see Figures 2.6 and 2.8). These have been seen by dress

---

Snodin and John Styles, *Design and the Decorative Arts: Britain, 1500–1900* (London, 2001), pp. 315–17.

[39]   In a lithograph published c.1850, Prince Albert wears a kilt and Garter regalia in a moorland setting. V&A image number 22182, illustrated in Snodin and Styles, *Design*, p. 315.

[40]   Two portraits by Franz Xaver Winterhalter, *Albert Edward, Prince of Wales, with Prince Alfred in Highland dress* (Royal Collection RCIN 403121) and *Prince Alfred and Princess Helena* (Royal Collections RCIN 400872). The latter was engraved for sale in 1850; Ormond and Blackett-Ord, *Franz Xaver Winterhalter*, number 33, p. 193.

[41]   Alison Matthews David, 'Decorated Men: Fashioning the French Soldier, 1852–1914', *Fashion Theory*, 7/1 (2003), p. 12.

[42]   Phyllis Cunnington and Anne Buck, *Children's Costume in England 1300–1900* (London, 1965), p. 173.

[43]   William D.F. Vincent, *The Cutter's Practical Guide: Part I, Juvenile, Youths and Young Men* (London, 1890), Plate 18.

[44]   See Clare Rose, *Children's Clothes Since 1750* (London, 1989) p. 48; Nicole Pellegrin, *Les Vêtements de la liberté, Abécédaire des pratiques vestimentaires en France de 1780 à 1800* (Aix, 1989), p. 127.

historians as the result of Veblenian emulation of the royal family. Elizabeth Ewing summed up the process of emulation:

> The first full-scale uniforms to be worn widely by boys of all ages were variations of Highland dress ... when, in 1851, Queen Victoria opened the Great Exhibition ... Bertie was in full Highland dress ... soon hordes of small boys everywhere were following suit ... It was Britain's proud boast that she ruled the seas and her navy was the proudest symbol of that rule and of her far-flung Empire. Small boys decked out as sailors brought a parental and symbolic glow of pride into every home and the Royal lead was followed with such zeal that the sailor suit became the main fashion for boys. [45]

The sailor suit worn by the Prince was based on those worn on the Royal Yacht, which were used as the model for the new uniform for naval ratings introduced in 1857.[46]

The 1850s was also a period when seaside holidays were becoming established as a feature of middle-class British life, boosted by advances in transport. Brighton had been established as a seaside resort in 1815, but after the arrival of the railway in 1840 its population expanded by 50 per cent in ten years. By 1850 Brighton was receiving up to 73,000 visitors per week in the season, and this expansion was echoed in resorts around the coast.[47] The status of the seaside holiday as a phenomenon of fashionable life was confirmed by William Frith's 1854 painting *Ramsgate Sands*, voted Painting of the Year at the Royal Academy, reproduced as an engraving, then finally purchased by Queen Victoria.[48] Thus both royal precedents and leisure associations would be expected to make the boys' sailor suit fashionable in the 1850s.

In fact, it does not seem to have been widely worn until the late 1860s. The earliest extant non-royal example dates from 1855, but was worn in the unusual context of a long sea voyage from India back to Britain.[49] The earliest photograph of a boy wearing a sailor suit for leisure (not as uniform) dates from 1865.[50] *Punch*, an acute observer of middle-class life, published many cartoons of children on the beach, but it was not until 1868 that they were depicted wearing sailor suits.[51] In 1870, a pattern for a boys' sailor suit was published in a dressmaking magazine,

---

[45]   Elizabeth Ewing, *History of Children's Costume* (London, 1977), pp. 83–7.

[46]   Amy Miller, *Dressed to Kill: British Naval Uniform, Masculinity and Contemporary Fashions, 1748–1857* (Greenwich, 2007), p. 10.

[47]   John Walvin, *Beside the Seaside: A Social History of the Popular Seaside Holiday* (London, 1978), p. 39.

[48]   Mark Bills and Vivien Knight, *William Powell Frith, Painting the Victorian Age* (New Haven and London, 2006), p. 12.

[49]   MOL 1942.20.

[50]   Miles Lambert, *Fashion in Photographs 1860–1880* (London, 1991), no. 74.

[51]   Cartoon by George Du Maurier, *Punch*, 19 December 1868, p. 260.

and a ready-made version was registered by Donald Nicoll.[52] By 1874 sailor suits were described as a favourite style for children, and patterns for women's sailor blouses were also available.[53]

Yet when the *Tailor and Cutter* discussed sailor suits in 1875, it was as novelties inspired by Royal precedent: 'What do you think of the change in juvenile attire, as seen now on every little gentleman, since the cartoon in Punch, representing our young Prince in "The ship boy's semblance" giving a glass of grog to a Jack Tar?'[54] Royal precedents were highly visible in 1875, when the Prince of Wales had his five children photographed wearing sailor suits.[55] Yet ascribing the fashion to royal influence oversimplifies the development of the style since 1865, a time when there were no royal juveniles to wear it.[56]

Highland outfits for boys were on sale as early as 1850,[57] but do not seem to have been widely worn at this time. As late as 1877, they were described as novelties: 'a new style of juvenile dress ... In style it may be classified with the Highland dress.'[58] They were not discussed in terms of their national symbolism until 1890, when the *Cutter's Practical Guide* classified Highland and sailor suits as 'historic, national and artistic styles'.[59]

Sailor and Highland Suits in Advertising

Advertising material, as discussed in Chapter 3, acted as an intermediary between retailers and customers, and would be expected to highlight any symbolic associations that would help to sell the garments. The commercial documents in the Stationers' Hall archive, the John Johnson Collection and elsewhere yielded 228 images of sailor suits and 60 of Highland outfits. These images presented some problems of interpretation, the foremost of which was that there was usually no accompanying text other than information on prices and sizes. Images intended for use in newspaper advertisements or small flyers were purely functional, with

[52]   Dressmaking pattern sheet from *Young Ladies Journal*, 1870, exhibited in *Sailor Chic*, National Maritime Museum, July–December 2007. Sailor suit by D. Nicoll, BT 43/13 238638 (1870), TNA, illustrated in Sarah Levitt, *The Victorians Unbuttoned* (London, 1986), p. 98.

[53]   *Tailor and Cutter*, June 1874. Nancy Bryk, *American Dress Pattern Catalogs 1873–1909* (New York, 1988), p. 24. This pattern would have been available in Britain as Butterick had opened a London office in 1873.

[54]   *Tailor and Cutter*, March 1875, p. 105: 'Tom Jones' Diary, or Tailoring of the Past and Present Generation'. A search of *Punch* between 1870 and 1875 failed to identify this image, so the reference may be spurious.

[55]   NPG x96023, x96035, x96036, x96037.

[56]   See Rose, 'Meanings of the late-Victorian Sailor Suit'.

[57]   L. Hyam and Co., *The Gentleman's Illustrated Album of Fashion for 1850*, London and provinces (JJ MC 4/9).

[58]   *Tailor and Cutter*, February 1877 p. 1.

[59]   Vincent, *Cutter's Practical Guide*, p. 51.

figures arranged against a blank background (see Figures 3.1 and 7.3). Elaborate groups printed in full colour in a landscape setting were produced as display posters by some manufacturers and wholesalers (Figures 3.2 and 3.3). Few of these indicated the age ranges or associations of different styles, although the figures wearing sailor suits appear younger than those in other suits.[60] A third category of images, intended for retailers' multi-page catalogues, depicted figures with accessories and settings that suggest the intended uses and meanings of specific garment types (Figures 3.4 and 7.1).

Figure 7.1   A page from the catalogue of Frederick Watts & Co., 1897 [Copy 1 134/220]. Courtesy of The National Archives, Kew.

---

[60]   Notably in a poster by Wesley Petty, Stationers' Hall Archive (Copy 1) Books Commercial (BC) 971/17475 (1899), The National Archives (TNA); see Illustration 5.25, p. 331 in Clare Rose, 'Boyswear and the Formation of Gender and Class Identity in Urban England, 1840–1900' (unpublished PhD thesis, University of Brighton, 2006).

In the case of sailor suits the settings of the images referred overwhelmingly to seaside holidays, with boys posed on cliff-tops, by sea walls, or on the sand with a toy spade.[61] References to nautical activities were limited to play with a toy yacht, and sailor-suited boys were also shown engaged in other amusements, such as playing horses. Another catalogue image showed two young boys in sailor suits (one made of velvet, one of dark wool) and a third in formal Highland dress in a drawing-room setting (Figure 7.1).[62] This image is interesting as it places both sailor and Highland suits in the context of a formal social event. Other images of Highland suits had references to Scots national identity, through golf or Highland sword dances.[63] Interestingly, both of these activities were presented as play, with walking sticks substituted for claymores and golf clubs.

In all of these images the only context given for sailor and Highland suits was that of middle-class leisure.[64] Specifically Imperial references for these garments were found in only a handful of commercial documents registered in 1900. A sheet of copyrighted images registered by Wesley Petty gave prominent place to an image of a sailor-suited boy riding on a lion while waving a Union Jack (Figure 7.2).[65] The combination of the British Lion and the flag make the Imperial message of this image very clear. This message also permeates other images in the set: a young boy in a tunic holds a Union Jack and military bugle, a middling boy stands in front of a military tent, and an older boy has an air-rifle and a flag. These images were used in a catalogue for the retailer Logan of Leamington Spa, which refers to 'khaki caps' and 'latest speciality – khaki suits, trimmed red'. [66]

The reference to khaki locates the document very precisely in the context of the Boer War, the first campaign in which khaki-coloured uniforms were in general use by British troops.[67] The South African conflict had begun in 1899, and early in 1900 there were a series of notable advances by the British troops, including the relief of Kimberley in February and the capture of Bloemfontein in March, and

---

[61]   For example, the coloured cover of a catalogue for the Scotch House, London, by Gardiner & Co., Copy 1 BC/975/18647 (1899), TNA, showed a boy in a sailor suit standing on a sea wall and playing with a hoop. See Rose, 'Boyswear', illustration 5.24, p. 331.

[62]   From a catalogue for F. Watts & Co., Copy 1 134/220 (1897), TNA; Rose, 'Boyswear', illustration 5.26, p. 332.

[63]   Golf, Copy 1 BC 974/18528 (1899), TNA, colour cover of a catalogue for Southcott of Hull by Wesley Petty; see Rose, 'Boyswear', illustration 5.27, p. 333. For sword dance, see Copy 1 128a/58 (1896), TNA, by Richard Taylor.

[64]   This fits with the stress on pleasure in French advertising images of the 1890s; see Paul Jobling and David Crowley, *Graphic Design: Reproduction and Representation since 1800* (Manchester, 1996), esp. Chapter 3.

[65]   Petty sheet, Copy 1 163/134, TNA.

[66]   Logan catalogue, Copy 1 BC 975/18747, TNA; Rose, *Boyswear* illustrations 5.30 and 5.31 p. 336.

[67]   The term 'khaki' was used as shorthand for the British troops by civilians on both sides; Tabitha Jackson, *The Boer War* (London, 1999), pp. 138–9.

Figure 7.2   Boys' clothes in a catalogue for Logan of Leamington Spa, 1900 [Copy 1 BC 975/18747]. Courtesy of The National Archives, Kew.

culminating in the relief of Mafeking in May.[68] The Petty images were registered on 20 March 1900, and were evidently designed to capitalise on the patriotic fervour aroused by this stage of the campaign. Other retailers went even further: Baker & Co. offered khaki suits and hats styled after those worn by the City of London Imperial Volunteers (CIV) to fit boys aged six to twelve (Figure 7.3).[69] Another retailer presented their February 1900 sales leaflet as a 'Special War Edition' with an image of a khaki-clad soldier on the front.[70] As Frederick Willis recollected, 'Everybody went khaki mad. There were khaki ties, khaki braces, khaki dresses, blouses, handkerchiefs, hats and stockings.'[71]

In these advertising images we see that the Imperial and militaristic references were not particular to the sailor suit, but to a specific moment in 1900, when they were applied to all clothing from a toddler's tunic to a lady's costume. The use of patriotic images in advertising seems to have been a common tactic at the outset of a war, documented by Schorman for America in 1898, and by Ugolini for Britain in 1914.[72] The one significant exception was the Highland kilt: the example in the Logan catalogue is posed on a rocky hillside, with no military or patriotic accessories. As kilts were worn on active duty in the Boer War by regiments such as the Argyll and Sutherland Highlanders, the avoidance of military references in this case appears to be deliberate.[73]

---

[68]   Thomas Pakenham, *The Boer War* (London, 1982), pp. 321–418.

[69]   Khaki suits by C. Baker & Co., Copy 1 BC 975/18721 (1900), TNA. The CIV was raised in late 1899 and served during 1900, returning to an ecstatic welcome in October 1900. See Richard Price, *An Imperial War and the British Working Class: Working-Class Attitudes and Reactions to the Boer War, 1899–1902* (London, 1972), pp. 178–80, 191–6.

[70]   London House, Llandudno, Copy 1 BC 974/18322 (1900), TNA; see also the images reproduced in Michael Paris, *Warrior Nation: Images of War in British Popular Culture, 1850–2000* (London, 2000), pp. 46–7.

[71]   Frederick Willis, *A Book of London Yesterdays* (London, 1960), p. 88. Khaki products in the Copy 1 archives include dressmaking fabric, AMB Ltd, Copy 1 162/17 (1900), TNA; 'khaki creams' sweets, Backhouse of York, Copy 1 BC 974/18440 (1900), TNA; BP boot polish (with portrait of Robert Baden-Powell), Copy 1 BC 977/19702 (1900), TNA. For the 'khaki election' of 1900, see Price, *Imperial War*, pp. 97–131.

[72]   For America, see Rob Schorman, *Selling Style: Clothing and Social Change at the Turn of the Century* (Philadelphia, 2003), pp. 102–16; for Britain, see Laura Ugolini, *Men and Menswear: Sartorial Consumption in Britain, 1880–1939* (Aldershot, 2007), pp. 77–8 and 156–7.

[73]   For the difficulties and dangers created by kilts on South African battlefields, see Jackson, *Boer War*, pp. 59–64.

C.I.V. HATS.
In Khaki,
Scarlet, and
other
colours.
3/6

KHAKI
CAPS,
from
1/-

KHAKI SUITS.

**For Boys from 6 to 12 years of
age.**

Height 3ft. 7 3ft. 9 4ft.   4ft. 3.
        6/11 6/11 7/11   7/11

        4ft. 5. 4ft. 7. 4ft. 10.
        8/11 8/11 9/11

Figure 7.3   Khaki suits and hats based on those worn by the City of London
Imperial Volunteers, catalogue by Baker, 1900 [Copy 1 BC
975/18721]. Courtesy of The National Archives, Kew.

Social Distinctions in Sailor and Highland Suits

Nineteenth-century texts made frequent references to the need to match different versions of the sailor and Highland suit to different social settings. As early as 1875 *Myra's Journal* commented in a review of the stock of H.D. Nicoll:

> For little boys' best suits, the Highland, the Parisian, the Swiss, and the Scarboro' styles are the most suitable; for every-day or seaside wear, the Sailor, the American Sailor, the Brighton, Norfolk, and Spanish are most commendable. The American Sailor differs from the ordinary sailor's suit, it is trimmed more 'taut'.[74]

The recommendation of sailor suits for the seaside was based on more than an association of ideas. As the principal site for middle-class family holidays in the mid-nineteenth century, the seaside was a location for both active leisure and social display, requiring clothing that was 'free looking, combined with elegance'.[75] The loose sailor blouse was more comfortable to wear than a fitted jacket or bodice, and the navy serge or undyed cotton traditionally used would withstand sun and salt water. Some versions of the sailor suit were recommended for their practical advantages, like that by Capper of Gracechurch Street, 'made of the thick army serge, which never wears out'.[76]

However, the availability of practical versions tended to devalue the style in the eyes of wealthier consumers, who looked for variants that would express their social status. This was discernible as early as 1878, when Myra stated: 'this pattern is given at the request of several of our subscribers, who appear to be almost weary of sailor and man-of-war suits for their little boys.'[77] Choosing exclusive or high-priced versions of a common style was one way of distinguishing oneself from social inferiors, and this strategy was recommended by fashion advisors. The sailor suits by H.D. Nicoll that *Myra* praised in 1875 had a starting price of 21s, equivalent to the weekly income of many families (see Table 4.1). In 1888, Jane Emily Panton stated that 'sailor suits can be bought best of Redfern, at Cowes, in the Isle of Wight'.[78] Evidently the 'much-copied Jack Tar suit' was only acceptable if purchased from this elite retailer which also had branches in Bond Street and the Rue de la Paix, Paris.[79]

---

[74]   *Myra's Journal*, May 1875.

[75]   *Tailor and Cutter*, June 1874.

[76]   *Myra's Mid-Monthly Journal*, January 1878, p. 10.

[77]   *Myra's Mid-Monthly Journal*, October 1878, p. 306.

[78]   Jane Emily Panton, *From Kitchen to Garrett: Hints for Young Householders* (London, 1888), p. 200.

[79]   Susan North, 'John Redfern and Sons, 1847–1892', *Costume*, 42 (2008), pp. 145–69; Lou Taylor, 'Wool Cloth and Gender: The Use of Woollen Clothing in Women's Dress in Britain, 1865–85', in Amy de la Haye and Elizabeth Wilson, *Defining Dress: Dress as*

Social distinctions could also be maintained by the use of exclusive fabrics for a standard outfit. In 1878, *Myra* stated that 'dressy sailor suits are made of [fine wool] cloth or black velveteen, with bands of black silk on the sides of the short trousers, and silk collars with gilt anchors at the corners'.[80] These unwashable, non-utilitarian fabrics distinguished sailor suits made for the drawing room from those made for the beach. Trimmings could also add value to an outfit, either through their added cost or through reference to a transient fashion that added an element of planned obsolescence. All of these factors are implied in the 1878 description of suits with costly silk and gilt trimmings that followed a current fashion for contrast stripes on trousers. These fashionable additions also separated boys' sailor suits from adult uniforms.

As mentioned in Chapter 6, sailor suits were understood by consumers in the 1890s as a distinguishing mark of young childhood. The kilt might also be interpreted as a transitional garment between the dresses worn by unbreeched boys and suits with jackets and shorts. This interpretation, rather than its references to military uniforms, can be seen in texts such as *The Boy and How to Suit Him* (see Figure 6.1). It recommends a Highland suit for boys aged three to four, with a preference for the 'undress' version in tweed.[81] Then:

> He has arrived at the interesting age of four to six years, and the fond mother ...
> has arrived at the conclusion that her offspring must be 'breeched' forthwith ...
> If a 'Sailor' suit be decided upon, shall it be in the 'regulation' style as shown
> here ... At this age the 'Highland' or other kilt may still be worn if thought
> desirable, or the little boys may be put into the 'Man O' War' in which the full-
> length trouser takes the place of the knicker.[82]

This text classifies the Highland suit as an 'unbreeched' garment worn primarily by boys under four, while the sailor suit with short trousers is presented as the normative choice for boys aged four to six. Panton, in 1896, saw the two suits as equally suitable for young boys, although 'when school-time comes the kilt must go'.[83]

Object, Meaning and Identity (Manchester, 1999), p. 35. Edwina Ehrman, 'Fashion in the Age of Imperialism: 1860–90', in Christopher Breward, Edwina Ehrman and Caroline Evans (eds), *The London Look: Fashion from Street to Catwalk* (London, 2004), pp. 53–4.

[80]   *Myra's Mid-Monthly Journal*, May 1878, p. 138.

[81]   Richard Taylor, *The Boy and How to Suit Him!! A Suitable Little Treatise in 5 Chaps*, Copy 1 BC 971/17475 (1899), TNA, p. 3.

[82]   Ibid., pp. 5–6.

[83]   Given the middle-class audience, this may refer to entering boarding school at age eight, rather than infants' school at age four or five; Panton, *The Way They Should Go*, p. 98.

Masculinity in Surviving Boys' Garments

Social Status in Sailor Suits

As indicated in these texts, sailor suits could be used to present a number of overlapping meanings about the wearer's age and social status. These are brought into focus by an examination of the surviving sailor suits which form the largest category of late nineteenth-century boys' garments in museum collections (Table 7.1). The twenty examples identified demonstrate the marking of social status by choice of materials, by cut, by trimming and by choice of retailer. The first surviving example is the one worn by Prince Edward in 1846, made as a replica of an actual uniform.[84] However, the next, made on board a ship in 1855, showed a degree of fantasy in the decoration of the shirt and trousers with contrast fabric and embroidery.[85] Sailor suits from the 1870s varied from uniform in cut as well as trimming, with short trousers trimmed with a contrast band down the side seam or at the knee.[86] One suit, worn in 1876, has a jacket based on military rather than naval uniform, but made up in fabrics normally used for sailor suits (Figure 7.4).[87] This example is machine-sewn and well finished, and was probably commercially produced. If so, it shows the realisation of the hybrid designs discussed in Chapter 2. Another example, probably dating from the 1870s but undocumented, has short trousers and blouse edged with strips of wool braid rather than fabric.[88]

Even when boys' sailor suits were more correctly cut there were still subtle variations that differentiated them from naval uniform and from each other. Some examples had contrasting facings in red or pale blue rather than the orthodox navy blue, and others had collars and cuffs that could be detached for washing.[89] Detachable elements would allow the wearer to vary the appearance of the suit, but would add to the cost. Others were made of fabrics that were decorative but washable, like striped wool flannel or checked linen. Sailor suits made of blue wool serge also showed substantial variations from naval orthodoxy, as with the examples registered in the Board of Trade (BT) documents discussed in Chapter 2 with celtic or art-nouveau style trimmings. The only surviving examples made of wool diverged even further: one was made from machine-knitted fabric machine-

---

[84] NMM UNI0293 and UNI0294/ F4848-001. See Miller, *Dressed to Kill*, pp. 87–8; Ormond and Blackett-Ord, *Winterhalter*, p. 192.

[85] MOL 1942.20; another suit made on board a ship in the 1880s (BATH IV.24.8) is closer to uniform in its construction and trim.

[86] As in a plate in the *Tailor and Cutter*, June 1873; see Rose, 'Boyswear', illustration 3.44, p. 207.

[87] V&A Museum of Childhood (VAMC) Misc.85A,B&C-1979.

[88] Gallery of Costume, Manchester City Galleries (GCM), 1947.2029.

[89] Hampshire County Museums Service (HCMS) CRH 1969.102b and CRH 1969.102c; GCM 1954.953 and 1959.297.

stitched together, probably by a manufacturer in Leicester where it is preserved.[90] The other suit had a double-breasted jacket of fine blue wool trimmed with gilt buttons and a detachable blue cotton sailor collar.[91]

Table 7.1   Boys' sailor suits, 1846–c.1900, in museum collections

Source	Date	Fabric	Trousers	Maker or retailer
NMM UNI0293	1846	cotton; blue cotton	long sailor	Royal Yacht *Britannia*
MOL 1942.20	1855	linen; blue cotton	long sailor	Earl Balcarras crew
VAMC 1979.M85	1876	cotton	short	
VAMC 1961.T137	c.1875	navy velvet	short	Clack, Ludgate Hill
GCM 1947.2029	c.1880	cotton	short	
BATH IV.24.8	1880s	cotton	long	made on board RN ship
VAMC 1952.T17	1880–1900	cotton	long sailor	
VAMC 1979.M352	c.1880–1900	striped cotton	long sailor	
VAMC 1938.T63	1880–c.1900	cotton	long sailor	
VAMC 1970.T83	c.1890	linen	long sailor	Rowe of Gosport, 106 New Bond St
BOW 1949.18	c.1890	blue velvet	short	
GCM 1978.184	c.1890	navy velvet	short	Kempton & Co., 32 Argyll St
GCM 1957.297	c.1890	cotton	long	
BOW 1983.6.3	c.1895	striped flannel	short	
GCM 1954.952	1898	navy wool	short	Barran regd no. 331385
GCM 1954.953	1898	cotton	long	Barran?
HCMS CRH 1969.102a	c.1900	cotton	short	Bon Marché Brixton
HCMS CRH 1969.102c	c.1900	cotton	long	Peter Robinson
LEIC 1979.133	c.1900	navy wool jersey	short	
LEIC 1979.134	c.1900	check linen	short	

Sources: BATH – Museum of Costume, Bath; BOW – Bowes Museum, Barnard Castle; GCM – Gallery of Costume, Manchester; HCMS – Hampshire County Museums Service; LEIC – Leicester City Museums; MOL – Museum of London; NMM – National Maritime Museum; VAMC – V&A Museum of Childhood.

---

[90]   Leicester Museums, 1979.133.
[91]   GCM 1954.952.

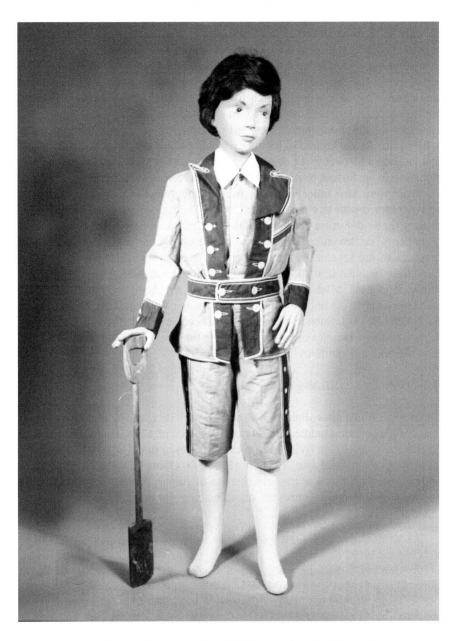

Figure 7.4   A linen and cotton suit combining naval and military elements, worn in 1876. Courtesy of the Victoria and Albert Museum.

This suit can be linked to the manufacturer Barran of Leeds through a BT copyright number stamped on the waistcoat lining (see Figures 3.9 and 3.10), and its careful finish and optional accessories (including a gilt whistle) imply a high selling price. By contrast, the knitted wool of the Leicester suit would need less careful tailoring as it would stretch to fit the wearer, and would also be more liable to snag or wear out than the woven wool used both for standard serge sailor suits and for the more formal version by Barran. These factors imply a lower selling price for the knitted suit. Other surviving sailor suits have retailers' labels that indicate a hierarchy of prices – from the Bon Marché Brixton, through Peter Robinson in the Strand, to Rowe of Gosport and New Bond Street.[92]

There were also sailor suits that were definitely non-utilitarian, made from velvet trimmed with lace and fancy buttons.[93] The lace imitated early eighteenth-century 'point de venise', which was the type of trimming most associated with 'Fauntleroy' or 'Vandyke' velvet suits. Its use invoked references to aristocratic practices of the seventeenth century, and also to the popular novel *Little Lord Fauntleroy* published in 1886 and presented on stage in 1888.[94] The 'Fauntleroy' reference in these sailor suits placed them two steps above common wool sailor suits, since they were not only made of an impractical material and liable to wear out but also tied to fashion and hence liable to become outdated. The BT50 designs include several examples of velvet sailor suits from between 1884 and 1892,[95] but only one with a 'Fauntleroy' trimming, dated 1892.[96]

Boys' Dresses: Establishing Masculinity

The ways in which masculinity was expressed in clothing can be illuminated more clearly by examining toddler boys' tunics. A search of 17 museum collections in England revealed 37 surviving examples of dresses or tunics known to have been worn by boys and dated approximately 1870–1900 (Table 7.2).[97] One aspect which united these garments was the selective use of colour: thirteen were made from cotton or wool in non-colours such as white, cream or beige. This lack of colour

---

[92]   VAMC T83.1970; HCMS CRH 1969.102b; HCMS CRH 1969.102c; GCM 1954.953 and 1959.297.

[93]   GCM 1978.184, with a label from Kempton & Co., 32 Argyll Street, Glasgow; Bowes Museum 1949.18, worn by Mr H. Surtees.

[94]   Ewing, *History of Children's Costume*, p. 91; Willis, *London Yesterdays*, p. 42, mentions wearing a 'Fauntleroy' suit before starting school aged five, c.1890.

[95]   Board of Trade (BT) 50 18366 (1884), TNA; BT 50 194760 (1892), TNA, both registered by Barran & Sons.

[96]   BT50 186441 (1892), TNA, by Barran & Sons.

[97]   A further 51 dresses were found that were very similar in cut and trimming to the documented examples, but that had no documentation. These were omitted from the analysis in order not to prejudge the results. See Appendix 1 for an account of the collections visited.

aligned them with the washable white cotton dresses worn by infants at this time, even when the boys' garments were made of non-washable wool.[98] There were six red garments made from either wool or silk fabric, or a mixture; four in dark blue and one pale blue; four in dark brown (velvet or wool); and three in tartan or plaid. There were also single examples of garments in dark green, maroon, pale pink and magenta.[99] This sombre palette could have been chosen on pragmatic grounds, as dark fabrics would not show dirt and might also be more suitable for remodelling and handing down.[100] The main exceptions were three tunics in bright red wool, trimmed in graphic patterns of interlaced black braid or bold strips of black velvet.[101] Both the fabric and the trimming referred to full-dress military uniforms, of the type still worn by the guards at Buckingham Palace. The 1860 painting *The Volunteers* by Frederick Daniel Hardy makes this reference explicit, showing an off-duty soldier in red jacket watching his young son in a red tunic playing at soldiers.[102] Yet this identification was clouded by the periodic appearance of red (usually in a darker shade, ruby or wine) as a fashionable female colour: in 1887, *Myra's Journal* predicted, 'Red is likely to be very much worn by little girls and by babies.'[103] Colour in itself does not seem to have been a determining factor in establishing the masculine status of boys' dresses, as evidenced by surviving examples in pale pink and bright magenta.[104]

---

[98]   See Chapter 5, note 44.

[99]   Magenta was a bright purple derived from coal tar, synthesised for the first time in 1856, and a high-fashion colour for women in the 1860s. A fashionable dress of c.1870 in this dye (V&A T118-1979) is pictured on the front cover of Lucy Johnston, *Nineteenth-Century Fashion in Detail* (London, 2005).

[100]   The maroon wool dress, York BA926, is made of fabric trimmed with interlaced black braid in a style popular c.1870, but the museum records state that it was worn in 1903 and made by the wearer's grandmother. Some seams have been resewn and it could be an example of a garment remade a generation after its original use.

[101]   For a boy's dress of red cloth and black velvet dated c.1860 (VAMC T83.1966), see Rose, *Children's Clothes*, plate 5.

[102]   Painting in York City Art Gallery; see Trev Lynn Broughton and Helen Rogers, 'The Empire of the Father', in Broughton and Rogers (eds), *Gender and Fatherhood in the Nineteenth Century* (Basingstoke, 2007), pp. 1–30.

[103]   *Myra's Journal*, May 1887 p. 246.

[104]   The association of pale pink with girls and pale blue with boys was not fixed until well into the twentieth century: a 1921 dressmaking course published by the Women's Institute of Domestic Science in Scranton, Pennsylvania, recommended pink for boys and blue for girls. See also Jo Paoletti and Carol Kregloh, 'The Children's Department', in Claudia Kidwell and Valerie Steele (eds), *Men and Women: Dressing the Part* (Washington DC, 1989), pp. 22–41. For colour symbolism for infants in European cultures, see Heide Nixdorff and Heidi Muller, *Weisse Westen, Rote Roben: von den Farbordnungen des Mittelalters zum individuellen Farbgeschmack* (Berlin, 1983), pp. 136–40.

Table 7.2   Dresses known to have been worn by boys, c.1870–1900, in museum collections

Museum number	Date	Age	Wearer	Fabric	Trim
YOR 1956/198/16a	1871		Armstrong family	red wool	black velvet
YOR 1956/198/16b	1871		Armstrong family	blue wool	white braid
YOR BA1013	1872	2	William Ferrand	blue wool	buttons
GCM 1962.197	1872–73		Mr Martin	cotton pique	black braid
GCM 1956.164	c.1872		Mr Brown (b. 1870)	linen; blue silk	cutwork embroidery
YOR 125.1965	1873		Boy	cotton pique	braid pattern
YOR BA183	1873	2	Rawson family	tartan	black velvet; buttons
GCM 1956.70	1873–74		Mr Smith	tartan	'waistcoat'; mop buttons
GCM 1961.61	1873–76		Mr Gibson (b. 1870)	tartan wool/ silk	buttons
VAMC M158-1979	1875		Boy	magenta wool	brown braid
VAMC M481-1978	1875		Henley Hon A M	cotton brod anglaise	embroidery
YOR 116.1943	c.1875		Brown Mr	red wool	braid pattern
VAMC T47.1958	1880		General ?	machine lace	pink silk & chiffon
NOR 171.1970.73	1880	5	John Walker	cotton check	bias yoke
WOR 1962.468	1880		Boy	navy check wool	navy satin; buttons
WOR 1984.138	1880		Boy	brown velveteen	crochet; pleats
YOR 189.1955.2	1880s		Mr Puttick	cream wool	cream braid; narrow ribbon; lace
YOR 282.1955	1880s		Mr Puttick	cream wool	wool lace; tucks
YOR 515.1947	1881	6	Dr Lister	brown stripe wool	narrow velvet ribbon
GCM 1965.145	1881–83		John Brierly (b. 1878)	white wool	diagonal; floral embroidery
WOR 1967.1023	1882		Evans twins	brown velveteen	brown ribbon; lace
BOW 1963.30	1882	2	MrDent	red wool	black velvet & lace
LON 1946.20	1883		Mr Myers	blue velvet; satin	diagonal; crochet lace
LON 1933.228	1885		Hon. M. Brett	cotton	embroidery

Museum number	Date	Age	Wearer	Fabric	Trim
GCM 1964.2	1885–87		A.P.S. Smith (b. 1883)	olive wool	pink smocking
GCM 1959.198	1886	5	Oscar Ashcroft (b. 1881)	red silk	buttons; lace; red velvet
NOR 209.1980	1886	3	J.Whiting	cotton pique	braid
VAMC Misc493-1984	1888	2	J.H. Judd	cotton brod anglaise	embroidery
NOR 37.1964	1888	3	Norwich Sunday school boy	black silk	lined red
VAMC Misc336-1979	c.1889		Boy	blue wool twill	blue velvet cape
BOWES 1966.35	c.1890		Boy	cotton	
GCM 1962.186	1890–92		Mr Parry (b. 1888)	red satin	lace
NOR 10.1966	1893	3	Boy	red wool	black braid
LEIC 160-1981	1894	2	A.E. Cholerton	cotton	embroidery, tucks
BOW 1981.30.3	1895		Richardson Jackson	brown velveteen	gold ricrac
YOR 299.1957.1	1897		Boy	pink cotton	Lace
YOR BA926	1903		Mr Walker	maroon wool	braid pattern

Sources: BATH – Museum of Costume, Bath; BOW – Bowes Museum, Barnard Castle; GCM – Gallery of Costume, Manchester; HCMS – Hampshire County Museums Service; LEIC – Leicester City Museums; MOL – Museum of London; NMM – National Maritime Museum; NOR – Norwich Museums; VAMC – V&A Museum of Childhood; WOR – Worthing Museum; YOR – York Castle Museum.

The shape of these boys' dresses was linked to fashions for young girls, and moved from a defined bodice and full skirts in the 1870s, to a bodice with low waist and narrow skirts in the 1880s, to a smock shape in the 1890s. At each of these periods, boys' dresses would have been distinguished from girls' by being looser in the waist, and by having skirts made with broad pleats and plain hems rather than gathers and ruffles.[105] These differences were comparative rather than absolute, however, and did not exclude features such as necklines cut low over the shoulders.[106] There were only two features that were exclusive to boys' dresses: one was a kilt skirt with a flat front and pleats at the sides and back, and the other was a diagonal opening (or applied trim) from shoulder to hem. The

---

[105]   'Boys' [dress] bodies are always cut straight at the waist, and not sloped.' 'Clothing for children of six years', in *Cassell's Household Guide* (London, 1869–71), vol. I, p. 370. Surviving examples include GCM 1965.145 (1882) and MOL 1946.20 (1883).

[106]   Seen in a surviving boy's dress in York Castle Museum (BA1013), worn by William Ferrand in 1873.

diagonal opening was recommended in *Cassell's* and in other texts, and was seen in surviving garments up to the 1880s.[107] No reason was given for its function as a marker of masculinity, although there may have been a reference to the diagonal sashes worn by military commanders in the seventeenth century, codified in Garter regalia from the eighteenth century onwards.[108]

The kilt references in young boys' dresses are easier to link with forms of masculinity, especially as they were often reinforced by the use of tartan fabric. However, these garments also showed a surprising divergence from standard Highland dress.[109] They were made of tartan woven from silk and wool mixture or in non-traditional colours, and trimmed with velvet, broderie anglaise and fancy buttons (Figure 7.5).[110] They adjusted the kilt and jacket shaping to follow fashionable dress shapes, with low-cut bodices and bustled skirts.[111] This is consistent with the way that Highland references were discussed in dressmaking magazines:

> A pretty costume for a little boy of three is of green plaid with a kilted skirt, plain in front, over which fall tabs of plaid edged with scarlet. The costume buttons down the front with small red buttons, and is trimmed in front with red bias bands, the belt being edged in red. A very large lace collar completely covers the shoulders, the wide parements [trimmings] being to match.[112]

In this description the military references implicit in the kilt suit were blurred by shifting the fabric, cut and trim of the suit to align it with fashionable women's clothing. A similar shift was seen in some designs published in the *Tailor and Cutter* in the 1870s, in which the kilt suit was radically revised to form a fitted tunic trimmed with braided scrolls (Figure 7.6).[113]

---

[107]   Anon., *The Mother's Thorough Resource-book* (London, 1860), p. 150; *Cassell's Household Guide*, vol. I. p. 370. GCM 1965.145 (1882) and MOL 1946.20 (1883), known to be worn by boys, have diagonal trim, as does the undocumented MOL 1931.91.17 (1870).

[108]   In the group portrait by Franz Xaver Winterhalter, *The Royal Family in 1846* (Royal Collections RCIN 405413), the diagonal opening of the tunic worn by Prince Edward echoes the Garter sashes worn by his parents. For the military sash, see the portrait of Rupert, Prince Palatine, as a military commander (unknown engraver, after van Dyck), NPG D18156.

[109]   GCM 1956.70 (1873) and 1961.61 (1875); York BA183 (1873).

[110]   Silk tartan with embroidered trim and pearl buttons, GCM 1961.61; velvet trim and pearl buttons, York BA183; pearl buttons, GCM 1956.70 (Plate 15 in *Picture Book Number Seven: Children's Costume*, Manchester, 1959).

[111]   Notably GCM 1956.70, where the kilt pleats are confined to a narrow area at the back to give a bustled effect.

[112]   *Myra's Mid-Monthly Journal*, September 1882, p. 265; see also pattern no. 380 in *Myra's Journal*, August 1890, Rose, 'Boyswear', illustration 5.23, p. 328. The 1890 design is very close to one published in the Paris journal *Le Caprice* in 1887; see Musée Galliera, *La mode et l'enfant 1780–2000* (Paris, 2001), p. 88.

[113]   *Tailor and Cutter,* November 1877, p. 348.

Figure 7.5   A 'Highland' style dress worn by a young boy in 1873–74 [1956.70].
© Manchester City Galleries.

Figure 7.6   Design for a kilt variant, *Tailor and Cutter*, 1875. Courtesy of the
NAL, Victoria and Albert Museum, London 2009.

Masculine Symbolism in Boys' Clothes

The analysis of images, texts and surviving garments in this chapter has shown that the symbolic language of masculinity in nineteenth-century boys clothing was largely unarticulated. Texts aimed at middle-class women were able to assume a shared understanding of the norms for young boys' dresses without needing to spell out what these were or how they differed from girls' dresses. There were some types of cut (such as the loose tunic) and trimmings (such as diagonal openings) specific to young boys in the 1870s. However, by the 1880s there seemed to be much less of an emphasis on gender differentiation either in surviving garments or in dressmaking texts. In any case, the signifiers of gender in young boys' dresses were apparently arbitrary and self-referential. References to masculine archetypes such as soldiers were notable by their absence. Even the Highland kilt was substantially modified in cut, fabric and trim to conform to a fashionable aesthetic based on women's dresses.

Sailor suits and kilts worn by older boys were also visually differentiated from the versions worn as military uniform. Kilts worn with tweed, broadcloth or velvet jackets were clearly distinct from the uniform of Highland regiments, worn with tunics in either bright red or (after 1899) khaki.[114] Some were even further from military uniform, like the all-black kilt made for Prince Leopold in 1862 when mourning the death of his father Prince Albert.[115] Sailor suits had fancy braid edgings and motifs on the collar, vest and sleeves, and often included shorts rather than naval bell-bottoms. Both sailor and Highland suits were separated by age from military uniforms, as they were mainly worn by boys under eleven, or even younger. As boys were only able to join the navy from age fourteen, the age limit of eleven would establish boys' sailor suits as fantasy wear rather than uniforms.[116] The fact that sailor tops might also be worn by girls further distanced them from uniforms.[117]

The royal associations of both sailor suit and the Highland kilt have proved weaker than has been assumed, undermined by the twenty-year delay between their use by royalty and their widespread adoption. Texts and images in the 1880s and 1890s used surprisingly few royal or patriotic references when discussing these outfits, talking instead about their suitability in terms of age and social position. The anxiety expressed in Panton's 1896 text made it clear that the symbolic value of these garments was not absolute, but directly related to their

---

[114]　For Highland regiments' uniforms in this campaign, see Jackson, *The Boer War*, pp. 64 and 96; also www.argylls.co.uk.

[115]　Made from dull black wool and silk crape; MOL 1954.137. Other surviving kilt suits in museums are an example worn by Prince Edward in 1843, MOL 1933.202; a kilt with black broadcloth jacket worn by Justinian Laczkovic, 1883, VAMC. B.82:27-1995.

[116]　See Miller, *Dressed to Kill*, Fig. 79, p. 89, a seaman aged fourteen.

[117]　The V&A Museum of Childhood has a white sailor top and skirt worn by a girl to match her brother's sailor top and shorts in 1927: M266.1978.

social exclusivity. Seaside holidays had become more widely available since Frith's 1854 painting, boosted by developments such as the August Bank Holiday for clerical and commercial workers, and mill holidays in the cotton districts of Lancashire. Increased leisure led to greatly increased numbers of seaside visitors: on the first Bank Holiday in 1871, 'Margate jetty was simply blocked so far as to be impassable'.[118] The changing character of seaside visitors can be gauged from the development of working-class resorts, typified by Blackpool which trebled in size between 1880 and 1890.[119]

The development of maritime references in clothing seems to have followed the same chronology as the development of seaside holidays. In the 1850s these were a middle-class pastime, and the clothes worn were chosen with a view to social display rather than practicality, as can be seen in the fashionable dresses in Frith's painting.[120] Specialised seaside ensembles were made from materials that would resist sun and water damage, with no references to sailor suits.[121] Sailor-styled garments became fashionable only in the early 1870s, at a time when seaside visits were becoming more available to the mass of the population and losing their elite character.

By the 1890s, sailor-styled clothes had spread from the seaside to everyday use and in doing so their meaning had been diluted. The availability of multiple variants of the mass-produced sailor suit made it a normative garment rather than one that was specially chosen to express social standing. Instead, families could invoke social distinction by wearing versions with costly fabric or trim, or by buying from exclusive high-fashion retailers. Boys could be dressed in a wardrobe of sailor suits appropriate for different social occasions: serge for school, velvet for parties and white cotton for seaside holidays.

The use made of the Highland kilt was superficially similar to the sailor suit, but differed in important respects. It was adapted for wear by very young 'unbreeched' boys in the 1860s and 1870s, but in hybrid forms that diluted its masculine and military references. Kilts for older boys were aligned with leisure rather than warfare by being sold with expensive velvet or cashmere jackets. The images used to sell them also referenced middle-class leisure, even at the height of patriotic fervour for the Boer War. Kilt suits, by virtue of their higher cost, were intrinsically more prestigious than sailor suits, but there was still a hierarchy within kilt types, as was recognised by both Panton and Richard Taylor. While the cost of a tweed

---

[118] *News of the World*, August 1871, cited in Walvin, *Beside the Seaside*, p. 61.

[119] John K Walton, *Lancashire A Social History, 1558–1939* (Manchester, 1987), p. 295.

[120] Coloured fabrics, and silk, would be damaged by salt water and sunlight, so wearing them at the seaside was a form of conspicuous consumption. See Deirdre Murphy, '"The Girls in Green": Women's Seaside Dress in England, 1850–1900', *Costume*, 40 (2006): 56–66.

[121] For an example, see Jean Druesdow, *In Style Celebrating Fifty Years of the Costume Institute* (New York, 1987), p. 36.

kilt was comparable to that of a tweed suit for a boy of the same age, a full-dress version in tartan with a velvet jacket might cost three times as much.[122]

As Christina Bates has pointed out, garments widely adopted in the age of mass manufacturing were those which presented economic advantages for manufacturers, retailers and, ultimately, consumers.[123] The advantages of sailor suits for manufacturers and retailers lay in the constant demand for the style, which meant that prices could be kept low. They were also easier to cut than fitted styles such as the lounge suit. At the same time the potential for variation meant that different versions were available in different seasons or from different shops.

The case study of the sailor suit and the kilt has raised the issue of the role of mass producers in shaping and directing taste, and the role of mass consumers in selecting from available goods. Revisions to the design of both sailor and Highland suits removed them from the timeless state of uniforms, as described by Jennifer Craik,[124] and inserted them in the fashion system, where they could be further varied to express nuances of age, gender and social status. It seems to have been the variability rather than the uniformity of these styles that constituted their appeal for clothing producers: 'For a style of dress designated with a common name there is no other that admits of such variety … the variation in the trimming, in changes of form and colour is practically boundless.'[125] By the 1890s the sailor suit could be seen not as a reference to British naval prowess but as a fashion item whose ready availability rendered it 'odious, common'.

In the sailor suit, the kilt and the toddler boy's tunic we see how the gender connotations of clothing were modulated by considerations of age and class (Figure 7.7). There was not a polarisation between masculine and feminine clothing styles, more a continuum. Changes in practice seem to have been driven less by emulation of an elite than by a fashion cycle instigated by mass manufacturers. Moreover, the presentation of boys' garments was permeated by an element of play or fantasy which undermines any attempt at a simple interpretation of masculinity in this material.

---

[122]   For example, 16s 6d for tweed and 42s for full-dress versions from Harrod's in Alison Adburgham, *Victorian Shopping: Harrod's Catalogue, 1895* (Newton Abbot, 1972), p. 980. A surviving tweed kilt suit in Manchester (GCM 1951.317) has a price label for 14s 6d.

[123]   Christina Bates, 'How to dress the Children? A Comparison of Prescription and Practice in Late Nineteenth-Century North America', *Dress*, 24 (1997), p. 51.

[124]   Jennifer Craik, *Uniforms Exposed: From Conformity to Transgression* (Oxford, 2005).

[125]   *Tailor and Cutter*, June 1874.

Sailor Blouse, Fig. 51   Kilt Frock, Fig. 52.   Jack Tar Suit, &c., Fig. 53. Girl's Kilt   Frock, Fig. 52a.

Figure 7.7   A sailor/kilt hybrid for a young boy and sailor suit for a girl, *Cutter's Practical Guide*, 1891. Courtesy of the NAL, Victoria and Albert Museum, London 2009.

Chapter 8
Conclusions and Contexts

Boys (especially working-class boys) and their clothing could be seen as marginal subjects: marginal to masculinity because of their youth, to consumption because of their low economic status, to fashion because of their masculinity, to clothing history because of their association with cheap mass-production.[1] This study has made these marginalised figures into subjects in every sense, and located them at the centre of a network of familial, social, commercial and intellectual practices and debates. Doing so set up comparisons in a wider geographical and chronological frame, some of which will be dealt with below. The large number of visual documents used required new interpretative frameworks and new methodologies, which have important implications for the understanding of the history of dress, and of the clothing industry.

Making Boys' Clothes

The investigations of Chapman, Godley and Honeyman into the history of ready-to-wear clothing production had previously established the importance of this sector as early as 1850, particularly in London and in Leeds.[2] This was amply confirmed by the documents registered by manufacturers in the Board of Trade (BT)43, BT45 and BT50 archives at The National Archives. What was surprising was the volume of designs for boys, and the location of major manufacturers outside Leeds in Wigan and Walsall. Firms such as Coop of Wigan, who employed 500 workers in a factory built for them in 1872, were present in local histories but absent from overviews of the industry.[3] This demonstrated the need for further

---

[1] See Clare Rose, 'Alla ricerca della cenciosità' ('In Search of Raggedness'), in Tiziano Bonazzi (ed.), *Riconoscimento ed Esclusione* (Rome, 2003), pp. 156–80.

[2] Stanley Chapman, 'The Innovating Entrepreneurs in the British Ready-made Clothing Industry', *Textile History*, 24/1, (1993): 5–25; Andrew Godley, *The History of the Ready-Made Clothing Industry* (Leeds, 1997); Katrina Honeyman, *Well Suited: A History of the Leeds Clothing Industry, 1850–1990* (Oxford, 2000).

[3] John Hannavy and Chris Ryan, *Working in Wigan Mills* (Wigan, 1987), p. 12. Sarah Levitt does not mention Coop in her survey of the BT 43 documents in *The Victorians Unbuttoned* (London, 1986).

work to establish the scope of ready-to-wear production for boys, men, women and girls in centres such as Manchester and Bradford.[4]

The writing-out of firms like Coop of Wigan may have been hastened by their focus on boys' clothing, which can be deduced from their publicity posters. In fact, many of the firms now recognised as leaders in mass-production specialised in boys' clothing, as both Levitt and Honeyman noted.[5] Levitt categorises Barran as 'one of the largest wholesale ready-made clothing manufacturers in the country ... from the start it is likely that his staple product was boys' clothing.'[6] She speculated that the two factors were related, as boys' clothing opened up the ready-to-wear trade for middle-class families.[7] The dominance of designs for boys in documents registered by both manufacturers and retailers suggests that boyswear may have been crucial in the development of mass-production and mass marketing techniques for the industry as a whole.

Another key finding from the Registered Designs was the importance of fashion in boys' ready-to-wear clothing. This is contrary to Fine and Leopold's assertion that 'a tailored fit in menswear took precedence over, and to a great extent crowded out, the demands of fashion'.[8] The multiple variations in trimming in BT43 and BT50 correspond to Fine and Leopold's definition of 'changes dictated by fashion.'[9] The manufacturers themselves were very clear about the importance of surface trimming: 'The novelty consists in the ornamental design.'[10] Honeyman and Godley have shown that Leeds clothing manufacturers often subcontracted out the trickier aspects of garments, and this may have encouraged the division between standardised shapes and varied trimmings.[11] It appears from the designs that manufacturers may have operated a batch system, with basic garment shapes made up in a range of different fabrics to provide variety of appearance (and of

---

[4]   Based on documents registered by Bradford Manufacturing Co., Stationers' Hall Archive, Copy 1 968 (1898); Pollard's of Bradford, Copy 1 968 (1898); John Noble, Manchester, Copy 1 127/144 (1896); Hyam, Leeds Copy 1 974/18528 (1899), The National Archives (TNA).

[5]   Honeyman, *Well Suited*, pp. 21, 33, and fig 2.8.

[6]   Levitt, *Victorians Unbuttoned*, pp. 103–4.

[7]   Ibid., p. 101.

[8]   Ben Fine and Ellen Leopold, *The World of Consumption* (London, 1993), p. 234. It is also different from Andrew Godley's attribution of Leeds' success to cut; *The History of the Ready-Made Clothing Industry* (Leeds, 1997), p. 7.

[9]   Fine and Leopold, *The World of Consumption*, p. 235.

[10]   Wilkinson & Chorlton, Wholesale Clothiers, St Pauls Street, Leeds, design no. 39868 (1885).

[11]   Honeyman, *Well Suited*, p. 22; Andrew Godley, 'Development of the UK Clothing Industry, 1850–1950: Output and Productivity Growth', *Business History*, 37/4 (1995), p. 57.

price points) with minimal effort.[12] This variety would be especially attractive to the small independent retailer, using the publicity material of a firm like Coop to indicate 'his' range of styles.[13]

Christina Bates and Farid Chenoune (working on clothes for girls and for men) have found that garments which were widely adopted in the age of mass manufacturing were those which presented economic advantages for manufacturers, retailers, and ultimately consumers.[14] The boys' styles most heavily promoted by mass manufacturers of boyswear were ones which suited their production practices, such as sailor suits. As early as 1880, the *Tailor and Cutter* recognised that 'the best styles which are now being introduced' originated from a ready-to-wear firm, Macbeth of Manchester, and that bespoke tailors needed to follow Macbeth's lead in order to remain competitive.[15] This suggests that the role of mass tailors as innovators and arbiters of style may have begun not with Montague Burton in the 1920s but with firms such as Macbeth and C. Baker & Co. in the 1890s.[16]

The Hidden Role of Mass Manufacturers

One reason why the design qualities of mass-produced clothes have been overlooked lies in the difficulty of identifying the origins of the garments that are featured in retailers' catalogues or that survive in museum collections. Manufacturers such as Coop and Barran did not attach permanent labels to garments,[17] and were not named in publicity material even when these were designed by them.[18] This was a surprising finding, as we would expect manufacturers who sought to safeguard

---

[12]   See Barran's design BT50/194760 (1892) where the swatch of trimming and the photograph of the finished garment are in different fabrics; Fig. 1, p. 4 in Clare Rose, '"The novelty consists in the ornamental design": Design Innovation in Mass-produced Boys' Clothing, 1840–1900', *Textile History*, 38/1 (2007): 1–24.

[13]   It may be significant here that major garment-producing centres (Leeds, Manchester, Wigan and Walsall) were well positioned on national rail networks for distributing goods.

[14]   In girls' clothing, the loose smock dress; Christina Bates 'How to dress the Children? A Comparison of Prescription and Practice in Late Nineteenth-Century North America', *Dress*, 24 (1997), p. 51. In menswear, the loose 'paletot' jackets of the 1850s, which did not need careful fitting; Farid Chenoune, *A History of Men's Fashion* (Paris, 1993), p. 66.

[15]   *Tailor and Cutter*, 17 June 1880, p. 219.

[16]   See Laura Ugolini, *Men and Menswear: Sartorial Consumption in Britain, 1880–1939* (Aldershot, 2007), pp. 178–84, for the fashion advantages offered by multiple tailors. For Burton's claims to primacy, see Eric Sigsworth, *Montague Burton: The Tailor of Taste* (Manchester 1990).

[17]   As demonstrated by sailor suit GCM 1954.952, identified with Barran only by a stamped registration number (see waistcoat in Figure 3.4).

[18]   The only exception was the poster by W. Shannon & Son, Walsall, Copy 1 093/094 (1891), TNA.

their designs by registration would also seek to safeguard their reputation by the use of trademarks or labelling.[19]

Labelling practice seems to have been determined instead by the needs of retailers. The survey of surviving garments in Chapter 3 showed that when they had permanently attached labels (as opposed to card sales tags) these identified the retailer not the manufacturer. We know from Mayhew's investigations that Nicoll, one of the first ready-to-wear retailers to label their clothing, relied on a network of small subcontractors who sometimes shaded into 'sweaters'; these small manufacturers would not be in a position to advertise their own work.[20] Nicoll was alive to the importance of publicity and spent heavily on advertisements, although none of these were registered.[21]

Schorman has identified a similar tension between the needs of manufacturers and the needs of retailers in the USA, where retailers were reluctant to admit to selling mass-produced goods.[22] This resulted in advertising material that stressed the 'individual', 'traditional' and even 'tailor-made' qualities of ready-to-wear garments. Manufacturers themselves seem to have been party to this sleight-of-hand, as we see in Coop's posters, modelled on tailors' fashion plates (though with a small image of the factory of origin). Yet in doing so they erased the evidence of their own contribution to the democratisation of fashion.

The Limits of Home Sewing

At the other extreme from the mass manufacturers were the (female) dressmakers who produced individual garments to order. In spite of some excellent studies, there is as yet no overview of the scope of professional dressmaking practice.[23] The picture is further confused by the tendency of nineteenth-century needlework texts to address the concerns of a double audience, both amateur and professional.

---

[19]   By 1907 Barran issued a booklet of copyrighted images of their garments for retailers to use in advertisements. However, these were not signed and could only be linked to the manufacturer through the booklet, not available to consumers; a rare example survives at York Castle Museum. See Clare Rose, *Children's Clothes Since 1750* (London, 1989), Fig. 107, p. 143; Alison Adburgham, *Yesterday's Shopping: Army and Navy Stores Catalogue, 1907* (Newton Abbot, 1969), pp. 884–8.

[20]   Cited in David Green, *From Artisans to Paupers* (Aldershot, 1995), p. 163; J. Ashelford, *The Art of Dress: Costume and Society, 1500–1914* (London, 1996), p. 265. Both authors spell the name 'Nicholl'.

[21]   Andrew Godley, 'The Development of the Clothing industry: Technology and Fashion', *Textile History*, 28/1 (1997), p. 6.

[22]   Rob Schorman, *Selling Style: Clothing and Social Change at the Turn of the Century* (Philadelphia, 2003), pp. 18–33 and 148.

[23]   Barbara Burman (ed.), *The Culture Of Sewing: Gender, Consumption And Home Dressmaking* (Oxford, 1999); Wendy Gamber, *The Female Economy: The Millinery and Dressmaking Trades, 1860–1930* (Urbana, 1997); Beth Harris (ed.), *Famine and Fashion: Needlewomen in the Nineteenth Century* (Aldershot, 2005).

Moreover, the practice of dressmaking was fluid, and it is likely that women were both consumers and producers at different times and for different garments. The close analysis of texts for dressmakers in Chapter 2 provided some surprising insights into their practices. Firstly, the school textbooks that claimed to provide girls with all the needlework skills necessary to make and repair a family's clothes did no such thing, dealing only with underwear and baby clothes made of lightweight cotton. Secondly, after 1870 there was a flood of dressmaking patterns, including many for boys and young men. However, these were expensive, and making them up would require considerable skills in construction and fitting.

It seems that the skills to make boys' clothes at home were noticeably lacking: references to them in autobiographies are associated with a sense of embarrassment. H.G. Wells and his brother 'under the pressure of our schoolfellows' derision ... rebelled against something rather naive in the cut'.[24] The visible difference between individualised home-made garments and the standardised shop-bought ones seems to have been at the root of this. This calls into questions assertions like those in the *Cornhill* articles about the practice of home sewing for the family; further study is needed to establish the extent, and norms, of dressmaking practice.

Buying and Selling Boys' Clothes

The information provided by the archives of advertising material was crucial in several respects. Firstly, their images showed the dissemination of particular garment types over time, and across a range of manufacturers and retailers. Secondly, the catalogue pages and flyers included in both archives provided important evidence for the pricing of boys' clothes by different retailers. Thirdly, the quantity, variety, and visual quality of the material in Copy 1 indicated the sophistication of the advertising industry in the 1890s, and the importance of boys' clothing within it. Finally, the repeated images of outfits such as the sailor suit gave a basis for examining how they were understood as referring to concepts of militarism and patriotism.

The documents from retailers revealed the importance of boys' clothing in the development of ready-to-wear retailing, multiple retailing, and mail order. There were firms in each of these categories who specialised in boys' clothing, from Lynes in the 1870s to the Don Clothing Company in the 1890s. Even firms like Baker & Co. and Marychurch & Blackler who sold clothing for men issued specialist catalogues for boys. These created a virtual selling space analogous to the children's departments initiated in large American stores in the 1920s.[25] The provision of dedicated spaces for selling boys' clothes in large stores is a

---

24   Ugolini, *Men and Menswear*, pp. 208–9.

25   Daniel Cook, *The Commodification of Childhood: The Children's Clothing Industry and the Rise of the Child Consumer* (Durham NC, 2004), pp. 112–20.

topic which requires further investigation, and which could illuminate issues of gendered practice in retailing.

Both Breward and Ugolini have stressed the importance of advertising and publicity practices in menswear retailing, even before 1914.[26] Changes in the appearance, layout and management of shops seem to have been instigated by large multiple firms from the 1880s, and copied by independent tailors.[27] This tended to blur the dividing line between bespoke and ready-to-wear businesses, which was still further blurred by the gradual encroachment of mail-order and 'wholesale bespoke' practices.[28] The operation of specialist commercial publishers such as Clements Newling, Richard Taylor and Wesley Petty may have been crucial to this process.

The variety of formats found in the Copy 1 archive, from four-inch-wide novelty shapes, through flyers and booklets to large posters indicated the maturity of advertising practice by 1890. The dominance of men's and boys' images in this material implied that advertising was structurally linked to mass manufacturing, which was also dominated by menswear.[29] Moreover, the need for illustrations shows that customers were interested in style and the details of trimming, not just price. The visual sophistication of these images suggests that the interaction between aesthetics, culture and commerce identified by Jobling, Crowley and Breward in *fin-de-siècle* advertising for adults was also needed to sell boys' clothes.[30] The mass-production and mass-reproduction of advertising images may in themselves have contributed to the establishment of the *habitus* of boys' clothing, as Schorman postulates.[31]

The detachment of commercial publishers like Richard Taylor from the manufacturing process could be seen in his provision of catalogues for different retailers using the same images and layout.[32] If the catalogue images were intended for general use rather than based on a particular manufacturer's products, they

---

[26]   Ugolini, *Men and Menswear*, esp. pp. 178–84; Christopher Breward, *The Hidden Consumer: Masculinities, Fashion and City Life, 1860–1914* (Manchester, 1999), esp. pp. 100–151.

[27]   Ugolini, *Men and Menswear*, pp. 148–9.

[28]   Ibid., pp. 13–15 and 147–53.

[29]   The exception to both these generalisations is found in Alfred Stedall, a London manufacturer and wholesaler of women's cloaks and mantles, who was a very prolific registrant in Copy 1. There were also some advertising documents for women's clothing registered by manufacturers operating mail-order services, such as the Bradford Manufacturing Co., Copy 1 968 (1898); Pollard's of Bradford, Copy 1 968 (1898); John Noble, Manchester, Copy 1 127/144 (1896); Hyam, Leeds, Copy 1 974/18528 (1899).

[30]   Paul Jobling and David Crowley, *Graphic Design: Reproduction and Representation since 1800* (Manchester, 1996).

[31]   Schorman, *Selling Style*, p. 149.

[32]   Southcott of Hull, Copy 1 974/18528 and Logan of Leamington Spa, Copy 1 975/18747.

must have represented recognisable types of garments. This is interesting in itself, as it implies that a number of manufacturers were producing variations on the same theme.

Boys' Clothes and the Cost of Living

Retailers' documents also provided important information on clothing prices, which fell both in cash terms and as a fraction of family budgets between 1870 and 1900.[33] This is a remarkable finding, especially when we consider that the documents analysed were aimed at middle-class consumers and that there was probably another price level below them. The price drop is a strong indication of the involvement of mass manufacturers, with their economies of scale, in the provision of boys' clothing. It would have been a precondition for the pattern of consumption revealed in the Barnardo's entry photographs, with a consensus in clothing practices across a broad social range. It may have also have been this drop in the cost of standard garments that provided the impetus for more elaborate and costly variations such as the lace-trimmed velvet sailor suit.

Research on nineteenth-century France by Phillipe Perrot has shown a comparable price drop in clothing prices, to the extent that second-hand clothing dealers went out of business.[34] The effects were also seen in increased clothing consumption, even in poor rural households, as demonstrated by Diana Crane's analysis of Le Play's household budgets.[35] We would expect the democratisation of dress to be even more marked in Britain, which was more urbanised and less socially stratified than France at this time. Harold Perkin has identified the period from 1873 to 1900 as one of falling prices and rising real incomes.[36] He discusses the fall in the cost of basic foodstuffs through imports, but not changes in the pricing of manufactured goods such as clothing. The data obtained from the retailers' catalogues supports Perkin's model, and indicates the potential of such case studies for adding to the cost of living debate.

---

[33]   The fall in prices from 1850 to 1900 was even more striking. The cheapest suit for a small boy listed in the catalogue of E. Moses & Son in 1850 cost about 3/6d, and by 1900 the cheapest small boy's suit cost 2s 11d. See Clare Rose, 'Boyswear and the formation of gender and class identity in urban England, 1840–1900' (unpublished PhD dissertation, University of Brighton, 2006), Fig. 4.4, p. 234.

[34]   Phillipe Perrot, *Fashioning the Bourgeoisie: A History of Clothing in the Nineteenth Century* (Princeton, 1994), pp. 70–71.

[35]   Diana Crane, *Fashion and its Social Agendas* (Chicago, 2000), Chapter 2.

[36]   Harold Perkin, *The Rise of Professional Society: England since 1880* (London, 1989), pp. 36–40.

Interpreting Boys' Clothes

Boys' Clothes and Social Identities

As Laura Ugolini has found in her detailed examination of male clothing consumption:

> Most men did not choose their clothes primarily in order to express their unique individuality ... Rather they sought to chart a course through the social environments within which they spent their days and their lives. Reflecting the ways in which identities were – and are – constructed and reinforced, primarily by reference to 'others', sartorial identities showed both who the individual was and who he was not, where he belonged and where he did not.[37]

This is even more applicable to boys, where the consumption process was carried out at one remove, with the parent acting on behalf of the boy. This mediation seems to have been generally accepted, up to and even beyond the age of puberty and wage-earning.[38] It could be seen as an extension of the practice (particularly in poor households) of the pooling of resources, with consumption decisions made by parents on behalf of all.[39] What seems to have aroused resentment was the attempt by parents to control or subvert clothing purchases made from funds earmarked for personal use.[40] Another source of resentment was the imposition of a cheaper (often home-made) substitute for the normative choice of garment, since this acted as a public statement of the family's lack of funds.[41]

The pressure towards conformity was particularly important in the use of clothing to define age groups. This practice was particularly visible in Board Schools, where clothing norms were not imposed from above, but created by families in a classic example of Bourdieu's *habitus*. Moreover, they were enforced and maintained through peer pressure, as when Frederick Willis picked on a schoolfellow who was dressed inappropriately for his age: 'I remember one boy who wore a sailor suit and hat suitable for a boy two or three years his junior. Naturally I thought I could fight such a boy and as his sailor outfit got on my nerves I challenged him one day by saying dreadful things.'[42] The use of clothing to divide the period of ten or more years between infancy and adolescence into

---

[37]   Ugolini, *Men and Menswear*, pp. 44–5.

[38]   Ibid., pp. 62–3 and 210–11.

[39]   Ellen Ross, *Love and Toil: Motherhood in Outcast London, 1870–1918* (Oxford, 1993), esp. pp. 148–60.

[40]   See George Acorn, *One of the Multitude: An Autobiography of a Resident of Bethnal Green* (London, 1911), pp. 135–7.

[41]   Ugolini cites two examples of home-made football shorts, particularly noticeable in a team sport; *Men and Menswear,* pp. 51–2 and 206.

[42]   Frederick Willis, *A Book of London Yesterdays* (London, 1960), p. 54.

briefer stages implies an understanding of child development as a process rather than a single event.

Daniel Cook has identified the promotion of age-appropriate clothing styles (primarily for girls) as one of the means by which manufacturers and retailers consolidated their position as 'cultural brokers' of childhood in 1920s America:

> American girlhood and to a lesser extent American boyhood underwent a transformation, from a grossly defined stage of the early life course to one in which various named age-size clothing designations made for finely grained distinctions within a trajectory of childhood.[43]

It is therefore doubly interesting to see this process taking place in Britain in the 1880s and 1890s, and with boys. In fact, age-graded clothing has also been integral to non-industrialised societies such as the Kalabari of Nigeria.[44] This suggests that the link between clothing and the cultural construction of childhood needs further study.

The practice of age-grading in clothing was not absolute but modified by pragmatic considerations of cost and availability, and also by the symbolic considerations of expressing family membership. This aspect of children's clothing is apparent in elite family portraits from at least 1600 onwards,[45] and was still associated with the social elite in the 1870s.[46] Autobiographies suggested that in poorer families, handing-down and remaking of clothing was universal.[47] Yet the presence of 100 pairs of brothers in the Barnardo's entry photographs wearing matching or near-matching clothes suggests that this practice was widespread.[48] The importance of clothing that 'underlined the primacy of family ties over individual identity' has been recognised in France, and needs to be re-examined in Britain.[49]

The potential of sibling matching as a marketing tool does not seem to have been addressed by retailers until the 1930s, when Cook highlights several advertisements

---

[43]   Cook, *The Commodification of Childhood*, pp. 14 and 97

[44]   Catherine Daly, "'Ah, a real Kalabari Woman!'": Reflexivity and the Conceptualization of Appearance', *Fashion Theory*, 3/3 (1999): 343–62; Susan Michelman and Tonye Erekosima, 'Kalabari dress in Nigeria', in Ruth Barnes and Joanne Eicher (eds), *Dress and Gender: Making and Meaning* (Oxford, 1993), pp. 164–82.

[45]   See the portrait of the family of the Earl of Leicester, c.1600, plate 1 in Elizabeth Ewing, *History of Children's Costume* (London, 1977).

[46]   Notably the children of the Prince of Wales; NPG x96036 (1875).

[47]   See Ugolini, *Men and Menswear*, pp. 210–11, for examples.

[48]   Jackets of the same style but different fabrics on boys of different ages, as in Barnardo's numbers 11276–7 (1891), suggests a deliberate choice rather than a pragmatic adoption of the cheapest or most easily available option. See Rose, 'Boyswear', illustration 5.6, p. 307.

[49]   Catherine Join-Diéterle, 'Le vêtement comme illustration des liens familiaux', in Musée Galliera, *La mode et l'enfant, 1780–2000* (Paris, 2001), p. 152.

on this theme – but addressed to the trade rather than to consumers.[50] This is surprising, as the practice is a highly visible form of conspicuous consumption. Again, there is a parallel in Nigeria today, where guests at events such as weddings are encouraged to wear 'aso ebi' or matched clothing to indicate both membership of a peer group of workmates or school friends and social status.[51]

The Embodiment of Masculinity in Clothes

One area of enquiry that proved very elusive was the ways in which boys' clothing embodied masculinity. The texts examined in Chapter 6 and Chapter 7 did not articulate this relationship. Those concerned with clothing provision (such as the *Tailor and Cutter*) tended to focus closely on details of cut and trim, without addressing the relationship of these to boys' developmental stages. Conversely, educational texts (for teachers in either private or state schools) focused on boys' intellectual and spiritual development, with little attention to their bodies.[52] The texts that most consistently discussed clothing appropriate for different stages of boyhood were aimed at middle-class mothers, but these were still limited in their scope.

Even when there were major changes in the age-related dress codes, as there were in the 1880s, the rationale behind either system, or behind the change, was not addressed. On the face of it, the lowering of the age of 'breeching' from eight to four between 1871 and 1899 suggests a change in the view of masculinity.[53] Jo Paoletti, a dress historian, agrees with cultural historians John Tosh and Christine Nelson in seeing a growing essentialism in attitudes to masculinity at this time, reflected in a 'masculinisation' of young boys' clothes.[54] However, this perceived 'essentialism' in 1880s boys' clothing is undermined by retailers' tendency to provide overlapping age ranges for each stage of clothing. Indeed it would be more accurate to speak of 'breeching' as a process that extended over a period of ten years or more, from the toddler's short trousers to the adolescent's long ones.

Nor were 'essentialist' attitudes to masculinity visible in texts dealing with boys' clothes, which tended to focus on changes in detail from season to season, ignoring

---

[50]   Trade advertisements from *Earnshaw's Infants and Children's Merchandiser* by Kiddies Pal (1933), and by Iserson Imports (1936) in Cook, *The Commodification of Childhood*, pp. 109–10.

[51]   The cost of this practice increases its social prestige, and its function as a marker of status for participants; see Judith Perani and Norma H. Wolff, *Cloth Dress and Art Patronage in Africa* (Oxford, 1999), pp. 29–30. For further examples, see *Ovation International* (Lagos), http://ovationinternational.com.

[52]   E. Lyttleton, *Mothers and Sons; or, problems in the home training of boys* (London, 1892).

[53]   Compare, for example, *Cassell's Household Guide* (London, 1869–71), vol. I, p. 370; vol. II, p. 361; Richard Taylor, *The Boy and How to Suit Him!! A Suitable Little Treatise in 5 Chaps* (London, 1899), p. 6.

[54]   Jo B. Paoletti, 'Clothes Make the Boy, 1869–1910', *Dress*, 9 (1983), p. 19.

the major shift in clothing systems. This focus on surface details was particularly noticeable in dressmaking texts such as *Myra's Mid-Monthly Journal*, which gave precise indications of the gender and age range for all garments, but never explained what made a dress suitable for a three-year-old boy rather than his sister. This silence suggests that the marks of difference were arbitrary and governed by unspoken convention rather than any explicit rationale. As there was no explicit linkage, changes in signs could take place without affecting the deeper symbolism of masculinity. The unspoken nature of the conventions governing boys' dresses also allowed them to function as a tool of social distinction and a form of 'cultural capital'.

Symbolic Meanings of Clothes

Because texts were silent on the rationale for age and gender codes, the study of clothing practices in family portraits, school groups, and Barnardo's entry images became even more important. The images in retailers' documents provided material for qualitative and quantitative analysis of the meanings associated with specific garment types, particularly the sailor suit and the Highland kilt. The analysis of the photographs showed that the age at which sailor suits was typically worn (four to eight) was much more restricted than the ages for which they were available from retailers (three to eleven). However, the retailers' images confirmed the association of sailor suits with youth and play, typically showing boys in holiday settings.[55]

The military and nationalistic references of the Highland kilt suit were minimised in texts and catalogues. Retailers' catalogues depicted kilt-clad boys in playful versions of Scottish activities, imitating golf or Highland dancing but with walking sticks substituted for golf clubs and ceremonial swords. There were also kilt variants adapted for very young boys, some with considerable changes to fabric and cut. These changes, like the elaborate braiding of boys' sailor suits, tended to distance the garments from adult male prototypes and align them with fashionable female clothing.

The commercial documents demonstrated that retailers were keenly aware of the importance of 'lifestyle marketing' to reinforce sales. Advertising material acted as an intermediary between retailers and customers, and would be expected to highlight any symbolic associations that would help to sell the garments. The patriotic references in advertising images in 1899 reflect not a constant theme but a topical response to the Boer War. Schorman and Ugolini have identified a similar response at the start of the Spanish-American war in 1898, and the Great War in 1914.[56] The relationship between advertising and the popular perception of an ongoing conflict is an area that would repay further investigation.

---

[55] Cheryl Buckley noted the dominance of play or holiday imagery in advertisements for young children's clothing in the 1990s; 'Children's clothes: design and promotion', in Pat Kirkham (ed.), *The Gendered Object* (Manchester, 1996), pp. 103–11.

[56] Schorman, *Selling Style*, pp. 102–16; Ugolini, *Men and Menswear*, pp. 77–8 and 156–7.

Variation in Styles and 'Distinction'

The availability of multiple versions of the same style, even within the same catalogue, has important implications for our understanding of standard styles such as the sailor suit. Was it true that 'small boys decked out as sailors brought a parental and symbolic glow of pride into every home', as Ewing claimed, or were the symbolic associations dulled by repetition? [57] Did variations on the 'correct' style, present from the 1870s (see Figure 7.4) maintain the patriotic associations, or dilute them?

For customers, multiple variations on the sailor or Greenwich suit offered greater possibilities of 'distinction'. The workings of this process were evident in the surviving sailor suits examined in Chapter 7, which ranged from washable cotton drill to non-washable velvet and lace. Marks of 'distinction' based on fabric would tend to be constant year on year, but marks of distinction based on trimming would be subject to shifts in fashion. This would allow the fashionable elite to distinguish their sons from the merely respectable masses. The provision of multiple variants both of garments and of advertising images for the same style also allowed retailers to distinguish themselves from their competitors', even when they were supplied by the same manufacturers and advertising agents.

Panton's 1896 characterisation of the 'odious common sailor suit'[58] pays oblique testimony to the success of clothing manufacturers in establishing the sailor suit as a garment that fitted their production processes, and that was capable of stylistic variations that kept it in fashion from 1875 to 1900 and beyond. The attention given to these variations, rather than to the underlying forms (even in advisory texts such as Panton's), suggests that the rationale behind changes in practice was not directly related to changes in paediatric theories. If these were present, they were mediated by commercial texts and practices so that changes in ideas were perceived as changes in fashion.

Moreover, the changes in clothing practice, with trouser suits worn at a younger age, corresponded neatly to the interests of mass manufacturers, whose production was dominated by just these garments. It is possible that, through their sophisticated use of visual material and their adoption of consistent age ranges, manufacturers and retailers helped to establish a coherent model of age-related practice for boys across all classes. Yet producers and retailers, no matter how sophisticated, could only advise consumers.

---

[57]   Ewing, *History of Children's Costume*, pp. 83–7. For further discussion of the meanings of sailor suits, see Clare Rose, 'The Meanings of the Late Victorian Sailor Suit,' *Journal of Maritime Research*, http: //www.jmr.nmm.ac.uk/server/show/ ConJmrArticle.270/, online September 2009.

[58]   Jane Emily Panton, *The Way They Should Go* (London, 1896), p. 99.

Clothes and Social Status

The relationship between clothing and social status was axiomatic in nineteenth-century England, central to the opposition between 'raggedness' and 'respectability' that shaped bodies like the Ragged School Union. It was also at the centre of the publicity images issued by all the 'child rescue' charities, such as Barnardo's and the Church of England Waifs and Strays Society (CEWSS). As shown in Chapter 1, these institutions had a broadly consistent way of presenting 'raggedness', to the extent of borrowing key images from each other, but their imagining of 'respectability' in dress was surprisingly varied. Boys wore ill-fitting corduroys in the Workhouse, smart wool suits with collars and ties in the charities. There was a further distinction between the charities, with Barnardo's issuing uniform outfits and the CEWSS varied ones. These distinctions reflected different practices in sourcing the garments: from contractors for the Workhouse, from their own workshops by Barnardo's, from middle-class well-wishers by the CEWSS.[59]

These practices in themselves revealed profound differences between the three organisations in terms of both the current needs of their charges and their future occupations. These differences were both conscious and reflexive, with the CEWSS appealing for individual donations of clothing in order to distinguish itself from 'great institutions, in which all training must be more or less mechanical, and all personal influence unknown', a coded reference to the Workhouse system.[60] This differentiation suggests a process closer to 'distinction' than to an opposition between 'raggedness' and 'respectability'. These key concepts proved unexpectedly hard to define in practice.[61] There seem to have been no rules excluding children from attending Board Schools in clothing that was ragged, dirty or otherwise unsuitable (like mill overalls).[62]

---

[59] Manufacturers making clothes for institutions included Arthur Lynes: *Merriment and Modes* (London, 1872), p. 96, JJ MC Box 4/19. Both Barnardo's and the London Poor Law schools dressed boys in uniform clothing which they aimed to make in their own workshops. See Lydia Murdoch, *Imagined Orphans: Poor Families, Child Welfare and Contested Citizenship in London* (New Brunswick, 2006), pp. 123–8. For the CEWSS, see *Our Waifs and Strays*, March 1887, p. 2.

[60] Address by the Bishop of Bedford, *Our Waifs and Strays*, December 1887, p. 5.

[61] This issue is explored in Rose, 'Alla ricerca'. See also Freda Millett, *Up at Rive: Voices of the Half-timers in Oldham's Cotton Mills* (Oldham, n.d.).

[62] Because cotton mills were kept very warm and humid, workers wore thin cotton clothing and sometimes worked barefoot. This created issues of decency as well as cleanliness when mill clothes were worn outside. A case study was made of the clothing worn at schools in Oldham, a district where many schoolchildren worked 'half-time' in the cotton mill. The logbooks for St Peter's Infants (1876–95), St Domingo Street Wesleyan Mixed (1893–1901), and Wellington Street (1883–90) were examined (Box B/CBO 12/OBC, Oldham Local Studies Centre). These contained some references to half-time pupils, but none to half-timers' clothing or cleanliness.

Even the Ragged Schools had ragged clothing as only one of their thirteen criteria for eligibility.[63]

The search for visual evidence of raggedness in Barnardo's entry photographs and school group photographs complicated the issue still further. Barnardo's entrants were more visibly ragged and less 'respectable' than the schoolboys, but not exclusively so: 30 per cent of the Barnardo's entrants wore collars, and only 53 per cent of the schoolboys. The blurred focus and crowding of the school groups hindered the identification of raggedness in this source, so the gap between the two was probably even narrower.

The importance of the white collar could be seen in instances where it was added to an otherwise ragged ensemble as a means of differentiating the wearer from those without even a pretension of respectability.[64] The degree to which clothing was understood as indicating respectability is demonstrated by examples of children who were dressed in donated or loaned garments before presenting themselves for admission to Barnardo's.[65] The involvement of the community in presenting a child speaks of a shared understanding of what this entailed. Finally, the 'dressing-up' of children confirms that entrance to Barnardo's was often instigated by families, rather than by the charity.[66]

The Barnardo's entry photos also provided evidence for age-related clothing practice within families. This showed that the age of 'secondary breeching' (going from short to long trousers) varied, but most often happened at age twelve or thirteen. The age of thirteen was used in retailers, dressmakers' and tailors' documents at this period as a dividing line between boys' and youths' clothing, probably related to the growth spurt of puberty.[67] However, it is clear that the progression from boys' clothing to men's was not necessarily tied to progression from school to work, which happened around the age of eleven.

Notwithstanding references by autobiographers to purchasing new clothes as part of the job-seeking process,[68] there was no evidence in the Barnardo's photographs that potential wage-earners were better dressed. Indeed, a close

---

[63]   Claire Seymour, *Ragged Schools, Ragged Children* (London, 1995), p. 5.

[64]   For the importance of such distinctions within the working class, see Perkin, *The Rise of Professional Society*, pp. 101–7.

[65]   For example, John Roddy/McHugh, 1888, cited in Gillian Wagner, *Barnardo* (London, 1979), p. 229. It is possible that some of the white collars worn with ragged jackets were donated by neighbours.

[66]   For parents requesting Barnardo's places for their children, see Murdoch, *Imagined Orphans*, pp. 87–91.

[67]   Which would itself vary depending on the boy's family income and level of nutrition; see Roderick Floud, Kenneth Wachter and Annabel Gregory, *Height, Health and History: Nutritional Status in the United Kingdom, 1750–1980* (Cambridge, 1990), pp. 186–7.

[68]   See Jack Lanigan in John Burnett (ed.), *Destiny Obscure: Autobiographies of Childhood, Education and Family from the 1820s to the 1920s* (London, 1982), p. 90;

examination of the presentation of raggedness within sibling groups in this data showed several examples where school-age younger brothers were better dressed than working-age elder ones. These examples suggest that different conventions governed clothing in the workplace and in schools. They also uphold Ross's finding that additional income from adolescent children was used to benefit the whole family, not for marks of individual status such as new clothes.[69]

Children and Consumption

The acquisition of clothing for children with no or little earning power is a tricky subject for theories of consumption, and one that is only beginning to be addressed with studies of the twentieth century.[70] There have been recent discussions in the press of parents purchasing 'designer' clothing and equipment for young children, or on children exerting 'pester power' in order to obtain clothing and shoes that they see as particularly desirable. These practices have been presented as worrying on both financial and moral grounds, in articles with titles like 'Designer babywear costs parents an arm and a leg'.[71] There has been a consensus that excessive consumption is a reaction to, or outgrowth of, late twentieth-century ways of life: 'with these restrictions on childhood it's no wonder kids seek refuge in consumerism.'[72] A more reflective view of the issues has been taken by researchers in the Cultures of Consumption project, who have concluded that 'Consumption of clothing seems to act as a tool for children in defining a sense of individual or group identity'.[73] Yet children's clothing is also used as a means for parents

---

Acorn, *One of the Multitude*, p. 121; further examples in Ugolini, *Men and Menswear*, pp. 62–3.

[69]   Ellen Ross, '"Fierce Questions and Taunts": Married Life in Working-class London, 1870–1914', *Feminist Studies*, 8/3 (1982), p. 576.

[70]   Cook, *Commodification of Childhood*; Alison Clarke, 'Maternity and Materiality: Becoming a Mother in Consumer Culture', in Linda Layne, Janelle Taylor and Danielle F. Wozniak (eds), *Consuming Mothers* (Camden, NJ, 2004), pp. 55–71; *eadem*, 'Mother Swapping: The Trafficking of Nearly New Children's Wear', in Peter Jackson, Michelle Lowe, Daniel Miller and Frank Mort (eds), *Commercial Cultures: Economies, Practices, Spaces* (Oxford, 2000), pp. 85–100.

[71]   Alexandra Frean, 'Designer babywear costs parents an arm and a leg', *Times* online, 6 July 2005; 'Designer labels more likely to be worn by baby than yummy mummy', *Times* online, 13 June 2006; Alice Miles, 'Don't just sit there, do nothing', *Times* online, 8 May 2004; Lisa Armstrong, 'Good taste doesn't count for anything much. Being "stylish" has become much more important', *Times* online, 17 March 2007.

[72]   India Knight, 'Mollycoddle curse of the middle class', *Times* online, 2 March 2008.

[73]   Sharon Boden, Christopher Pole, Jane Pilcher and, Tim Edwards, 'New Consumers? The Social and Cultural Significance of Children's Fashion Consumption', *Cultures of Consumption Working Papers*, 16 (2004), online at www.consume.bbk.ac.uk.

to define their own group identity through vicarious consumption, leading to complex negotiations.[74]

Historic consumption for children provides a useful perspective from which to address these issues. Fashion magazines in the past were unapologetic in describing children as 'those big, moving, shiny dolls which mothers amuse themselves in dressing',[75] or recommending for young boys 'lovely frocks of muslin and embroidery with all the adornments of finely gauged plastrons [bodice fronts] and wide sashes of folded surah [silk]' designed to harmonise with their mothers'.[76] Bringing nineteenth-century boys into consumption theory would force us to evaluate the role of group identity as against personal, gender and age identity. One model for this is Emma Tarlo's work on contemporary India, where clothing practice acts as a way of articulating and balancing caste, family and personal identities.[77]

Use of Sources

As the review of the literature in the Introduction indicated, there are many different approaches to the interpretation of dress.[78] These tend to prioritise different types of source material: economic history approaches may use the records of businesses, while cultural studies approaches may use family photographs and personal memories. This creates gaps and inconsistencies between different accounts of the same terrain, and leaves the validity of different sources unexamined.[79] This is particularly problematic for children's clothing, where there are few preceding studies.

This project used a wide variety of sources, comparing information derived from texts, images and actual garments against each other. This allowed me to build up a multi-dimensional picture of the making, selling and wearing of boys' clothing, and also to test the validity of different types of sources against each other. Retail catalogues, were analysed comparatively and gave new and surprising

---

[74]   Clarke, 'Mother swapping'; Ragnhild Brusdal, '"If it is good for the child's development then I say yes almost every time": How Parents Relate to Their Children's Consumption', *International Journal of Consumer Studies*, 31/4 (2007): 391–6.

[75]   *Femina*, 1903 (author translation), cited in Catherine Join-Diéterle, 'Introduction', in Musée Galliéra, *La mode et l'enfant, 1780–2000* (Paris, 2001), p. 14.

[76]   *Myra's Mid-Monthly Journal*, July 1882, p. 201.

[77]   Emma Tarlo, *Clothing Matters: Dress and Identity in India* (London, 1996).

[78]   There is a sampler of these in *Fashion Theory*, 2/4 (1998), and a fuller analysis in Joanne Entwistle, *The Fashioned Body: Fashion, Dress and Modern Social Theory* (London, 2000), Chapter 2, pp. 40–77. The development of the discipline is the subject of Lou Taylor, *The Study of Dress History* (Manchester, 2002).

[79]   Good examples of cross-disciplinary practice include the work of Christopher Breward, Lou Taylor and Laura Ugolini.

evidence of a sharp fall in boys' clothing prices by the 1890s. The very large sets of documents from the archives of Barnardo's, the Board of Trade and Stationers' Hall were analysed using quantitative methods. This gave a firm evidential base for the discussion of clothing practices and their meanings. Quantitative analysis modifies the interpretation of individual documents: our understanding of patriotic advertisements for sailor suits changes when we know that their (literal) flag-waving was a topical reference rather than a constant feature.[80] Quantitative analysis was particularly important in opening up the Barnardo's entry images, seen as paradigms of Foucauldian surveillance, to alternative interpretations.[81] This opens up the potential of other such photographs, such as those in criminal records.

Personal documents such as autobiographies and garments survived in small numbers, and were analysed comparatively and by reference to the quantitative data. Doing this showed up some of the problems of the sources; for example, that the commonest type of sailor suit in museum collections was not the type most frequently worn.[82] Autobiographies, which offer seemingly unmediated evidence of past practice, were shown to be somewhat unreliable, as John Walton warned of oral histories: 'they supply illustrations and cautionary examples; but we generalise from them at our peril.'[83]

Final Conclusions

Cunningham's and Davin's understanding of childhood experience as not unitary but modulated by age, gender and social status has deep implications for the study of children's clothing. Previous studies of this area (including my own) tended to over-emphasise the experience of elite families, for whom data is readily available. The relationship between elite and mass practice was either framed as a trickling-

---

[80]   See Schorman, *Selling Style: Clothing and Social Change at the Turn of the Century* (Philadelphia, 2003), pp. 102–16, and Ugolini, *Men and Menswear*, pp. 156–7.

[81]   John Tagg, *The Burden of Representation: Essays on Photographies and Histories* (Basingstoke, 1988) pp. 83–5.

[82]   Similar problems were found in a study of eighteenth-century women's quilted petticoats; Clare Rose, 'Bought, stolen, bequeathed, preserved: sources for the study of 18th-century petticoats', in Maria Hayward and Elizabeth Kramer (eds), *Textiles and Text: Re-establishing the Links Between Archival and Object-based Research* (London, 2007), pp. 114–21.

[83]   John K Walton, *Lancashire: A Social History, 1558–1939* (Manchester, 1987), p. 294. Barbara English, described the paradigmatic autobiography *Lark Rise to Candleford* as 'not an artless production, rather a very skilful piece of special pleading'; 'Lark Rise and Juniper Hill: A Victorian Community in Literature and in History', *Victorian Studies*, 28 (1985), p. 33.

down or left unexamined.[84] The evidence presented here has supported Davin's view of working-class practice as accommodating and even adopting forms of behaviour originally established by the middle-classes. The subcultural resistance to hegemonic norms described by Humphries was not visible in these sources.[85] This is partly a function of the age group studied, since boys under fifteen had little discretion in clothing choice. However, it should also make us question how vivid descriptions of 'monkey parades' and other subcultural displays have been shaped by their origins as popular journalism for middle-class readers with a preconception of working-class difference.[86]

A close examination of clothing practice within families revealed how clothing was used to embody family relationships, attitudes to masculinity, and educational status. Clothing also acted to assert the identity of the boy as part of a group, whether family, institution or school. In all of these areas 'distinction' (between male and female, older and younger, toddler and scholar) could be discerned. However, these distinctions were not binary but incremental: even the category of gender was not absolute, but modified by considerations of age.

The concept of 'distinction', or of variation within a norm, can also be used as an explanatory framework for the ways in which the clothing industry viewed boys' garments. The numerous registered designs, and the unknown number of designs made without Registration, indicate that mass manufacturers needed to distinguish their products from their competitors'. By the 1890s design was largely in the hands of factory-based professionals, and the role of the client was reduced to that of consumption. This loss of consumer involvement was masked by the offering of numerous alternatives, and by strategies such as Barran's sailor suits with interchangeable collars and cuffs. Texts written for consumers indicated how they could satisfy their wish for 'distinction' from other families, while still observing social conventions.

As Panton stated so clearly, a garment that was widely available would lose its attraction for the elite and become 'odious, common'.[87] One way that manufacturers could combat this overfamiliarity was by increasing the element of fashion, which involves constant change and updating. Thus the needs of the mass consumer and the needs of the mass producer worked together to increase rather than decrease the sophistication of the product.

The high-fashion content of mass-produced boys' suits belies historians' views of male clothing as 'standardised, machine-made garments',[88] or as 'semi-durable

---

[84]   Ewing, *History of Children's Costume*; Rose, *Children's Clothes*; Anne Buck, *Clothes and the Child: A Handbook of Children's Dress in England, 1500–1900* (Bedford, 1996).

[85]   Stephen Humphries, *Hooligans or Rebels? An Oral History of Working-Class Childhood and Youth, 1889–1939* (Oxford, 1981).

[86]   Breward, *Hidden Consumer*, pp. 206–10.

[87]   Panton *The Way They Should Go*, p. 99.

[88]   Fine and Leopold, *World of Consumption*, p. 236.

products'.[89] This may reflect a difference between the adult and child markets based on the ephemeral nature of boyhood. As the Barnardo's photographs demonstrate, any attempt to treat boys' garments as 'semi-durable' would be frustrated by the wearers' tendency to grow out of them, or wear through them. If a different set of clothes were needed to accommodate each year's growth, the presence of fashionable markers would indicate to all whether the garments were actually new, or handed down.

The degree to which the families entering Barnardo's reflect the clothing practices seen in Board Schools also suggests the workings of Bourdieu's *habitus*, the 'reasonable', 'common-sense' behaviours.[90] Because these behaviours are internalised and rarely verbalised, they can only be understood through practices rather than texts. This was certainly the case for the presentation of masculinity through clothing, which was rarely addressed directly in any of the texts examined. The practice of each period was presented as self-evident and logical, even when there had been major changes from the previous period. Changes in practice were explained not in terms of paediatric theory, but as changes in fashion. Thus fashion, 'where individual psychology meets the social organisation of a group, a class, an age',[91] can affect the ways that we understand and express fundamental human relationships.

---

[89]   Katrina Honeyman, 'Style Monotony and the Business of Fashion: The Marketing of Menswear in Inter-war England', *Textile History*, 34/2 (2003), p. 171.

[90]   Pierre Bourdieu, *The Logic of Practice* (Cambridge, 1990), pp. 55–6.

[91]   Elizabeth Wilson and Lou Taylor, *Through the Looking Glass: A History of Dress from 1860 to the Present Day* (London, 1989), p. 13.

Appendix 1
Sources and Research Methodologies

This Appendix will give detailed information on the archives and sources used for this thesis, and on the methods of sampling and analysis applied. In some cases changes in the presentation of data over the period studied meant that different sampling methods had to be applied for different sections of a single source. Sources providing evidence for the consumption of clothing by individuals (surviving garments, photographs, autobiographical texts) will be discussed first. Sources providing evidence for the production and retailing of clothing (registered designs, dressmaking patterns, shop catalogues) will be discussed subsequently. The largest sources (registered designs, Barnardo's photographs) will be discussed separately, while smaller ones will be grouped together.

Sources for Consumption

Surviving Garments

The analysis of surviving garments for this thesis builds on research carried out in 1987 for the book *Children's Clothes Since 1750*, using museum collections in Exeter, London, Bath, Bristol, Stoke, Leicester, Nottingham, Manchester, Carlisle and County Durham. Major archives in Manchester, London, Bath, York and County Durham were revisited during 1999–2000 (with a grant from the Pasold Research Fund), and collections in Leeds, Leicester, Winchester and Worthing were visited for the first time. Collections were searched manually to identify all garments of potential interest, and supporting documentation was searched to clarify the date and gender of questionable items. In many cases the documentation was inadequate, owing to the limitations of donors' knowledge and of museum procedures. In at least one museum, information about original wearers had been actively suppressed in order to concentrate on the generic attributes of dress.[1]

Boy toddlers' dresses dominated museum collections to a surprising extent, with 87 examples found.[2] Unfortunately surviving dresses had often been catalogued as 'child', with no indication of gender. In order to clarify the issue of gender

---

[1] Some museums deliberately suppressed all data about original wearers: see Jane Tozer and Sarah Levitt, 'Cunnington's Attitude to Collecting', *Costume*, 20 (1986): 1–17.

[2] For the complete dataset, see Clare Rose, 'Boyswear and the Formation of Gender and Class Identity in Urban England, 1840–1900' (unpublished PhD disertation, University of Brighton, 2006), Table 4.9.

codes only garments documented as male were selected for analysis in Chapter 6. The 50 dresses tentatively identified as masculine on the basis of similarity to documented examples, or to illustrations in dressmaking texts, were excluded. Of the 37 surviving dresses identified as worn by boys 31 were linked to a named individual and 27 were associated with specific dates (either a date of wearing or the wearer's date of birth). The remaining garments had looser dates supplied either by the donor or by the curator.

Some collections with large numbers of boys' dresses contained no trouser suits from the period 1870–1900. The main collections with holdings of boys' suits were Bethnal Green Museum of Childhood (13 examples) and the Gallery of Costume at Manchester (12 examples). Altogether 43 surviving trouser suits believed to date before 1900 were identified, although the lack of documentation made it hard to be sure of the end date for this group.[3]

Garments were catalogued in a series of databases, and photographs and brief descriptions were taken to enable stylistic analysis and comparison. A preliminary overview of the data showed a preponderance of exceptional garments; 20 of the 43 trouser suits were made from velvet or silk, and a further 14 were light cotton or linen sailor suits of a kind worn on middle-class seaside holidays. This distribution of garment types was not found in any other source, not even family photographs. Thus a quantitative analysis was unlikely to be productive, or to provide points for comparison with other sources. Instead, the surviving garments were analysed qualitatively in Chapter 7 to assess how boys' dresses and sailor suits encoded masculine symbolism, and how consumers distinguished between different subtypes of garments.

Information on the class status of wearers was rarely available, but the garments found in museum collections appeared to be exclusively middle-class. This was true even of collections with a special interest in working-class lives such as the North of England Open Air Museum at Beamish. The only known example of a corduroy suit of the type worn by working boys was recently purchased by a museum without any documentation.[4] Information on the production of surviving garments was also very patchy. This was particularly noticeable with the dresses and tunics, where the only information was 'made by mother'. Boys' trouser suits were better documented through the presence of retailers' labels. This allowed individual garments to be linked to the discussion of retailing in Chapter 3.

Photographs

Many photographs of children have been published, but the material remains problematic as it is often inadequately documented. National archives, such as the National Media Museum, Bradford, the V&A Museum of Childhood, London, and the Museum of Education at the University of Leeds, did not have systematic

---

[3]   See ibid., Table 4.10, for the complete dataset.
[4]   Museum of London (MOL) 1985.236.

collections of school group or individual photographs. Regional archives in the north and south of England were also consulted. Each archive contained some photographs of children, but many of these were unusable owing to inadequate documentation. For example, all of the school group photographs in Oldham Local Studies Centre were undated, and many were only vaguely localised.[5] The same was true of the archives of The Museum of English Rural Life, Reading University.

The London Metropolitan Archives contain documents from London bodies including the School Board for London. These include many original photographs taken at London schools, both class portraits and 'action shots' of teaching in progress; however, only 13 of these had documented dates before 1900. The Documentary Photography Archive, Manchester is another very large archive, containing 80,000 images of family and social groups from the north-west of England. Many of these images came as part of family collections or albums and the archive aimed to record the names, birth dates and social status of the family members.[6] Unfortunately, there was less information attached to photographs before 1900 than for later images. Although there were 18 school group photographs with supporting documentation in this archive. it was not possible to read the details of these from the very small copy photographs (5cm × 3cm) made available to researchers. The legibility of images also created problems at the North of England Open Air Museum at Beamish, County Durham, where images were again available only in a reduced format. A private collection of photographs held by Mr F.P. Raine, a local historian from Barnard Castle,[7] included three dated examples from Cotherstone Wesleyan School, near Darlington. (Visits to these collections were aided by a grant from the Pasold Research Fund.[8])

The largest single source of family photographs used was the National Portrait Gallery (available online at www.npg.org.uk). This is biased towards the social and intellectual elite but has the advantage of being well documented. Smaller collections were found in Beamish Museum, the Documentary Photography Archive, Worthing Museum and Art Gallery, and Winchester City Museum. Many of these images were not fully documented, and those without dates were not used for analysis. A few additional images were found in publications on the history of

---

[5] Several undated group photographs from St Paul's School Royton are held in box LS1/910.

[6] 'Each deposit is accompanied by detailed documentary records which include background information about the family, subject content of each individual photograph and data on how or why the photograph was taken': http://www.gmcro.co.uk/Photography/DPA/collections.htm (accessed 17 December 2003).

[7] I am grateful to Joanna Hashagen of the Bowes Museum for providing the introduction.

[8] For a complete listing of the school group photographs used see Table 2.1 in Rose, 'Boyswear'.

dress, the history of photography, or local history.[9] Altogether 80 family portraits of boys were found; in 72 of these the ages of sitters were documented. The portraits were analysed for information on consumption practices in Chapter 5 and for age-related expressions of masculinity in Chapter 6.

Dr Barnardo's Entry Photographs

Images of poor boys disseminated by charities had been identified by Cunningham as important in both shaping and reflecting nineteenth-century ideas of childhood. Lloyd, Green-Lewis, and Lindsay Smith had identified Dr Barnardo's Homes as the chief user of this form of publicity, with the Church of England Waifs and Strays Society (now the Children's Society) as another important example. These two charities are still extant, and their archives were investigated for images that had been influential in forming concepts of 'raggedness'. At the Children's Society the main source consulted was the journal *Our Waifs and Strays*, which published images of groups of boys both before and after 'rescue'.[10] These images were analysed to indicate normative practice in charitable fundraising. Photographs of individuals were held in case files and not available to researchers.[11]

The images in the Barnardo's archive were much more numerous (500,000 in total; 42,000 prior to 1900) and included record photographs of every child on entrance and exit.[12] These images for internal use are readily distinguishable from groups and posed photographs used for publicity purposes.[13] Record photographs are stored separately from the case notes, which are subject to access restrictions under the Data Protection Act 1998.[14] Although the original case notes were not available, indicative examples were found in publications by Wagner

---

[9]   Madeleine Ginsburg, *Victorian Dress in Photographs* (London, 1982); Miles Lambert, *Fashion in Photographs 1860–1880* (London, 1991); E. Roberts, *In and Around Alresford in Old Photographs* (Alresford 1975); J. Norwood, *Victorian and Edwardian Hampshire & the Isle of Wight from Old Photographs* (London, 1973); *Owslebury, A Village School: 150 Years 1840–1990* (no imprint, 1990); John Wilshere, *Leicester Portrait Photographers before 1900* (Leicester, 1988).

[10]   Seen at the Society's archive, Tower Bridge Business Complex, Bermondsey, London.

[11]   A website has since been set up, reproducing a few individual images from casebooks, www.hiddenlives.org.uk (accessed 28 June 2005).

[12]   Held in the photographic archives at Barnardo's headquarters, Tanner Lane, Barkingside, Ilford, Essex.

[13]   Examples of these are also held in Barnardo's photographic archives; Boxes 1–35 contain approximately 900 images of groups, or of individuals grouped in albums. A small selection from these are reproduced on the website www.topfoto.co.uk.

[14]   Access to records of individuals was normally restricted to their descendants or family members.

and Murdoch.[15] The photographic files were made freely available, and included enough information (name, date, age) to make them a useful source.

Before sampling the images it was necessary to distinguish entry from exit photographs as these were numbered in a single sequence up to 1888. These were differentiated by clear visual codes: children entering were posed full-face on a rough wooden box, while children leaving were posed in three-quarters view on a polished drawing-room chair. The different staging of the two types of photographs acts as a paradigm for the class status of the children on entrance and exit, with entry images similar to police or prison 'mug shots', and exit images to middle-class portraits.[16] After 1888 the child's record number was inscribed on the photograph, clarifying the status of images.

Between 1874 and 1899 there were approximately 21,000 entrants to Barnardo's, most of them boys. This resulted in over 21,000 entry photographs, which were preserved as prints measuring about 9 × 6cm pasted into large ledgers, 12 per page. These were searched manually and sampled by selecting two sheets from a winter month and two from a summer month in each year. It was not possible to use the same month each year as some sections of the ledgers were dominated by exit photographs. In addition, all the sheets from January and all from July of 1890 and 1895 were recorded. Entry photographs of boys were selected from these sheets. From 1888 Barnardo's photographed sibling groups together as well as individually.[17] Group photographs were easily identified on the ledger pages and all were included in the sample.

Each of the sheets or images selected was recorded in a copy photograph, giving a sample of 1,874 individuals.[18] Images adjacent to sibling groups were sometimes recorded in the copies, and these were included in the sample for analysis. Four quantitative visual analyses were applied. The first, discussed in Chapter 1, evaluated the incidence of visible 'raggedness' and compared this with the same indicators in school group photographs. The second analysis, discussed in Chapter 5, looked at the type of jacket worn by each boy as evidence of consumption for comparison with the analysis of garment types in manufacturers' documents.

The third analysis used the ages of boys (recorded on the photographs after 1886) to providing data about age-related clothing codes. Boys identified as over sixteen were excluded as they were probably over the age of puberty. Infants aged under three years old were also excluded as below the age of toilet training. These

---

[15]   Lydia Murdoch, *Imagined Orphans: Poor Families, Child Welfare, and Contested Citizenship in London* (New Brunswick, 2006); Gillian Wagner, *Barnardo* (London, 1979).

[16]   See Murdoch, *Imagined Orphans,* pp. 36–9.

[17]   The family names of individuals were written on the photographs but have not been included in accordance with Barnardo's Data Protection policies.

[18]   I am extremely grateful to the photography staff at Barnardo's at this time, Paul Carr and Marisa Dowling, for their help and encouragement. See Rose, 'Boyswear', Table 5.6, for the complete dataset.

two physical events were selected as representing the upper and lower parameters of boyhood. Excluding the eldest and youngest boys, and those whose age was not recorded, gave a sample of 1,520 images. In Chapter 6 these were analysed to show evidence of age-related dress codes. Finally, sibling pairs were categorised as either 'respectable', 'ragged', 'anomalous' or 'neutral' in terms of dress, and each subgroup was examined separately. This provided detailed information on the relationship between age, earning capacity and clothing.

Autobiographies

Autobiographies have been seen as a key source of information for social historians wishing to question the assumptions implicit in more formal texts. As John Burnett states: 'The outstanding merit of autobiography lies in the fact that it is the direct, personal record of the individual himself … without the intermediary of another person who may change the situation or misread the experience.'[19] However, its use as evidence for practices affecting children is complicated by several factors. One is the paucity of references to clothing in childhood (as opposed to adolescence) in written accounts. This may be related to the lack of children's involvement in clothing choice.[20] A further problem is the vagueness over periodisation created when writers look back over decades to experiences in early childhood.

A more serious problem is created by the wish of writers to select and shape their memories. Burnett warned that: 'Autobiographers may suppress or misrepresent the truth, may exaggerate or sensationalize, may tell only half the story and thereby make the part that is told misleading.'[21] Barbara English's case study of Flora Thompson's often-cited *Lark Rise to Candleford* identified the effects of selection and revision: 'Lark Rise is not an artless production, rather a very skilful piece of special pleading. Thompson told her story with a purpose … the changes of fact or changes of emphasis … were made in order to reinforce her theme.'[22]

It is possible to overcome these drawbacks by using large numbers of autobiographies, and by examining them for evidence of attitudes as much as practices. In this project autobiographers' accounts were compared with evidence from photographs, and from commercial documents, to clarify what was normative and what was exceptional. The main model for my use of autobiographies, and a source of many references, was Laura Ugolini's *Men and Menswear*.[23] Further

---

[19]   John Burnett (ed.), *Destiny Obscure: Autobiographies of Childhood, Education and Family from the 1820s to the 1920s* (London, 1982), p. xi.

[20]   See Gwen Raverat, *Period Piece* (Cambridge, 1952), pp. 253–6.

[21]   Burnett, *Destiny Obscure*, p. xii.

[22]   Barbara English, 'Lark Rise and Juniper Hill: A Victorian Community in Literature and in History', *Victorian Studies*, 28 (1985), p. 33.

[23]   Laura Ugolini, *Men and Menswear: Sartorial Consumption in Britain, 1880–1939* (Aldershot, 2007).

sources were the work of Anna Davin, David Vincent, John Burnett and the individual autobiographies cited in the bibliography.[24]

Sources for Clothing Production and Retailing

Manufacturers' Registered Designs: BT43 and BT45, 1842–83

Manufacturers' designs registered under the terms of Design and Copyright Acts from 1842 onwards, held at The National Archives, had been identified as an important source by Sarah Levitt.[25] In 1842, designs were divided into two main categories, 'ornamental' and 'useful'. Ornamental designs were subdivided into 13 classes by material and manufacturing process, with 'useful' designs in a single series.[26] Ornamental classes 6–13 were for different types of textiles; references in Levitt (1986) indicated that garments were registered in Board of Trade (BT) 43 Class 12 (Other Fabrics) and BT 43 Class 13 (Lace). These were recorded in two sets of ledgers: Representations, with sample or sketches of the item registered; and Registers with the names and addresses of the proprietors. Class 12 covered Representations volumes BT 43/382–406 and Registers BT 44/29–30, while Class 13 was in Representations volumes BT 43/416–432 and Registers BT 44/33–38. The registration of 'Useful' designs, BT 45, ran in parallel with 'Ornamental' (BT 43) between 1842 and 1883. BT 45 consisted of a single series of 6,740 designs in 30 volumes. In 1883, a new Act of Parliament changed the recording system for registered designs, which were entered into a single series of ledgers. The 367,200 entries for the period 1883–1900 were lodged in 408 volumes of Representations, catalogued as BT50.

Levitt published a table of reference numbers for garment designs she had found in these records between 1842 and 1900, including some for boys.[27] It was hoped that the listings of designs by Levitt, and the listing of Leeds clothing manufacturers by Honeyman, would permit a targeted search of the documents

---

[24]   John Burnett, David Mayall and David Vincent, *The Autobiography of the Working Class: An Annotated Critical Bibliography, vol. 1, 1790–1200* (Brighton, 1984); David Vincent, *Bread, Knowledge and Freedom: A Study of Nineteenth-Century Working-Class Authobiography* (London, 1981).

[25]   Sarah Levitt, *The Victorians Unbuttoned* (London, 1986).

[26]   This classification is similar in spirit, though different in detail, from the classification of exhibits at the Great Exhibition in 1851. See John Gloag (ed.), *The Crystal Palace Exhibition: Illustrated catalogue, London 1851 ... [etc.]* (Facsimile reprint of: 'The Industry of All Nations, 1851, the Art-Journal illustrated Catalogue' [London: Virtue for the Art -Journal, 1851]; New York; Dover Publications, 1970).

[27]   Levitt, *Victorians Unbuttoned*, pp. 227–8.

using the Index of Proprietors.[28] However, an initial check of the Index against references from Levitt and Honeyman showed substantial discontinuities, with documents in the Index that were not referenced in Levitt or Honeyman, and references in Levitt that were not in the Index. It was therefore decided that it would be simpler to work directly from the volumes of Representations for the period 1842–83 (BT43 and BT50).

Registrations of boys' garments in BT43 and BT45 were identified by visually examining every page of each volume, and registrations of men's and women's garments were also noted for quantitative comparison. The three categories together yielded 322 designs for boys' outer garments, with the bulk of these in BT43 Class 13, and these were tabulated in Excel databases. Each Registration included an image of all or part of a garment, and each image was recorded by photocopy or sketching. Names and addresses of proprietors were taken from the registration form pasted into the ledger with the sample or picture representing the design to be registered. Name of registrant and place of business were used as sorting criteria, enabling me to quantify the involvement of different firms and different manufacturing centres.

BT50, 1883–1900

The Copyright Act of 1883 changed the procedure for design registration. Designs were still classified, but entered into a single series of 367,200 designs in 408 volumes. These volumes, measuring up to 27in × 15 in × 12in thick and weighing about 20lb each, were difficult to handle, making it doubly impractical to search them directly. The Index proved unsatisfactory because of the lack of information on firms listed, making it impossible to identify manufacturers unless their names were already known. Instead the 103 volumes of Registers (BT 51) were searched, and entries of interest were noted for checking. From January 1884 to December 1887 the register volumes had brief descriptions of the designs that gave some idea of the final product; these are transcribed in Appendix 2.[29] The presence of these descriptions meant that of the 134 references selected for 1883–87, 97 were in fact boys' garments. Information from the Registers was entered into a database with the same format as had been used for BT 43 and BT45 data and images of garments or garment trims were also recorded.

From January 1888 the brief descriptions of designs in the registers were discontinued and this made it much harder to know whether or not the references were for boys' clothes. References were instead selected for checking according to several criteria. The first was the recognition of the name of the firm from previously assembled data. A database of firms known to have produced boys'

---

[28]   Katrina Honeyman, *Well Suited: A History of the Leeds Clothing Industry, 1850–1990* (Oxford, 2000); Stanley Chapman, 'The Innovating Entrepreneurs in the British Ready-made Clothing Industry', *Textile History*, 24/1 (1993): 5–25.

[29]   See Appendix 2 for manufacturers' descriptions of their designs.

garments was made from documents identified in BT43 and BT45 and BT50 before 1887, and references to manufacturers from Honeyman and Chapman. The second criterion used was the manufacturers' self-descriptions in the Registers: designs from firms described as clothiers, tailors, outfitters or hosiers (like Corah of Leicester) were selected. The third criterion was the allocation of designs to 14 categories analogous to the Classes in BT43. Designs from known clothing manufacturers were assigned to categories X and XIV, so all designs in these categories were noted.

Using all of these criteria (previous registrations, self-description and category) gave a total of 122 firms who might be involved in manufacturing boys' garments, and 591 references of potential interest distributed across 252 volumes of the BT50 series. As the references from the initial database were checked in the Representation volumes, a revised database was created. Some of the firms identified were not in fact engaged in garment manufacturing and they were removed from the database. Other firms that had registered garments in BT43 or BT45 had changed their practice and were registering only accessories in BT50.[30] The self-descriptions given by firms were also used to filter out entries that were less likely to be of interest.[31] By eliminating references that were likely to be irrelevant it was possible to reduce the number of volumes that had to be consulted. Even so, of the 600 BT50 references checked, only 355 were for main garments; 262 of these were for boys, and 93 were for men. It was not possible to count all garment registrations for men.

Retailers' Documents

Retailers' documents and catalogues have not been systematically collected by the copyright libraries, so several major archives were searched for documents relating to the sale of boys' clothing.[32] The most useful was the John Johnson Collection at the Bodleian Library, Oxford. Based on a personal collection of retailing ephemera, this archive held more than 90 catalogues and pricelists of

---

[30]   For example, Welch Margetson of Cheapside had registered three men's garments in BT45, but their first entry in BT50 (50/9417) was for a man's collar and the next (50/97718) was for a man's made-up tie.

[31]   For example, firms describing themselves as 'warehousemen' in the BT50 Registers (Welch Margetson of Cheapside, J. & R. Morley of Wood Street) were only registering accessories and luggage. The same was true of 'outfitters' such as Grant & Watson of Buchanan Street, Glasgow.

[32]   For example, partial sets of catalogues for the well-known retailer E. Moses & Son are held by the National Art Library, the British Library, the John Johnson Collection of the Bodleian and the Gallery of Costume Manchester; it is not known when the catalogues began or ceased.

interest, including several unique survivals.[33] The Evanion Collection of the British Library contains 5,000 items of ephemera dated before 1895, seven of which were flyers selling boys' clothing.[34] The House of Fraser Archive at the University of Glasgow contains material on the Army and Navy Stores, London, from 1872 onwards. However, only two documents in this set had information on boys' clothes other than underwear.[35] Retailers' advertisements were also sought in the popular press but proved less frequent than expected; for example the *Illustrated London News* (1840–1900) and the *Graphic* (1869–1900) contained only a handful of advertisements for boys' clothing with images and prices.[36]

Each document from these archives was given a single entry in an Excel database. The format and content of the documents varied, from a six-line newspaper advertisement to a 20-page illustrated catalogue. The contents of each document were indicated in the 'notes' column with the number of different garment types available, and whether or not there were prices and illustrations for these. Where the document had a distinguishing title this was also noted to aid identification. Many of the documents were undated; more detailed dating was possible through a comparison with documents from the Copy 1 archive discussed below.

The Stationer's Hall Archive (Copy 1)

The Stationers' Hall Archive (held at The National Archives) is composed of commercial documents registered for copyright protection at Stationers' Hall, London, from 1862.[37] This archive has only been partially published and is consequently little known.[38] It is a comprehensive archive, holding samples of all commercial paper goods, from price tickets through posters to photographs for sale. From 1883 this material was subdivided, and 'books commercial' (booklets

---

[33]   Now available online at http://johnjohnson.chadwyck.co.uk/marketing.do (by subscription).

[34]   Available online at http://www.bl.uk/catalogues/evanion/.

[35]   This archive also holds catalogues for Dallas's of Glasgow, 1900–1920; McDonalds of Glasgow, 1912–16; Dickens & Jones, London, 1892 (drapery only); Jolly's, Bath (women's fashions). These were viewed but material from them has not been included in this thesis.

[36]   Samuel Brothers, 1883; Baker & Co., 1886. Advertisements with text describing garments, but no images and no prices, were more numerous but could not be used for comparison with other material.

[37]   I would like to thank Hugh Alexander of the Image Library, for introducing me to this archive and for encouraging my work on Copy 1.

[38]   See Clare Rose, 'Advertising Ready-made Style: The Evidence of the Stationers' Hall Archive', *Textile History*, 40/2 (2009): 185–201. See also Michael Jubb, *Cocoa and Corsets: A Selection of Late Victorian and Edwardian Posters and Showcards from the Stationers' Company Copyright Records Preserved in the Public Record Office* (London, 1984); further images are online at www.nationalarchives.gov.uk/imagelibrary/victoriana/default.htm.

or folded sheets) were registered separately from the main category of 'paintings drawings and photographs'.[39] There are 170 boxes in the main series (Copy 1/1–170) between 1862 and 1900, and a further 90 boxes of 'Books Commercial' between 1883 and 1900, with a total of about 96,000 items.

The index of registrants (Copy 3) was consulted to see if it could be used for sampling documents. It was, however, neither fully alphabetic nor fully chronological, and relying on it would have run the risk of missing potentially valuable data. Books Commercial were sampled from 1898 to 1900 (boxes 966 to 977) in the hope that they would provide a higher proportion of retailers' catalogues than the more general 'paintings drawings and photographs'. Of the approximately 3,000 documents in the sample of ten boxes,[40] 116 were for firms selling clothing, and 19 of these were selling boyswear; however, 44 were represented only by the front cover of what had been a multi-page catalogue. This included 9 of the 19 documents referring to boyswear. It was extremely frustrating to see an index to pages of boys' clothing that had not been preserved.

The Paintings and Drawings and Books Commercial documents had both been used by firms to deposit sets of images at regular intervals. This suggested that both categories of Stationers' Hall registrations were seen as commercially important by their users. There were even instances of the same images being registered in both, first for the catalogue designers and secondly for a particular retailer.[41] The Copy 1 registration forms included spaces for the 'proprietor' of the copyright, 'Parties to Agreement' (such as the client commissioning a document) and 'Author of Work' (the commercial artist). These provide scope for further research, for example on the activity of freelance commercial artists.[42]

The Paintings, Drawings and Photographs section of Copy 1 included publicity images used by retailers, from billheads and catalogue illustrations to large wall posters. Boxes 1–100 of this section had been transferred to microfilms that could be photocopied; Boxes 101–170 and Books Commercial could be recorded by photography for quantitative visual analysis. Boxes 1–170 were viewed in total, and documents designed to sell clothing were recorded. These ranged from price tickets, to advertising novelties, to catalogue illustrations, catalogue pages and wall pages. Because these were only lightly attached to the registration form, it was often possible to gain additional information from the reverse of the document. As

---

[39] Books Commercial (BC) were defined by the Copyright Act: 'The term "Book" means and includes every *volume*, part or division of a volume, pamphlet, sheet of letterpress, sheet of music, map, chart, or plan, separately published.'

[40] Documents registered before December 1898 did not have individual record numbers and so the total number of documents is unclear.

[41] For example, Copy 1 163/135 and BC 975/18747, with images by Wesley Petty & Sons of Leeds. Petty was responsible for 16 of the 116 clothing documents registered in Books Commercial.

[42] See Rose, 'Advertising Ready-made Style', p. 196.

the Books Commercial documents were incomplete, it was decided to concentrate on the Paintings and Drawings series.

Not all of the 196 firms registering fashion images of clothing in Copy 1 were retailers.[43] The most frequent registrant in Copy 1 was Alfred Stedall, with 980 entries, each representing a single garment for a woman. The most frequent registrant showing garments for men, boys, and women was Richard Taylor & Co., with 268, followed by H.J. Nicoll with 254, and John Williamson with 135. Interestingly, these three firms each had different roles in the clothing industry.

Stedall, whose name was not known to me from published sources, described themselves on document Copy 1 972/17696 of 1899 as 'Wholesale and export Manufacturers'. Their publicity material was directed at retailers: 'this sheet supplied to a limited number of customers, one per town, with their own names and prices'.[44] They produced fancy capes, mantles, jackets and suits for women. The remaining firms were not directly involved in clothing manufacture. Richard Taylor & Co. were printers of publicity material for retailers. Some of these were themselves registered under the name of a particular firm (for example, Frederick Watts & Co., Copy 1 120/27–46), but more often they were generic products to be personalised as required. John Williamson was the firm responsible for *The Tailor and Cutter*, available by subscription only to bespoke tailors. The full-page fashion plates in each issue represented not existing garments, but suggestions for styles that might be made up for particular clients.

Because of these discrepancies the different types of companies represented in the Copy 1 archives were analysed separately. Documents relating to manufacturers who did not sell direct to customers (such as Coop of Wigan) or to the practice of bespoke tailors (such as the *Tailor and Cutter*) was analysed in Chapter 2. Documents relating to the sale of clothing were analysed in Chapter 3. One of the aims of this analysis was to evaluate whether the manufacturers' designs in the BT archives were representative of goods available in shops. In order to maintain comparability the same garment categories were used as for the BT documents.

After documents registered by manufacturers and tailors' designers had been sifted out, 520 documents remained (420 from Copy 1 and 90 from John Johnson). Many of these documents were shop catalogues or posters containing up to 20 images of boys' garments, bringing the total number of images to over 1,200. The documents themselves ranged from text-based newspaper advertisements, to catalogues with images and explanatory text, to publishers' sheets of images with no text. In some catalogues multiple images were used to demonstrate the variety of goods offered by a retailer (for example, sailor suits in navy wool, white cotton, and brown velvet) while in other cases this function was performed by the

---

[43]   This was different from the BT archives, where all entries were made by manufacturers (some of whom were also retailers).

[44]   Text on reverse of Copy 1 972/17696. See also the fragmentary text on documents Copy 1 133/124–5, 1897, two images which have been cut from the same large sheet.

accompanying text. This made it difficult to count the number of garment types present in a document.

By any method of counting, the garments represented in the retailers' and advertisers' archives were more varied than those in the BT archives of manufacturers' documents. This meant that new categories had to be added to those used for the analysis in Chapter 2. In addition, catalogue descriptions pointed to the existence of further sub-categories for some styles: white cotton or black velvet sailor suits, tartan or grey tweed kilts. In order to maintain comparability with the BT material the sub-types were grouped together.

Tailors' Texts

The *Tailor and Cutter* was published from 1866 by The John Williamson Company, and claimed to be the leading trade journal in both London and New York. Williamson published both monthly and weekly editions, as well as books and display materials using the same illustrations.[45] *Tailor and Cutter* magazines from 1868 to 1877 were viewed at the National Art Library, where it was possible to record images for visual analysis. The Stationers' Hall Archive contained 218 fashion plates for tailors registered between 1883 and the end of 1900.[46] The John Williamson Company was the most prolific registrant with 135 documents, followed by Edme Guichard with 36 and two other firms with 24 and 23. Williamson's documents in this archive were plates intended for inclusion with the *Tailor and Cutter*, but surviving in the copies seen in the National Art Library. Guichard and the other firms registered large-format plates with multiple images that were apparently distributed without any periodical.[47] The intended use of the *Tailor and Cutter* plates can be understood by examining the 12 volumes of a handbook issued by Williamson in 1890.[48] All of the images in this text were included in the registered plates and had also been published in the magazine. The book added pattern diagrams, instructions for cutting and making up, and comments on the uses of each ensemble.

Dressmaking Publications

Finding a representative sample of this material was challenging, as dressmaking patterns and pattern catalogues fall outside the remit of both the British Library and the The National Archives and there is no comprehensive archive in the UK.

---

[45] Breward, *Hidden Consumer*, p. 25.

[46] These were identified by investigating the name and business of the registrant.

[47] Although Edme Guichard was apparently the publisher of the *Album of Ladies' Fashions*, copies of this have not survived. Information from *Kelly's London Directory* (1889).

[48] W.D.F. Vincent, *The Cutter's Practical Guide: Part I, Juvenile, Youths and Young Men* (London, 1890).

Up to 1875, information on dressmaking practice was obtained mostly from books, and after 1875 mostly from magazines. These two types of sources present their own evidential problems, as well as problems of comparability.

Dressmaking books were identified through a search of the British Library catalogue, using the keywords 'needlework', 'dressmaking' and 'sewing'. This returned 36 titles first published between 1840 and 1900. The contents of these were determined by their intended audience: texts for use in state-funded National and British Schools were limited both by the logistics of group teaching and by the requirements of the school syllabus and gave instructions only for baby clothes and underwear.[49]

The limitations of the elementary school needlework syllabus were addressed by the provision of evening or extension classes for older girls and women set up in the 1880s and 1890s by organisations such as the Recreative Evening Schools Association and the City and Guilds of London Institute.[50] Teaching manuals for these classes included *Dressmaking, A Technical Manual for Teachers* (1892), and *Needlework, Knitting and Cutting-Out for Evening Continuation Schools* (1894).[51] Other sewing books published in the 1890s sought a multiple audience, such as *The elements of modern dressmaking for the amateur and professional dressmaker: being also a handbook for the use of students and for candidates preparing for the examinations in dressmaking under the City and Guilds of London Institute* (1896).[52] There were also texts instructing in pattern drafting, probably for professional dressmakers.[53] However, all the extension class texts reviewed concentrated on women's dresses:

> The making of a dress will always be an interesting matter to women, and we hope by making this the starting point, to see the further taste developed for 'Household Sewing', i.e. mending and patching of garments and other household articles.[54]

---

[49]   See Annemarie Turnbull, 'Learning Her Womanly Work: the Elementary School Curriculum, 1870–1914', in Felicity Hunt (ed.), *Lessons for Life: The Schooling of Girls and Women, 1850–1950* (Oxford, 1987), pp. 83–100.

[50]   The perceived need for these was especially strong in factory areas where most women were in paid work; see Mrs Hyde, *How To Win Our Workers, A short account of the Leeds Sewing School for Factory Girls* (London, 1862).

[51]   Alethea Grenfell, *Dressmaking, A Technical Manual for Teachers* (London, 1892); Ellen Rosevear, *Needlework, Knitting and Cutting-Out for Evening Continuation Schools* (London, 1894).

[52]   J. Davis, *The elements of modern dressmaking* (London, 1896).

[53]   M. Boehmer, *French Scientific Dressmaking, with map of chart and full explanations and illustrations* (Glasgow, 1887).

[54]   Fanny. L. Calder, introduction, in Grenfell, *Dressmaking*, p. vii.

The only texts published before 1873 which gave detailed information on a range of clothes for children were guides for middle-class women. These framed their instruction on dressmaking in terms of the management of a well-regulated household. *Cassell's Household Guide: being a complete encyclopaedia of domestic and social economy, etc.*[55] dealt with clothing for women and children as an aspect of household management. The dressmaking sections were intended to provide a basic wardrobe for boys and girls from infancy to twelve, and patterns were given as sketches and diagrams with measurements for standard sizes.

From the late 1870s onwards there were an increasing number of dressmaking publications for self-instruction: *Dressmaking Lessons.. By Myra ... With numerous illustrations* (1877); *Easy Dressmaking. Containing diagrams, etc.* (1892); *Practical Dressmaking* (1895); *Dressmaking Simplified. Simple rules for measuring, marking, and cutting out a dress, etc.* (1895); *Hints on Practical Dressmaking, etc.* (1898); *Dressmaking for All. A handbook of dress and dressmaking* (1900).[56] Most of these texts did not include patterns, but when they did, as in *How to dress well on a shilling a day: a ladies' guide to home dressmaking and millinery* (1876), these were for women only.[57]

The major source for dressmaking patterns for boys was periodicals, but not all of these were helpful. For example, *The Englishwoman's Domestic Magazine*, a 'solidly bourgeois' publication, had advertisements for boys' patterns, but published few of their own.[58] More information on making boys' clothes was found in specialist dressmaking journals: *Myra's Journal of Dress and Fashion* (from 1875), *Myra's Mid-Monthly Journal and Children's Dress* (1877), *Mrs Schild's Monthly Journal of Parisian Dress Patterns and Needlework* (1879), *Schild's Mother's Help and Little Dressmaker* (1878), *Weldon's Illustrated Dressmaker* (1880) or *Mrs Leach's Children's and Young Ladies' Dressmaker* (1882).[59] Each of these appeared monthly with an illustrated catalogue of up to 100 patterns

---

[55]   Published as a partwork; London, 1869–71.

[56]   Myra, *Dressmaking Lessons ... By Myra ... With numerous illustrations, etc.* (London, 1877 and 1888); F. White (Writer on Dressmaking), *Easy Dressmaking. Containing diagrams, etc.* (London, 1892); Mrs L. Smith, *Practical Dressmaking* (London, 1895); H. Green, *Dressmaking Simplified. Simple rules for measuring, marking, and cutting out a dress, etc.* (Walsall, 1895); Mrs A. Platts, *Hints on Practical Dressmaking, etc.* (Leeds, 1898); Anon., *Dressmaking for All: a handbook of dress and dressmaking* (London, 1900).

[57]   'S', *How to dress well on a shilling a day* (London, 1876).

[58]   Patterns advertised by Mme Letellier included 'Boy's Knickerbocker Suit, 2s 6d; Scotch Suit 2s 6d; Sailor Suit 2s; Tunic, High and Low 1s 6d'; *Englishwoman's Domestic Magazine*, April 1876.

[59]   Other titles dating back to 1868 are noted by Kevin Seligman in 'Dressmakers' Patterns: The English Commercial Paper Pattern Industry, 1878–1950', *Costume*, 37 (2003): 95–113, but it is not clear whether these published illustrated catalogues. For the audience of different magazines, see Christopher Breward, 'Patterns of Respectability: Publishing, Home Sewing and the Dynamics of Class and Gender 1870–1914', in Barbara Burman

produced by the parent company, and a few full-size diagram patterns for tracing. The number and variety of patterns was the same in each publication, but the 'Myra' journals presented them in most detail. The largest number of patterns for boys was found in issues of *Myra's Mid-Monthly Journal and Children's Dress*, published 1877–82; *Myra's Journal of Dress and Fashion* was used for the periods 1875–77 and 1882–1900.[60]

It was not possible to view a complete run of pattern catalogues for this period as these are not held by any library. The National Art Library has a sample of Butterick's *Metropolitan Catalogue of Fashions* from August to October 1886. This was a large-format publication (15in × 19in) with large illustrations (up to 6in high) and detailed supporting text. An advertisement in the main Butterick catalogue suggests that the *Metropolitan Catalogue* was intended for professionals: 'Dressmakers will find it of the greatest assistance to them in interchanging ideas with their customers.'[61] This publication was helpful in showing whole outfits composed from jacket, skirt and trouser patterns sold separately in the main catalogues from 1873 and 1882, which were available as reprints. Butterick were the only American pattern publisher known to have agents in Britain; patterns from other companies such as Demorest were available but were not used. British pattern companies appear not to have published catalogues other than the linked magazines.

Uses of Data

One of the aims of this project was to establish the *habitus* of nineteenth-century boys' clothing practice. The data from different sources had to be evaluated and analysed in the same way in order to avoid the situation where a narrative is constructed from one type of data and illustrated using another. The quantitative visual analysis developed for this study was applied to all the major categories of data used: photographs of boys in families, school groups, and institutions; garment designs from mass manufacturers, tailors and dressmakers; and clothing retailers' catalogues. The findings from each source were expressed in percentage terms in order to permit comparisons between large and small datasets.

The size of the respective datasets, and the existence of any bias within them, was taken into account when interpreting discrepancies in the findings from each. A preliminary analysis of the surviving garments identified in museum collections indicated several strong biases in this set (towards toddlers; towards middle-class

---

(ed.), *The Culture of Sewing: Gender, Consumption and Home Dressmaking* (Oxford, 1999), pp. 21–32.

[60] A complete run of the *Mid-Monthly* (1877–82) is held by the National Art Library, and the *Journal* (1875–99) is available on microfilm.

[61] Nancy V. Bryk, *American Dress Pattern Catalogs 1873–1909* (New York, 1988), p. 71.

wearers; towards special-occasion wear). The documentation and date distribution of this set was also problematic, and so a quantitative analysis was not made. Instead the surviving garments were sorted into groups by type (tunic; sailor suit) and each group was analysed for evidence of 'distinction' within the type.[62]

Photographs of boys from schools and institutional archives are analysed first in Chapter 1. This analysis shows the importance of the concepts of 'raggedness' and 'respectability' in charities' publicity material, and the ways that this was understood by poor families. A comparison between the entry photographs taken by Barnardo's and school group photographs shows the validity of the former as a source. In Chapter 5 the garments portrayed in Barnardo's, school and family photographs are analysed to give a picture of clothing consumption. In Chapter 6 these photographs are examined for data on clothing worn by boys at different ages and with different earning abilities. Images of siblings from Barnardo's files are analysed in detail for evidence of clothing strategies within families.

Data from manufacturers and retailers was also used in several different ways. Information on the introduction and variation of garment styles by manufacturers, tailors and dressmakers is discussed in separate sections of Chapter 2. This data is then compared in order to evaluate the role of design innovation for each. The practice of mass manufacturers is compared with the practice of mass retailers who used catalogues. This gives a picture of the nature of the market in boys' clothing to be used as a foundation for the examination of consumption in Chapter 5.

Data from retailers is presented both as registered designs and as unregistered catalogues. The first set had clear dates but little consumption data (prices and sizes); the second set had prices and sizes, but fewer dates. The ways the different sources are used reflects this. Images and descriptions of garments were tabulated and used as evidence for clothing production in Chapter 2. Pricing information from retailers' catalogues was used in the analysis of garment costs in Chapter 4. From 1890 onwards, published retail catalogues gave age ranges for different styles, and these were used in the discussion of age-specific expressions of masculinity in Chapter 6.

In each chapter the data from each source is first presented separately in order to clarify the sampling and interpretive methods used. Data from different sources is then compared and evaluated in order to produce conclusions at the end of each chapter, and final conclusions in Chapter 8. Quantitative visual analysis has been a key methodological tool for this project, providing a powerful tool to evaluate the degree of consistency between the different manufacturers' and retailers' sources. It has allowed me to examine the ways in which the meanings of dress both derive and diverge from clothing practices.

[62]   See Rose, 'Boyswear', pp. 255–74.

Appendix 2

Manufacturers' Descriptions of Designs in Board of Trade 51 Registers, 1883–7

50/236, 1884, Joseph May, Park Mills, Wellington St. Leeds, Wholesale Clothier: The arrangement of Kilting or Pleating work shewn at front and back of boy's jacket

50/39, 1884, Barran & Sons, St Paul's St. Leeds: A Pattern Consisting of two Silk Braids in close juxtaposition of different colours as shewn in specimen machine stitched in rows upon Boys' 'Man O' War' or 'Naval' Suits as shewn in photograph

50/397, 1884, Barran & Sons, St Paul's St. Leeds: A Pattern consisting of two Silk Braids in close juxtaposition of the same of different colours as shewn in specimens, machine stitched in rows upon Boys' 'Man O' War' or 'naval' Collars & Vests as shewn in photographs (set)

50/1469, 1884, J Hepworth, Leeds, Wholesale Clothiers: Braided rib and kilting set on down front running parallel with each other, turned over pocket to conceal it, for boy's suit

50/1470, 1884, J Hepworth, Leeds: Kilting as shown on boys suit with belt round waist

50/3651, 1884, G Macbeth & Son, King St. Manchester, Clothiers: The design consists in the shape and ornamentation of a boys' suit

50/9167, 1884, Barran & Sons, St Paul's St. Leeds, Clothing Manufacturers: Pattern consisting of a design in Tubular or other braid of like character as in photo: style of suit to be applied to shewn in photograph

50/9168, 1884, Barran & Sons, St Paul's St. Leeds: Pattern, consisting of eight straps or frillings on cloth as shewn in photograph

50/9173, 1884, Barran & Sons, St Paul's St. Leeds: Pattern; consisting of 'Frillings' of Silk upon Velvet Juvenile Jackets as shown in photograph

50/9174, 1884, Barran & Sons, St Paul's St. Leeds: Pattern, consisting of straps and frillings of cloth back and front of overcoat (Juvenile) as shown in photograph

50/9175, 1884, Barran & Sons, St Paul's St. Leeds: Pattern – worked in Russia Braids as shewn in photograph. Juvenile Jacket

50/9176, 1884, Barran & Sons, St Paul's St. Leeds: Pattern worked and stitched in various braids as shewn in photograph – Juvenile Jacket

50/9177, 1884, Barran & Sons, St Paul's St. Leeds: Pattern, consisting of 'straps' or 'frillings' of braids on back and front of Juvenile Overcoat

50/9178, 1884, Barran & Sons, St Paul's St. Leeds: Pattern of Machine Stitching upon Front and back of Juvenile Overcoat as shewn in photographs

50/9179, 1884, Barran & Sons, St Paul's St. Leeds: Pattern of Collar, Pockets and Back as shewn in photograph – Juvenile Overcoat

50/9268, 1884, Barran & Sons, St Paul's St. Leeds: Pattern, consisting of straps, or Frillings, of Braids, as shown in photograph

50/13210, 1884, Rhodes & Clay, Quebec St. Leeds: Design applicable for the pattern of coat

50/13211–2, 1884, Rhodes & Clay, Quebec St. Leeds: Design applicable for the pattern of jacket

50/14966, 1884, Buckley & Sons, Leeds: Applicable for the corded pattern on jacket

50/14967, 1884, Buckley & Sons, Leeds: Applicable for the plaited pattern on jacket

50/16303–4, 1884, Coop & Co., Wigan: Design for plaiting the fronts of children's clothing

50/16305–6, 1884, Coop & Co., Wigan: Design for braiding the fronts of children's clothing

50/16865–6, 1884, Coop & Co., Wigan: Design for the braiding of children's clothing

50/17053–4, 1884, Coop & Co., Wigan: Design for the braiding of children's clothing

50/18252, 1884, Barran & Sons, St Paul's St. Leeds, Clothing Manufacturers: A pattern being an arrangement in rows of different kinds of braids for ornamentation of Juvenile Garments, as shewn in Photograph and example

50/18253, 1884, Barran & Sons, St Paul's St. Leeds, Clothing Manufacturers: A pattern – being an arrangement of different kinds of braids for ornamentation of Juvenile Garments as shown in photograph and example

50/18254, 1884, Barran & Sons, St Paul's St. Leeds, Clothing Manufacturers: A pattern – being an arrangement of tubular braids for the ornamentation of Juvenile garments as shown in Photograph and example

50/18255, 1884, Barran & Sons, St Paul's St. Leeds, Clothing Manufacturers: A pattern – being an arrangement of Braids for the ornamentation of Juvenile Garments as shewn in Photograph and Example

50/18366, 1884, Barran & Sons, St Paul's St. Leeds, Clothing Manufacturers: A pattern in braids for the ornamentation of juvenile garments

50/18881, 1884, Barran & Sons, St Paul's St. Leeds, Clothing Manufacturers: A pattern – being an arrangement of Braids and Velvet applied to 'Blouse Naval' (or Juvenile Sailor) Jackets as shown in Photograph and example

50/18889, 1885, Buckley and Sons, Leeds, Tailors: Applicable to Braided pattern on, and shape of, Jacket

50/10048, 1885, Gaunt & Hudson, Grace St. Mills, Leeds, Clothiers: It is the pattern that we desire to register

50/21946, 1885, Welch & Sons, Gutter Lane, London, Manufacturers and Warehousemen: The shape of the sleeves whereby the clothes can be fastened around the child without twisting the arms

50/39868, 1885, Wilkinson & Chorlton, St Paul's St. Leeds, Wholesale Clothiers: The novelty consists in the ornamental design formed by the kilted or pleated work extending over the shoulder and continued down the back of the jacket as shown

50/39870, 1885, Wilkinson & Chorlton, St Paul's St. Leeds, Wholesale Clothiers: The novelty consists in the ornamental design formed by the kilted or pleated work

50/39871, 1885, Wilkinson & Chorlton, St Paul's St. Leeds, Wholesale Clothiers: The novelty consists in the ornamental design formed by the kilted or pleated work extending over the shoulder and continued down the back of the jacket as shown

50/39759–68, 1885, Coop & Co., Wigan: Plaiting and braiding for coats

50/40529–30, 1886, Dawson Hardy & Co. 1–2 Bedford St. Leeds, Wholesale Clothiers: For the pattern, that is, an ornamented portion let in and the surrounding braid or stitching on each side of the breast of the jacket or coat

50/42664–5, 1886, Buckley & Sons, Greek St. Leeds: For the kilted pattern on coat as shown

50/45265, 1886, W. Dixon, 32 Houndgate Nottingham: Pattern of a boy's jacket

50/47690, 1886, G.A. Macbeth, Juvenile Tailor, 255 Regent St. London: Pattern of a child's jacket

50/54041, 1886, Barran & Sons, St Paul's St. Leeds, Clothing Manufacturers: Coloured braids of rainbow hues arranged and stitched

50/61861–4, 1886, Buckley & Sons, Leeds, Cap Manufacturers: Patterns on boys' jackets

50/62473, 1886, Dawson, Hardy & Co., 1–2 Bedford St. Leeds: Boy's garment with curved or waved straps or pleats

50/63146–9, 1886, Barran & Sons, St Paul's St. Leeds, Clothing Manufacturers: An arrangement of braids as shown to be used upon wearing apparel

50/63561, 1886, Rhodes & Clay, Quebec St. Leeds, Wholesale Clothiers: Pattern of an ornamented jacket front

50/63924, 1886, Barran & Sons, St Paul's St. Leeds: A pattern consisting of a combination of coloured Russia braids arranged in the juxtaposition shown in example, to be applied to juvenile 'Naval' or 'Sailors' suits

50/68409, 1887, Redman Brothers, Hebden Bridge Leeds, Wholesale Clothiers: For the pattern

50/74707–12, 1887, Rhodes & Co., Oxford Row Leeds: Pattern and shape of boy's coat

50/87264, 1887, Barran & Sons, St Paul's St. Leeds: A pattern in cords or braids for the ornamentation of collars of juvenile garments as shown in photograph

50/87265, 1887, Barran & Sons, St Paul's St. Leeds: A pattern in braids and buttons for the ornamentation of collar of juvenile garment as shown in photograph

50/89372, 1887, Shannon & Son, George St. Walsall, Wholesale Clothiers: Rows
    of diagonal piping and vertical straps
50/89766, 1887, May & Son, Park Mills, Leeds, Clothiers: Pattern of the garment

Bibliography

Primary Sources

A Lady [Maria Wilson?], *The Workwoman's Guide, by a Lady* (London: Simpkin, Marshall, 1838; reprint Doncaster: Bloomfield Books, 1975).

A Lady [M.W. Cook], *How to Dress on £15 a Year, as a Lady* (London: Frederick Warne & Co., 1873).

Anon., *The Mother's Thorough Resource-book* (London: Ward & Lock, 1860).

Anon., *Dressmaking for All: a handbook of dress and dressmaking* (London: H. Marshall & Son, 1900).

Acorn, George, *One of the Multitude: An Autobiography of a Resident of Bethnal Green* (London: William Heinemann, 1911).

Adburgham, Alison, *Yesterday's Shopping: Army and Navy Stores Catalogue, 1907* (Newton Abbot: David & Charles, 1969)

———, *Victorian Shopping: Harrod's Catalogue, 1895* (Newton Abbot: David & Charles, 1972).

Barnardo, Dr, *'Taken out of the Gutter.' A true incident of child life on the streets of London, etc.* (London:Haughton & Co, 1881).

Baxter, Robert Dudley, *National Income: The United Kingdom* (London: Macmillan, 1868).

Boehmer, M., *French Scientific Dressmaking, with map of chart and full explanations and illustrations* (Glasgow: Privately published, 1887).

Booth, Charles (ed.), *Life and Labour of the People in London, Series I: Poverty, Series II, Industry* (London: Macmillan, 1892–97).

Bray, R.A., 'The Boy and the Family', in E.J. Urwick, *Studies of Boy Life in Our Cities* (London: J.M. Dent & Co., 1904).

———, *The Town Child* (London: Fisher Unwin, 1907).

———, *Boy Labour and Apprenticeship* (London: John Constable & Co., 1911).

Bryk, Nancy Villa, *American Dress Pattern Catalogs 1873–1909* (New York: Dover, 1988).

Burnett, John (ed.), *Destiny Obscure: Autobiographies of Childhood, Education and Family from the 1820s to the 1920s* (London: Routledge, 1982).

Burnett, John, David Mayall and David Vincent, *The Autobiography of the Working Class: An Annotated Critical Bibliography, vol 1, 1790–1900* (Brighton: Harvester, 1984).

Butterick & Co., *Metropolitan Fashions* (London and New York: Butterick & Co., 1886).

Cassell & Co., *Cassell's Household Guide: being a complete encyclopaedia of domestic and social economy, etc.* (London: Cassell & Co., 1869–71; 2nd edn 1885).

———, *Cassell's Book of the Household, A Work of Reference on Domestic Economy* (London: Cassell & Co., 1889).

Chaplin, Charles, *My Autobiography* (London: The Bodley Head, 1964).

Couts, Joseph, *A Practical Guide for the Tailor's Cutting–Room, being a treatise on Measuring and Cutting Clothing in all styles, and for Every Period of Life from Childhood to Old Age* (Glasgow: Blackie & Son, 1850).

Davis, J., *The elements of modern dressmaking* (London: Cassell & Co., 1894).

Finch, Lady E., *The Sampler; or, A System of teaching plain needlework in schools* (London: G.C. Caines, 1850, 1855).

Gloag, John (ed.), *The Crystal Palace Exhibition: Illustrated catalogue, London 1851 ... [etc.]* (Facsimile reprint of 'The Industry of All Nations, 1851, the Art-Journal illustrated Catalogue' [London: Virtue for the Art -Journal, 1851]; New York; Dover Publications, 1970).

Green, H., *Dressmaking Simplified. Simple rules for measuring, marking, and cutting out a dress, etc.* (Walsall: T Kirby & Son., 1895).

Grenfell, Alethea, *Dressmaking, A Technical Manual for Teachers* (London, Macmillan & Co., 1892)

Haw, George, *From Workhouse to Westminster: The Life Story of Will Crooks, MP* (London: Cassell & Co, 1909).

Hill, Miranda, 'Life on Thirty Shillings a Week', *Nineteenth Century* 23 (1888): 458–63.

Hyde, Mrs, *How To Win Our Workers, A short account of the Leeds Sewing School for Factory Girls* (London: Macmillan & Co., 1862).

Jones, E.G., *A Manual of Plain Needlework and Cutting Out* (London: Hughes & Co.,1884).

Layard, George, 'How to Live on £150 a Year', *Cornhill Magazine* May 1901, reprinted in E. Royston Pike (ed.), *Human Documents of the Age of the Forsytes* (London: Allen & Unwin, 1969), pp. 161–5.

Levi, Leone, *Wages and Earnings of the working classes: with some facts illustrative of their economic condition, drawn from authentic and official sources* (London: John Murray, 1867).

Lynes & Son, Arthur, *New Winter Magazine* (London, 1870)

———, *Summer Journal* (London, 1870).

———, *Smiles and Styles* (London, 1871).

———, *Wit and Wear* (London, 1871).

———, *Mirth and Modes* (London, 1872).

———, *Fiction and Fashion* (London, 1872).

———, *Stories and Styles* (London, 1873).

———, *Novelettes and Novelties* (London, 1873).

———, *Twice a Year* (London, 1875).

———, *Merriment and Modes* (London, 1876).

————, *Romance and Reality* (London, 1876).

May, Phil, *Guttersnipes* (London: Macmillan & Co., 1896).

Mayhew, H., *The Unknown Mayhew,* ed E. Yeo and E.P. Thompson, (London: Merlin Press, 1971).

Morrison, Arthur, 'How to Live on 30s a Week', *Cornhill Magazine* (May 1901), in E. Royston Pike (ed.), *Human Documents of the Age of the Forsytes* (London: Allen and Unwin, 1969), pp. 157–60.

Myra, *Dressmaking Lessons. By Myra . With numerous illustrations, etc.* (London: M. & A. Goubaud, 1877).

————, *Dressmaking Lessons . By Myra . With numerous illustrations, etc.* (London: Myra & Son, 1888).

Panton, Jane Emily, *From Kitchen to Garrett: Hints for Young Householders* (London: Ward & Downey, 1888).

————, *The Way They Should Go* (London, Downey & Co., 1896).

Platts, Mrs A., *Hints on Practical Dressmaking, etc.* (Leeds: S. Grant, 1898).

Pritchett, Victor S., *A Cab at the Door* (Harmondsworth: Penguin, 1980).

Raverat, Gwen, *Period Piece* (Cambridge: Faber, 1952).

Reeves, Maud Pember, *Round About a Pound a Week* (London: G. Bell & Sons Ltd, 1913).

Richmond, Ennis, *Through Boyhood to Manhood, a plea for ideals* (London: Longmans, Green & Co., 1899).

Rolph, Cecil Hewitt, *London Particulars* (Oxford: Oxford University Press, 1980).

Rosevear, Ellen, *A Text-Book of Needlework, Knitting and Cutting-Out with Methods of Teaching* (London: Macmillan, 1893).

————, *Needlework, Knitting and Cutting-Out for Evening Continuation Schools* (London: Macmillan, 1894).

Rowntree, B.S., *Poverty, A Study of Town Life* (London: Macmillan, 1901).

Russell, C.E.B., *Manchester Boys, Sketches of Manchester Lads at Work and Play* (Manchester: Manchester University Press, 1905).

Smith, Amy K, *Needlework for student teachers: intended for the use of pupil teachers, scholarship candidates and certificate students (1st and 2nd year),* 4th edn (London: City of London Book Depot, 1897)

Smith, Mrs L.E., *Practical Dressmaking* (London: Bemrose & Sons, 1895).

Sylvia, *How to dress well on a shilling a day: a ladies' guide to home dressmaking and millinery* (London: Ward, Lock & Tyler,1876).

————, *The Lady's Guide to Home Dressmaking and Millinery* (London: Ward, Lock & Co., 1883).

Synge, Margaret Bertha, *Simple Garments for Children (from 4 to 14)* (London: Longmans & Co. 1913).

Taylor & Co., Richard, *The Boy and How to Suit Him!! A Suitable Little Treatise in 5 Chaps* (London: Richard Taylor & Co., 1899).

T.H.P., *The Standard Needlework Book, a System for graduated instruction in plain Needlework in which arithmetic is brought to bear practically. Designed chiefly for use in primary schools and as a handbook for inspectors* (London: Longmans, Green & Co., 1871).

————, *The Standard Needlework Book, a System for graduated instruction in plain Needlework in which arithmetic is brought to bear practically. Arranged in six standards each distinguished by its colours, containing also plans on a reduced scale, by inch or metric measure, and knitting rules. For use in schools and families, and as a handbook for inspectors*; sixth edition, enlarged and revised (London: Longmans, Green and Co., 1885).

Tennant, Dorothy [Mrs H.M. Stanley], *London Street Arabs* (London: Cassell & Co., 1890).

Urwick, E.J., *Studies of Boy Life in Our Cities* (London: J.M Dent & Co., 1904).

Victoria, Queen, *Leaves from the Journal of our Life in the Highlands, from 1848 to 1861. To which are prefixed and added, extracts from the same journal, giving an account of earlier visits to Scotland, and tours in England and Ireland, and yachting excursions*, ed. Sir Arthur Helps (London: Smith, Elder & Co., 1868).

Vincent, William *The Cutter's Practical Guide. Part I, Juvenile, Youths and Young Men* (London: John Williamson & Co., 1890).

White, F., *Easy Dressmaking. Containing diagrams, etc.* (London: J.Smith, 1892).

Willis, Frederick, *Peace and Dripping Toast* (London: Phoenix House, 1950).

————, *A Book of London Yesterdays* (London: Phoenix House, 1960).

Periodicals

Englishwoman's Domestic Magazine
The Gentleman's Magazine of Fashion
The Graphic
The Illustrated London News
Mrs Leach's Children's and Young Ladies' Dressmaker
Myra's Journal of Dress and Fashion
Myra's Mid-Monthly Journal and Children's Dress
Schild's Mother's Help and Little Dressmaker

Secondary Sources

Adburgham, Alison, *Shops and Shopping 1800–1914* (London: Barrie & Jenkins, 1989).

Ashelford, Jane, *The Art of Dress: Clothes and Society 1500–1914* (London: The National Trust, 1996).

Barnes, Ruth and Joanne Eicher, *Dress and Gender: Making and Meaning* (Oxford: Berg, 1992).

Bates, Christina, 'How to dress the Children? A Comparison of Prescription and Practice in Late Nineteenth-Century North America', *Dress* 24 (1997): 43–54.

Beetham, Margaret, *A Magazine of Her Own? Domesticity and Desire in the Woman's Magazine, 1800–1914* (London: Routledge, 1996).

Benson John, *Production, Consumption and History: The British Working Class* (Wolverhampton: PUBLISHER, 1994). Can't find it – may be alternate title for *The Working Class in Britain, 1850-1939* (London: Longman, 1989).

———, *The Rise of Consumer Society in Britain, 1880–1980* (London: Longman, 1994).

Benson, John and Laura Ugolini, *A Nation of Shopkeepers, Five Centuries of British Retailing* (London: I B Tauris, 2003).

Berg, Maxine and Elizabeth Eger, *Luxury in the Eighteenth Century: Debates, Desires and Delectable Goods* (Basingstoke: Palgrave, 2003).

John Berger, *Ways of Seeing* (London: BBC Books/Penguin, 1972).

Bills, Mark, and Vivien Knight, *William Powell Frith, Painting the Victorian Age* (New Haven and London:, Yale University Press, 2006).

Boden, Sharon, Christopher Pole, Jane Pilcher and Tim Edwards, 'New consumers? The social and cultural significance of children's fashion consumption', *Cultures of Consumption Working Papers* 16 (2004), online at www.consume.bbk.ac.uk.

Bodleian Library, *A Nation of Shopkeepers, Trade Ephemera from 1654 to the 1860s in the John Johnson Collection* (Oxford: Bodleian Library, 2001).

Bourdieu, Pierre, *Distinction, a Social Critique of the Judgement of Taste* (London: Routledge & Kegan Paul, 1984).

———, *The Logic of Practice* (Cambridge: Polity Press, 1990).

Boyd, Kelly, 'Knowing Your Place, The tensions of manliness in boys' story papers, 1918–39', in Michael Roper and John Tosh (eds), *Manful Assertions: Masculinities in Britain Since 1800* (London: Routledge, 1991), pp. 145–67.

Bressey, Caroline, 'Forgotten Geographies: Black Women, Victorian London and the Black Atlantic' (unpublished PhD dissertation, University College London, 2002).

———, 'Forgotten Histories: Three Stories of Black Girls from Barnardo's Victorian Archive', *Women's History Review* 111/3 (2002): 351–74.

Breward, Christopher, 'Cultures, Histories, Identities; Fashioning a Cultural Approach to Dress', *Fashion Theory* 2/4 (1998): 310–14.

———, *The Hidden Consumer: Masculinities, Fashion and City Life in 1860–1914* (Manchester: Manchester University Press, 1999).

———, 'Patterns of Respectability: Publishing, Home Sewing and the Dynamics of Class and Gender 1870–1914', in Barbara Burman (ed.) *The Culture of Sewing: Gender, Consumption and Home Dressmaking* (Oxford: Berg, 1999), pp. 21–31.

Brewer, John and Roy Porter, *Consumption and the World of Goods* (London, Routledge, 1993).

Briggs, Asa, *Friends of the People, The Centenary History of Lewis's* (London: B.T. Batsford, 1956).

Brogden, Ann, 'Clothing Provision by the Liverpool Workhouse', *Costume* 36 (2002): 50–55.

———, 'Clothing Provision by Liverpool's Other Poor Law Institution: Kirkdale Industrial Schools', *Costume* 37 (2003): 71–4.

Broughton, Trev Lynn and Helen Rogers (eds), *Gender and Fatherhood in the Nineteenth Century* (Basingstoke: Macmillan, 2007).

Brusdal, Ragnhild, 'If it is good for the child's development then I say yes almost every time: How Parents Relate to their Children's Consumption', *International Journal of Consumer Studies* 31/4 (2007): 391–6.

Anne Buck, *Dress in Eighteenth-Century England* (London: B.T.Batsford Ltd., 1979)

———, *Clothes and the Child, A Handbook of Children's Dress in England 1500–1900* (Bedford: Ruth Bean Books, 1996).

Buckley, Cheryl, 'Children's clothes: design and promotion', in Pat Kirkham (ed.), *The Gendered Object* (Manchester: Manchester University Press, 1996), pp. 103–11.

Burman, Barbara (ed.), *The Culture of Sewing: Gender, Consumption and Home Dressmaking* (Oxford: Berg, 1999).

Calvert, Karen, *Children in the House: The Material Culture of Early Childhood, 1600–1900* (Boston: Northeastern University Press, 1992).

Campbell, Colin, 'The Meaning of Objects and the Meaning of Actions, a Critical Note on the Sociology of Consumption and Theories of Clothing', *Journal of Material Culture* 1/1 (1996): 93–105.

———, 'When the Meaning Is not a Message: A Critique of the Consumption as Communication Thesis', in Mica Nava et al. (eds), *Buy This Book: Studies in Advertising and Consumption* (London: Routledge, 1997), pp. 340–52.

Chapman, Stanley, 'The Innovating Entrepreneurs in the British Ready-made Clothing Industry', *Textile History* 24/1 (1993): 5–25.

———, *Merchant Enterprise in Britain from the Industrial Revolution to World War I* (Cambridge: University Press, 1992).

Chenoune, Farid, *A History of Men's' Fashion* (Paris: Flammarion, 1993).

Childs, Michael J., *Labour's Apprentices: Working-Class Lads in Late Victorian and Edwardian England* (Montreal: McGill-Queen's University Press, 1992)

Church, R., *The Emergence of Modern Marketing* (London: Frank Cass, 2003).

Clark, Anna, *The Struggle for the Breeches: Gender and the Making of the British Working Class* (Berkeley: University of California Press, 1995).

Clarke, Alison, 'Mother Swapping: The Trafficking of Nearly New Children's Wear', in Peter Jackson et al. (eds), *Commercial Cultures: Economies, Practices, Spaces* (Oxford: Berg, 2000), pp. 85–100.

———, 'Maternity and Materiality: Becoming a Mother in Consumer Culture', in Linda Layne, Janelle Taylor and Danielle F. Wozniak (eds), *Consuming Mothers* (Camden: Rutgers University Press, 2004), pp. 55–71.

Cook, Daniel, *The Commodification of Childhood: The Children's Clothing Industry and the Rise of the Child Consumer* (Durham, NC: Duke University Press, 2004).

———, 'The Missing Child in Consumption Theory', *Journal of Consumer Culture* 8/2 (2008): 219–243.

Coopey, Richard, Sean O'Connell and Dilwyn Porter, *Mail Order Retailing in Britain: A Business and Social History* (Oxford: University Press, 2005).

Copeland, Barbara and Gavin Thompson, 'The "Boy Labour Problem" in Lancashire', in Michael Winstanley (ed.), *Working Children in Nineteenth-Century Lancashire* (Preston: Lancashire County Books, 1995), pp. 93–114.

Craik, Jennifer, *Uniforms Exposed: From Conformity to Transgression* (Oxford: Berg, 2005).

Crane, Diana, *Fashion and its Social Agendas* (Chicago: Chicago University Press, 2000).

Crompton, Frank, *Workhouse Children: Infant and Child Paupers under the Worcestershire Poor Law, 1780–1871* (Stroud: Sutton Publishing, 1997).

Crowther, Michael A., *The Workhouse System 1834–1929: The History of an English Social Institution* (Athens, GA: University of Georgia Press, 1981).

Cunningham, Hugh, *The Children of the Poor: Representations of Childhood since the Seventeenth Century* (Oxford: Blackwell, 1991).

———, 'Histories of Childhood', *American Historical Review* 103/4 (1998): 1195–208.

Cunningham, Hugh and Michael Morpurgo, *The Invention of Childhood* (London: BBC Books, 2006).

Cunningham, Patricia, 'Beyond Artifacts and Object Chronology', *Dress* 14 (1988): 76–82.

Cunnington, Phillis and Anne Buck, *Children's Costume in England 1300–1900* (London: A. & C. Black, 1965).

Cunnington, Phillis and Catherine Lucas, *Charity Costumes of Children, Scholars, Almsfolk, Pensioners* (London: A. & C. Black, 1978).

Daly, Catherine, '"Ah, a real Kalabari Woman!": Reflexivity and the Conceptualization of Appearance', *Fashion Theory* 3/3 (1999): 343–62.

David, Alison Matthews, 'Decorated Men; Fashioning the French Soldier, 1852–1914', *Fashion Theory* 7/1 (2003): 3–38.

Davidoff, Leonore and Catherine Hall, *Family Fortunes: Men and Women of the English Middle Class, 1780–1850* (London: Hutchinson, 1987)

Davin, Anna, 'Imperialism and Motherhood', *History Workshop Journal* 5 (1978): 9–66

———, 'When is a Child not a Child?', in L. Jamieson and H. Corr (eds), *The Politics of Everyday Life* (London: Macmillan, 1990), pp. 37–57.

———, *Growing Up Poor: Home, School and Street in London 1870–1914* (London: Rivers Oram, 1996).

———, 'Waifs' Stories', *History Workshop Journal* 52/2 (2001): 86–97.

Dawson, Graham, *Soldier Heroes: British Adventure, Empire, and the Imagining of Masculinity* (London: Routledge, 1994).

De Marly, Diana, *Fashion for Men, An Illustrated History* (London: B.T. Batsford, 1985).

Digby, Anne and Peter Searby, *Children, School and Society in Nineteenth-Century England* (London: Macmillan, 1981).

Di Girolamo, Vincent, 'Redressing the Ragged Newsboy: Clothing, Character, and Coercion in Pre-World War I Britain' (unpublished seminar paper, Rutgers University, 1994).

Driver, Felix, *Power and Pauperism: The Workhouse System, 1834–1884* (Cambridge: University Press, 1993).

Druesdow, Jean, *In Style: Celebrating Fifty Years of the Costume Institute* (New York:Metropolitan Museum of Art, 1987).

Duke, Francis, 'Pauper Education', in Derek Fraser (ed.), *The New Poor Law in the Nineteenth Century* (Basingstoke: Macmillan, 1976), pp. 67–86

Ehrman, Edwina, 'Clothing a world city: 1830–60', in Christopher Breward, Edwina Ehrman and Caroline Evans, *The London Look: Fashion from Street to Catwalk* (London and New Haven: Yale University Press, 2004), pp. 31–44.

———, 'Fashion in the Age of Imperialism: 1860–90' in Christopher Breward, Edwina Ehrman and Caroline Evans, *The London Look Fashion from Street to Catwalk* (London and New Haven: Yale University Press, 2004), pp. 45–59.

Emery, Joy, 'Dreams on Paper: A Story of the Commercial Pattern Industry', in Barbara Burman (ed.), *The Culture of Sewing: Gender, Consumption and Home Dressmaking* (Oxford: Berg, 1999), pp. 235–54.

Englander, David, *Poverty and Poor Law Reform in Britain: From Chadwick to Booth, 1834–1914* (London: Longman, 1998).

English, Barbara, 'Lark Rise and Juniper Hill: A Victorian Community in Literature and in History', *Victorian Studies* 28 (1985): 7–34.

Entwistle, Joanne, *The Fashioned Body, Fashion, Dress and Modern Social Theory* (London: Polity Press, 2000).

Ewing, Elizabeth, *History of Children's Costume* (London: B.T. Batsford, 1977).

Fernandez, Nancy Page, 'Creating Consumers: Gender, Class and the Family Sewing Machine', in Barbara Burman (ed.), *The Culture of Sewing: Gender, Consumption and Home Dressmaking* (Oxford: Berg, 1999), pp. 157–68.

Fine, Ben and Ellen Leopold, *The World of Consumption* (London: Routledge, 1993).

Fleming, E McClung, 'Artifact Study: A Proposed Model', *Winterthur Portfolio* 16 (1981): 153–73.

Floud, Roderick, Kenneth Wachter and Annabel Gregory, *Height, Health and History: Nutritional Status in the United Kingdom, 1750–1980* (Cambridge: Cambridge University Press, 1990).

Forty, Adrian, *Objects of Desire: Design and Society 1750–1980* (London: Thames & Hudson,1986).

Fowler, Simon, *Workhouse: the People, the Places, the Life behind Doors* (Kew: The National Archives, 2007).

Franklin, G. and D. Bailey, *The Shaftesbury Story* (London: The Shaftesbury Society, 1979).

Fraser, Derek (ed.), *The New Poor Law in the Nineteenth Century* (Basingstoke: Macmillan, 1976).

Fraser, William Hamish, *The Coming of the Mass Market 1850–1914* (Basingstoke: Macmillan, 1981).

Gallery of English Costume, *Picture Book Number Seven: Children's Costume* (Manchester: Manchester City Art Galleries, 1959).

Gamber, Wendy, *The Female Economy: the Millinery and Dressmaking Trades, 1860–1930* (Urbana: University of Illinois Press, 1997).

Gardner, Phil, *The Lost Elementary Schools of Victorian England: The People's Education* (Beckenham: Croom Helm, 1984).

Gernsheim, Alison, *Fashion and Reality* (London: Faber & Faber, 1963).

Gernsheim, Helmut, *The History of Photography: From the Camera Obscura to the Beginning of the Modern Era* (London: Thames & Hudson, 1969).

Ginsburg, Madeleine, *Victorian Dress in Photographs* (London: B.T. Batsford, 1982).

Gittins, Diana, *The Child in Question* (Basingstoke: Macmillan, 1998).

Godley, Andrew, 'The Development of the UK Clothing Industry, 1850–1950: Output and Productivity Growth', *Business History* 37/4 (1995): 46–63.

———, 'The Emergence of Mass Production in the UK Clothing Industry', in Ian Taplin and Jonathan Winterton (eds), *Restructuring within a Labour Intensive Industry: The UK Clothing Industry in Transition* (Aldershot: Avebury, 1996), pp. 8–23.

———, *The History of the Ready-Made Clothing Industry* (Leeds: Pasold Research Fund, 1997).

———, 'The Development of the Clothing Industry: Technology and Fashion', *Textile History* 28/1 (1997): 3–9.

———, 'Comparative Labour Productivity in the British and American Clothing Industries, 1850–1950', *Textile History* 28/1 (1997): 67–80.

———, 'Homeworking and the Sewing Machine in the British Clothing Industry 1850–1905', in Barbara Burman (ed.), *The Culture of Sewing: Gender, Consumption and Home Dressmaking* (Oxford: Berg, 1999), pp. 255–68.

———, 'Foreign Multinationals and Innovation in British Retailing: 1850–1962', *Business History* 45/1 (2003): 80–100.

Green, David, *From Artisans to Paupers* (Aldershot: Scolar Press, 1995).

———, 'Pauper Protests: Power and Resistance in Early Nineteenth-century London Workhouses', *Social History* 31/2 (2006): 137–59.

Green-Lewis, Jennifer, *Framing the Victorians: Photography and the Culture of Realism* (Ithaca: Cornell University Press, 1996).

Hannavy, John and Ryan, Chris, *Working in Wigan Mills* (Wigan: Smiths Books, 1987).

Harris, Beth (ed.), *Famine and Fashion: Needlewomen in the Nineteenth Century* (Aldershot: Ashgate, 2005).

Harvey, John, *Men in Black* (Chicago: University of Chicago Press, 1995).

Helvenston, Sally, 'Advice to American Mothers on the Subject of Children's Dress, 1800–1920', *Dress*, 7 (1981): 30–46.

Hendrick, Harry, *Images of Youth: Age, Class and the Male Youth Problem 1880–1920* (Oxford: Clarendon Press, 1990).

Higonnet, Anne, *Images of Innocence, the History and Crisis of Ideal Childhood* (London: Thames & Hudson, 1998).

Hobsbawm, Eric, *Labouring Men, Studies in the History of Labour* (London: Weidenfeld & Nicolson, 1964).

Honeyman, Katrina, *Well Suited: A History of the Leeds Clothing Industry, 1850–1990* (Oxford: University Press / Pasold Research Fund, 2000).

———, 'Following Suit: Men, Masculinity and Gendered Practices in the Clothing Trade in Leeds, England, 1890–1940', *Gender and History* 14/3 (2002): 426–46.

———, 'Style Monotony and the Business of Fashion: The Marketing of Menswear in Inter-war England', *Textile History* 34/2 (2003): 171–91.

Hopkins, Eric, *Childhood Transformed: Working Class Children in Nineteenth-Century England* (Manchester: University Press, 1994).

Humphries Stephen, *Hooligans or Rebels? An Oral History of Working-Class Childhood and Youth 1889–1939* (Oxford: Blackwell, 1981).

Jackson, Peter, et al. (eds), *Commercial Cultures: Economies, Practices, Spaces* (Oxford: Berg, 2000).

Jackson, Tabitha, *The Boer War* (London: Channel 4 Books, 1999).

Jefferys, James, *Retail Trading in Britain 1850–1950: A Study of Trends in Retailing with Special Reference to the Development of Co-operative, Multiple Shop and Department Store Methods of Trading* (Cambridge: Cambridge University Press, 1954).

Jobling, Paul and David Crowley, *Graphic Design: Reproduction and Representation since 1800* (Manchester: Manchester University Press, 1996).

Johnson, Paul, *Saving and Spending: The Working-Class Economy in Britain 1870–1939* (Oxford: Clarendon Press, 1985).

Johnston, Lucy, *Nineteenth-Century Fashion in Detail* (London: V&A Publications, 2005).

Join-Diéterle, Catherine, 'Le vêtement comme illustration des liens familiaux', in Musée Galliera, *La mode et l'enfant, 1780–2000* (Paris: Paris Musées, 2001).

Jones, Edgar Y., *Father of Art Photography, O.G. Rejlander, 1813–1875* (Newton Abbot: David & Charles, 1973).

Jones, Peter, 'Clothing the Poor in Early Nineteenth-Century England', *Textile History* 37/1 (2006): 17–37.

Jubb, Michael, *Cocoa and Corsets: A Selection of Late Victorian and Edwardian Posters and Showcards from the Stationers' Company Copyright Records Preserved in the Public Record Office* (London: HMSO, 1984).

Kanitkar, Helen, '"Real true boys": Moulding the Cadets of Imperialism', in Andrea Cornwall and Nancy Lindisfarne (eds), *Dislocating Masculinity: Comparative Ethnographies* (London: Routledge, 1994).

Kidd, Alan, *State, Society and the Poor in Nineteenth Century England* (Basingstoke: Macmillan, 1999).

Kidwell, Claudia, 'Short Gowns', *Dress* 4 (1978): 30–65

Koven, Seth, 'Dr Barnardo's "Artistic Fictions": Photography, Sexuality, and the Ragged Child in Victorian London', *Radical History Review* 69 (1997): 6–45.

———, *Slumming: Sexual and Social Politics in Victorian London* (Princeton: Princeton University Press, 2004).

Kuchta, David, *The Three-Piece Suit and Modern Masculinity, England 1550–1850* (Berkeley: University of California Press, 2002).

Lambert, Miles, *Fashion in Photographs 1860–1880* (London: B.T. Batsford, 1991).

Lancaster, Bill, *The Department Store: A Social History* (Leicester: University Press, 1995).

Lansdell, Averil, *Fashion à la Carte 1860–1900: A Study of Fashion through Cartes-de-visite* (Aylesbury: Shire Publications, 1985).

Lemire, Beverly, *Dress, Culture and Commerce: The English Clothing Trade Before the Factory, 1660–1800* (Basingstoke: Macmillan, 1997).

Levitt, Sarah, *The Victorians Unbuttoned* (London: George Allen & Unwin, 1986).

———, 'Clothing Production and the Sewing Machine', *Textile Society Journal* 9 (1988): pp.2–12)

———, 'Cheap Mass-produced Men's Clothing in the Nineteenth and Early Twentieth Centuries', *Textile History* 22/2 (1991): 179–92.

———, 'Clothing', in Mary Rose (ed.), *The Lancashire Cotton Industry: A History Since 1700* (Lancaster: Lancashire County Council/Pasold Research Fund, 1996), pp. 154–86.

Linkman, Audrey, *The Victorians: Photographic Portraits* (London: Tauris Parke Books, 1993).

Lloyd, Valerie, *The Camera and Dr Barnardo* (London: The National Portrait Gallery, 1974).

Longmate, Norman, *The Workhouse* (London: Temple Smith, 1974).

Mackenzie, John, *Propaganda and Empir:, The Manipulation of British Public Opinion, 1880–1960* (Manchester: Manchester University Press, 1984).

——— (ed), *Imperialism and Popular Culture* (Manchester: Manchester University Press, 1986).

Marshall, Noreen, *A Dictionary of Children's Clothing* (London: V&A Publications, 2008).

Matthew, H.C.G., 'Edward VIII [*later* Prince Edward, duke of Windsor] (1894–1972)', in *Oxford Dictionary of National Biography* (Oxford: Oxford University Press, 2004); online edn (January 2008) http://www.oxforddnb.com/view/article/31061 (accessed 17 June 2008).

————, 'George VI (1895–1952)', in *Oxford Dictionary of National Biography* (Oxford: Oxford University Press, 2004); online edn (October 2007) http://www.oxforddnb.com/view/article/33370 (accessed 15 December 2008).

Matthew, Henry, 'George V, King of Great Britain', in *Dictionary of National Biography* (Oxford: Oxford University Press, 2007), vol. 21, p. 864.

McKendrick, Neil, John Brewer and J.H. Plumb, *The Birth of a Consumer Society: The Commercialization of Eighteenth-century England* (London: Europa, 1982).

McWilliam, Rohan, 'Melodrama and the historians', *Radical History Review* 78 (2000): 59–62.

Meacham, Standish, *A Life Apart, The English Working Class 1890–1914* (London: Thames & Hudson, 1977).

Mechling, Jay, 'Advice to Historians on advice to mothers', *Journal of Social History* 9 (1975): 44–63.

Michelman, Susan and Tonye Erekosima, 'Kalabari dress in Nigeria', in Ruth Barnes and Joanne Eicher (eds), *Dress and Gender: Making and Meaning* (Oxford: Berg, 1993), pp. 164–82.

Miller, Amy, *Dressed to Kill: British Naval Uniform, Masculinity and Contemporary Fashions, 1748–1857* (Greenwich: National Maritime Museum, 2007).

Miller, Daniel, *Material Culture and Mass Consumption* (Oxford: Basil Blackwell, 1987).

————, *Acknowledging Consumption* (London: Routledge, 1995).

———— (ed.), *Material Cultures, Why Some Things Matter* (London: University College London Press, 1996).

Millett, Freda, *Up at Five: Voices of the Half-timers in Oldham's Cotton Mills* (Oldham: Oldham Local Studies Library, n.d).

Moore, Doris Langley, *The Child in Fashion* (London: B.T. Batsford, 1953).

Mort, Frank, *Cultures of Consumption: Masculinities and Social Space in Late Twentieth Century Britain* (London; Routledge, 1996).

Murdoch, Lydia, *Imagined Orphans: Poor Families, Child Welfare and Contested Citizenship in London* (New Brunswick: Rutgers University Press, 2006).

Murphy, Deirdre, '"The Girls in Green": Women's Seaside Dress in England, 1850–1900', *Costume* 40 (2006): 56–66.

Musée Galliera, *La mode et l'enfant, 1780–2000* (Paris: Editions de musées de la ville de Paris, 2001).

Nelson, Claudia, *Boys Will Be Girls: The Feminine Ethic and British Children's Fiction, 1857–1917* (New Brunswick: Rutgers University Press, 1990).

Nevett, T.R., *Advertising in Britain: A History* (London: Heinemann, 1982).

Nixdorff, Heide and Heidi Muller, *Weisse Westen, Rote Roben: von den Farbordnungen des Mittelalters zum individuellen Farbgeschmack* (Berlin: Staatliche Museen, 1983).

North, Susan, 'John Redfern and Sons, 1847–1892', *Costume* 42 (2008): 145–69.

Norwood, J., *Victorian and Edwardian Hampshire & the Isle of Wight from Old Photographs* (London: B.T. Batsford, 1973).

Oddy, Nicholas, 'A Beautiful Ornament in the Parlour or Boudoir: The Domestication of the Sewing Machine', in Barbara Burman (ed.), *The Culture of Sewing: Gender, Consumption and Home Dressmaking* (Oxford: Berg, 1999), pp. 285–302.

O'Connell, Sean and Reid, Chris, 'Working-class consumer credit in the UK, 1925–60: The Role of the Check Trader', *Economic History Review* 58/2 (2005): 378–405.

Ormond, Richard and Caroline Blackett-Ord, *Franz Xavier Winterhalter and the Courts of Europe, 1830–70* (London: National Portrait Gallery, 1987).

Owslebury, A Village School: 150 Years 1840–1990 (no imprint, 1990).

Pakenham, Thomas, *The Boer War* (London: Macdonald, 1982).

Paoletti, Jo, 'Clothes Make the Boy, 1869–1910', *Dress* 9 (1983): 16–20.

Paoletti, Jo and Carol Kregloh, 'The Children's Department', in Claudia Kidwell and Valerie Steele (eds), *Men and Women: Dressing the Part* (Washington DC/ London: Smithsonian Institution, 1989), pp. 22–41.

Paris, Michael, *Warrior Nation, Images of War in British Popular Culture, 1850–2000* (London: Reaktion, 2000).

Parr, Joy, Labouring Children, *British Immigrant Apprentices to Canada, 1869–1924* (London: Croom Helm, 1980).

Partington, Angela, 'Popular Fashion and Working Class Affluence', in Juliet Ash and Elizabeth Wilson (eds), *Chic Thrills: A Fashion Reader* (London; Pandora, 1992), pp. 145–61.

Pellegrin, Nicole, *Les Vêtements de la liberté, Abécédaire des pratiques vestimentaires en France de 1780 à 1800* (Aix: Editions Alinea, 1989).

Perani, Judith and Norma H. Wolff, *Cloth, Dress and Art Patronage in Africa* (Oxford: Berg, 1999).

Perkin, Harold, *The Rise of Professional Society, England since 1880* (London: Routledge, 1989).

Perrot, Philippe, *Fashioning the Bourgeoisie: A History of Clothing in the Nineteenth Century* (Princeton: Princeton University Press, 1994).

Pollock, Linda, *Forgotten Children: Parent–Child relations from 1500 to 1900* (Cambridge: Cambridge University Press, 1983).

Porter, Bernard, *The Absent-Minded Imperialists: Empire, Society and Culture in Britain* (Oxford: Oxford University Press, 2004).

Price, Richard, *An Imperial War and the British Working Class: Working-Class Attitudes and Reactions to the Boer War, 1899–1902* (London: Routledge & Kegan Paul, 1972).

Prown, Jules, 'Mind in Matter: An Introduction to material Culture Theory and Method', in Susan Pearce (ed.) *Interpreting Objects and Collections* (London: Routledge, 1994), pp. 133–8.

Putnam, Tim, 'The Sewing Machine Comes Home', in Barbara Burman (ed.), *The Culture of Sewing: Gender, Consumption and Home Dressmaking* (Oxford: Berg, 1999), pp. 269–84.

Rexford, Nancy, 'Studying Garments for their Own Sake: Mapping the World of Costume Scholarship', *Dress* 14 (1988): 68–75.

Richmond, Tina Vivienne, '"No Finery": the Dress of the poor in Nineteenth-Century England' (unpublished PhD dissertation, Goldsmiths College, University of London, 2004).

Rickards, Maurice and Michael Twyman, *The Encyclopedia of Ephemera: A Guide to the Fragmentary Documents of Everyday Life for the Collector, Curator and Historian* (London: British Library, 2000).

Roberts, E., *In and Around Alresford in Old Photographs* (Alresford: Laurence Oxley, 1975).

Rose, Clare. *Children's Clothes Since 1750* (London: B.T. Batsford, 1989).

——, 'Alla ricerca della cenciosita' ('In Search of Raggedness'), in Tiziano Bonazzi (ed.), *Riconoscimento ed Esclusione* (Rome: Carocci Editore, 2003), pp. 156–80.

——, 'Boyswear and the Formation of Gender and Class Identity in Urban England 1840–1900' (unpublished PhD Dissertation, University of Brighton, 2006).

——, '"The novelty consists in the ornamental design": Design Innovation in Mass-produced Boys' Clothing, 1840–1900', *Textile History* 38/1 (2007): 1–24.

——, 'Bought, Stolen, Bequeathed, Preserved: Sources for the Study of 18th-century Petticoats', in Maria Hayward and Elizabeth Kramer (eds), *Textiles and Text: Re-establishing the Links Between Archival and Object-based Research* (London: Archetype Publications, 2007), pp. 114–21.

——, 'Advertising Ready-Made Style: the Evidence of the Stationers' Hall Archive', *Textile History* 40/2 (2009): 185–201.

——, 'The Meanings of the Late Victorian Sailor Suit', *Journal of Maritime Research*, http: //www.jmr.nmm.ac.uk/server/show/ConJmrArticle.270/, unpaginated, Autumn 2009.

Rose, June, *For the Sake of the Children: Inside Dr Barnardo's, 120 years of caring for Children* (London: Hodder & Stoughton, 1987).

Ross, Ellen, '"Fierce Questions and Taunts": Married Life in Working-class London, 1870–1914', *Feminist Studies* 8/3 (1982): 575–602.

——, 'Survival Networks: Women's Neighbourhood Sharing in London Before World War I', *History Workshop Journal* 15 (1983): 4–28.

——, *Love and Toil: Motherhood in Outcast London, 1870–1918* (Oxford: Oxford University Press, 1993).

Ryott, David, *John Barran's of Leeds, 1851–1951* (Leeds: Privately published, 1951).

Samuel, Raphael (ed.), *East End Underworld: Chapters in the life of Arthur Harding* (London: Routledge & Kegan Paul, 1981).

Scholliers, Peter (ed.), *Real Wages in 19th and 20th Century Europe: Historical and Comparative Perspectives* (New York: Berg, 1989).

Schorman, Rob, *Selling Style: Clothing and Social Change at the Turn of the Century* (Philadelphia: University of Pennsylvania Press, 2003).

Seligman, Kevin, 'Dressmakers' Patterns: The English Commercial Paper Pattern Industry, 1878–1950', *Costume* 37 (2003): 95–113.

Severa, Joan and Merrill Horswill, 'Costume as Material Culture', *Dress* 15 (1989): 51–64.

Severa, Joan, *Dressed for the Photographer: Ordinary Americans and Fashion, 1840–1900* (Kent, OH: Kent State University Press, 1995).

Seymour, Claire, *Ragged Schools, Ragged Children* (London: The Ragged School Museum Trust, 1995).

Sigsworth, Eric, *Montague Burton: The Tailor of Taste* (Manchester: Manchester University Press, 1990).

Smith, Lindsay, *The Politics of Focus: Women, Children and Nineteenth-century Photography* (Manchester: Manchester University Press, 1998).

Snodin, Michael and John Styles, *Design and the Decorative Arts: Britain, 1500–1900* (London: V&A Publications, 2001).

Springhall, John, 'Building Character in the British Boy: The Attempt to Extend Christian Manliness to Working-class Adolescents, 1880–1914', in Michael Roper and John Tosh (eds), *Manful Assertions: Masculinities in Britain since 1800* (London: Routledge, 1991), pp. 52–74.

———, *Youth, Empire and Society: British Youth Movements, 1883–1940* (London: Croom Helm, 1977).

Steedman, Carolyn, *Strange Dislocations: Childhood and the Idea of Human Interiority, 1780–1930* (Cambridge, MA: Harvard University Press, 1995).

Steele, Valerie, 'A Museum of Fashion is More than a Clothes Bag', *Fashion Theory* 2/4 (1998): 327–35.

Streets, Heather, *Martial Races: The Military, Race and Masculinity in British Imperial Culture, 1857–1914* (Manchester: Manchester University Press, 2004).

Stroud, John, *Thirteen Penny Stamps: The Story of the Church of England Children's Society (Waifs and Strays) from 1881 to the 1970s* (London: Hodder & Stoughton, 1971).

Styles, John, 'Dress in History: Reflections on a Contested Terrain', *Fashion Theory* 2/4 (1998): 383–9.

———, *The Dress of the People: Everyday Fashion in Eighteenth Century England* (New Haven/London: Yale University Press, 2007).

Tagg, John, *The Burden of Representation: Essays on Photographies and Histories* (Basingstoke: Macmillan, 1988).

Tarlo, Emma, *Clothing Matters: Dress and Identity in India* (London: Hurst & Co., 1996).

Taylor, Lou, 'Doing the Laundry? A Reassessment of Object-Based Dress History', *Fashion Theory* 2/4 (1998): 337–58.

———, 'Wool Cloth and Gender: The Use of Woollen Cloth in Women's Dress in Britain, 1865–85', in A. de la Haye and E. Wilson (eds), *Defining Dress: Dress* as Object, Meaning and Identity (Manchester: Manchester University Press, 1999), pp. 30–47.

——, *The Study of Dress History* (Manchester: University Press, 2002).

——, *Establishing Dress History* (Manchester: University Press, 2004).

Thompson, Andrew *The Empire Strikes Back? The Impact of Imperialism on Britain from the mid-Nineteenth Century* (Harlow: Pearson Education, 2005).

Tosh, John, 'Domesticity and Manliness in the Victorian Middle Class, the Family of Edward White Benson', in Michael Roper and John Tosh (eds), *Manful Assertions: Masculinities in Britain since 1800* (London: Routledge, 1991), pp. 44–74.

——, 'Authority and Nurture in Middle-Class Fatherhood: The Case of Early and mid-Victorian England', *Gender and History* 8/1 (1996): 48–64.

——, *A Man's Place: Masculinity and the Middle-Class Home in Victorian England* (New Haven: Yale University Press, 1999).

Tozer, Jane and Sarah Levitt, 'Cunnington's Attitude to Collecting', *Costume* 20 (1986): 1–17.

——, *Fabric of Society: A Century of People and their Clothes, 1770–1870* (Powys: Laura Ashley Ltd, 1983).

Treble J.H., *Urban Poverty in Britain 1830–1914* (London: B.T. Batsford, 1979).

Tulloch, Carol, '"Out of Many, One People": The Relativity of Dress Race and Ethnicity to Jamaica, 1880–1907', *Fashion Theory* 2/4 (1998): 359–82.

—— (ed.), *Black Style* (London: V&A Publications 2004)

Turnbull, Annemarie, 'Learning Her Womanly Work: the Elementary School Curriculum, 1870–1914', in Felicity Hunt (ed.), *Lessons for Life: The Schooling of Girls and Women, 1850–1950* (Oxford: Blackwell, 1987), pp. 83–100.

Turner, Michael and David Vaisey, *Oxford Shops and Shopping, A Pictorial Survey from Victorian and Edwardian Times* (Oxford: Blackwell, 1972).

Ugolini, Laura, 'Men, Masculinities and Menswear Advertising, c1890–1914', in John Benson and Laura Ugolini, *A Nation of Shopkeepers, Five Centuries of British Retailing* (London: I.B. Tauris, 2003), pp. 80–104.

——, *Men and Menswear: Sartorial Consumption in Britain, 1880–1939* (Aldershot: Ashgate, 2007).

Van der Kiste, John, 'Alfred, Prince, Duke of Edinburgh', in *Dictionary of National Biography* (Oxford: Oxford University Press, 2007), vol.1, p. 725.

Vincent, David, *Bread, Knowledge and Freedom: A Study of Nineteenth-Century Working-Class Autobiography* (London: Europa, 1981).

Wagner, Gillian, *Children of the Empire* (London: Weidenfeld & Nicolson, 1982).

——, *Barnardo* (London: Weidenfeld & Nicolson, 1979).

Walton, John K., *Lancashire, A Social History, 1558–1939* (Manchester: University Press, 1987).

Walvin, John, *Beside the Seaside: A Social History of the Popular Seaside Holiday* (London: Allen Lane, 1978).

Wilshere, Jonathan, *Leicester Portrait Photographers before 1900* (Leicester: Chamberlain Books, 1988).

Wilson, Elizabeth and Lou Taylor, *Through the Looking Glass: A History of Dress from 1860 to the Present Day* (London: BBC Books, 1989).

Winstanley, Michael, *Working Children in Nineteenth-Century Lancashire* (Lancaster: Lancashire County Books, 1995).

Wolff, Michael and C. Fox, 'Pictures from the Magazines', in H.J. Dyos and Michael Wolff (ed.), *The Victorian City: Images and Realities*, vol. 2 (London: Routledge & Kegan Paul, 1973).

Zelizer, Viviana, *Pricing the Priceless Child:, The Changing Social Value of Children* (New York: Basic Books, 1985).

Index

For Product Safety Concerns and Information please contact our
EU representative GPSR@taylorandfrancis.com Taylor & Francis
Verlag GmbH, Kaufingerstraße 24, 80331 München, Germany

Making, Selling and Wearing Boys' Clothes in Late-Victorian England

CLARE ROSE

Making, Selling and Wearing Boys' Clothes *is a significant contribution to the history of the material culture of childhood and the study of the production, marketing and consumption of clothing in nineteenth-century Britain. Clare Rose brings to the subject her meticulous attention to object-based and archival research and a rigorous engagement with theoretical and historiographical debates. It is a book that social, economic, cultural and dress historians will need to read.*

Christopher Breward, Head of Research,
Victoria and Albert Museum,
London, UK

Drawing on an impressive range of research, and making innovative use of visual data, not least from Barnardo's archive, Clare Rose's book is a compelling contribution to the history of consumption, and full of rich and unexpected findings. Broad in scope, the book explores the links between consumption and imperialism, household economics, gender, and childhood and adolescence. It will be essential reading for anyone interested in late-Victorian England, and has many resonances for twenty-first-century debates about children and the consumer market.

Hugh Cunningham, Professor of Social History,
University of Kent, UK

Drawing upon a remarkable variety of documentary evidence, this study argues that much of Britain's consumer culture and modern business practice was influenced by the ready-to-wear market in boys' clothes. Through a detailed visual and statistical analysis of these sources, linking the design and retailing of boys' clothing with social, cultural and economic issues, it shows that an understanding of the production and consumption of the boys clothing is central to debates on the growth of the consumer society, the development of mass-market fashion, and concepts of childhood and masculinity.

Cover illustration: Detail of advertisement for Chas. Baker & Co. From the 1897–8 edition of 'The ABC Guide to London'. Author's collection.

an **informa** business

ISBN 978-1-138-26186-0

9 781138 261860

Routledge
Taylor & Francis Group
www.routledge.com